Ace Phoenix Wright Attorney ™

VOLUME FIVE

Story by Kenji Kuroda
Art by Kazuo Maekawa
Supervised by CAPCOM

Translated and adapted by Alethea Nibley and Athena Nibley

Lettered by Christy Sawyer

KODANSHA
COMICS

This book is a faithful translation of the book
released in Japan on December 5, 2008.

A Kodansha Comics Trade Paperback Original

Phoenix Wright: Ace Attorney™ volume 5 copyright © 2008 CAPCOM/Kenji Kuroda/Kazuo Maekawa
English translation copyright © 2012 CAPCOM/Kenji Kuroda/Kazuo Maekawa

Published in the United States by Kodansha Comics, an imprint of Kodansha USA Publishing, LLC, New York.

Publication rights arranged through Kodansha Ltd., Tokyo.

First published in Japan in 2008 by Kodansha Ltd., Tokyo, as *Gyakuten Saiban*, volume 5.

ISBN 978-1-935429-61-6

Printed in the United States of America

www.kodanshacomics.com

2 3 4 5 6 7 8 9

Translator/Adapter: Aletha Nibley and Athena Nibley
Lettering: Christy Sawyer

CONTENTS

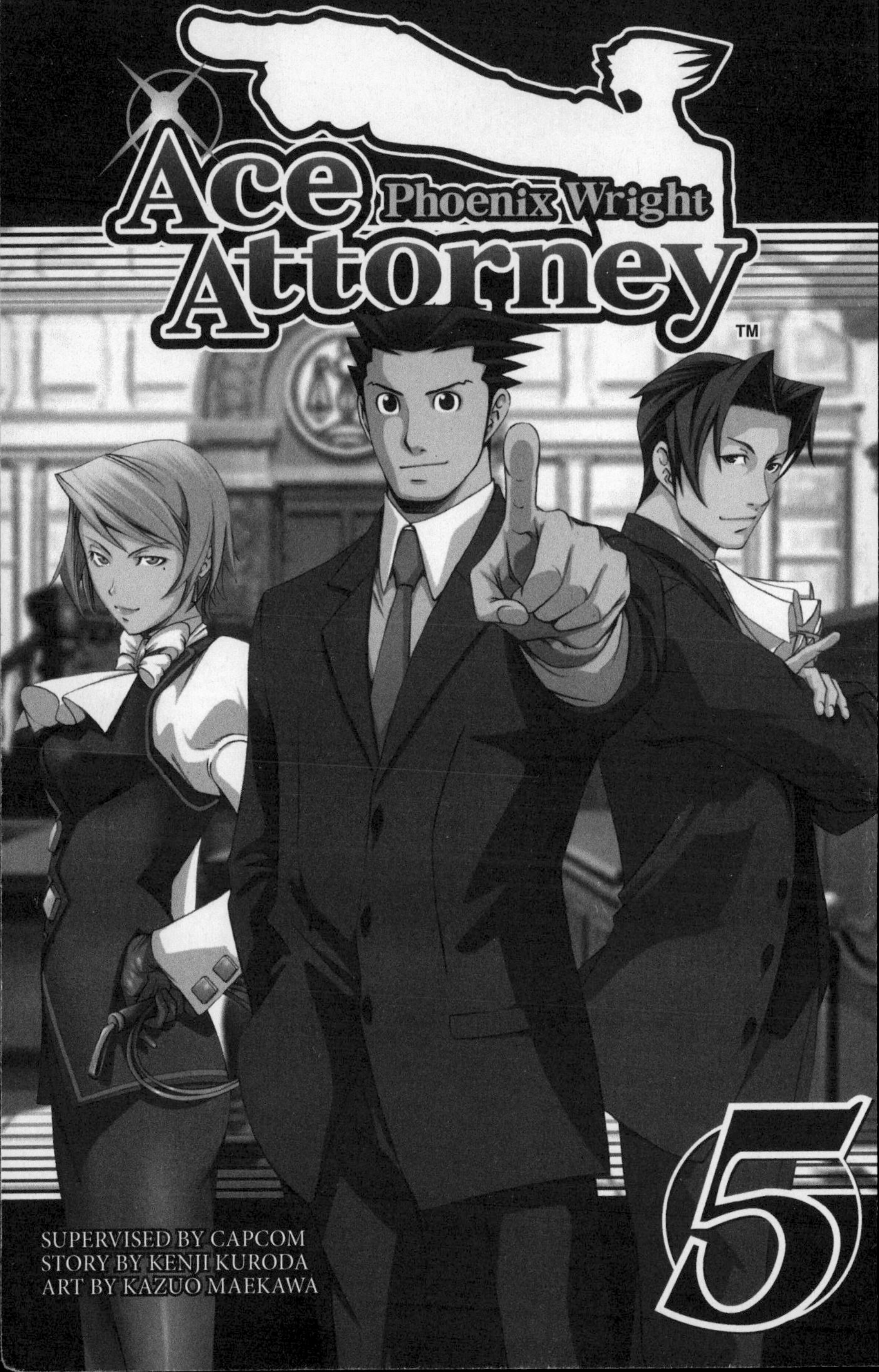
Ace Attorney
Phoenix Wright
TM
5
SUPERVISED BY CAPCOM
STORY BY KENJI KURODA
ART BY KAZUO MAEKAWA

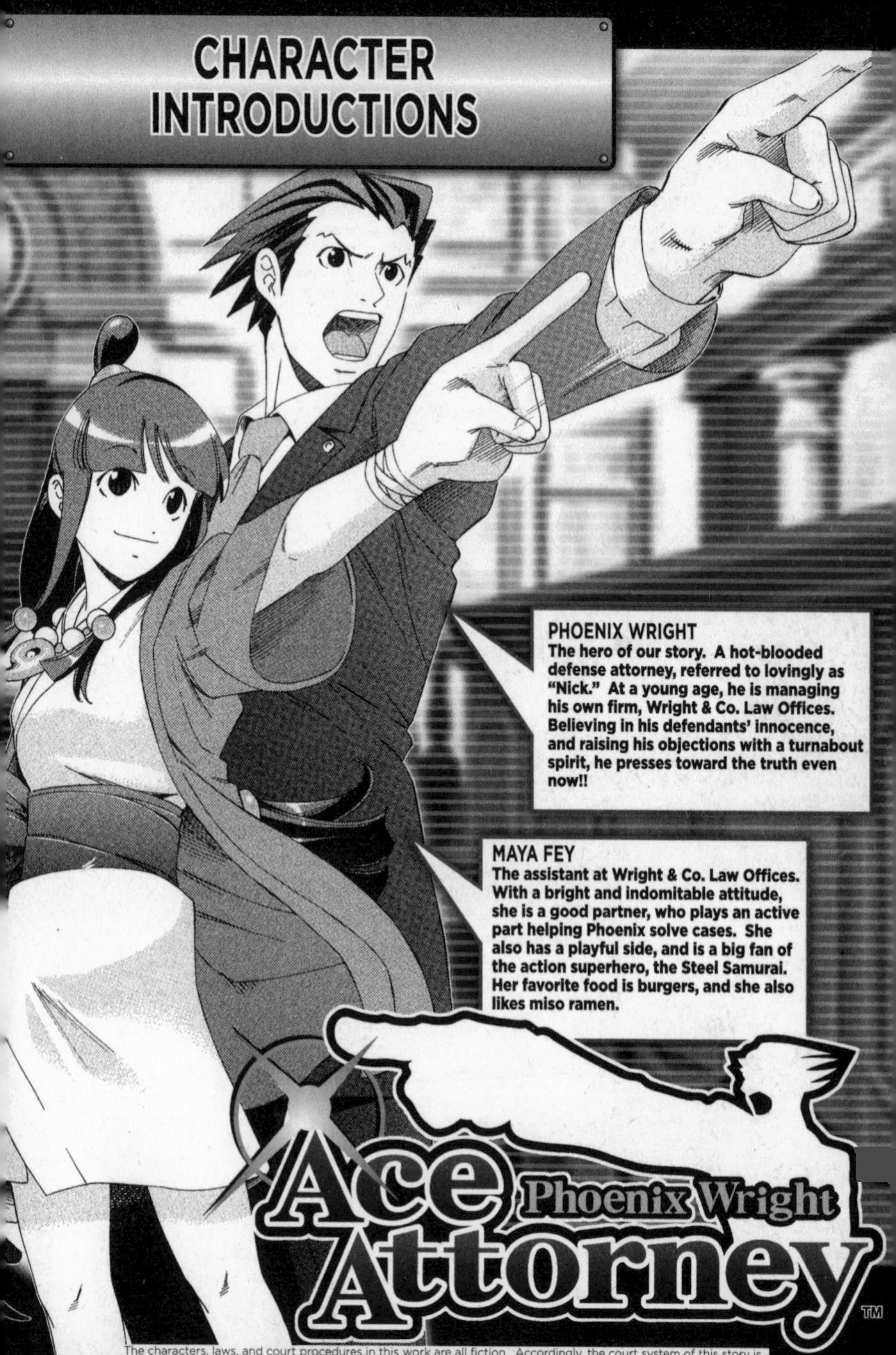
CHARACTER INTRODUCTIONS
PHOENIX WRIGHT
The hero of our story. A hot-blooded defense attorney, referred to lovingly as "Nick." At a young age, he is managing his own firm, Wright & Co. Law Offices. Believing in his defendants' innocence, and raising his objections with a turnabout spirit, he presses toward the truth even now!!
MAYA FEY
The assistant at Wright & Co. Law Offices. With a bright and indomitable attitude, she is a good partner, who plays an active part helping Phoenix solve cases. She also has a playful side, and is a big fan of the action superhero, the Steel Samurai. Her favorite food is burgers, and she also likes miso ramen.
Phoenix Wright
Ace Attorney
TM

The characters, laws, and court procedures in this work are all fiction. Accordingly, the court system of this story is

THE JUDGE
The court judge, who looks dignified but actually is not. He has a habit of gullibly swallowing every scenario fed to him by Phoenix or Edgeworth. His name is unknown.

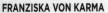

MILES EDGEWORTH
Phoenix's greatest rival. He has been known as a genius prosecutor ever since he started out in the profession. In fact, he and Phoenix knew each other as children, and were the best of friends, bound together by trust.

FRANZISKA VON KARMA
A strong-willed prosecutess whose goal is complete perfection. She will mercilessly flog anyone she dislikes with her beloved whip. Franziska sees Phoenix as her enemy, and so he, too, has been scourged by her lashings....

DICK GUMSHOE
A detective in charge of murder investigations. He's a few cards shy of a deck, and sometimes misses important clues. Every time he does, he gets a paycut, so his salary is very low.

WINSTON PAYNE
A veteran prosecutor, but he lacks presence, and is completely unreliable. Stress has caused his hairline to recede. In a word, he's dull.

TURNABOUT GURGITATION CASE FILE

MEET THE GORMAND FIGHTERS

MILO "FAIRPLAY" KENT (29)

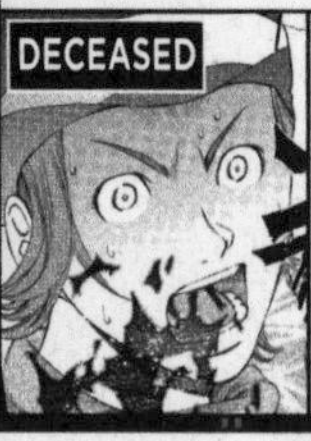
DECEASED

A miraculous champion, undefeated since his debut and loved by women for his good looks.

RISA IKO (28)

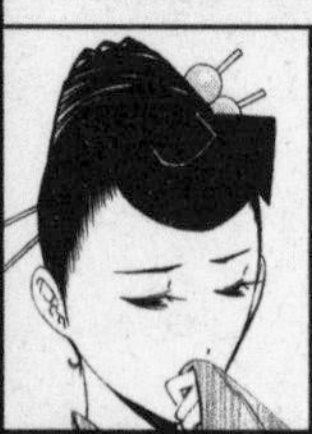

An ecologist who is using the Gormand Battle to teach the importance of caring for the environment.

ARNOLD "MUSCLES" BALBOA (34)

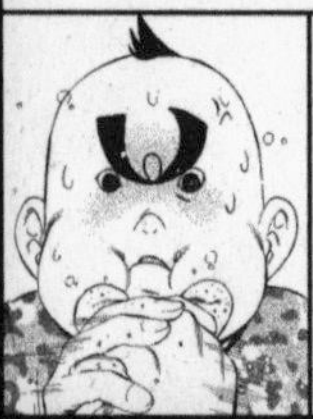

He crushes any dish in order to eat it at minimum volume. His body is covered in big muscles.

GALE CYCLONE (18)

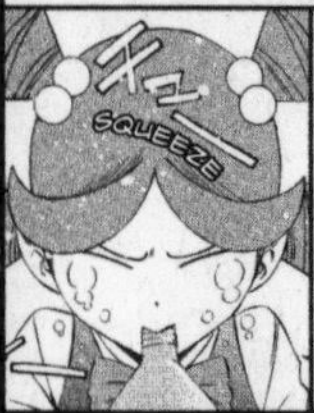
SQUEEZE

A huge lover of mayonnaise, she gets her name from the whirlwind of mayonnaise she applies to all her food.

CALIENTE DEL FUEGO

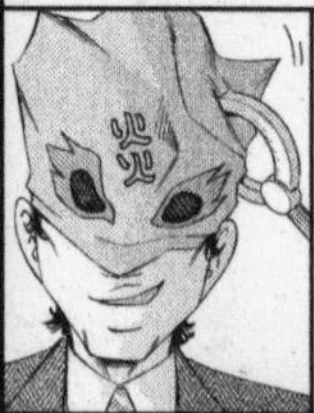

An extreme germophobe who roasts everything before eating. His true identity is that of the palm reader, Wally Flores.

CARL CAESAR (47)

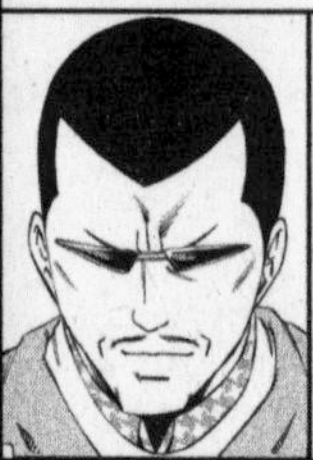

Producer at Stuffed! TV. He laments that his show might be canceled because of the murder.

KEVIN HATTORI (26)

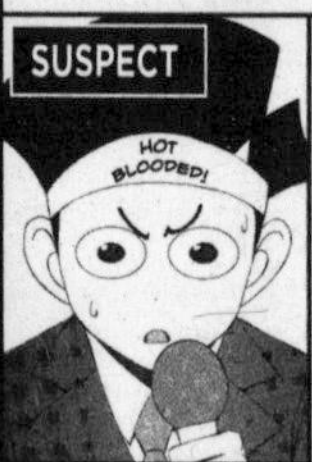
SUSPECT
HOT BLOODED!

Announcer at Stuffed! TV. He deeply respected Fairplay, but....

SUMMARY

The popular "Gormand Battle" TV show held its final battle to decide the ultimate King of Gurgitation, but the program ended in murder!

The undefeated champion, Milo "Fairplay" Kent, finished off his triple extra large bowl of red hot chili noodles and won the contest. But the next moment found him writhing in agony as he breathed his last. Traces of potassium cyanide were found in his bowl, and the announcer Kevin Hattori was arrested for murder. Fearing that his show would be canceled because the murderer was a member of his crew, the producer, Carl Caesar, hired Phoenix Wright to defend him. Phoenix will be facing off against Prosecutor Winston Payne in court.

Hattori had no motive for killing Fairplay, but the court determined that the poison was intended for Risa Iko. Everyone who worked on the show was aware of this fact, and because Hattori and Risa fought like cats and dogs, they all suspected Hattori as soon as the murder took place. Knowing that his show would be canceled if Hattori was arrested, Producer Caesar covered up the fact Risa was the killer's real target, and tried to make it look like an indiscriminate murder.

However, a threatening message was discovered, addressed to Risa Iko, and Caesar's attempts to hide the facts ended in failure. With overwhelming odds against his client, Phoenix begins to have his doubts about the entire Gormand Battle program. Are they keeping any more secrets? Do those secrets hold the key to revealing the true killer?

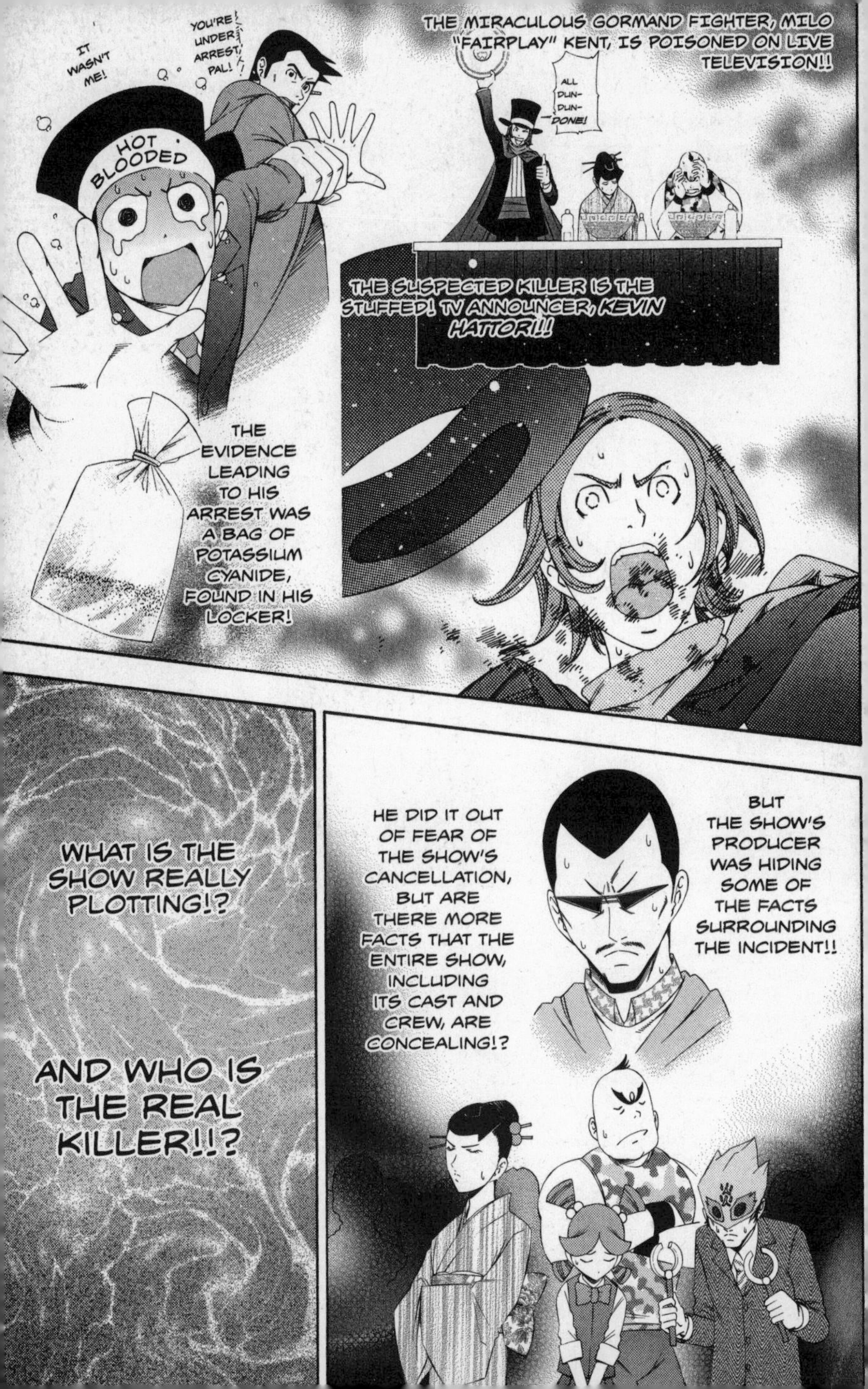
THE MIRACULOUS GORMAND FIGHTER, MILO "FAIRPLAY" KENT, IS POISONED ON LIVE TELEVISION!!
ALL DUN-DUN-DONE!
YOU'RE UNDER ARREST, PAL!
IT WASN'T ME!
HOT BLOODED
THE SUSPECTED KILLER IS THE STUFFED! TV ANNOUNCER, KEVIN HATTORI!!
THE EVIDENCE LEADING TO HIS ARREST WAS A BAG OF POTASSIUM CYANIDE, FOUND IN HIS LOCKER!
BUT THE SHOW'S PRODUCER WAS HIDING SOME OF THE FACTS SURROUNDING THE INCIDENT!!
HE DID IT OUT OF FEAR OF THE SHOW'S CANCELLATION, BUT ARE THERE MORE FACTS THAT THE ENTIRE SHOW, INCLUDING ITS CAST AND CREW, ARE CONCEALING!?
WHAT IS THE SHOW REALLY PLOTTING!?
AND WHO IS THE REAL KILLER!!?

CHAPTER 13
TURNABOUT GURGITATION (PART TWO)

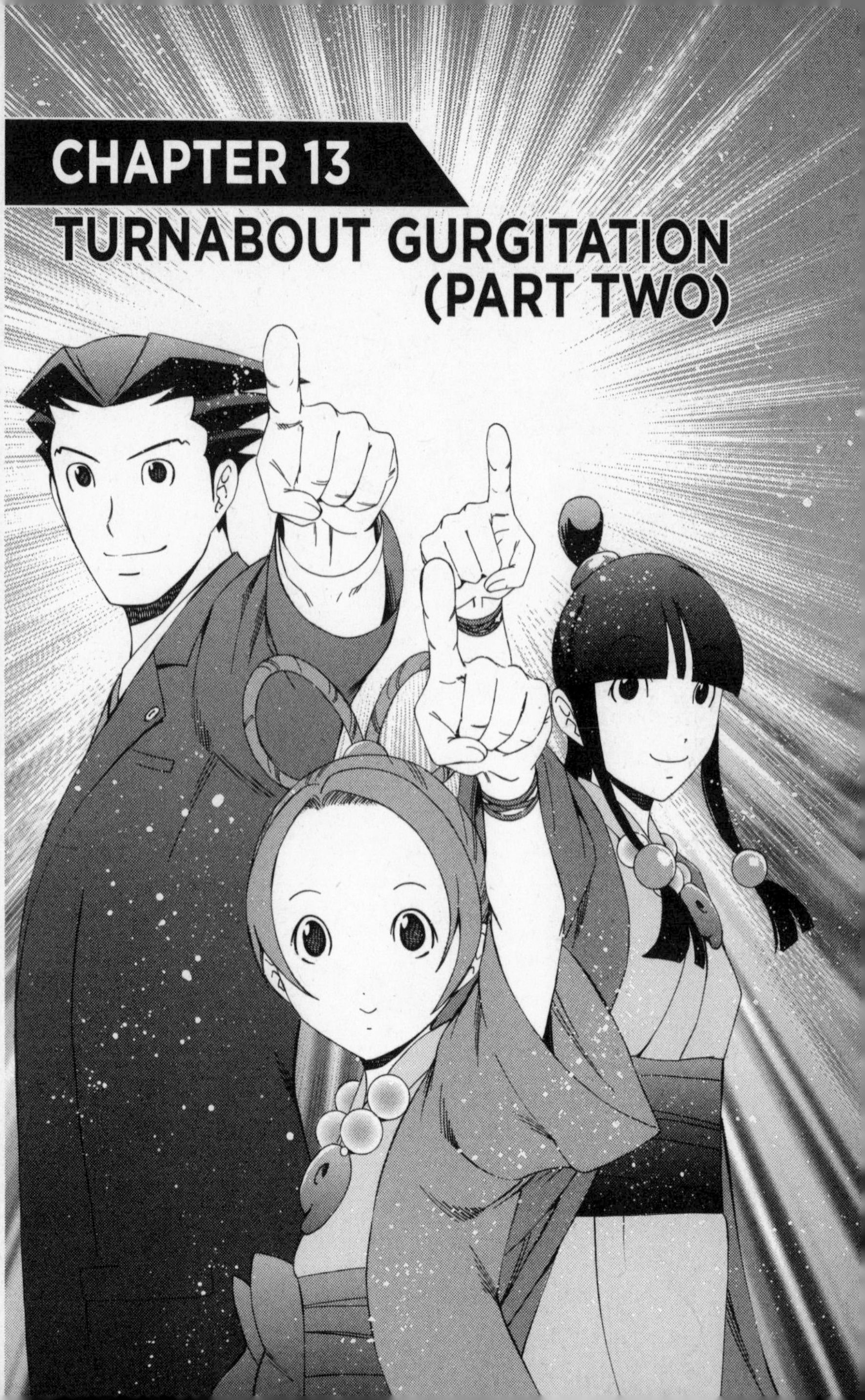

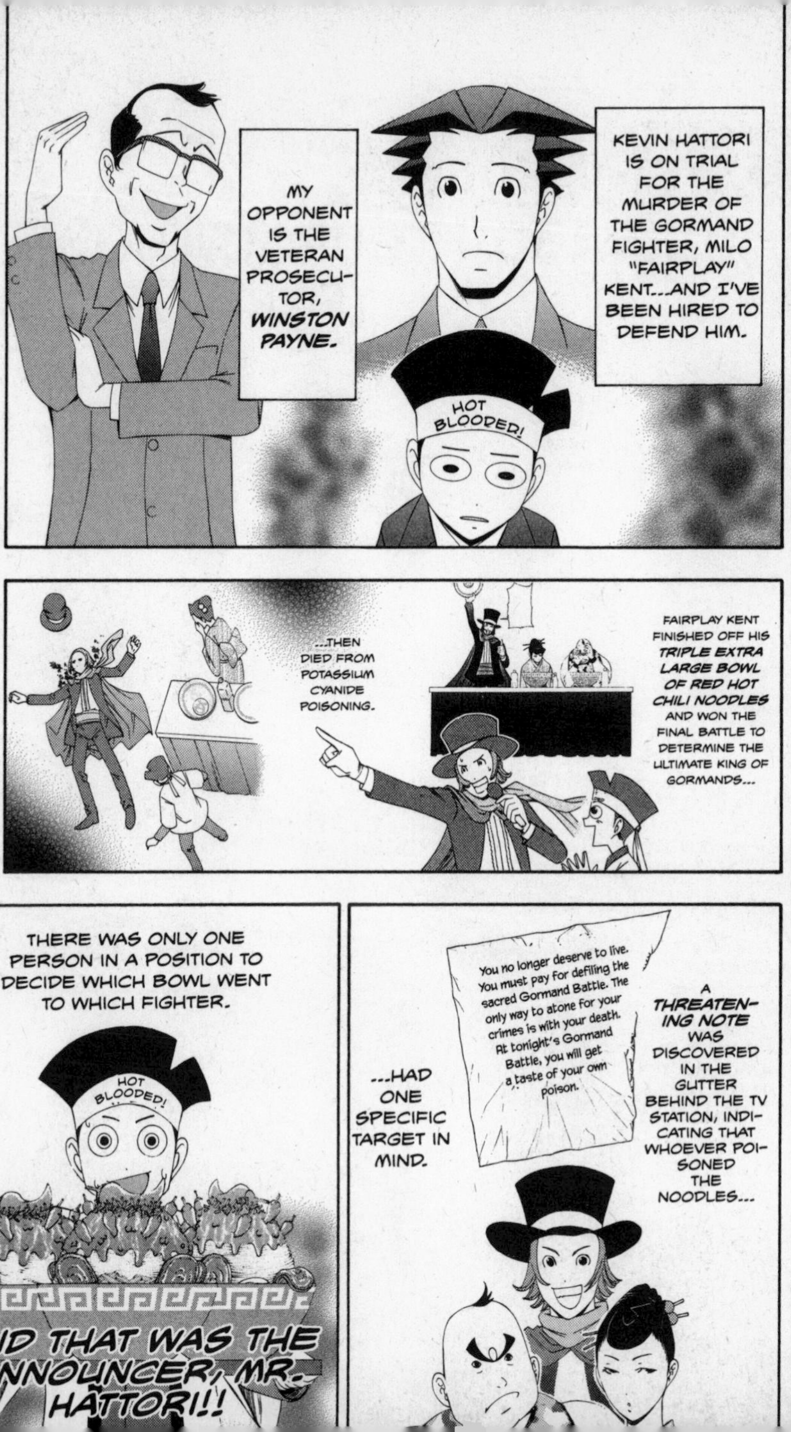

KEVIN HATTORI IS ON TRIAL FOR THE MURDER OF THE GORMAND FIGHTER, MILO "FAIRPLAY" KENT...AND I'VE BEEN HIRED TO DEFEND HIM.
MY OPPONENT IS THE VETERAN PROSECU-TOR, WINSTON PAYNE.
HOT BLOODED!
FAIRPLAY KENT FINISHED OFF HIS TRIPLE EXTRA LARGE BOWL OF RED HOT CHILI NOODLES AND WON THE FINAL BATTLE TO DETERMINE THE ULTIMATE KING OF GORMANDS...
...THEN DIED FROM POTASSIUM CYANIDE POISONING.
A THREATEN-ING NOTE WAS DISCOVERED IN THE GUTTER BEHIND THE TV STATION, INDI-CATING THAT WHOEVER POI-SONED THE NOODLES...
You no longer deserve to live. You must pay for defiling the sacred Gormand Battle. The only way to atone for your crimes is with your death. At tonight's Gormand Battle, you will get a taste of your own poison.
...HAD ONE SPECIFIC TARGET IN MIND.
THERE WAS ONLY ONE PERSON IN A POSITION TO DECIDE WHICH BOWL WENT TO WHICH FIGHTER.
HOT BLOODED!
AND THAT WAS THE ANNOUNCER, MR. HATTORI!!

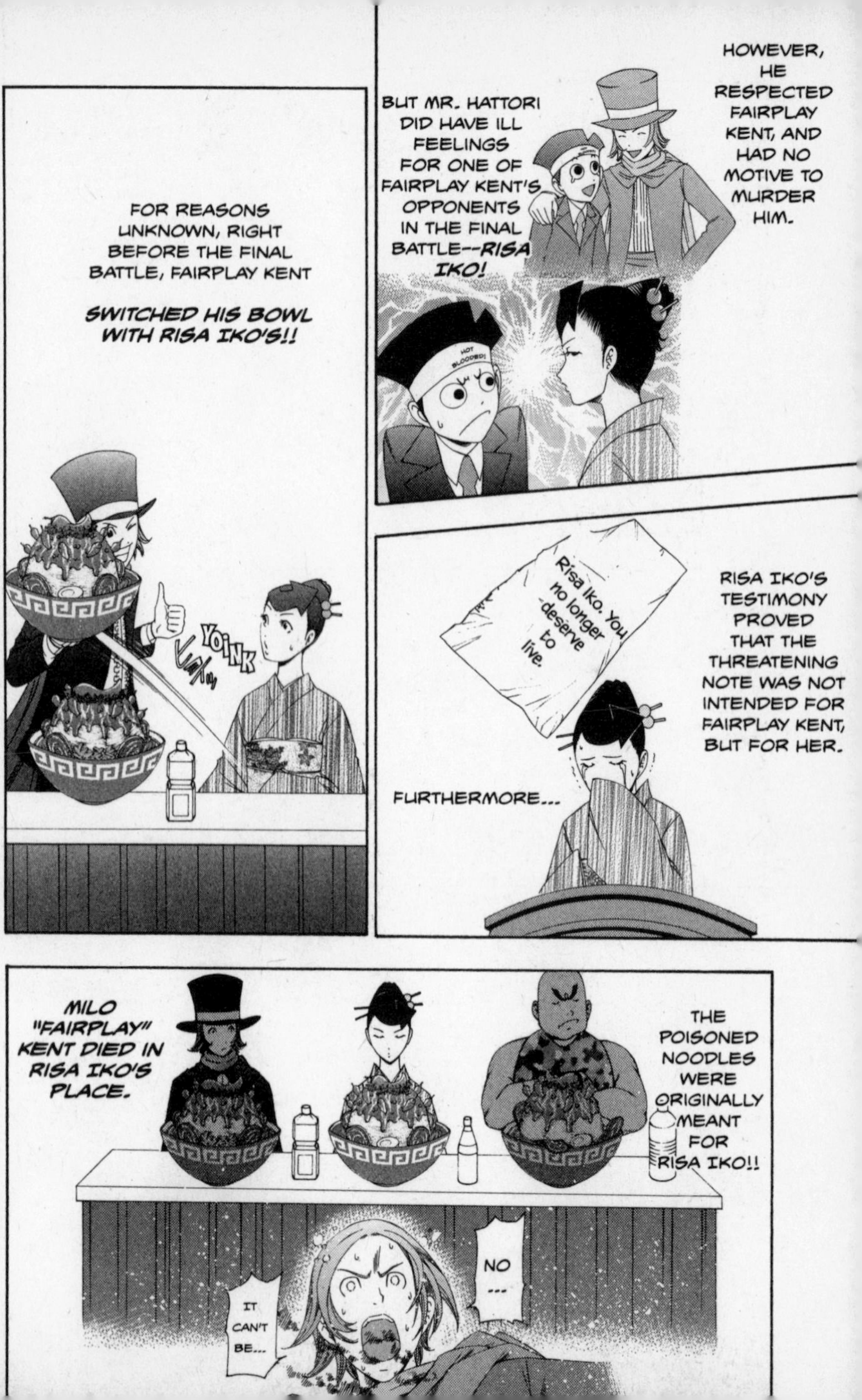
HOWEVER, HE RESPECTED FAIRPLAY KENT, AND HAD NO MOTIVE TO MURDER HIM.
BUT MR. HATTORI DID HAVE ILL FEELINGS FOR ONE OF FAIRPLAY KENT'S OPPONENTS IN THE FINAL BATTLE--RISA IKO!
HOT BLOODED!
RISA IKO'S TESTIMONY PROVED THAT THE THREATENING NOTE WAS NOT INTENDED FOR FAIRPLAY KENT, BUT FOR HER.
Risa Iko. You no longer deserve to live.
FURTHERMORE...
FOR REASONS UNKNOWN, RIGHT BEFORE THE FINAL BATTLE, FAIRPLAY KENT
SWITCHED HIS BOWL WITH RISA IKO'S!!
YOINK
THE POISONED NOODLES WERE ORIGINALLY MEANT FOR RISA IKO!!
MILO "FAIRPLAY" KENT DIED IN RISA IKO'S PLACE.
NO ...
IT CAN'T BE...

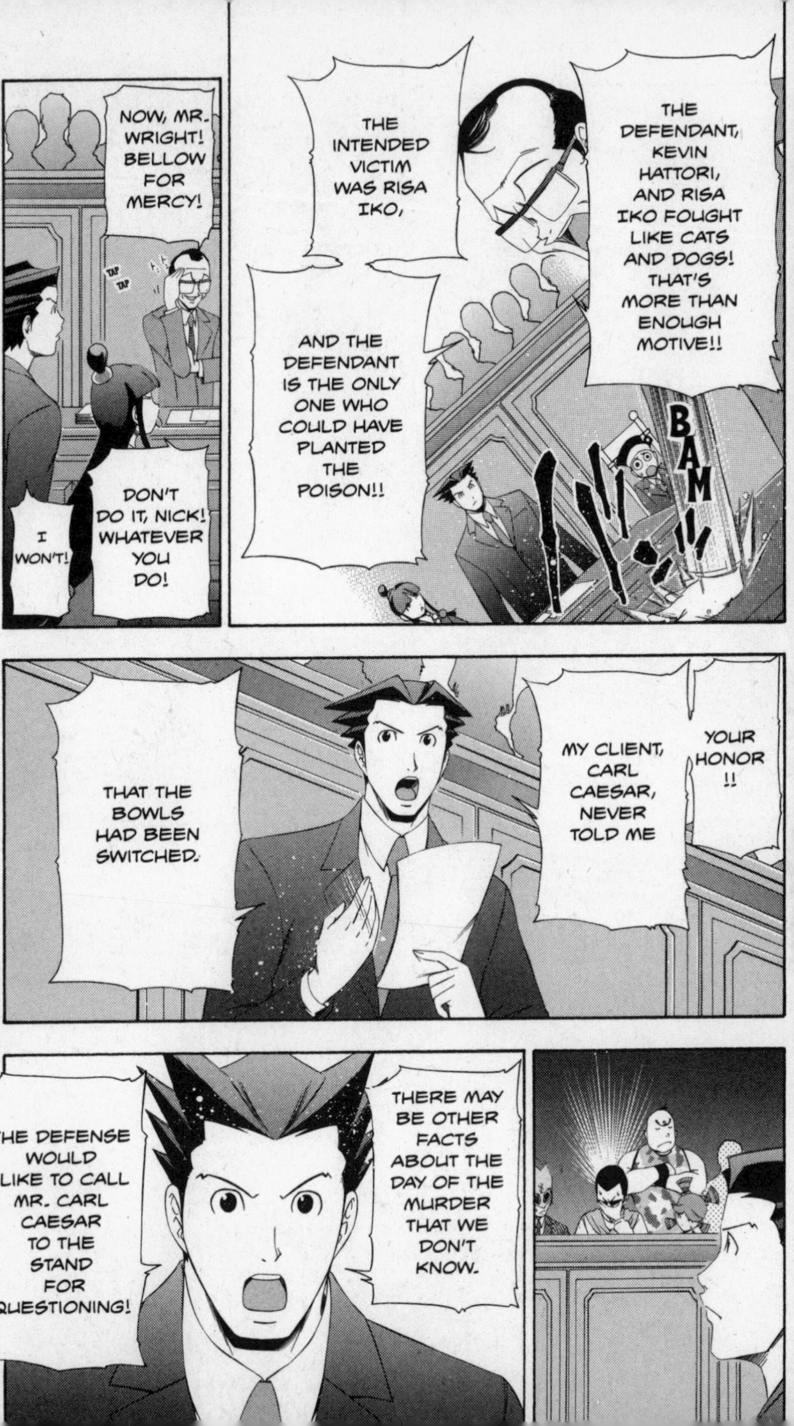
THE DEFENDANT, KEVIN HATTORI, AND RISA IKO FOUGHT LIKE CATS AND DOGS! THAT'S MORE THAN ENOUGH MOTIVE!!
THE INTENDED VICTIM WAS RISA IKO,
AND THE DEFENDANT IS THE ONLY ONE WHO COULD HAVE PLANTED THE POISON!!
BAM!!
NOW, MR. WRIGHT! BELLOW FOR MERCY!
TAP TAP
DON'T DO IT, NICK! WHATEVER YOU DO!
I WON'T!
YOUR HONOR!!
MY CLIENT, CARL CAESAR, NEVER TOLD ME
THAT THE BOWLS HAD BEEN SWITCHED.
THERE MAY BE OTHER FACTS ABOUT THE DAY OF THE MURDER THAT WE DON'T KNOW.
THE DEFENSE WOULD LIKE TO CALL MR. CARL CAESAR TO THE STAND FOR QUESTIONING!

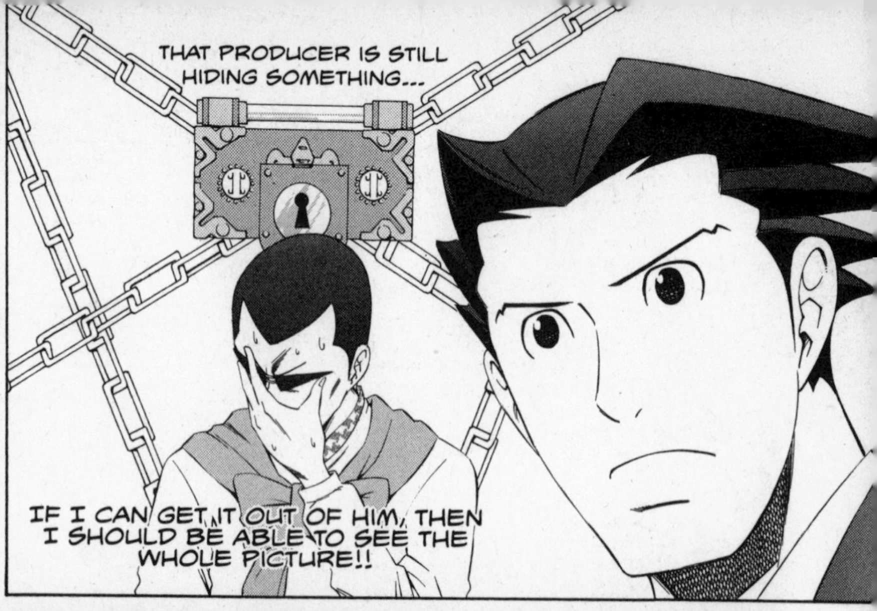
THAT PRODUCER IS STILL HIDING SOMETHING...
IF I CAN GET IT OUT OF HIM, THEN I SHOULD BE ABLE TO SEE THE WHOLE PICTURE!!

NOVEMBER 23, 11:54 AM
DISTRICT COURT
COURTROOM NO.3: CARL CAESAR'S TESTIMONY

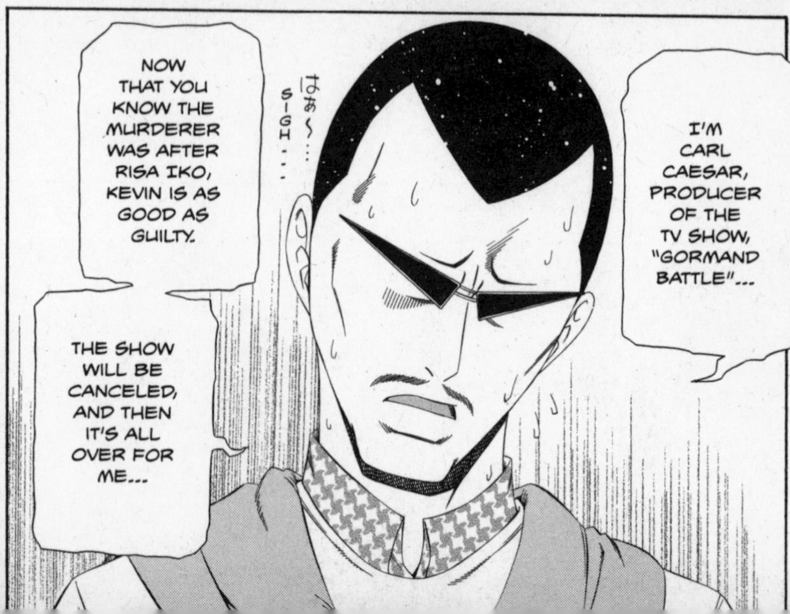
I'M CARL CAESAR, PRODUCER OF THE TV SHOW, "GORMAND BATTLE"...
はぁ~… SIGH...
NOW THAT YOU KNOW THE MURDERER WAS AFTER RISA IKO, KEVIN IS AS GOOD AS GUILTY.
THE SHOW WILL BE CANCELED, AND THEN IT'S ALL OVER FOR ME...

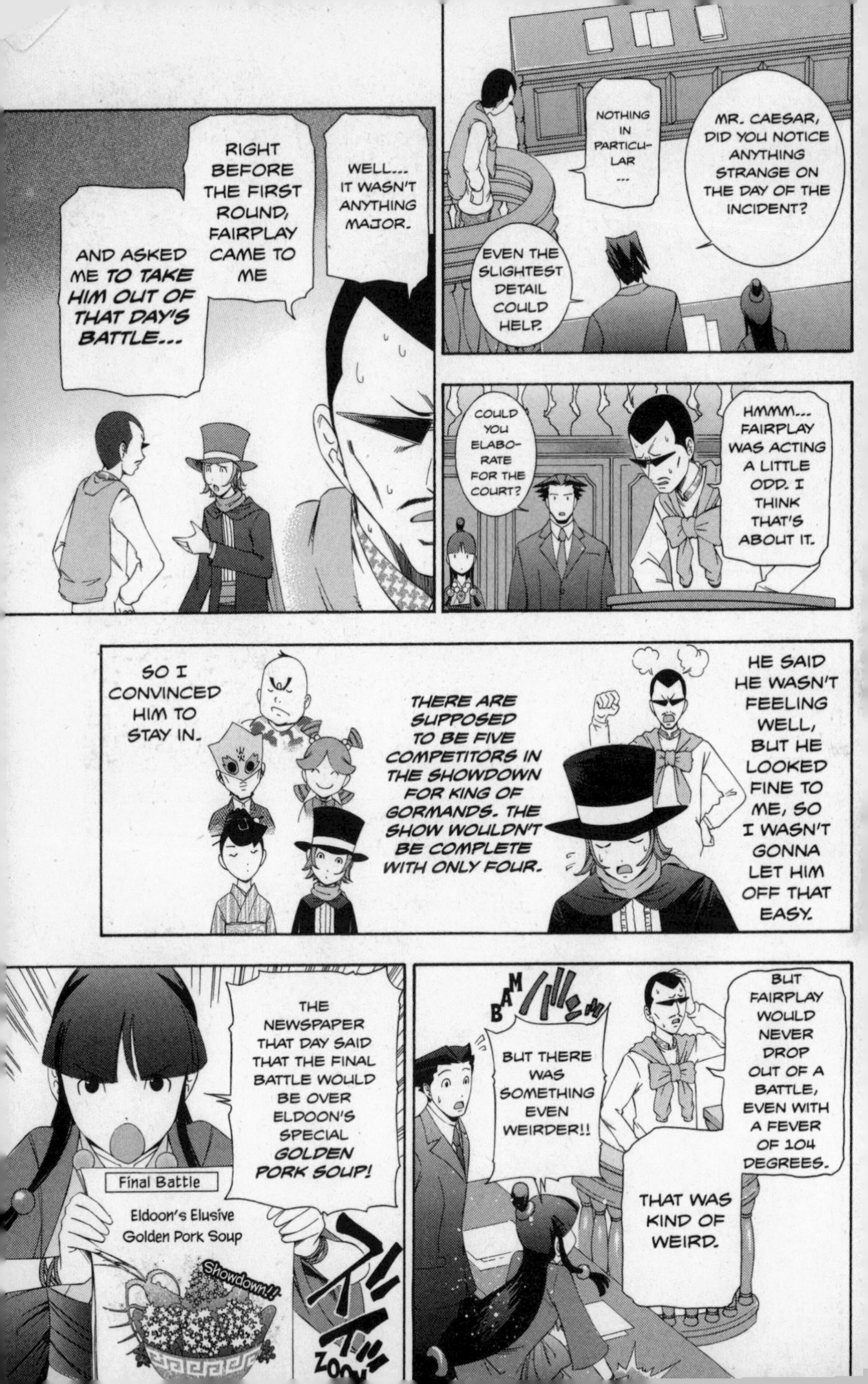
MR. CAESAR, DID YOU NOTICE ANYTHING STRANGE ON THE DAY OF THE INCIDENT?
NOTHING IN PARTICULAR...
EVEN THE SLIGHTEST DETAIL COULD HELP.
HMMM... FAIRPLAY WAS ACTING A LITTLE ODD. I THINK THAT'S ABOUT IT.
COULD YOU ELABORATE FOR THE COURT?
WELL... IT WASN'T ANYTHING MAJOR.
RIGHT BEFORE THE FIRST ROUND, FAIRPLAY CAME TO ME
AND ASKED ME TO TAKE HIM OUT OF THAT DAY'S BATTLE...
HE SAID HE WASN'T FEELING WELL, BUT HE LOOKED FINE TO ME, SO I WASN'T GONNA LET HIM OFF THAT EASY.
THERE ARE SUPPOSED TO BE FIVE COMPETITORS IN THE SHOWDOWN FOR KING OF GORMANDS. THE SHOW WOULDN'T BE COMPLETE WITH ONLY FOUR.
SO I CONVINCED HIM TO STAY IN.
BUT FAIRPLAY WOULD NEVER DROP OUT OF A BATTLE, EVEN WITH A FEVER OF 104 DEGREES.
THAT WAS KIND OF WEIRD.
BAM
BUT THERE WAS SOMETHING EVEN WEIRDER!!
THE NEWSPAPER THAT DAY SAID THAT THE FINAL BATTLE WOULD BE OVER ELDOON'S SPECIAL GOLDEN PORK SOUP!
Final Battle
Eldoon's Elusive Golden Pork Soup
Showdown!!

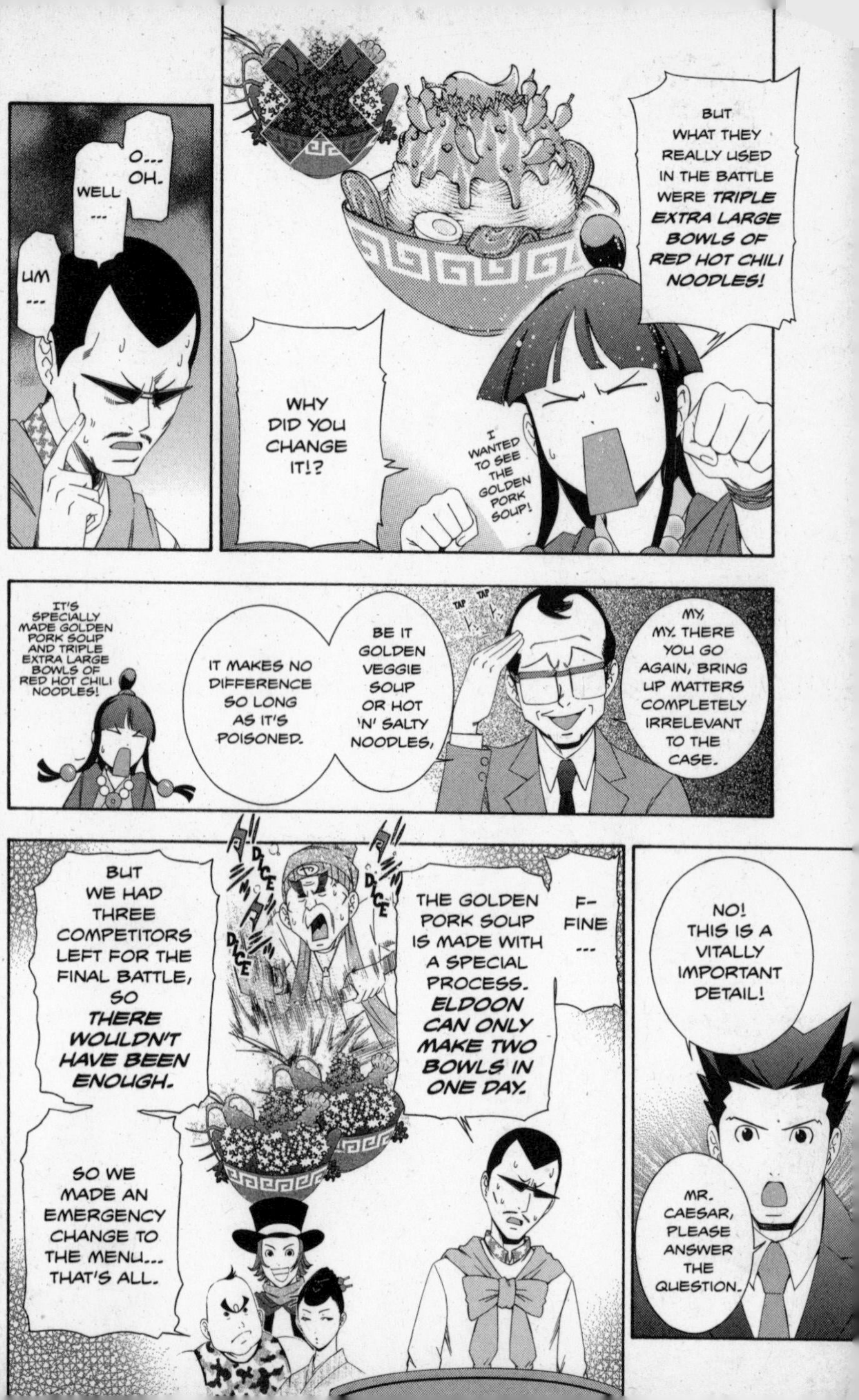
BUT WHAT THEY REALLY USED IN THE BATTLE WERE **TRIPLE EXTRA LARGE BOWLS OF RED HOT CHILI NOODLES!**
I WANTED TO SEE THE GOLDEN PORK SOUP!
WHY DID YOU CHANGE IT!?
O... OH.
WELL ...
UM ...
MY, MY. THERE YOU GO AGAIN, BRING UP MATTERS COMPLETELY IRRELEVANT TO THE CASE.
TAP TAP
BE IT GOLDEN VEGGIE SOUP OR HOT 'N' SALTY NOODLES,
IT MAKES NO DIFFERENCE SO LONG AS IT'S POISONED.
IT'S SPECIALLY MADE GOLDEN PORK SOUP AND TRIPLE EXTRA LARGE BOWLS OF RED HOT CHILI NOODLES!
NO! THIS IS A VITALLY IMPORTANT DETAIL!
MR. CAESAR, PLEASE ANSWER THE QUESTION.
F-FINE ---
THE GOLDEN PORK SOUP IS MADE WITH A SPECIAL PROCESS. **ELDOON CAN ONLY MAKE TWO BOWLS IN ONE DAY.**
DICE DICE DICE
BUT WE HAD THREE COMPETITORS LEFT FOR THE FINAL BATTLE, SO **THERE WOULDN'T HAVE BEEN ENOUGH.**
SO WE MADE AN EMERGENCY CHANGE TO THE MENU... THAT'S ALL.

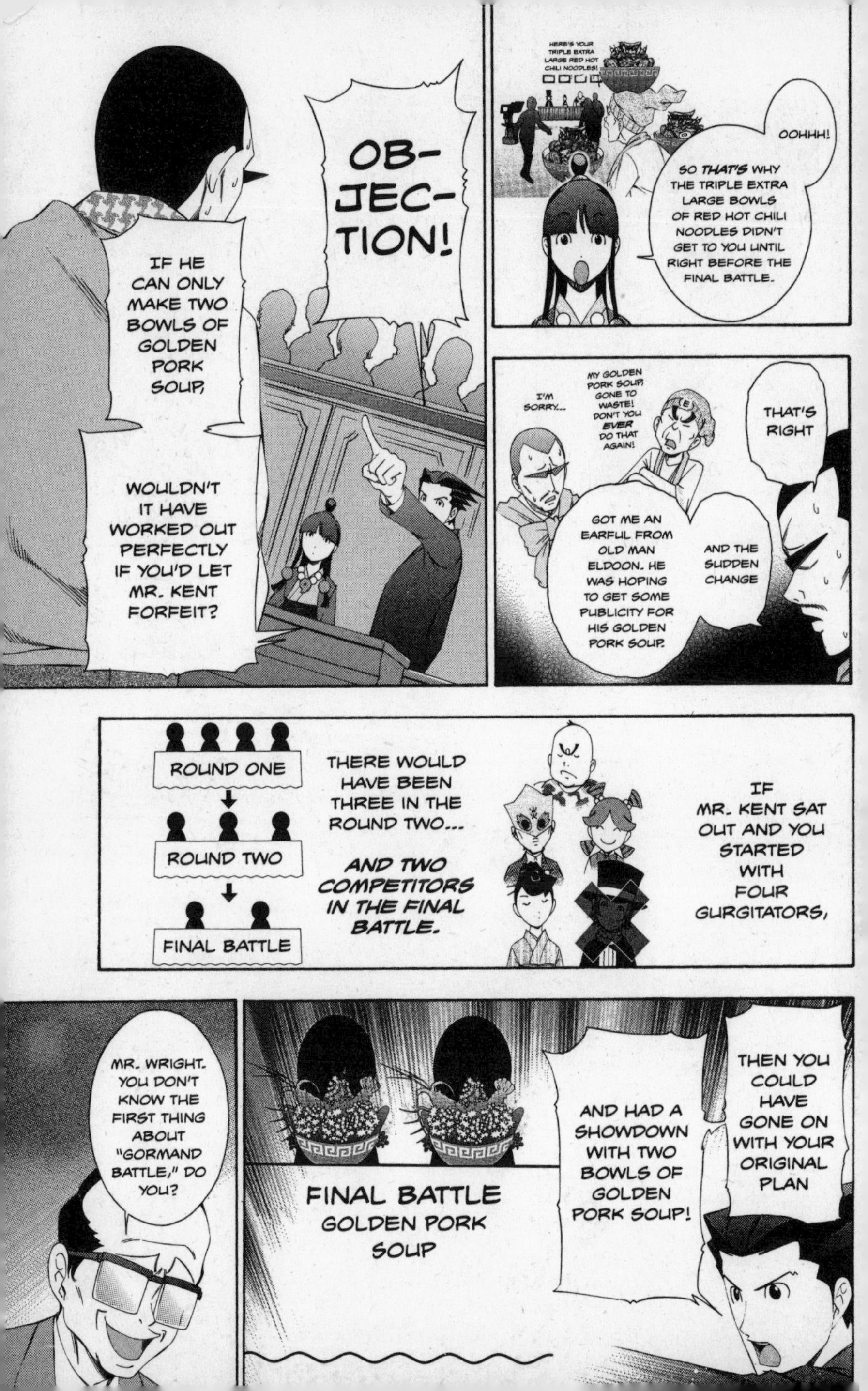
OOHHH!
SO THAT'S WHY THE TRIPLE EXTRA LARGE BOWLS OF RED HOT CHILI NOODLES DIDN'T GET TO YOU UNTIL RIGHT BEFORE THE FINAL BATTLE.
HERE'S YOUR TRIPLE EXTRA LARGE RED HOT CHILI NOODLES!
THAT'S RIGHT
AND THE SUDDEN CHANGE
GOT ME AN EARFUL FROM OLD MAN ELDOON. HE WAS HOPING TO GET SOME PUBLICITY FOR HIS GOLDEN PORK SOUP.
MY GOLDEN PORK SOUP, GONE TO WASTE! DON'T YOU EVER DO THAT AGAIN!
I'M SORRY...
OB-JEC-TION!
IF HE CAN ONLY MAKE TWO BOWLS OF GOLDEN PORK SOUP,
WOULDN'T IT HAVE WORKED OUT PERFECTLY IF YOU'D LET MR. KENT FORFEIT?
IF MR. KENT SAT OUT AND YOU STARTED WITH FOUR GURGITATORS,
THERE WOULD HAVE BEEN THREE IN THE ROUND TWO...
AND TWO COMPETITORS IN THE FINAL BATTLE.
ROUND ONE
ROUND TWO
FINAL BATTLE
THEN YOU COULD HAVE GONE ON WITH YOUR ORIGINAL PLAN
AND HAD A SHOWDOWN WITH TWO BOWLS OF GOLDEN PORK SOUP!
FINAL BATTLE GOLDEN PORK SOUP
MR. WRIGHT. YOU DON'T KNOW THE FIRST THING ABOUT "GORMAND BATTLE," DO YOU?

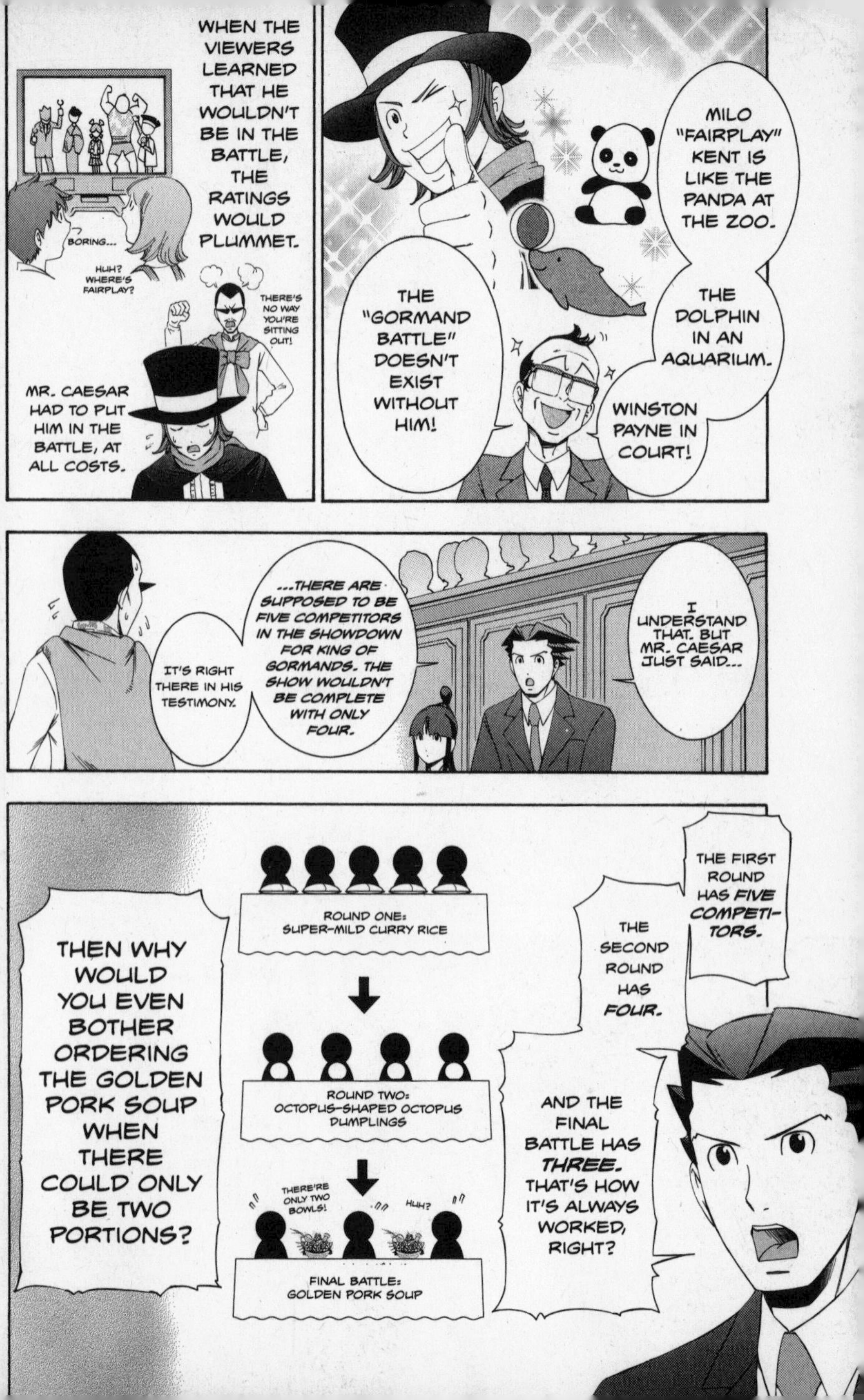
MILO "FAIRPLAY" KENT IS LIKE THE PANDA AT THE ZOO.
THE DOLPHIN IN AN AQUARIUM.
WINSTON PAYNE IN COURT!
THE "GORMAND BATTLE" DOESN'T EXIST WITHOUT HIM!
WHEN THE VIEWERS LEARNED THAT HE WOULDN'T BE IN THE BATTLE, THE RATINGS WOULD PLUMMET.
BORING...
HUH? WHERE'S FAIRPLAY?
THERE'S NO WAY YOU'RE SITTING OUT!
MR. CAESAR HAD TO PUT HIM IN THE BATTLE, AT ALL COSTS.
I UNDERSTAND THAT. BUT MR. CAESAR JUST SAID...
...THERE ARE SUPPOSED TO BE FIVE COMPETITORS IN THE SHOWDOWN FOR KING OF GORMANDS. THE SHOW WOULDN'T BE COMPLETE WITH ONLY FOUR.
IT'S RIGHT THERE IN HIS TESTIMONY.
THE FIRST ROUND HAS FIVE COMPETITORS.
THE SECOND ROUND HAS FOUR.
AND THE FINAL BATTLE HAS THREE. THAT'S HOW IT'S ALWAYS WORKED, RIGHT?
ROUND ONE: SUPER-MILD CURRY RICE
ROUND TWO: OCTOPUS-SHAPED OCTOPUS DUMPLINGS
HUH?
THERE'RE ONLY TWO BOWLS!
FINAL BATTLE: GOLDEN PORK SOUP
THEN WHY WOULD YOU EVEN BOTHER ORDERING THE GOLDEN PORK SOUP WHEN THERE COULD ONLY BE TWO PORTIONS?

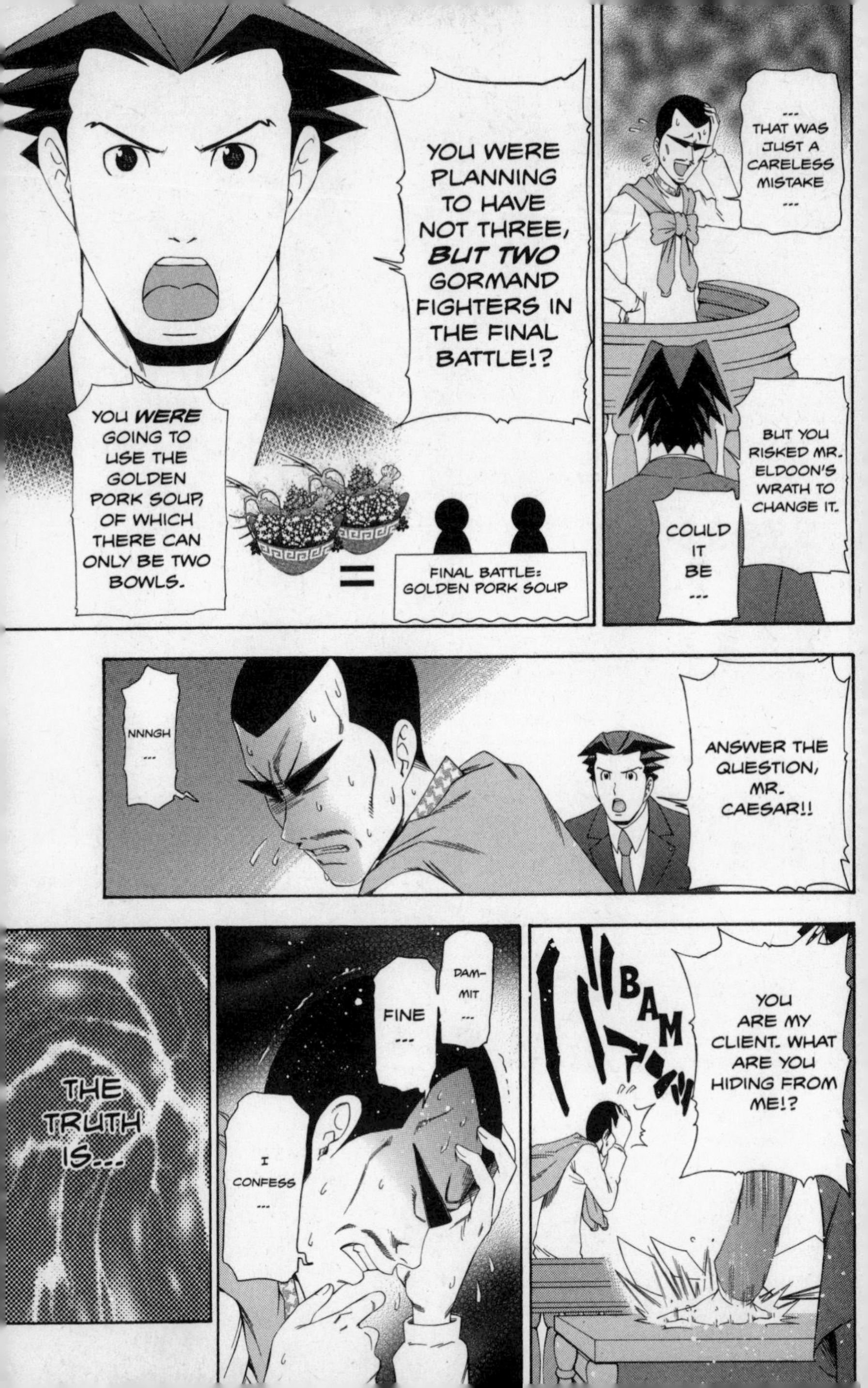
... THAT WAS JUST A CARELESS MISTAKE ...
BUT YOU RISKED MR. ELDOON'S WRATH TO CHANGE IT.
COULD IT BE ...
YOU WERE PLANNING TO HAVE NOT THREE, ***BUT TWO*** GORMAND FIGHTERS IN THE FINAL BATTLE!?
YOU ***WERE*** GOING TO USE THE GOLDEN PORK SOUP, OF WHICH THERE CAN ONLY BE TWO BOWLS.
FINAL BATTLE: GOLDEN PORK SOUP
ANSWER THE QUESTION, MR. CAESAR!!
NNNGH ...
BAM
YOU ARE MY CLIENT. WHAT ARE YOU HIDING FROM ME!?
DAM-MIT ...
FINE ...
I CONFESS ...
THE TRUTH IS...

WHAT!?

A... A THIRD ROUND!?

THERE WAS *A THIRD ROUND* THAT WE COULDN'T PUT ON THE AIR!!

ROUND THREE

FINAL BATTLE	

MR. WRIGHT IS CORRECT. WE WERE *PLANNING* TO HAVE TWO COMPETITORS IN THE FINAL BATTLE.

ROUND ONE				

ROUND TWO			

ROUND THREE			

FINAL BATTLE		

BUT *WE COULDN'T AIR ROUND THREE*, SO WE WENT ON TO THE FINAL BATTLE WITH THE SAME THREE FIGHTERS.

I HAD NO CHOICE! THE SPONSORS WOULD HAVE HAD MY NECK!

WH-WHY WOULD YOU HIDE THAT FACT!?

FAIRPLAY *WAS A DISGRACE* IN ROUND THREE!!

THAT'S WHY WE COULDN'T USE THE GOLDEN PORK SOUP—BECAUSE WE COULD ONLY GET TWO SERVINGS!

FINAL BATTLE		

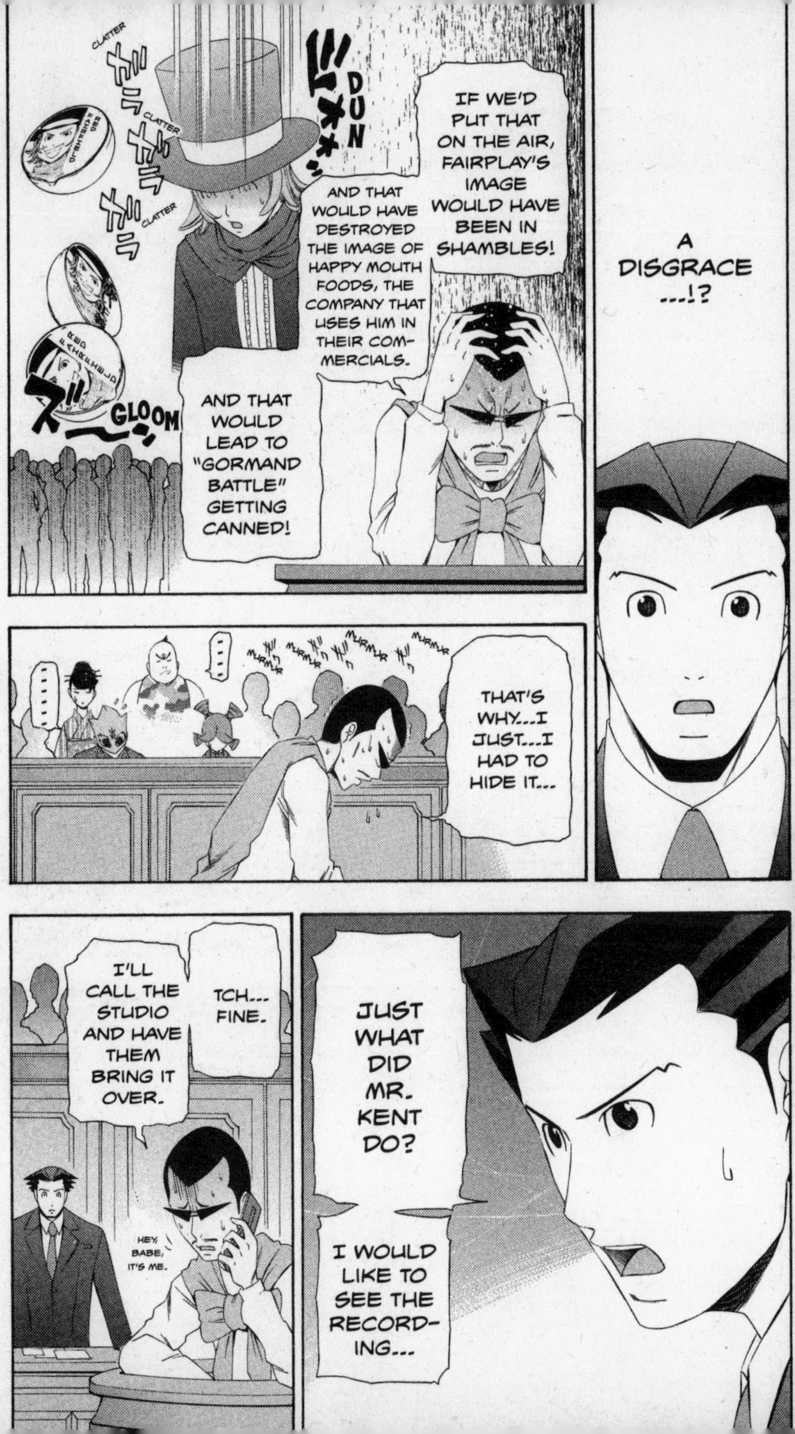
A DISGRACE ---!?
IF WE'D PUT THAT ON THE AIR, FAIRPLAY'S IMAGE WOULD HAVE BEEN IN SHAMBLES!
DUN
AND THAT WOULD HAVE DESTROYED THE IMAGE OF HAPPY MOUTH FOODS, THE COMPANY THAT USES HIM IN THEIR COM-MERCIALS.
CLATTER
CLATTER
CLATTER
AND THAT WOULD LEAD TO "GORMAND BATTLE" GETTING CANNED!
GLOOM
MURMUR
MURMUR
MURMUR
MURMUR
THAT'S WHY...I JUST...I HAD TO HIDE IT...
JUST WHAT DID MR. KENT DO?
I WOULD LIKE TO SEE THE RECORD-ING...
TCH... FINE.
I'LL CALL THE STUDIO AND HAVE THEM BRING IT OVER.
HEY, BABE, IT'S ME.

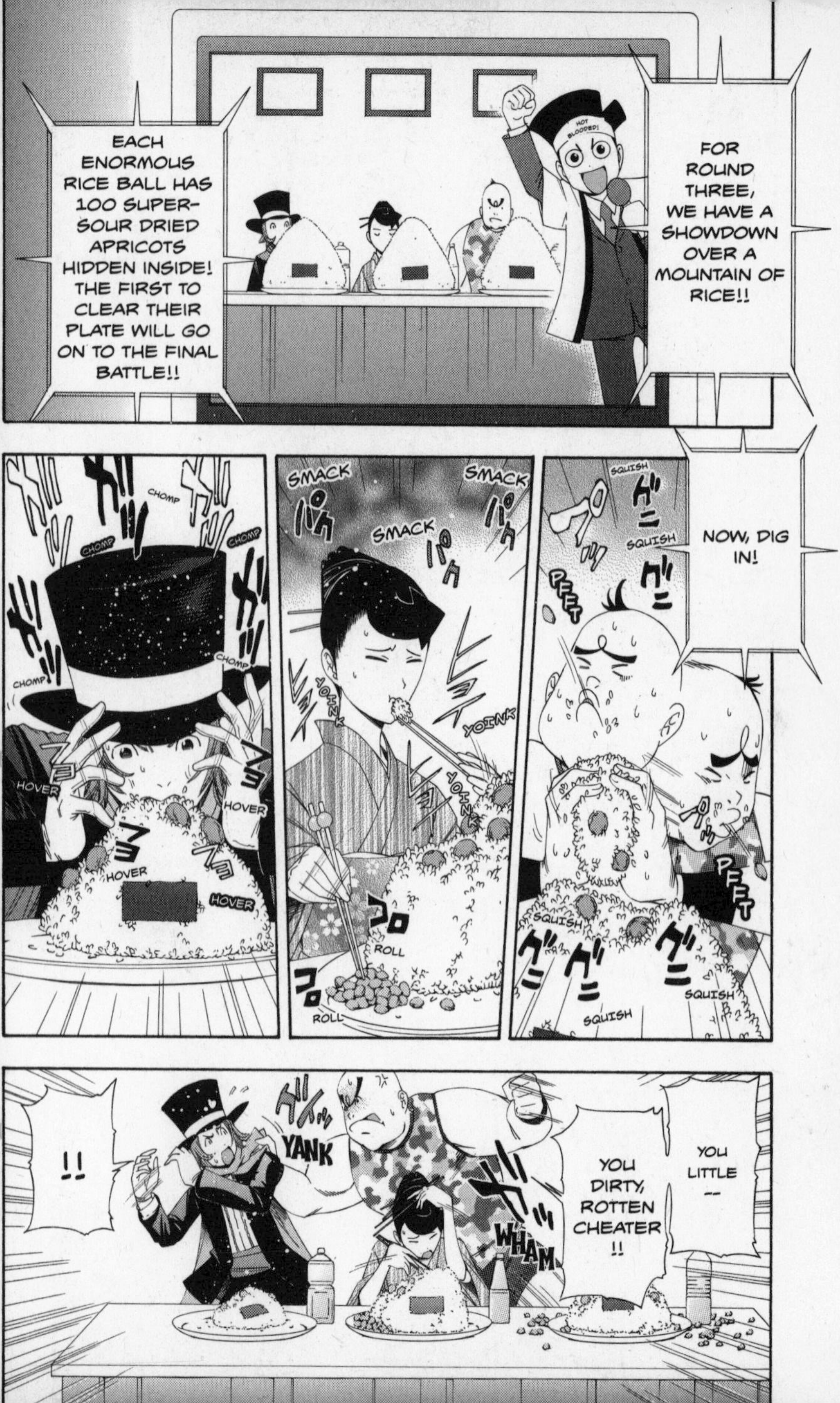
HOT BLOODED!
FOR ROUND THREE, WE HAVE A SHOWDOWN OVER A MOUNTAIN OF RICE!!
EACH ENORMOUS RICE BALL HAS 100 SUPER-SOUR DRIED APRICOTS HIDDEN INSIDE! THE FIRST TO CLEAR THEIR PLATE WILL GO ON TO THE FINAL BATTLE!!
NOW, DIG IN!
SQUISH
SQUISH
PFFT
PFFT
SQUISH
SQUISH
SQUISH
SMACK
SMACK
SMACK
YOINK
YOINK
YOINK
ROLL
ROLL
CHOMP
CHOMP
CHOMP
CHOMP
CHOMP
HOVER
HOVER
HOVER
HOVER
YOU LITTLE --
YOU DIRTY, ROTTEN CHEATER!!
WHAM
YANK
!!

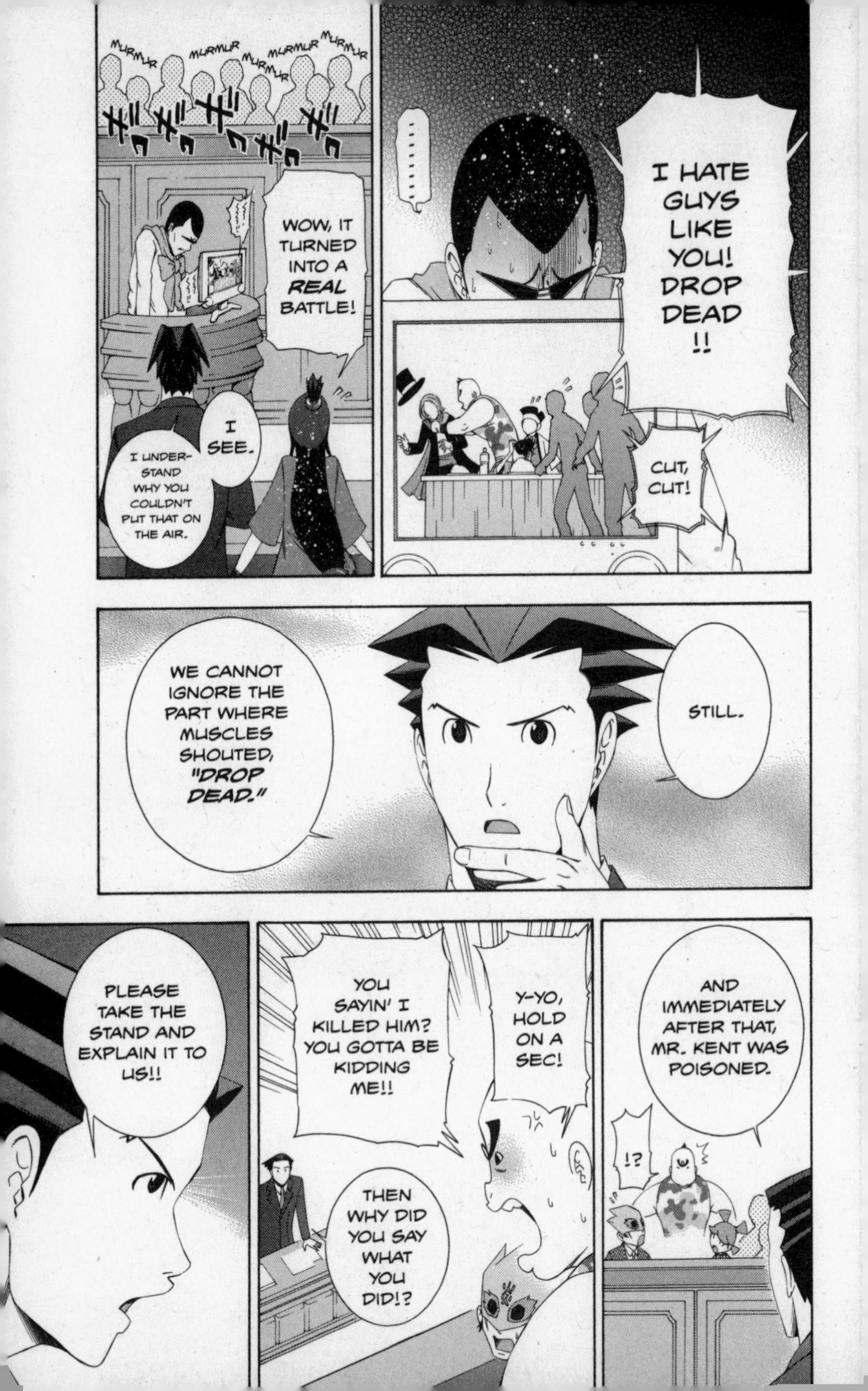
I HATE GUYS LIKE YOU! DROP DEAD!!
......
CUT, CUT!
MURMUR MURMUR MURMUR MURMUR MURMUR
WOW, IT TURNED INTO A *REAL* BATTLE!
I SEE.
I UNDERSTAND WHY YOU COULDN'T PUT THAT ON THE AIR.
STILL.
WE CANNOT IGNORE THE PART WHERE MUSCLES SHOUTED, *"DROP DEAD."*
AND IMMEDIATELY AFTER THAT, MR. KENT WAS POISONED.
!?
Y-YO, HOLD ON A SEC!
YOU SAYIN' I KILLED HIM? YOU GOTTA BE KIDDING ME!!
THEN WHY DID YOU SAY WHAT YOU DID!?
PLEASE TAKE THE STAND AND EXPLAIN IT TO US!!

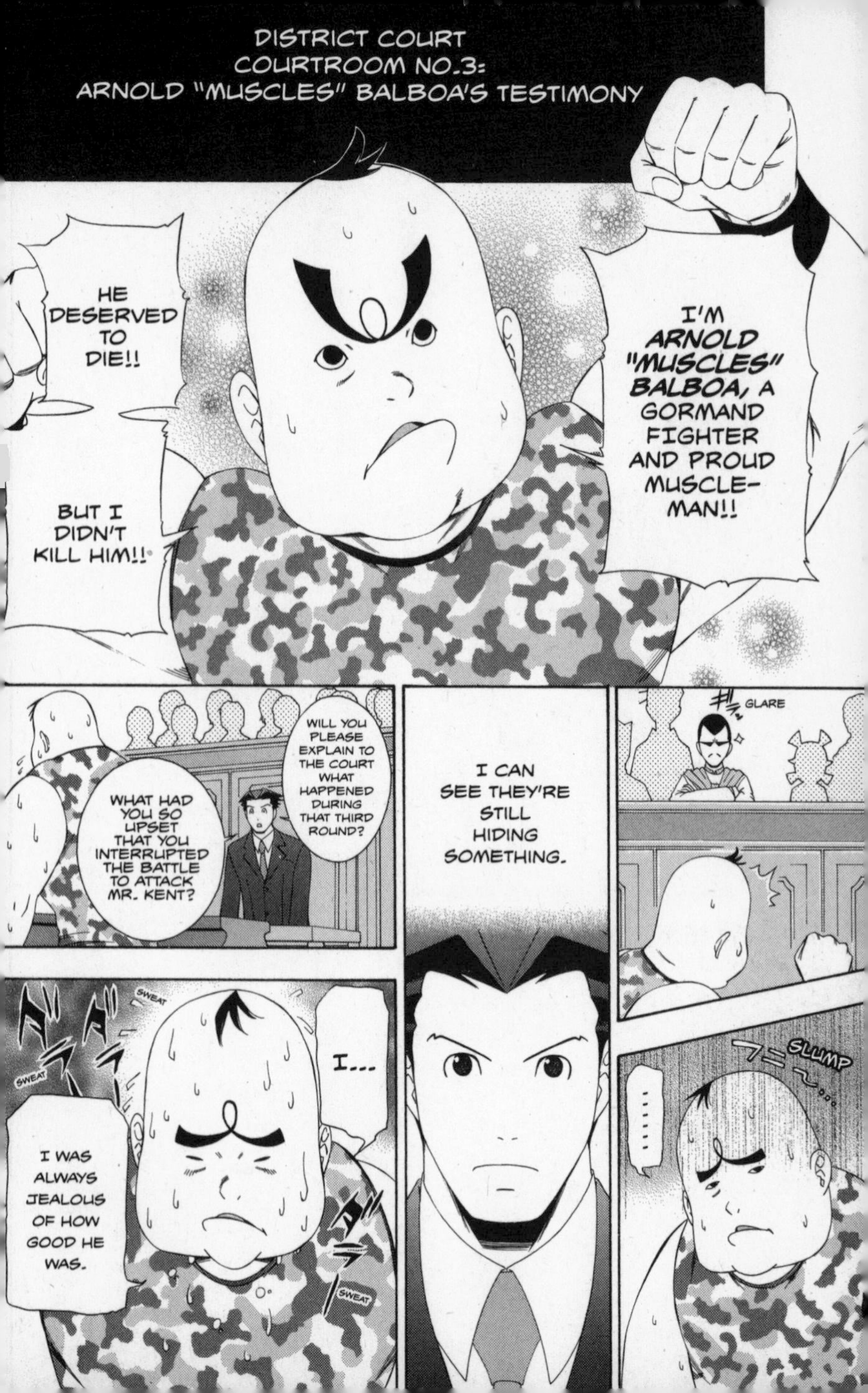
DISTRICT COURT
COURTROOM NO.3:
ARNOLD "MUSCLES" BALBOA'S TESTIMONY
I'M ARNOLD "MUSCLES" BALBOA, A GORMAND FIGHTER AND PROUD MUSCLE-MAN!!
HE DESERVED TO DIE!!
BUT I DIDN'T KILL HIM!!
GLARE
SLUMP
......
I CAN SEE THEY'RE STILL HIDING SOMETHING.
WILL YOU PLEASE EXPLAIN TO THE COURT WHAT HAPPENED DURING THAT THIRD ROUND?
WHAT HAD YOU SO UPSET THAT YOU INTERRUPTED THE BATTLE TO ATTACK MR. KENT?
SWEAT
SWEAT
I...
I WAS ALWAYS JEALOUS OF HOW GOOD HE WAS.
SWEAT

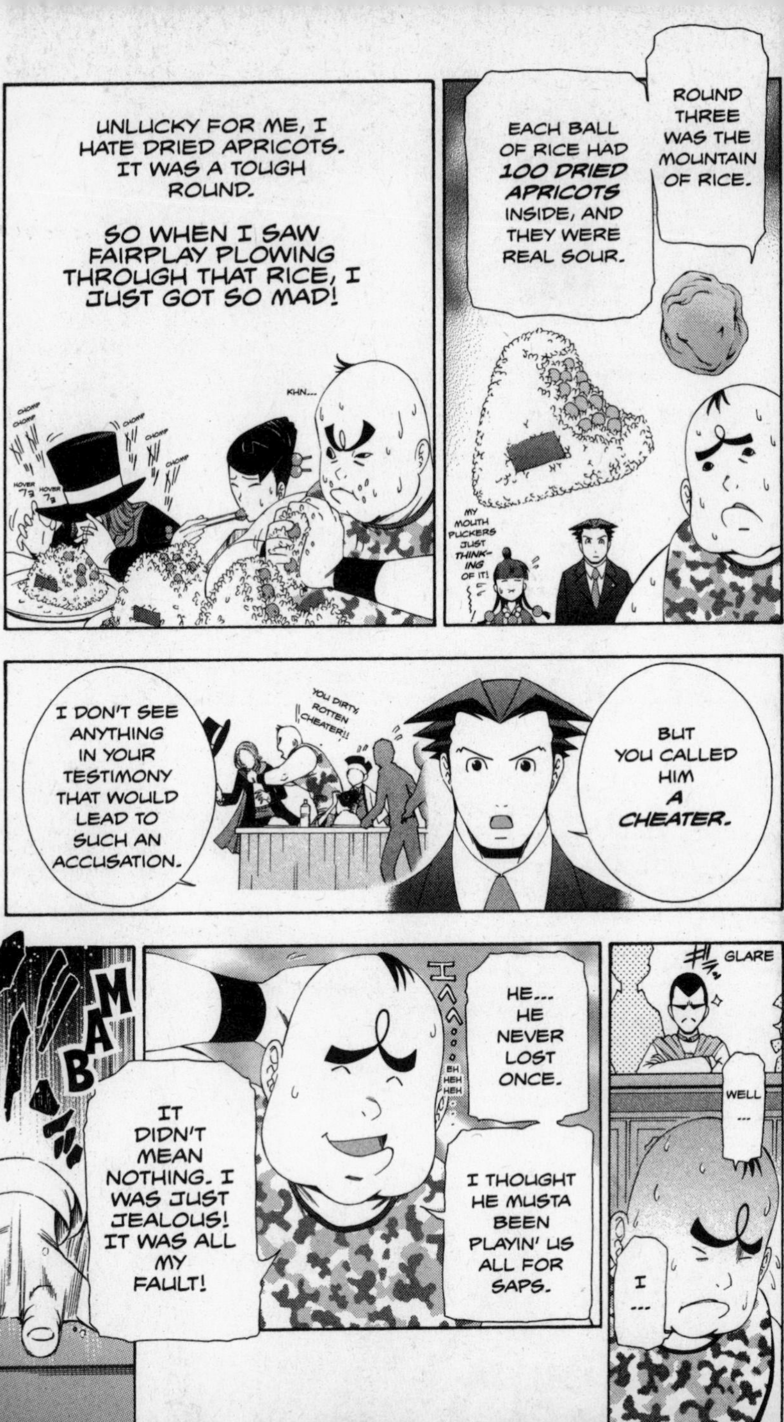
ROUND THREE WAS THE MOUNTAIN OF RICE.
EACH BALL OF RICE HAD 100 DRIED APRICOTS INSIDE, AND THEY WERE REAL SOUR.
MY MOUTH PUCKERS JUST THINKING OF IT!
UNLUCKY FOR ME, I HATE DRIED APRICOTS. IT WAS A TOUGH ROUND.
SO WHEN I SAW FAIRPLAY PLOWING THROUGH THAT RICE, I JUST GOT SO MAD!
KHN...
CHOMP CHOMP
CHOMP
CHOMP
CHOMP
HOVER
HOVER
BUT YOU CALLED HIM A CHEATER.
YOU DIRTY, ROTTEN CHEATER!!
I DON'T SEE ANYTHING IN YOUR TESTIMONY THAT WOULD LEAD TO SUCH AN ACCUSATION.
GLARE
WELL ...
I ...
HE... HE NEVER LOST ONCE.
EH HEH HEH
I THOUGHT HE MUSTA BEEN PLAYIN' US ALL FOR SAPS.
IT DIDN'T MEAN NOTHING. I WAS JUST JEALOUS! IT WAS ALL MY FAULT!
BAM

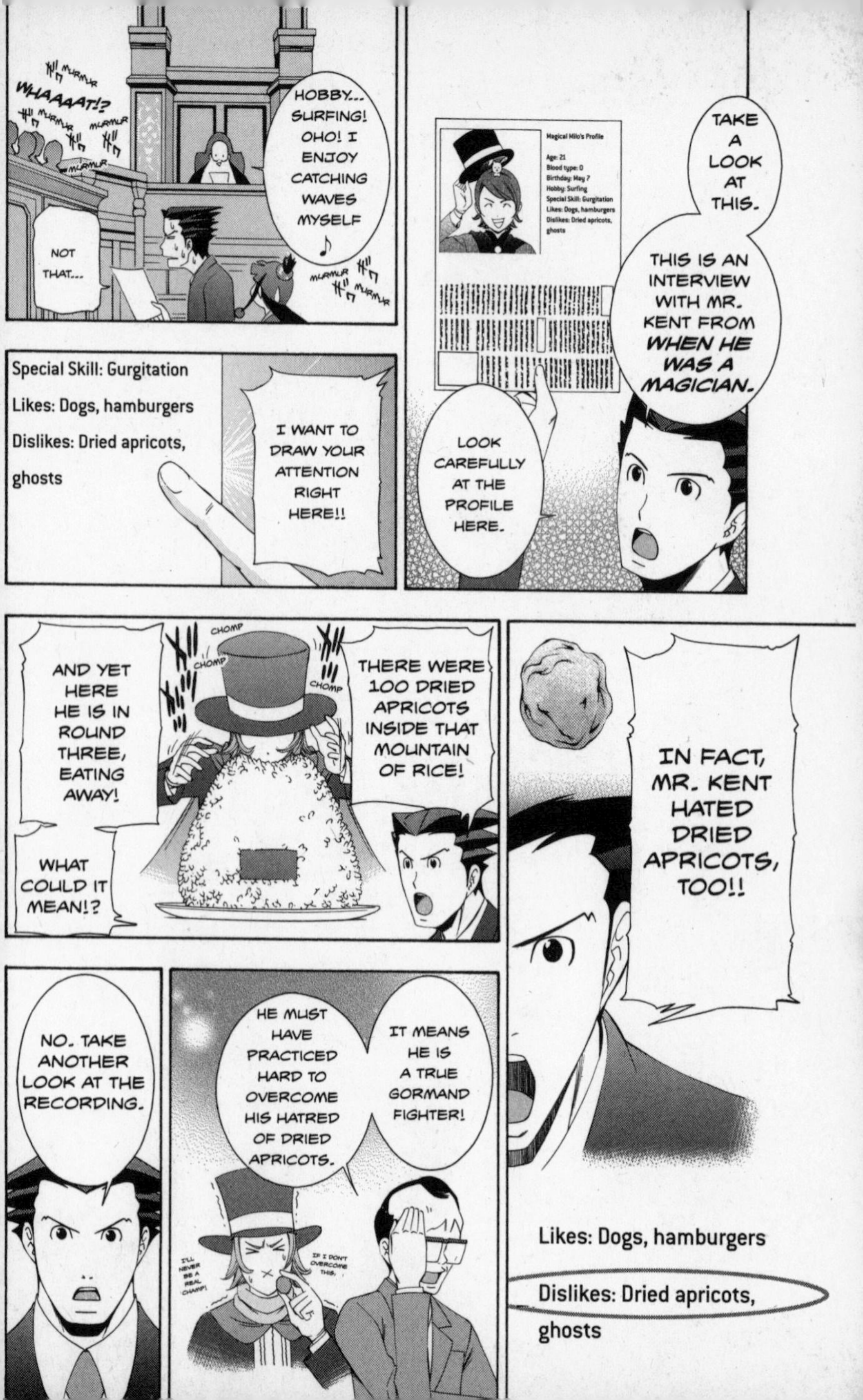
TAKE A LOOK AT THIS.
Magical Milo's Profile
Age: 21
Blood type: 0
Birthday: May 7
Hobby: Surfing
Special Skill: Gurgitation
Likes: Dogs, hamburgers
Dislikes: Dried apricots, ghosts
THIS IS AN INTERVIEW WITH MR. KENT FROM WHEN HE WAS A MAGICIAN.
LOOK CAREFULLY AT THE PROFILE HERE.
HOBBY... SURFING! OHO! I ENJOY CATCHING WAVES MYSELF ♪
MURMUR
WHAAAAT!?
MURMUR
MURMUR
MURMUR
NOT THAT...
MURMUR
MURMUR
Special Skill: Gurgitation
Likes: Dogs, hamburgers
Dislikes: Dried apricots, ghosts
I WANT TO DRAW YOUR ATTENTION RIGHT HERE!!
IN FACT, MR. KENT HATED DRIED APRICOTS, TOO!!
Likes: Dogs, hamburgers
Dislikes: Dried apricots, ghosts
THERE WERE 100 DRIED APRICOTS INSIDE THAT MOUNTAIN OF RICE!
CHOMP
CHOMP
CHOMP
AND YET HERE HE IS IN ROUND THREE, EATING AWAY!
WHAT COULD IT MEAN!?
IT MEANS HE IS A TRUE GORMAND FIGHTER!
HE MUST HAVE PRACTICED HARD TO OVERCOME HIS HATRED OF DRIED APRICOTS.
IF I DON'T OVERCOME THIS,
I'LL NEVER BE A REAL CHAMP!
NO. TAKE ANOTHER LOOK AT THE RECORDING.

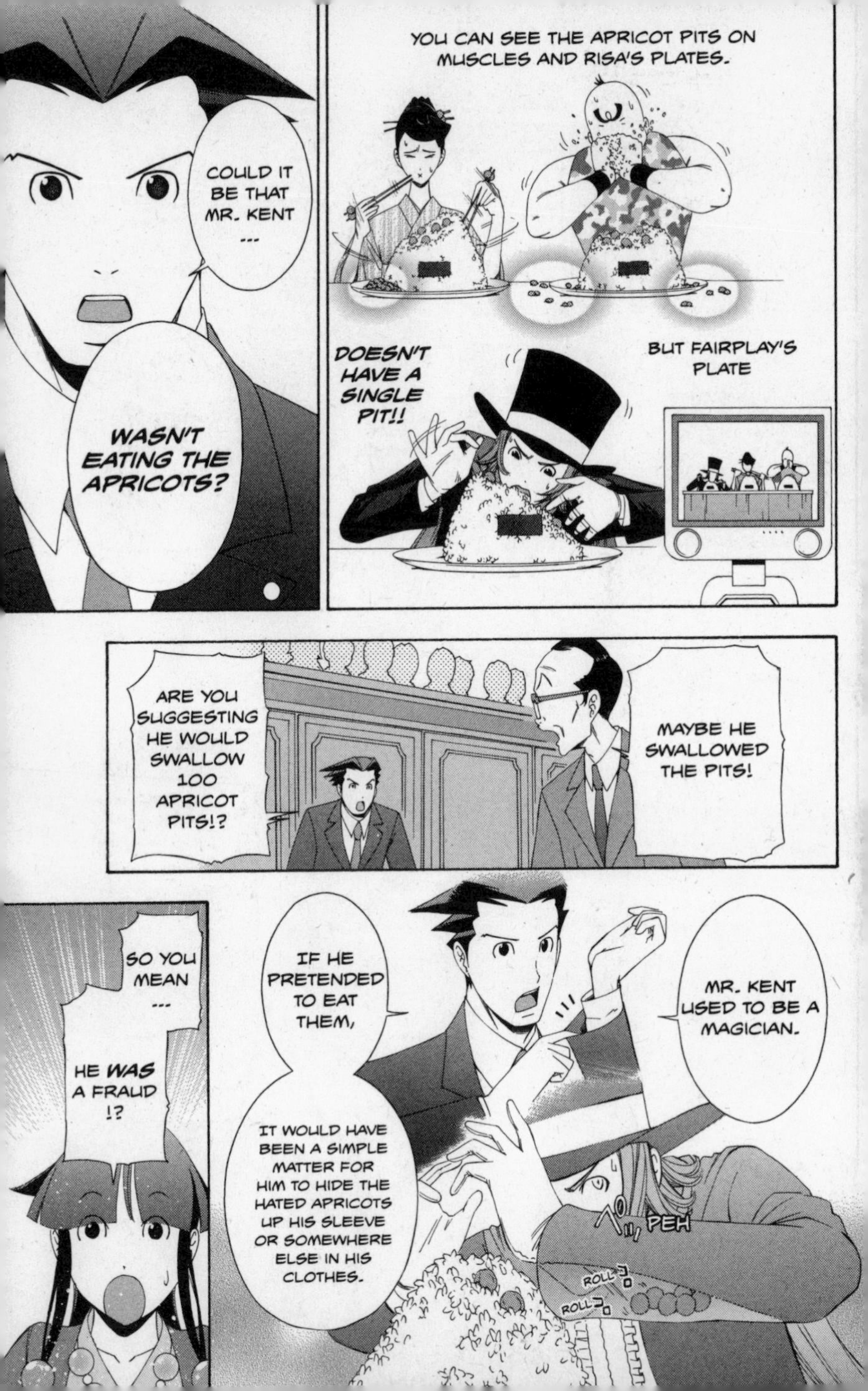
YOU CAN SEE THE APRICOT PITS ON MUSCLES AND RISA'S PLATES.
BUT FAIRPLAY'S PLATE
DOESN'T HAVE A SINGLE PIT!!
COULD IT BE THAT MR. KENT ---
WASN'T EATING THE APRICOTS?
MAYBE HE SWALLOWED THE PITS!
ARE YOU SUGGESTING HE WOULD SWALLOW 100 APRICOT PITS!?
MR. KENT USED TO BE A MAGICIAN.
IF HE PRETENDED TO EAT THEM,
IT WOULD HAVE BEEN A SIMPLE MATTER FOR HIM TO HIDE THE HATED APRICOTS UP HIS SLEEVE OR SOMEWHERE ELSE IN HIS CLOTHES.
PEH
ROLL
ROLL
SO YOU MEAN ---
HE *WAS* A FRAUD !?

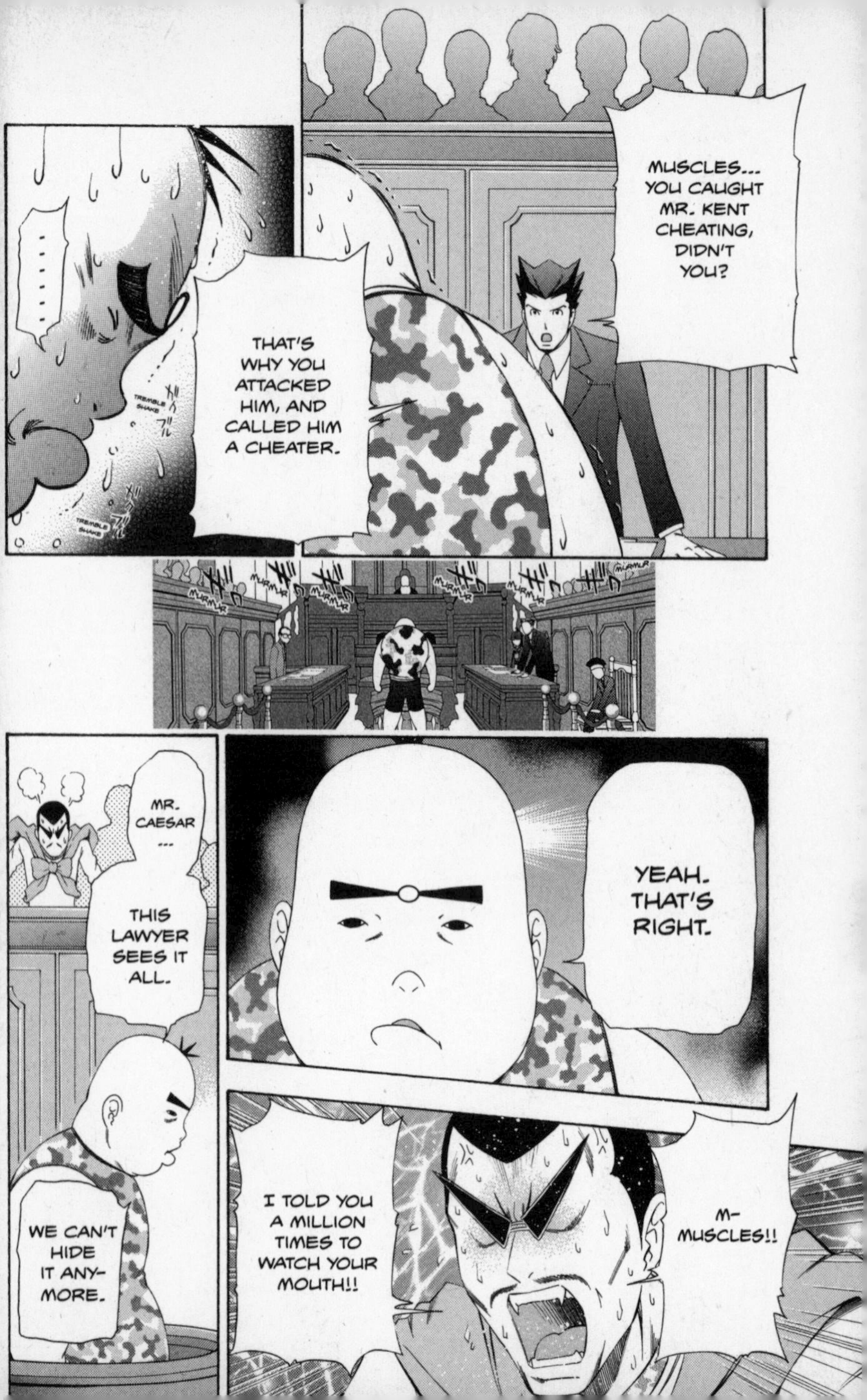

MUSCLES... YOU CAUGHT MR. KENT CHEATING, DIDN'T YOU?
THAT'S WHY YOU ATTACKED HIM, AND CALLED HIM A CHEATER.
......
TREMBLE SHAKE
TREMBLE SHAKE
MURMUR
MURMUR
MURMUR
MURMUR
MURMUR
MURMUR
YEAH. THAT'S RIGHT.
M-MUSCLES!!
I TOLD YOU A MILLION TIMES TO WATCH YOUR MOUTH!!
MR. CAESAR...
THIS LAWYER SEES IT ALL.
WE CAN'T HIDE IT ANYMORE.

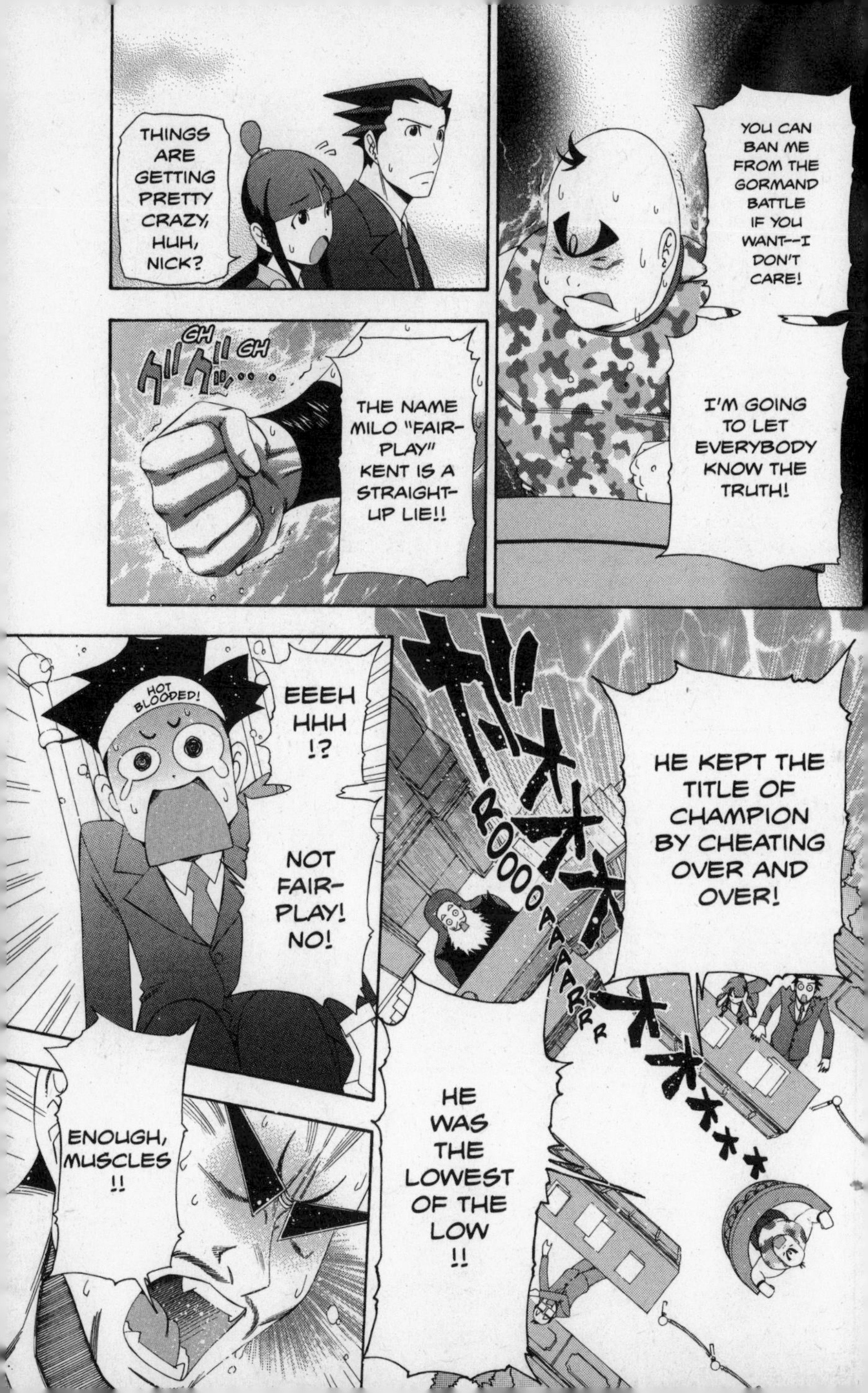
YOU CAN BAN ME FROM THE GORMAND BATTLE IF YOU WANT--I DON'T CARE!
I'M GOING TO LET EVERYBODY KNOW THE TRUTH!
THINGS ARE GETTING PRETTY CRAZY, HUH, NICK?
GH GH
THE NAME MILO "FAIR-PLAY" KENT IS A STRAIGHT-UP LIE!!
HE KEPT THE TITLE OF CHAMPION BY CHEATING OVER AND OVER!
ROOOOAAARRR
HE WAS THE LOWEST OF THE LOW!!
HOT BLOODED!
EEEH HHH!?
NOT FAIR-PLAY! NO!
ENOUGH, MUSCLES!!

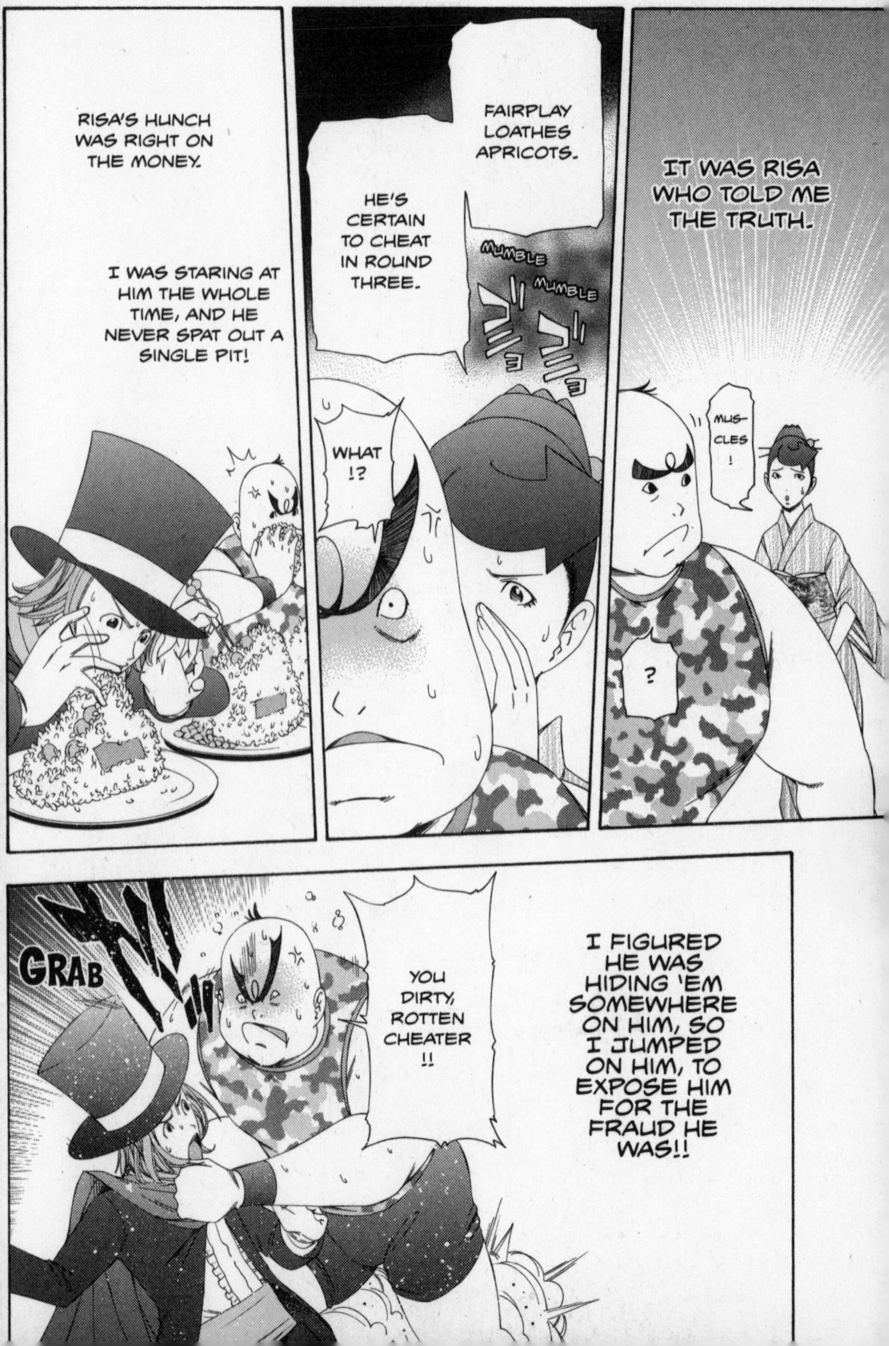
IT WAS RISA WHO TOLD ME THE TRUTH.
MUS-CLES!
?
FAIRPLAY LOATHES APRICOTS.
HE'S CERTAIN TO CHEAT IN ROUND THREE.
MUMBLE
MUMBLE
WHAT!?
RISA'S HUNCH WAS RIGHT ON THE MONEY.
I WAS STARING AT HIM THE WHOLE TIME, AND HE NEVER SPAT OUT A SINGLE PIT!
I FIGURED HE WAS HIDING 'EM SOMEWHERE ON HIM, SO I JUMPED ON HIM, TO EXPOSE HIM FOR THE FRAUD HE WAS!!
YOU DIRTY, ROTTEN CHEATER!!
GRAB

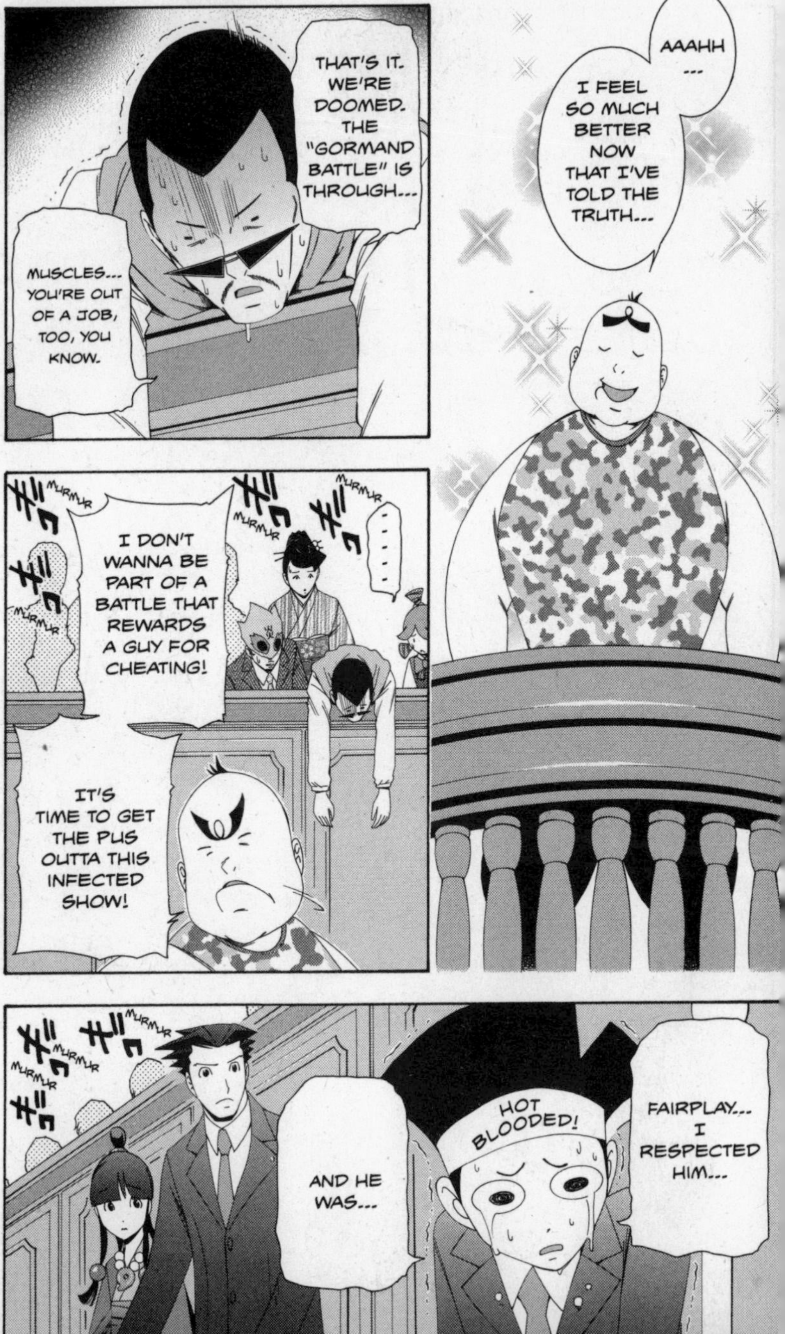
AAAHH ...
I FEEL SO MUCH BETTER NOW THAT I'VE TOLD THE TRUTH...
THAT'S IT. WE'RE DOOMED. THE "GORMAND BATTLE" IS THROUGH...
MUSCLES... YOU'RE OUT OF A JOB, TOO, YOU KNOW.
MURMUR
MURMUR
MURMUR
MURMUR
......
I DON'T WANNA BE PART OF A BATTLE THAT REWARDS A GUY FOR CHEATING!
IT'S TIME TO GET THE PUS OUTTA THIS INFECTED SHOW!
MURMUR
MURMUR
MURMUR
FAIRPLAY... I RESPECTED HIM...
HOT BLOODED!
AND HE WAS...

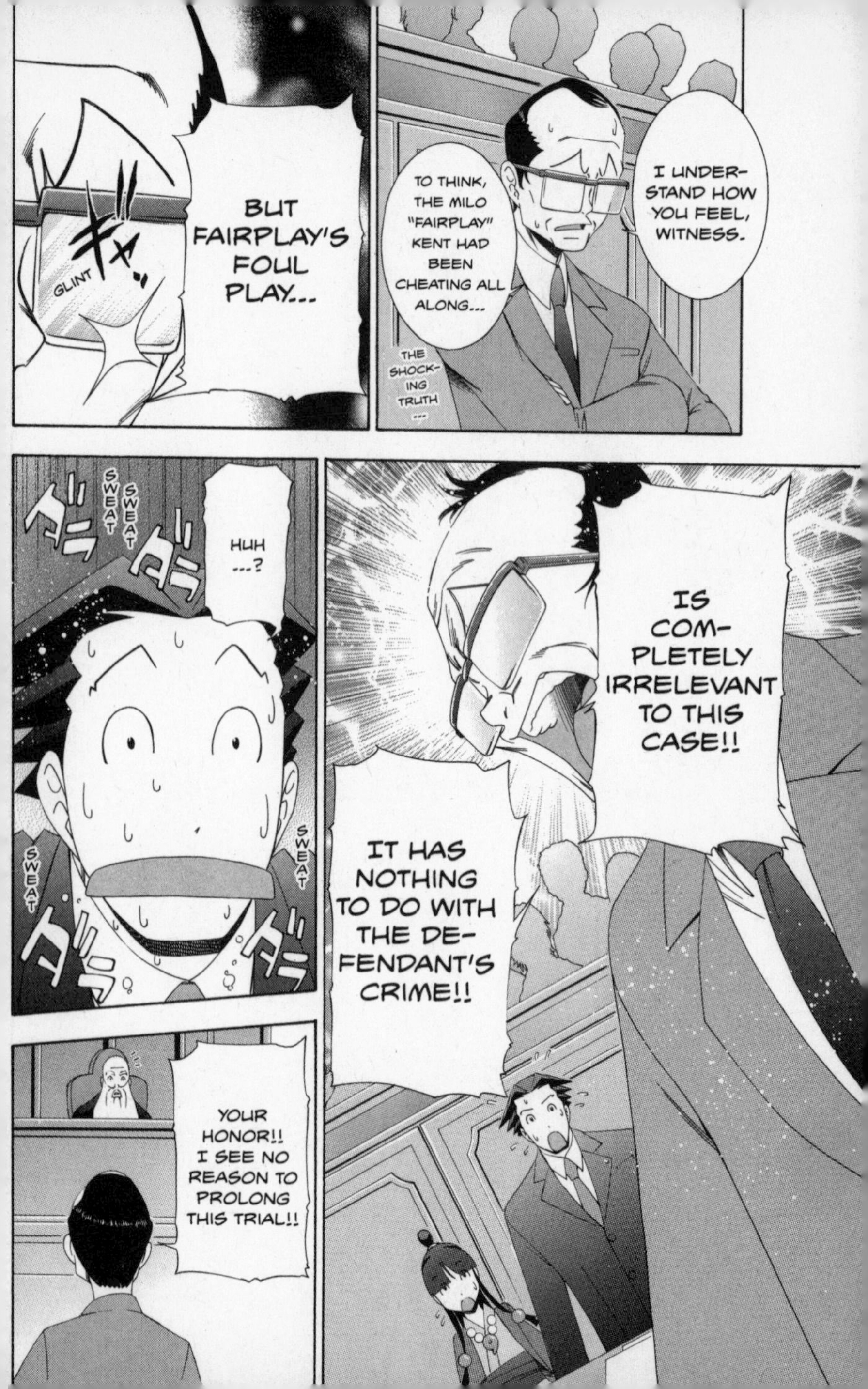
I UNDER-STAND HOW YOU FEEL, WITNESS.
TO THINK, THE MILO "FAIRPLAY" KENT HAD BEEN CHEATING ALL ALONG...
THE SHOCK-ING TRUTH ...
BUT FAIRPLAY'S FOUL PLAY...
GLINT
IS COM-PLETELY IRRELEVANT TO THIS CASE!!
IT HAS NOTHING TO DO WITH THE DE-FENDANT'S CRIME!!
SWEAT SWEAT
HUH ...?
SWEAT
SWEAT
YOUR HONOR!! I SEE NO REASON TO PROLONG THIS TRIAL!!

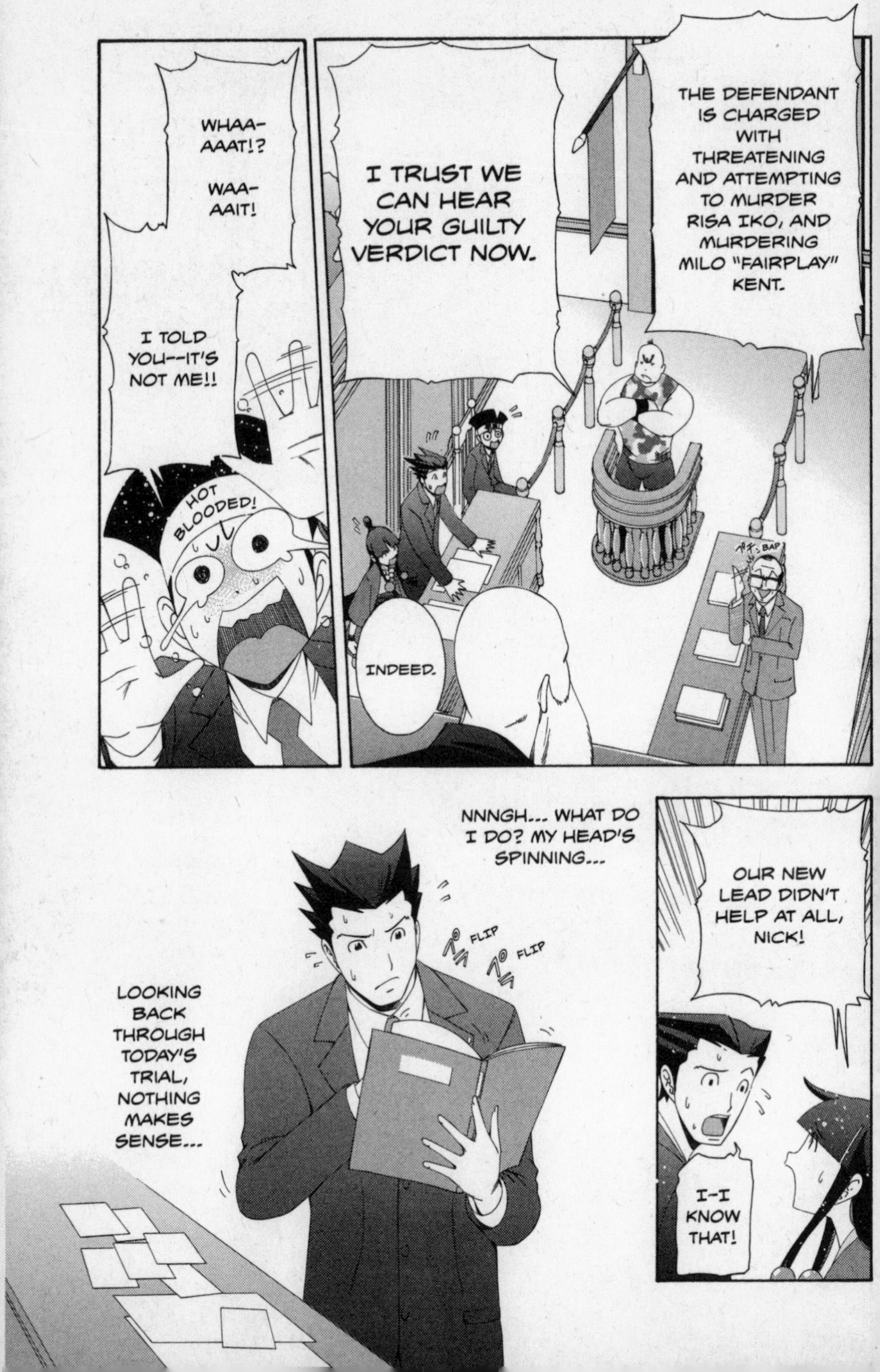
THE DEFENDANT IS CHARGED WITH THREATENING AND ATTEMPTING TO MURDER RISA IKO, AND MURDERING MILO "FAIRPLAY" KENT.
I TRUST WE CAN HEAR YOUR GUILTY VERDICT NOW.
BAP
INDEED.
WHAA-AAAT!?
WAA-AAIT!
I TOLD YOU--IT'S NOT ME!!
HOT BLOODED!
OUR NEW LEAD DIDN'T HELP AT ALL, NICK!
I-I KNOW THAT!
NNNGH... WHAT DO I DO? MY HEAD'S SPINNING...
FLIP
FLIP
LOOKING BACK THROUGH TODAY'S TRIAL, NOTHING MAKES SENSE...

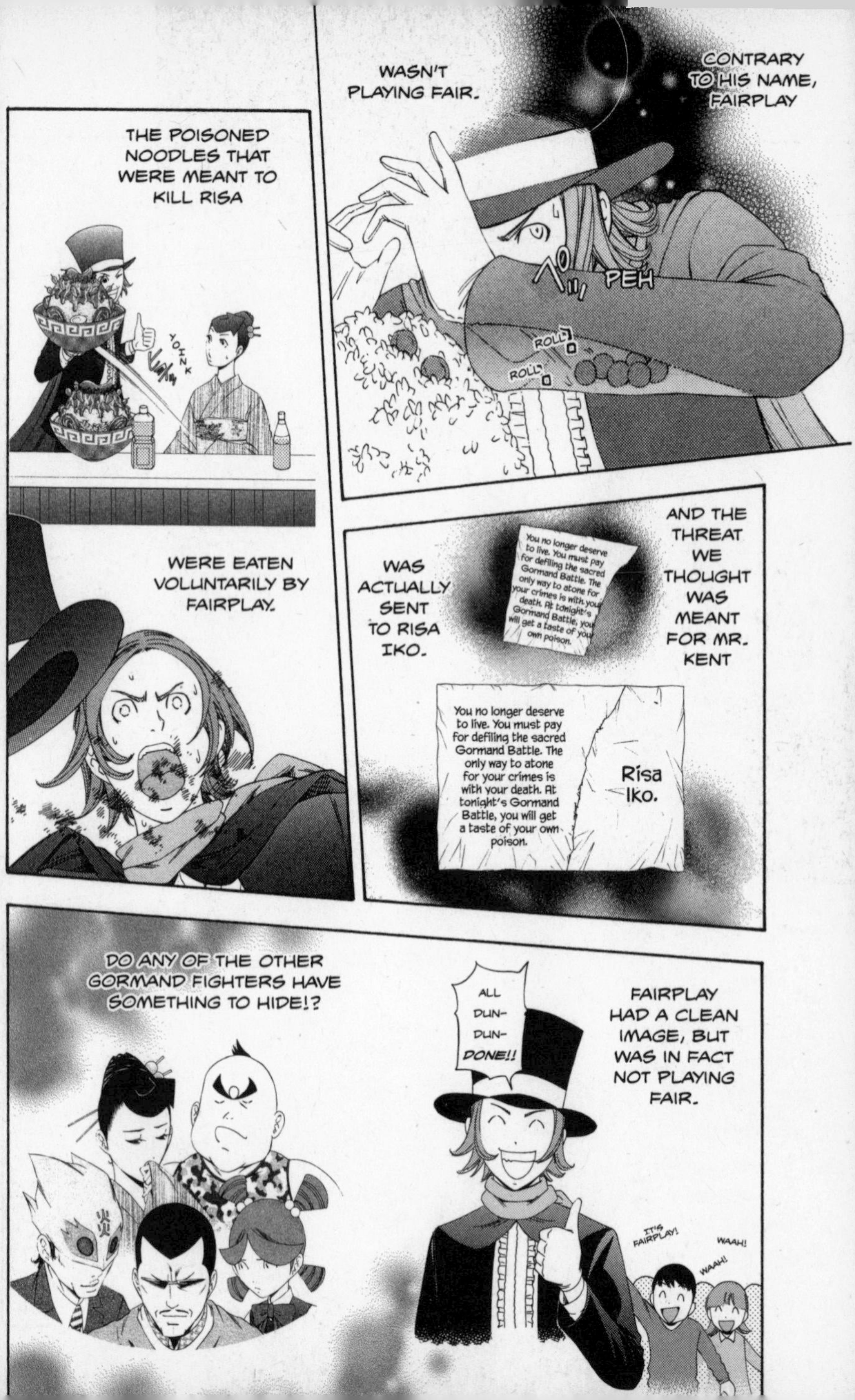

CONTRARY TO HIS NAME, FAIRPLAY
WASN'T PLAYING FAIR.
PEH
ROLL
ROLL
THE POISONED NOODLES THAT WERE MEANT TO KILL RISA
YOINK
AND THE THREAT WE THOUGHT WAS MEANT FOR MR. KENT
WAS ACTUALLY SENT TO RISA IKO.
You no longer deserve to live. You must pay for defiling the sacred Gormand Battle. The only way to atone for your crimes is with your death. At tonight's Gormand Battle, you will get a taste of your own poison.
You no longer deserve to live. You must pay for defiling the sacred Gormand Battle. The only way to atone for your crimes is with your death. At tonight's Gormand Battle, you will get a taste of your own poison.
Risa Iko.
WERE EATEN VOLUNTARILY BY FAIRPLAY.
FAIRPLAY HAD A CLEAN IMAGE, BUT WAS IN FACT NOT PLAYING FAIR.
ALL DUN-DUN-DONE!!
IT'S FAIRPLAY!
WAAH!
WAAH!
DO ANY OF THE OTHER GORMAND FIGHTERS HAVE SOMETHING TO HIDE!?

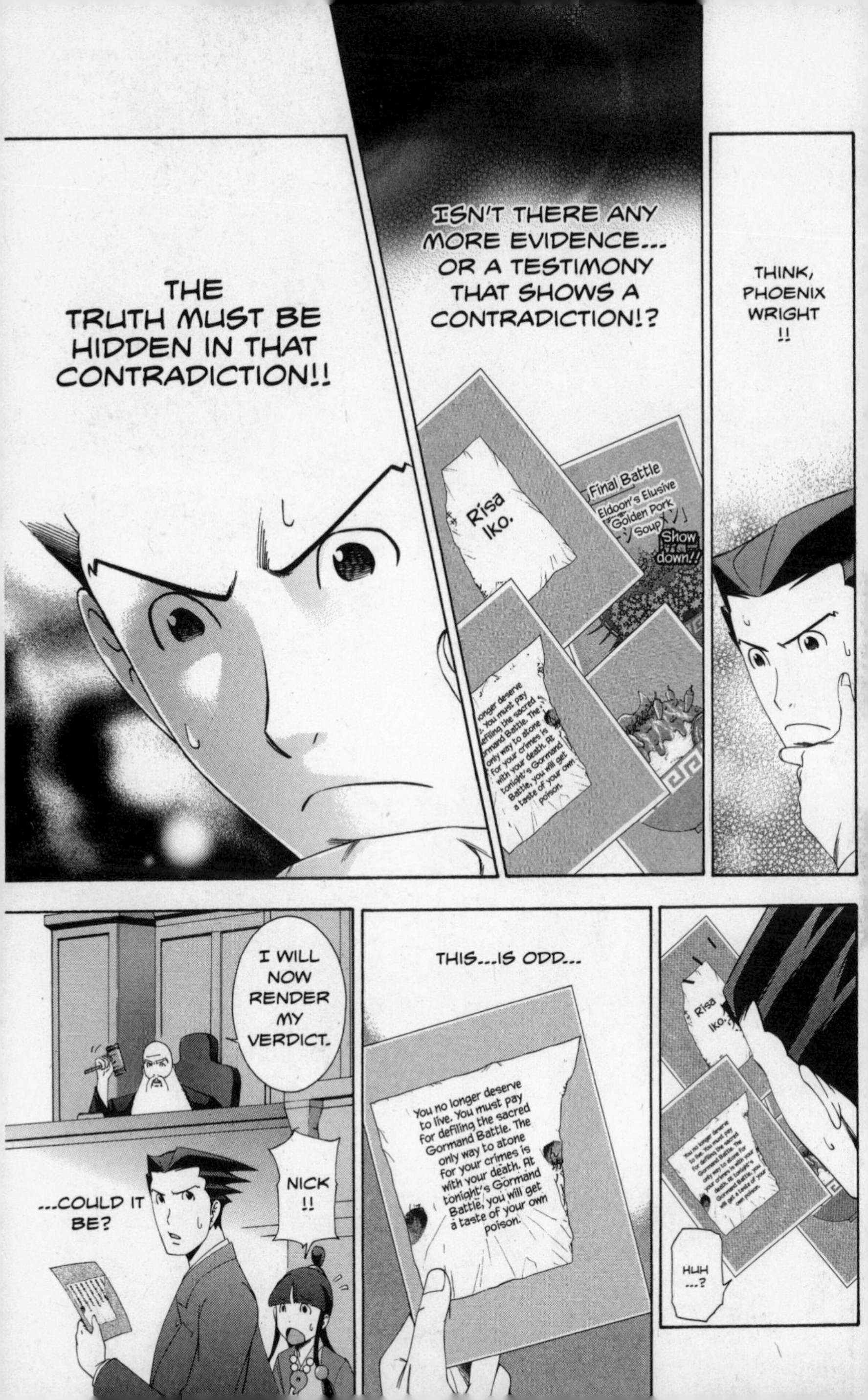
THINK, PHOENIX WRIGHT !!
ISN'T THERE ANY MORE EVIDENCE... OR A TESTIMONY THAT SHOWS A CONTRADICTION!?
Final Battle
Eldoon's Elusive Golden Pork Soup
Show down!!
Risa Iko.
THE TRUTH MUST BE HIDDEN IN THAT CONTRADICTION!!
Risa Iko.
HUH ...?
THIS...IS ODD...
You no longer deserve to live. You must pay for defiling the sacred Gormand Battle. The only way to atone for your crimes is with your death. At tonight's Gormand Battle, you will get a taste of your own poison.
I WILL NOW RENDER MY VERDICT.
NICK !!
...COULD IT BE?

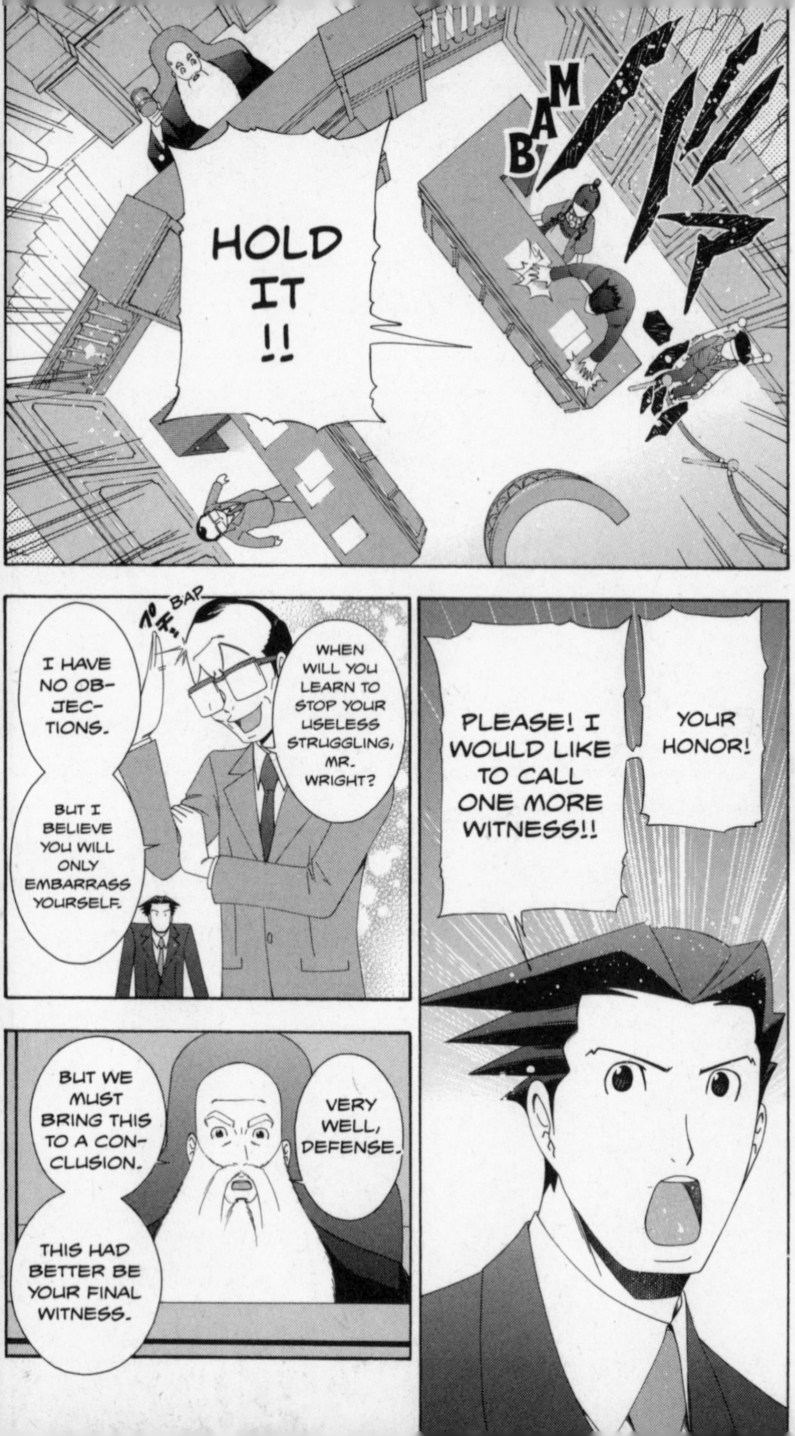
BAM
HOLD IT!!
YOUR HONOR!
PLEASE! I WOULD LIKE TO CALL ONE MORE WITNESS!!
BAP
WHEN WILL YOU LEARN TO STOP YOUR USELESS STRUGGLING, MR. WRIGHT?
I HAVE NO OBJECTIONS.
BUT I BELIEVE YOU WILL ONLY EMBARRASS YOURSELF.
VERY WELL, DEFENSE.
BUT WE MUST BRING THIS TO A CONCLUSION.
THIS HAD BETTER BE YOUR FINAL WITNESS.

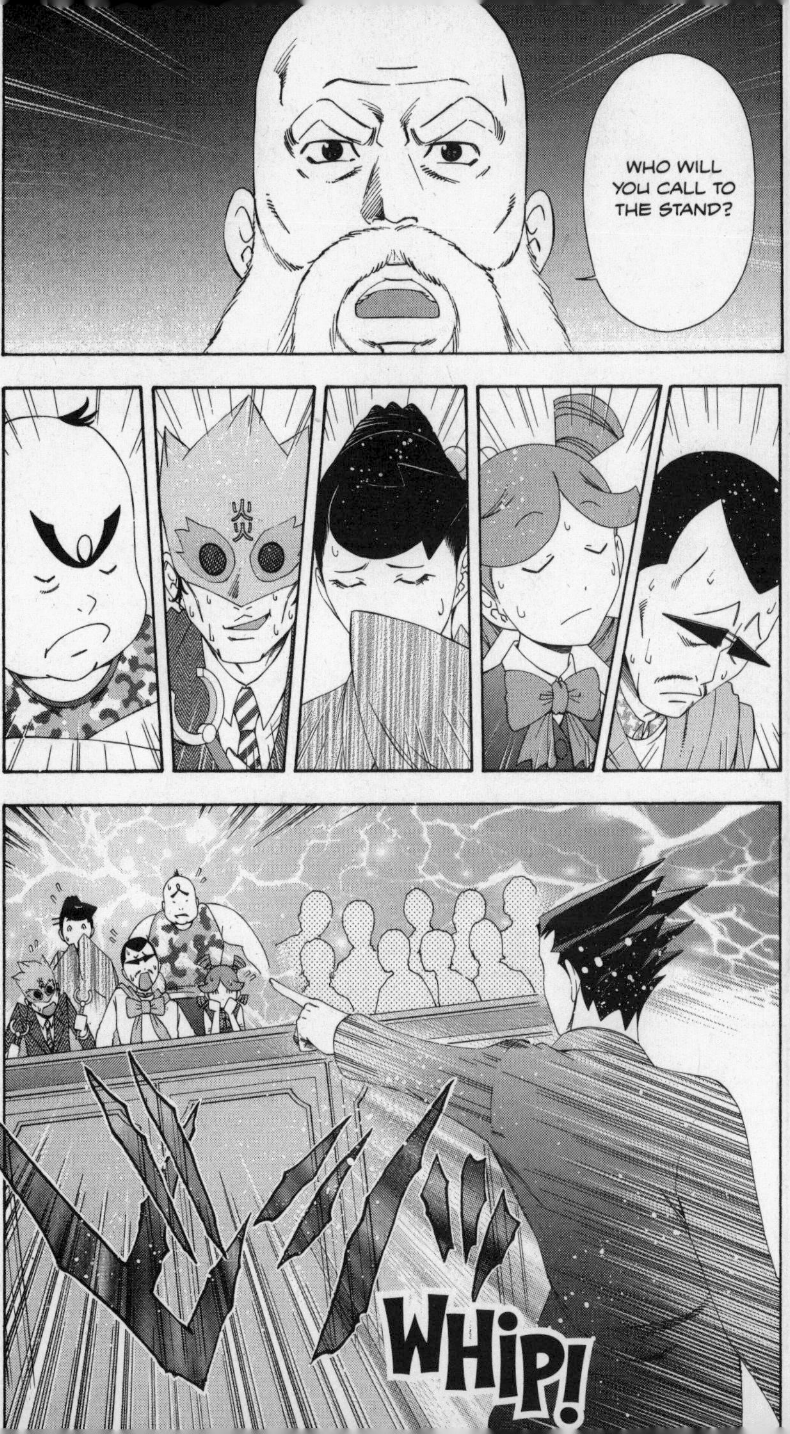
WHO WILL YOU CALL TO THE STAND?
WHIP!

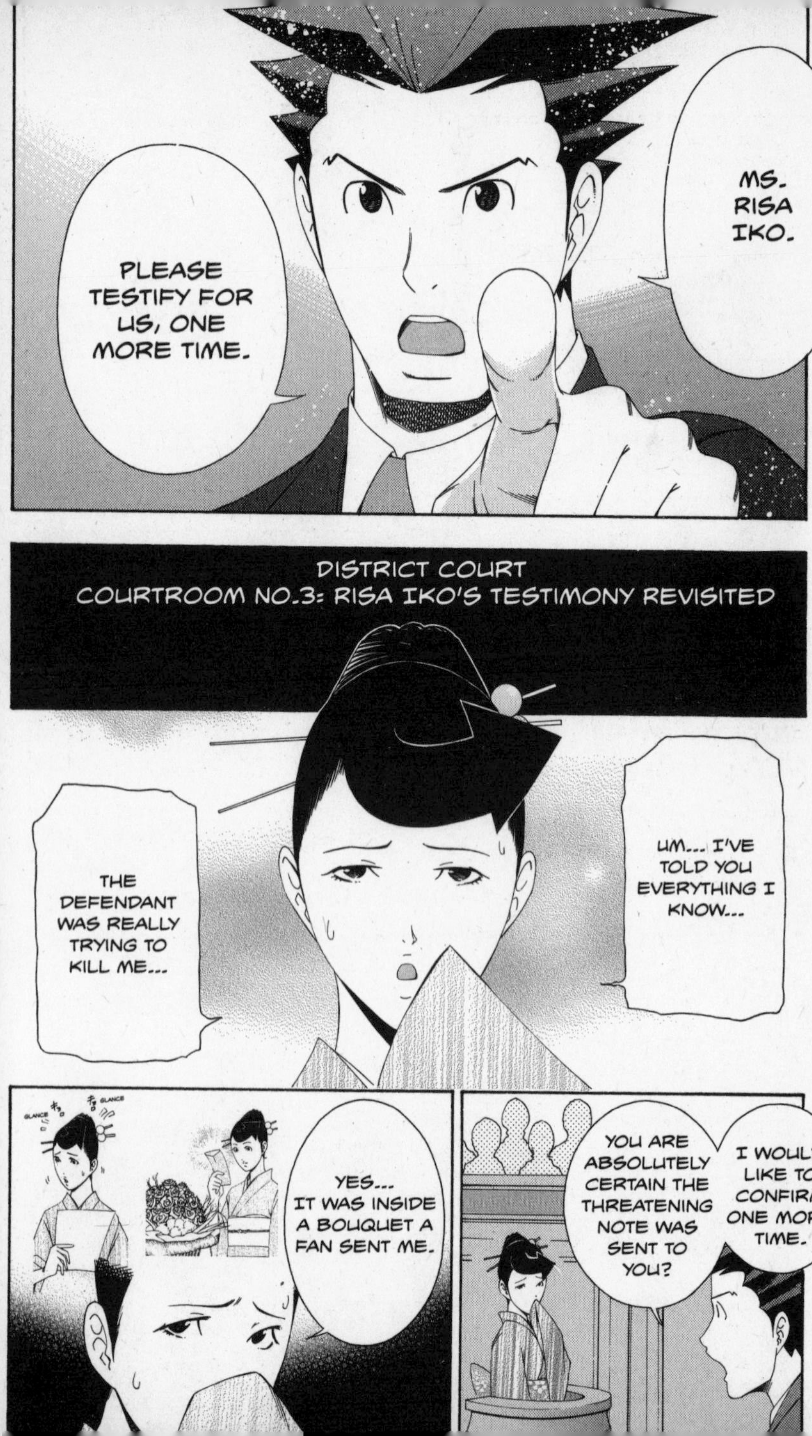
MS. RISA IKO.
PLEASE TESTIFY FOR US, ONE MORE TIME.
DISTRICT COURT
COURTROOM NO.3: RISA IKO'S TESTIMONY REVISITED
UM... I'VE TOLD YOU EVERYTHING I KNOW...
THE DEFENDANT WAS REALLY TRYING TO KILL ME...
I WOULD LIKE TO CONFIRM ONE MORE TIME.
YOU ARE ABSOLUTELY CERTAIN THE THREATENING NOTE WAS SENT TO YOU?
GLANCE
GLANCE
YES... IT WAS INSIDE A BOUQUET A FAN SENT ME.

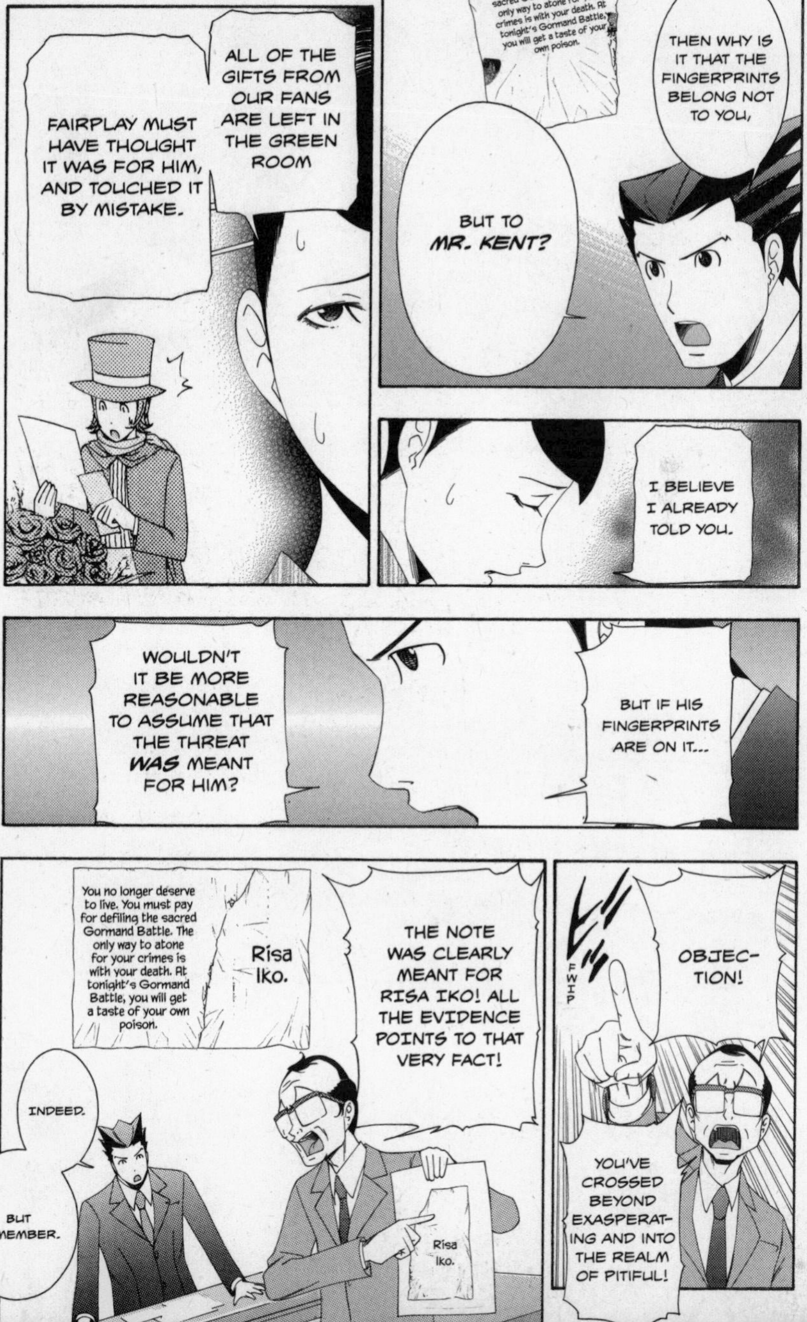
You no longer deserve to live. You must pay for defiling the sacred Gormand Battle. The only way to atone for your crimes is with your death. At tonight's Gormand Battle, you will get a taste of your own poison.
THEN WHY IS IT THAT THE FINGERPRINTS BELONG NOT TO YOU,
BUT TO MR. KENT?
I BELIEVE I ALREADY TOLD YOU.
ALL OF THE GIFTS FROM OUR FANS ARE LEFT IN THE GREEN ROOM
FAIRPLAY MUST HAVE THOUGHT IT WAS FOR HIM, AND TOUCHED IT BY MISTAKE.
BUT IF HIS FINGERPRINTS ARE ON IT...
WOULDN'T IT BE MORE REASONABLE TO ASSUME THAT THE THREAT WAS MEANT FOR HIM?
OBJECTION!
FWIP
YOU'VE CROSSED BEYOND EXASPERATING AND INTO THE REALM OF PITIFUL!
You no longer deserve to live. You must pay for defiling the sacred Gormand Battle. The only way to atone for your crimes is with your death. At tonight's Gormand Battle, you will get a taste of your own poison.
Risa Iko.
THE NOTE WAS CLEARLY MEANT FOR RISA IKO! ALL THE EVIDENCE POINTS TO THAT VERY FACT!
Risa Iko.
INDEED.
BUT REMEMBER.

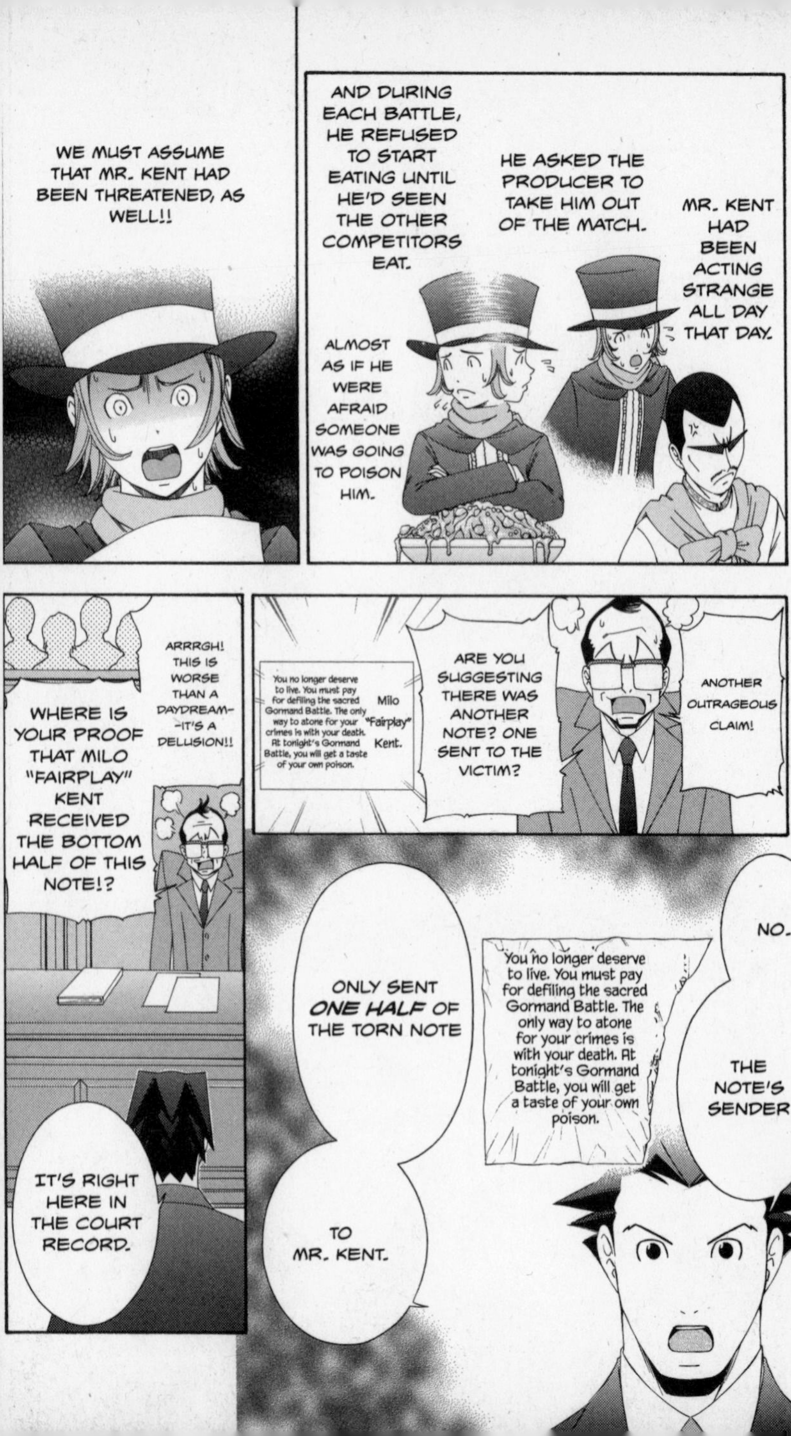
MR. KENT HAD BEEN ACTING STRANGE ALL DAY THAT DAY.
HE ASKED THE PRODUCER TO TAKE HIM OUT OF THE MATCH.
AND DURING EACH BATTLE, HE REFUSED TO START EATING UNTIL HE'D SEEN THE OTHER COMPETITORS EAT.
ALMOST AS IF HE WERE AFRAID SOMEONE WAS GOING TO POISON HIM.
WE MUST ASSUME THAT MR. KENT HAD BEEN THREATENED, AS WELL!!
ANOTHER OUTRAGEOUS CLAIM!
ARE YOU SUGGESTING THERE WAS ANOTHER NOTE? ONE SENT TO THE VICTIM?
You no longer deserve to live. You must pay for defiling the sacred Gormand Battle. The only way to atone for your crimes is with your death. At tonight's Gormand Battle, you will get a taste of your own poison.
Milo "Fairplay" Kent.
NO.
THE NOTE'S SENDER
ONLY SENT *ONE HALF* OF THE TORN NOTE
TO MR. KENT.
You no longer deserve to live. You must pay for defiling the sacred Gormand Battle. The only way to atone for your crimes is with your death. At tonight's Gormand Battle, you will get a taste of your own poison.
ARRRGH! THIS IS WORSE THAN A DAYDREAM—IT'S A DELUSION!!
WHERE IS YOUR PROOF THAT MILO "FAIRPLAY" KENT RECEIVED THE BOTTOM HALF OF THIS NOTE!?
IT'S RIGHT HERE IN THE COURT RECORD.

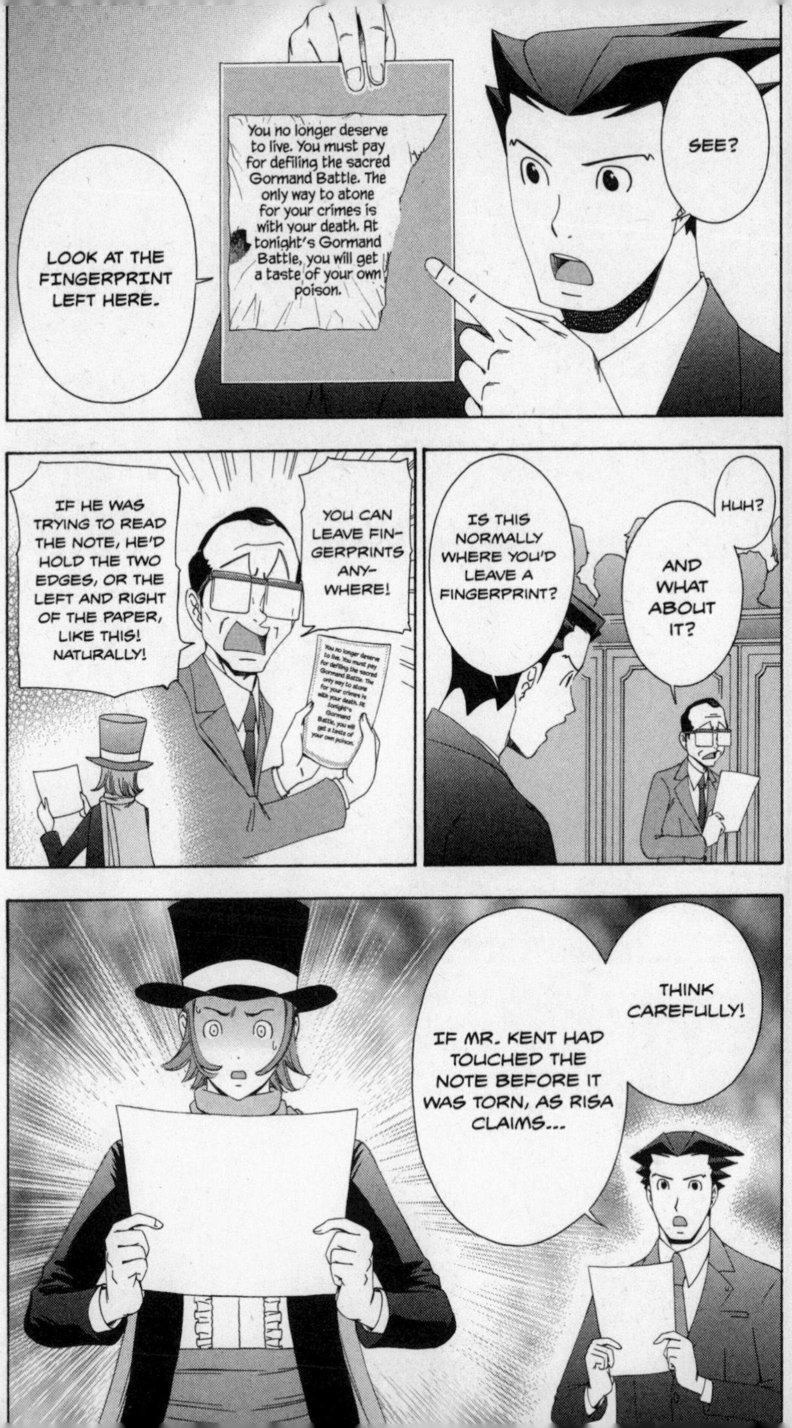
SEE?
You no longer deserve to live. You must pay for defiling the sacred Gormand Battle. The only way to atone for your crimes is with your death. At tonight's Gormand Battle, you will get a taste of your own poison.
LOOK AT THE FINGERPRINT LEFT HERE.
HUH?
AND WHAT ABOUT IT?
IS THIS NORMALLY WHERE YOU'D LEAVE A FINGERPRINT?
YOU CAN LEAVE FIN-GERPRINTS ANY-WHERE!
IF HE WAS TRYING TO READ THE NOTE, HE'D HOLD THE TWO EDGES, OR THE LEFT AND RIGHT OF THE PAPER, LIKE THIS! NATURALLY!
THINK CAREFULLY!
IF MR. KENT HAD TOUCHED THE NOTE BEFORE IT WAS TORN, AS RISA CLAIMS...

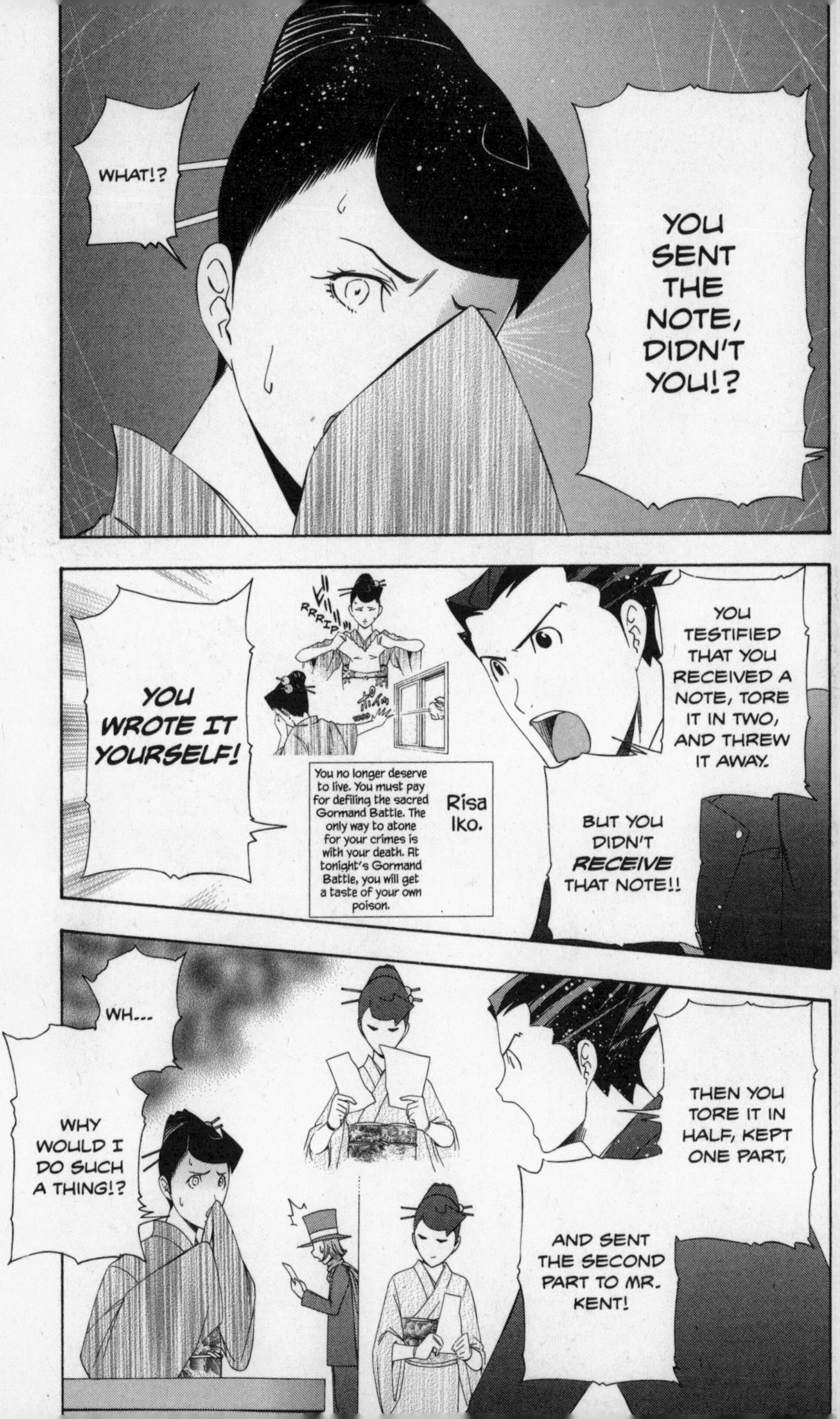
YOU SENT THE NOTE, DIDN'T YOU!?
WHAT!?
YOU TESTIFIED THAT YOU RECEIVED A NOTE, TORE IT IN TWO, AND THREW IT AWAY.
BUT YOU DIDN'T RECEIVE THAT NOTE!!
RRRIP
You no longer deserve to live. You must pay for defiling the sacred Gormand Battle. The only way to atone for your crimes is with your death. At tonight's Gormand Battle, you will get a taste of your own poison.
Risa Iko.
YOU WROTE IT YOURSELF!
THEN YOU TORE IT IN HALF, KEPT ONE PART,
AND SENT THE SECOND PART TO MR. KENT!
WH...
WHY WOULD I DO SUCH A THING!?

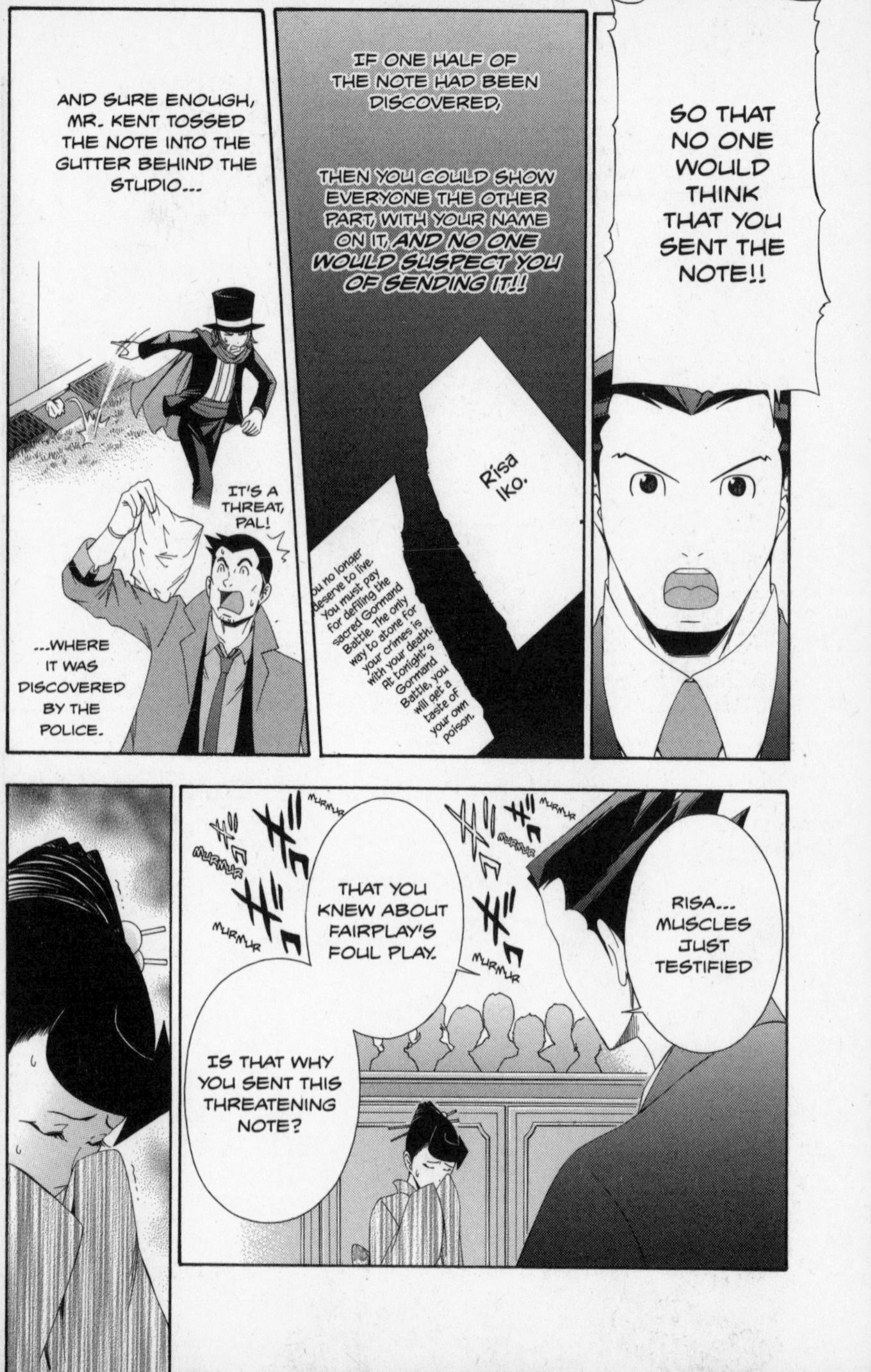
SO THAT NO ONE WOULD THINK THAT YOU SENT THE NOTE!!
IF ONE HALF OF THE NOTE HAD BEEN DISCOVERED,
THEN YOU COULD SHOW EVERYONE THE OTHER PART, WITH YOUR NAME ON IT, AND NO ONE WOULD SUSPECT YOU OF SENDING IT!!
Risa Iko.
ou no longer deserve to live. You must pay for defiling the sacred Gormand Battle. The only way to atone for your crimes is with your death. At tonight's Gormand Battle, you will get a taste of your own poison.
AND SURE ENOUGH, MR. KENT TOSSED THE NOTE INTO THE GUTTER BEHIND THE STUDIO...
IT'S A THREAT, PAL!
...WHERE IT WAS DISCOVERED BY THE POLICE.
MURMUR
MURMUR
RISA... MUSCLES JUST TESTIFIED
MURMUR
MURMUR
MURMUR
MURMUR
THAT YOU KNEW ABOUT FAIRPLAY'S FOUL PLAY.
IS THAT WHY YOU SENT THIS THREATENING NOTE?

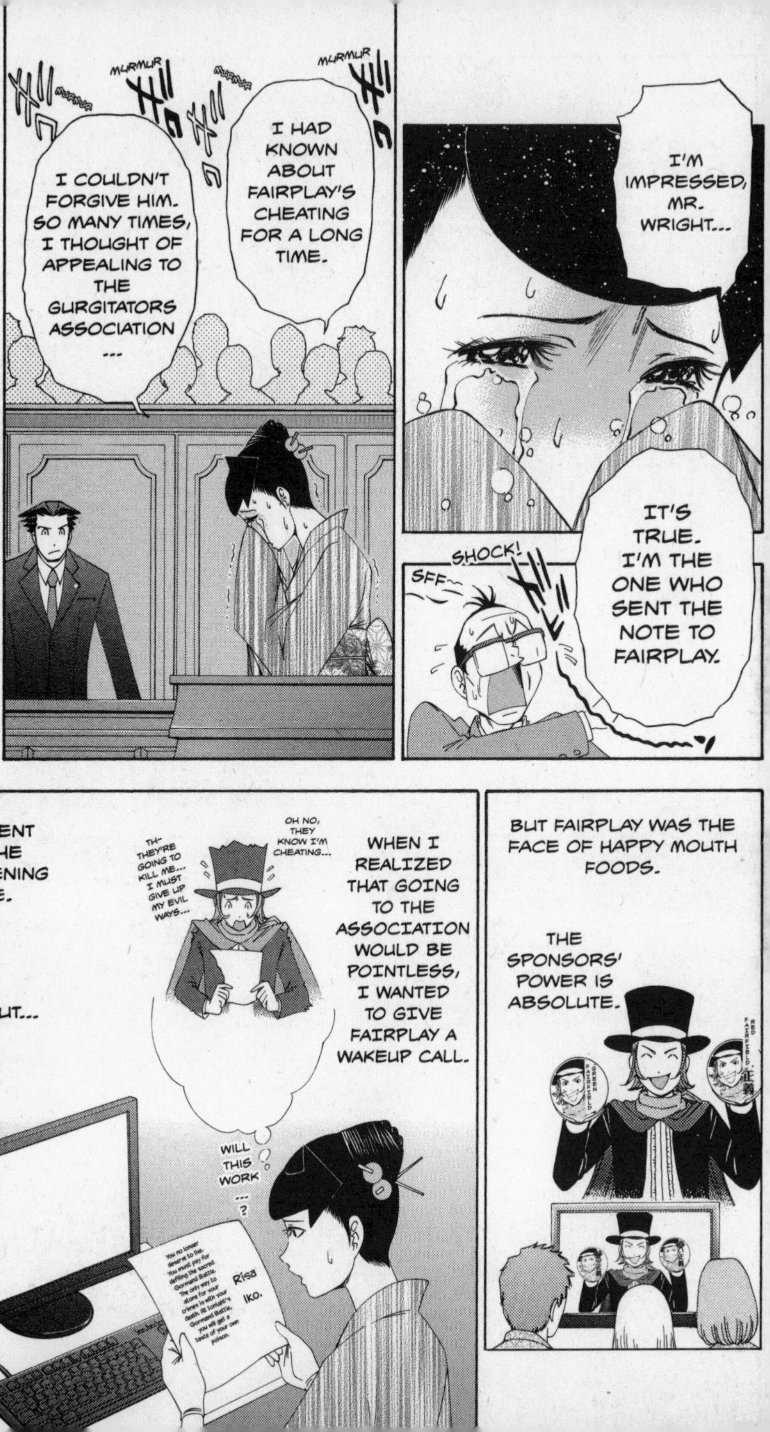
I'M IMPRESSED, MR. WRIGHT...
SHOCK!
SFF~
IT'S TRUE. I'M THE ONE WHO SENT THE NOTE TO FAIRPLAY.
MURMUR
MURMUR
MURMUR
MURMUR
I HAD KNOWN ABOUT FAIRPLAY'S CHEATING FOR A LONG TIME.
I COULDN'T FORGIVE HIM. SO MANY TIMES, I THOUGHT OF APPEALING TO THE GURGITATORS ASSOCIATION ...
BUT FAIRPLAY WAS THE FACE OF HAPPY MOUTH FOODS.
THE SPONSORS' POWER IS ABSOLUTE.
WHEN I REALIZED THAT GOING TO THE ASSOCIATION WOULD BE POINTLESS, I WANTED TO GIVE FAIRPLAY A WAKEUP CALL.
OH NO, THEY KNOW I'M CHEATING...
TH- THEY'RE GOING TO KILL ME... I MUST GIVE UP MY EVIL WAYS...
SO I SENT HIM THE THREATENING NOTE.
BUT...
WILL THIS WORK ...?
You no longer deserve to live. You must pay for defiling the sacred Gormand Battle. The only way to atone for your crimes is with your death. At tonight's Gormand Battle, you will get a taste of your own poison.
Risa Iko.

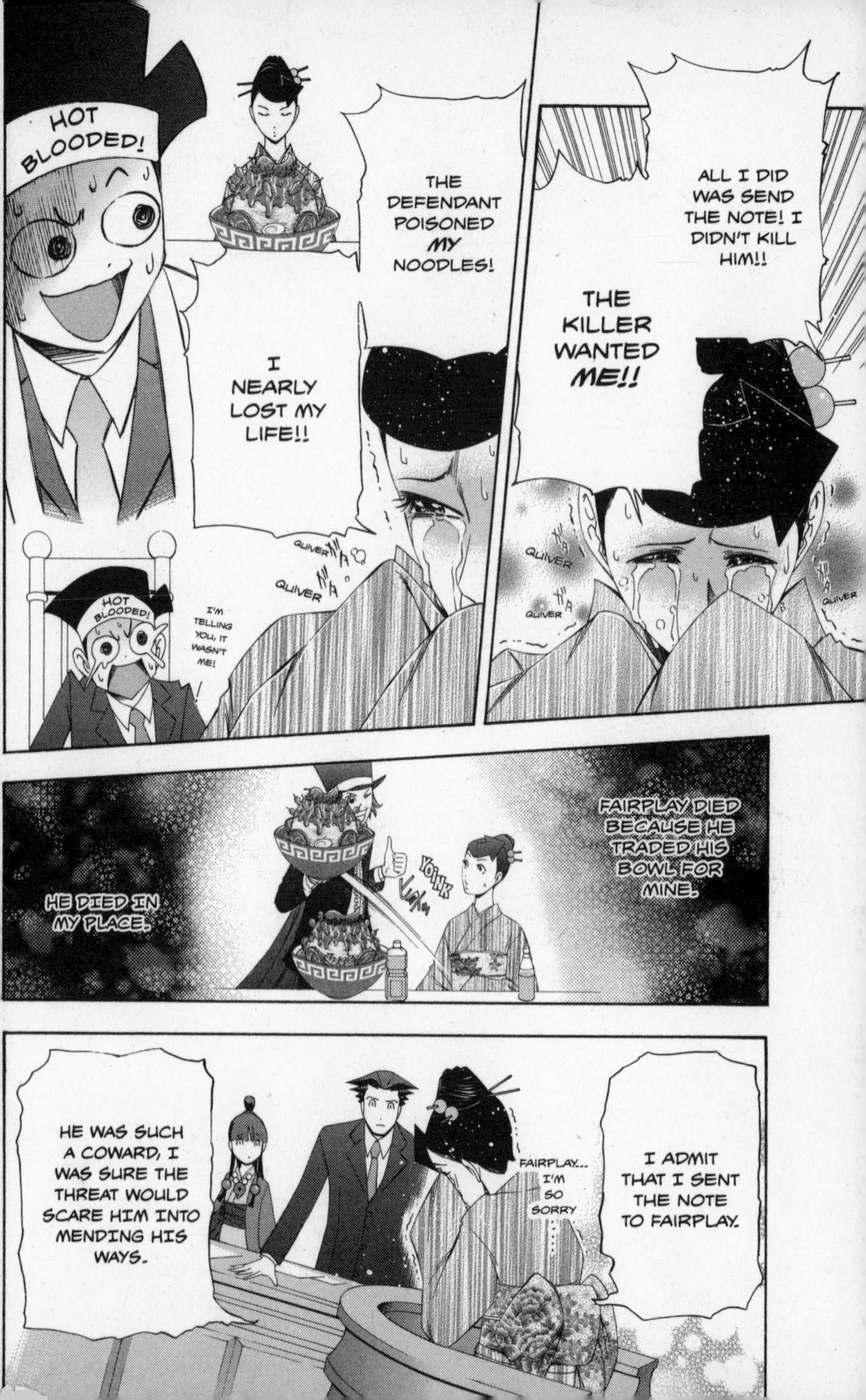

ALL I DID WAS SEND THE NOTE! I DIDN'T KILL HIM!!
THE KILLER WANTED *ME!!*
QUIVER
QUIVER
QUIVER
HOT BLOODED!
THE DEFENDANT POISONED *MY* NOODLES!
I NEARLY LOST MY LIFE!!
QUIVER
QUIVER
HOT BLOODED!
I'M TELLING YOU, IT WASN'T ME!
FAIRPLAY DIED BECAUSE HE TRADED HIS BOWL FOR MINE.
YOINK
HE DIED IN MY PLACE.
I ADMIT THAT I SENT THE NOTE TO FAIRPLAY.
FAIRPLAY... I'M SO SORRY
HE WAS SUCH A COWARD, I WAS SURE THE THREAT WOULD SCARE HIM INTO MENDING HIS WAYS.

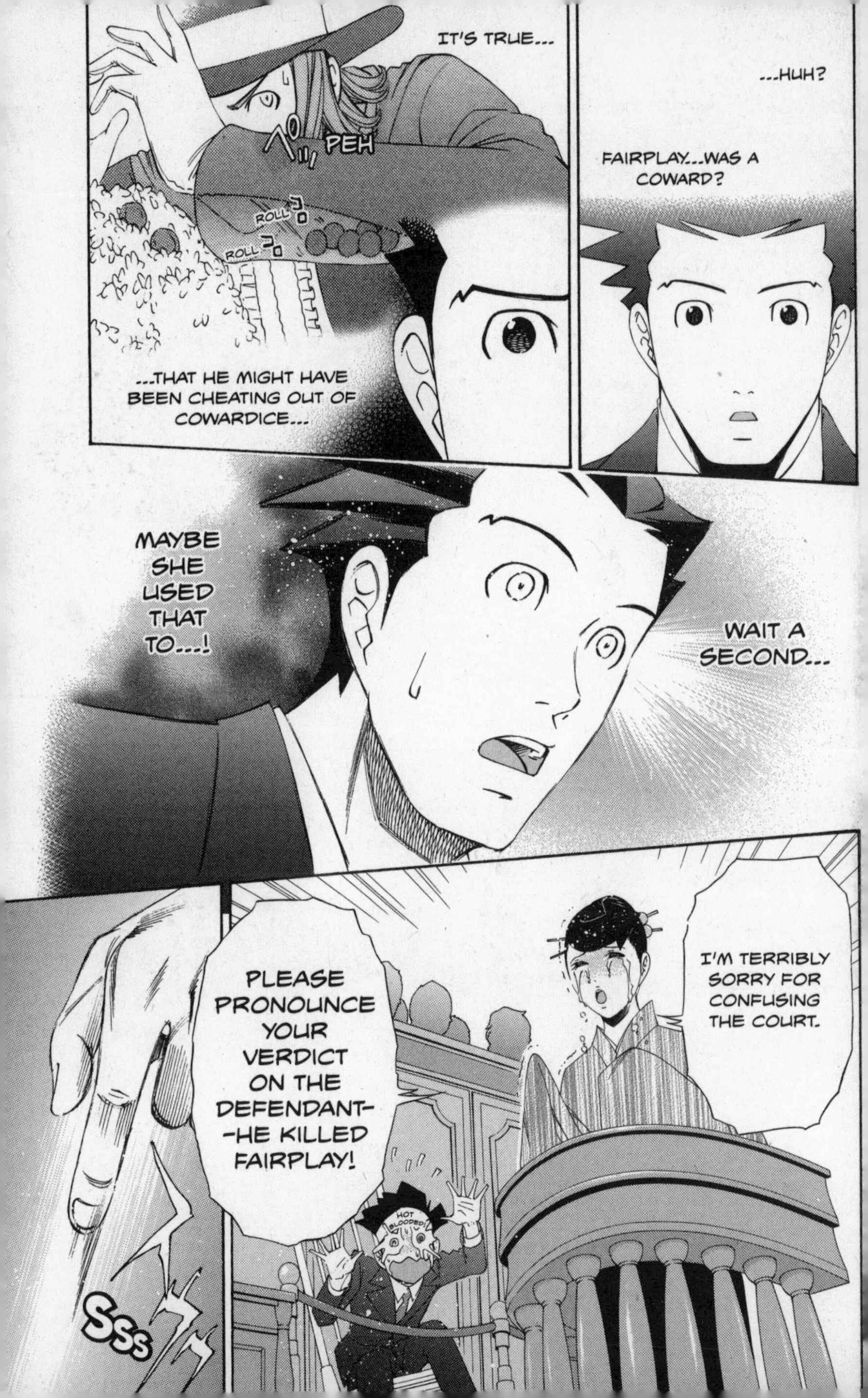
...HUH?
FAIRPLAY...WAS A COWARD?
IT'S TRUE...
PEH
ROLL
ROLL
...THAT HE MIGHT HAVE BEEN CHEATING OUT OF COWARDICE...
WAIT A SECOND...
MAYBE SHE USED THAT TO...!
I'M TERRIBLY SORRY FOR CONFUSING THE COURT.
PLEASE PRONOUNCE YOUR VERDICT ON THE DEFENDANT--HE KILLED FAIRPLAY!
HOT BLOODED!
SSS

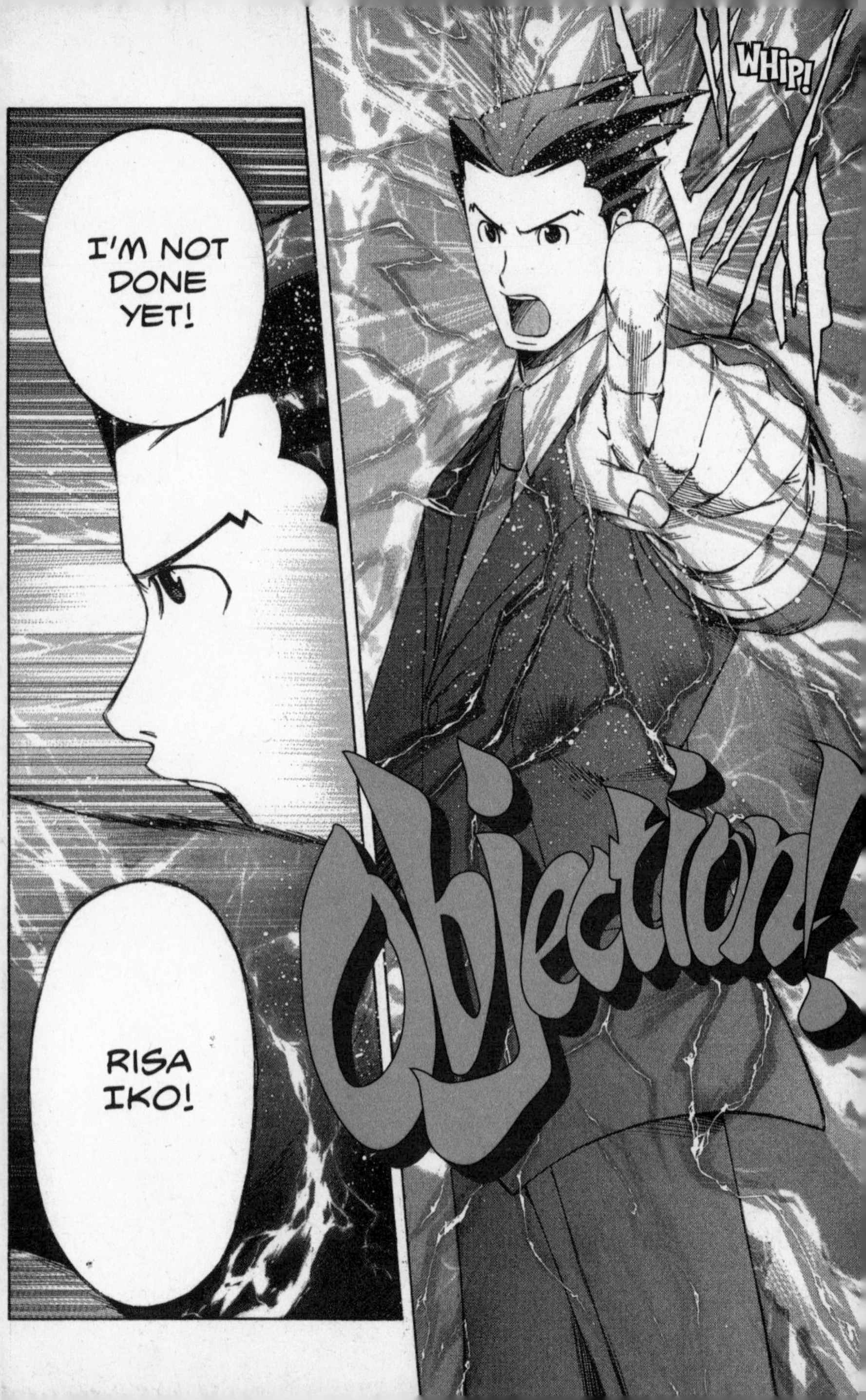
WHIP!
Objection!
I'M NOT DONE YET!
RISA IKO!

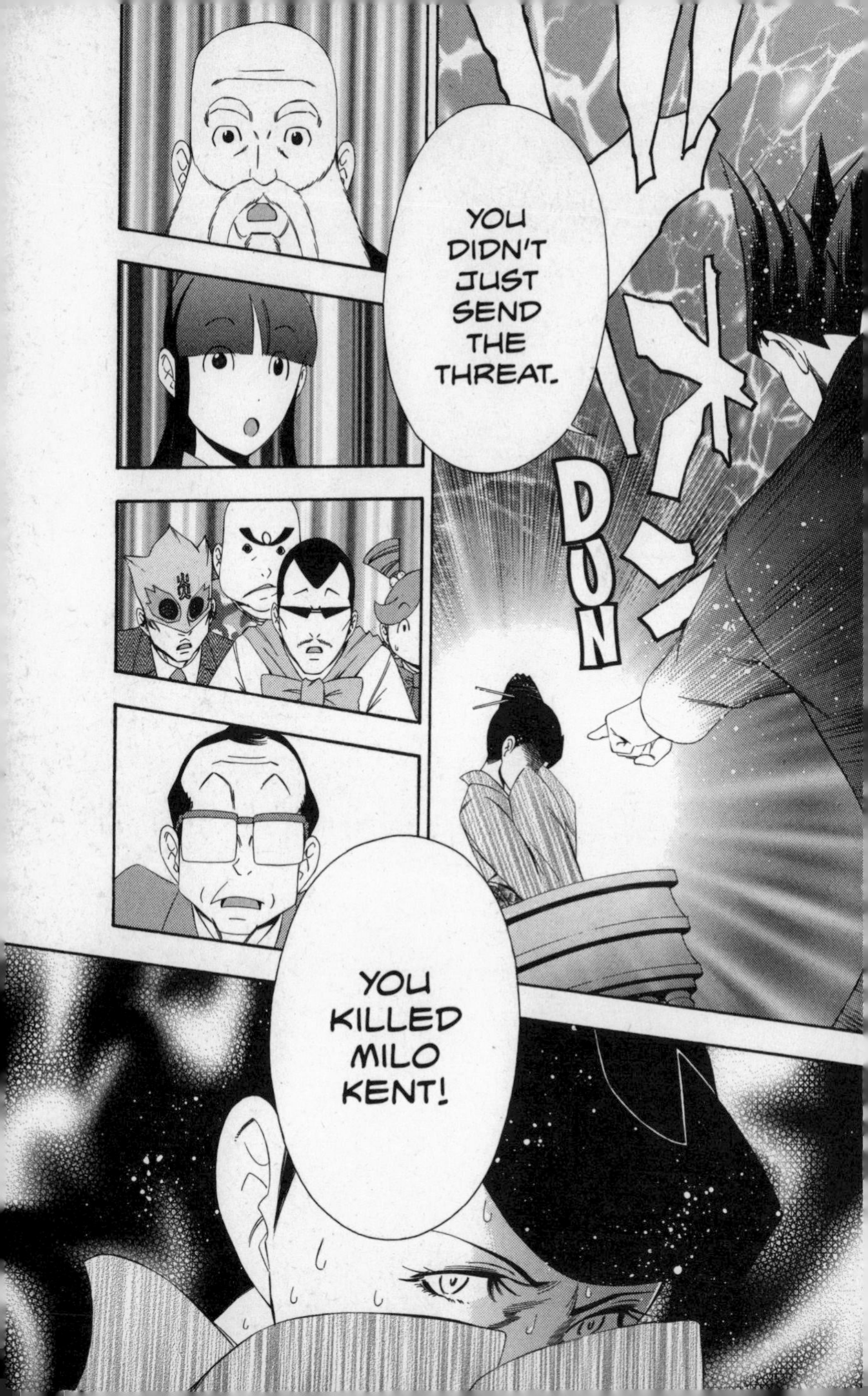
YOU DIDN'T JUST SEND THE THREAT...
DUN
YOU KILLED MILO KENT!

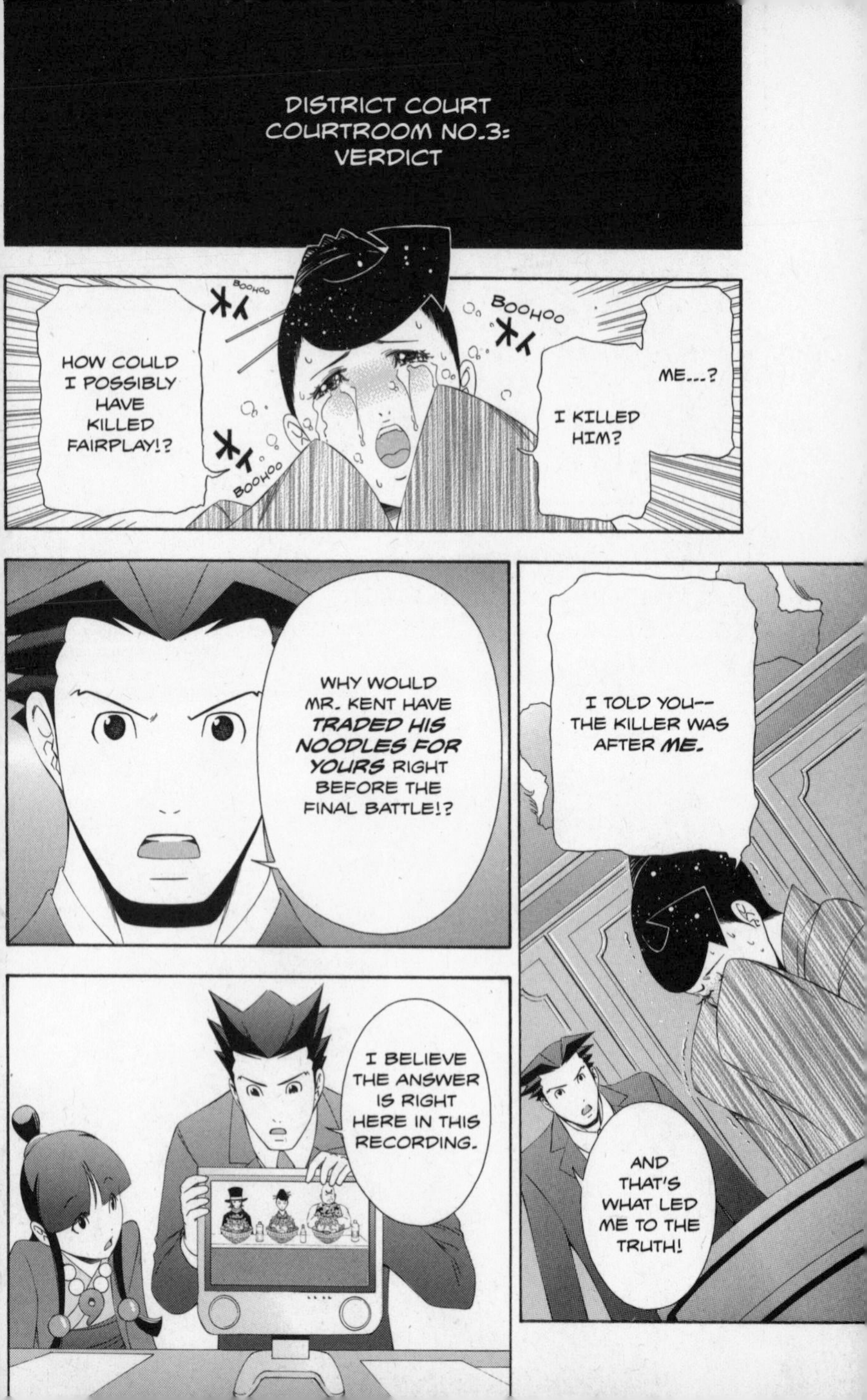
DISTRICT COURT COURTROOM NO.3: VERDICT
BOOHOO
ME...? I KILLED HIM?
BOOHOO
HOW COULD I POSSIBLY HAVE KILLED FAIRPLAY!?
BOOHOO
I TOLD YOU-- THE KILLER WAS AFTER *ME.*
WHY WOULD MR. KENT HAVE ***TRADED HIS NOODLES FOR YOURS*** RIGHT BEFORE THE FINAL BATTLE!?
I BELIEVE THE ANSWER IS RIGHT HERE IN THIS RECORDING.
AND THAT'S WHAT LED ME TO THE TRUTH!

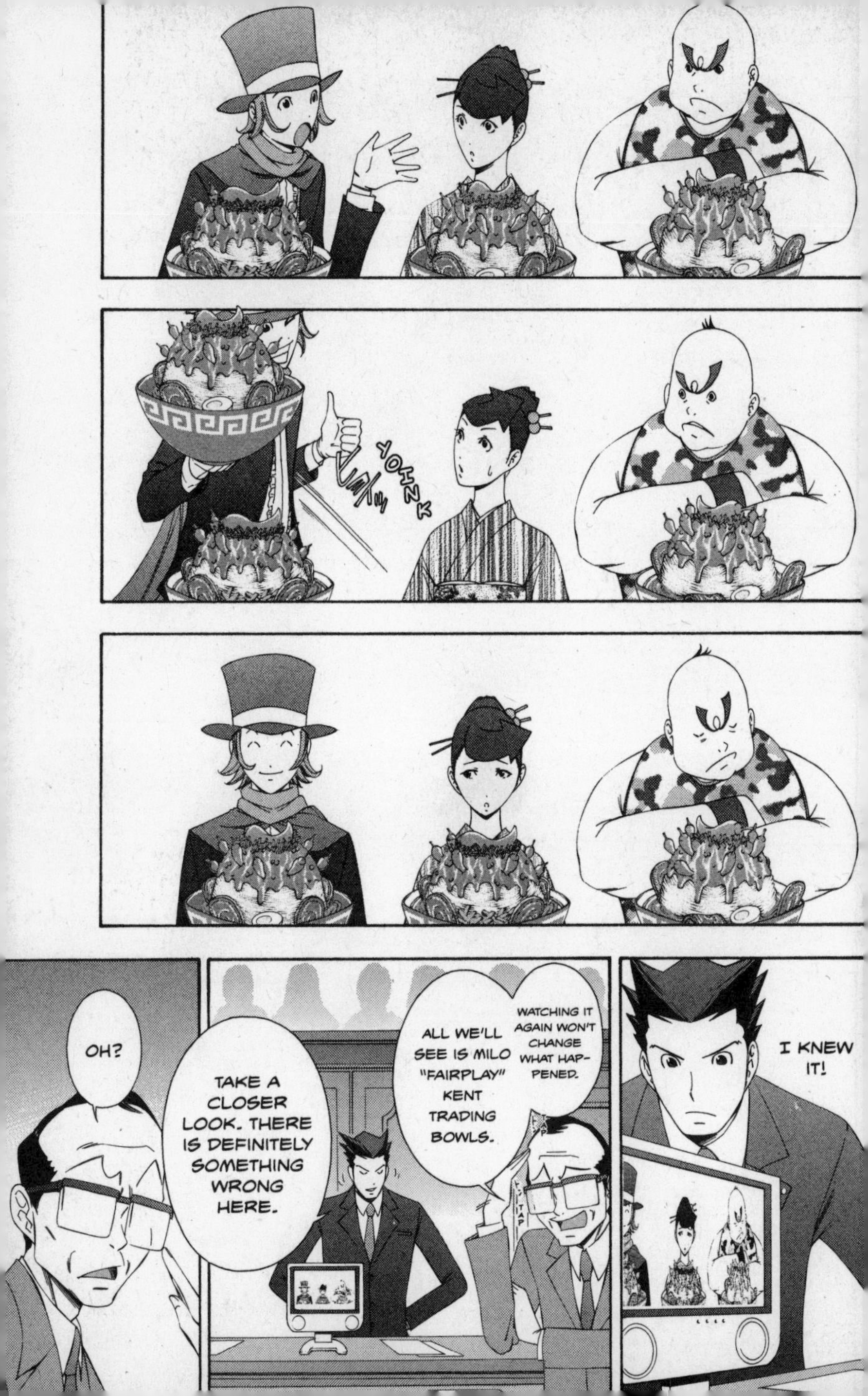
YOINK
I KNEW IT!
WATCHING IT AGAIN WON'T CHANGE WHAT HAP-PENED.
ALL WE'LL SEE IS MILO "FAIRPLAY" KENT TRADING BOWLS.
TAKE A CLOSER LOOK. THERE IS DEFINITELY SOMETHING WRONG HERE.
OH?

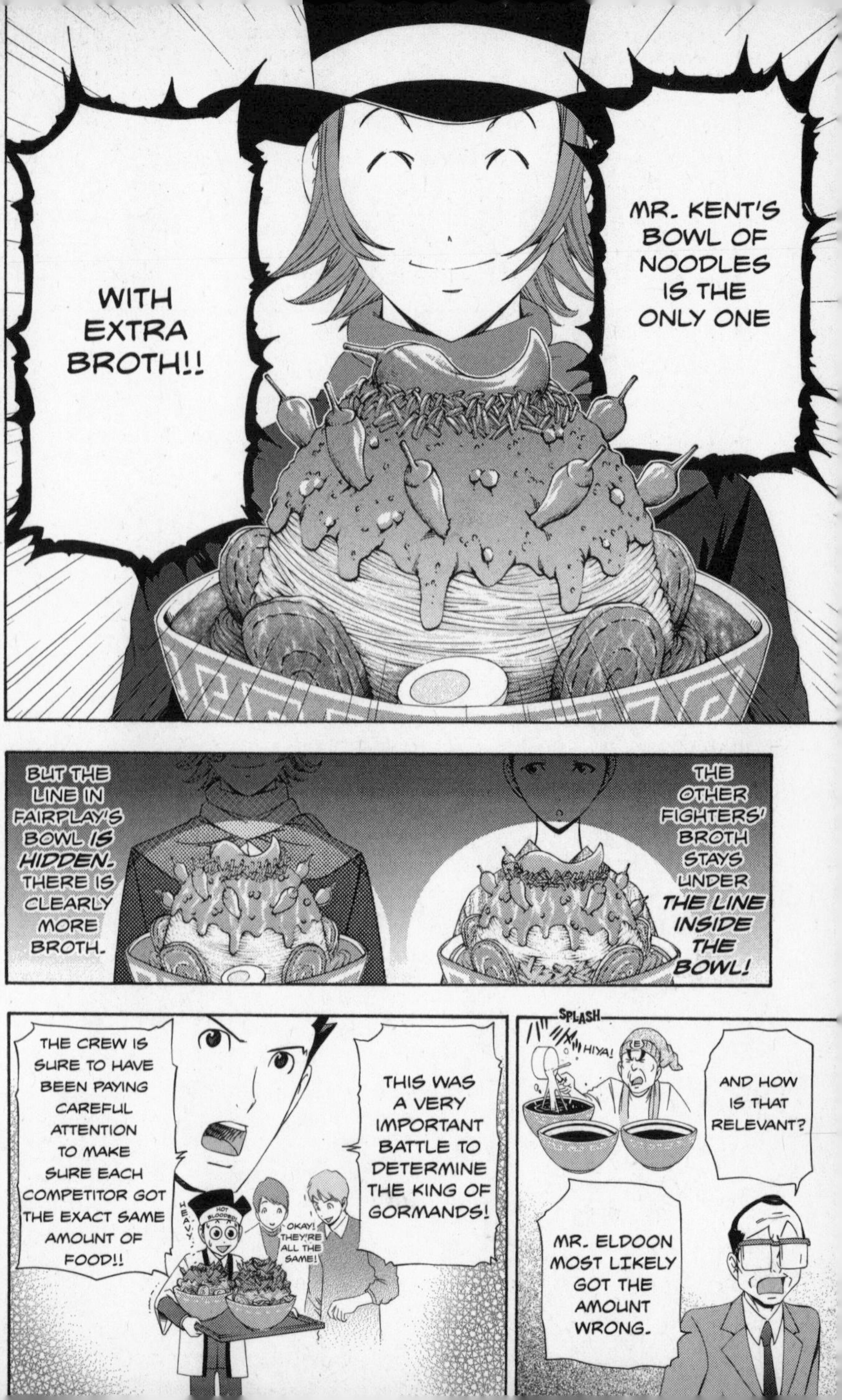
MR. KENT'S BOWL OF NOODLES IS THE ONLY ONE
WITH EXTRA BROTH!!
THE OTHER FIGHTERS' BROTH STAYS UNDER *THE LINE INSIDE THE BOWL!*
BUT THE LINE IN FAIRPLAY'S BOWL *IS HIDDEN.* THERE IS CLEARLY MORE BROTH.
SPLASH
HIYA!
AND HOW IS THAT RELEVANT?
MR. ELDOON MOST LIKELY GOT THE AMOUNT WRONG.
THIS WAS A VERY IMPORTANT BATTLE TO DETERMINE THE KING OF GORMANDS!
THE CREW IS SURE TO HAVE BEEN PAYING CAREFUL ATTENTION TO MAKE SURE EACH COMPETITOR GOT THE EXACT SAME AMOUNT OF FOOD!!
HOT BLOODED
HEAVY
OKAY! THEY'RE ALL THE SAME!

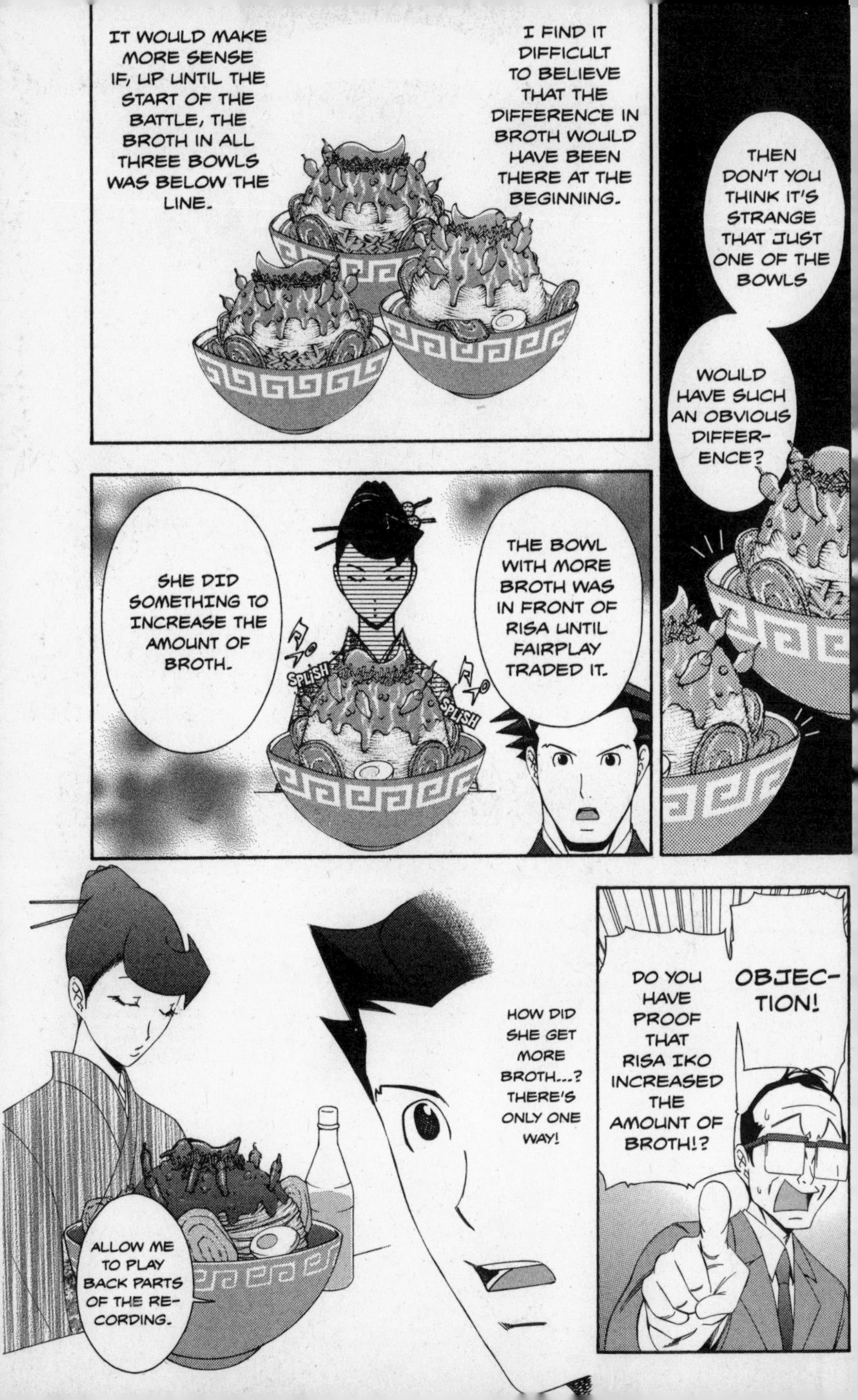
THEN DON'T YOU THINK IT'S STRANGE THAT JUST ONE OF THE BOWLS
WOULD HAVE SUCH AN OBVIOUS DIFFER-ENCE?
I FIND IT DIFFICULT TO BELIEVE THAT THE DIFFERENCE IN BROTH WOULD HAVE BEEN THERE AT THE BEGINNING.
IT WOULD MAKE MORE SENSE IF, UP UNTIL THE START OF THE BATTLE, THE BROTH IN ALL THREE BOWLS WAS BELOW THE LINE.
THE BOWL WITH MORE BROTH WAS IN FRONT OF RISA UNTIL FAIRPLAY TRADED IT.
SPLISH
SPLISH
SHE DID SOMETHING TO INCREASE THE AMOUNT OF BROTH.
OBJEC-TION!
DO YOU HAVE PROOF THAT RISA IKO INCREASED THE AMOUNT OF BROTH!?
HOW DID SHE GET MORE BROTH...? THERE'S ONLY ONE WAY!
ALLOW ME TO PLAY BACK PARTS OF THE RE-CORDING.

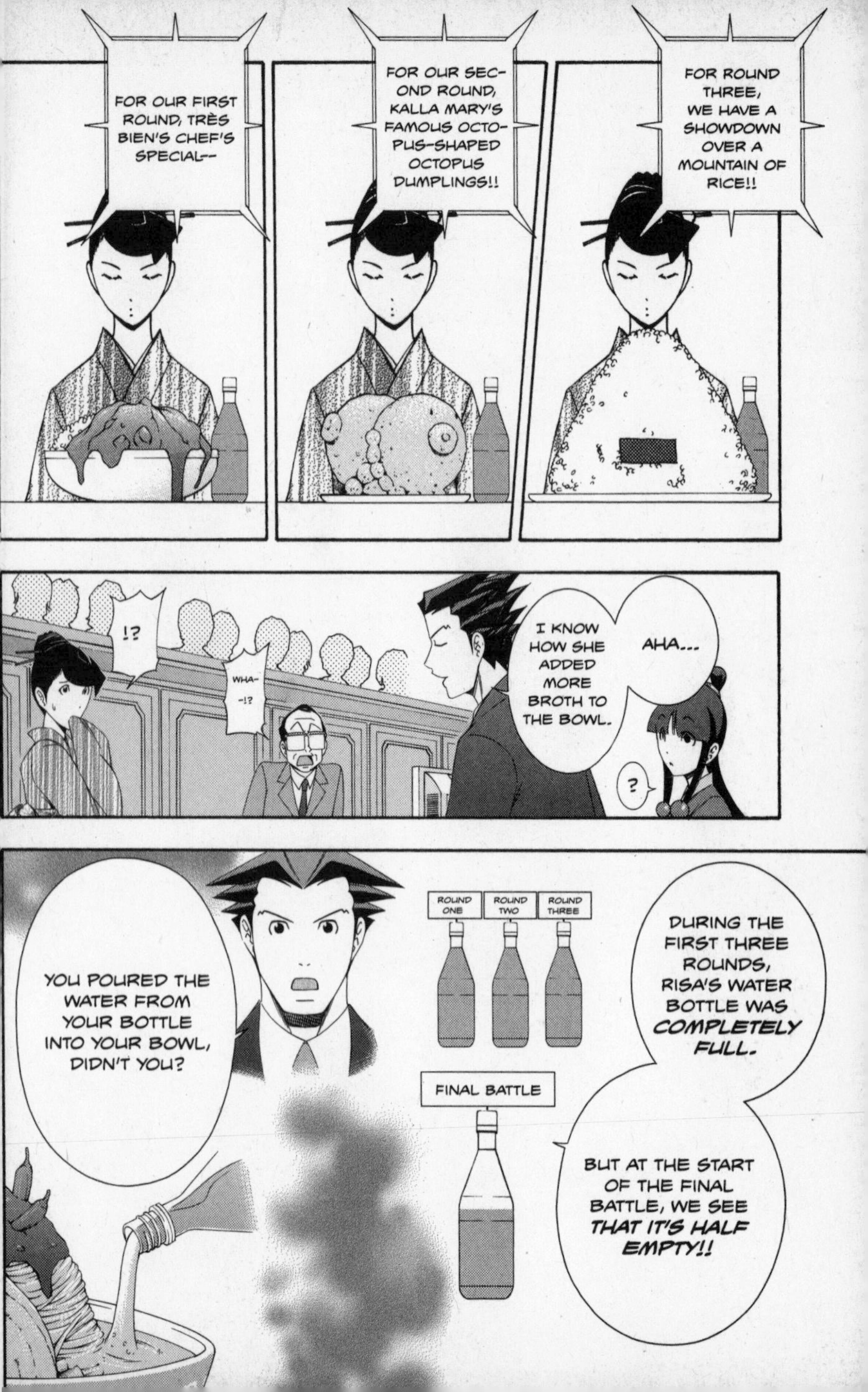
FOR ROUND THREE, WE HAVE A SHOWDOWN OVER A MOUNTAIN OF RICE!!
FOR OUR SECOND ROUND, KALLA MARY'S FAMOUS OCTOPUS-SHAPED OCTOPUS DUMPLINGS!!
FOR OUR FIRST ROUND, TRÈS BIEN'S CHEF'S SPECIAL--
AHA...
I KNOW HOW SHE ADDED MORE BROTH TO THE BOWL.
?
WHA--!?
!?
DURING THE FIRST THREE ROUNDS, RISA'S WATER BOTTLE WAS *COMPLETELY FULL.*
BUT AT THE START OF THE FINAL BATTLE, WE SEE *THAT IT'S HALF EMPTY!!*
ROUND THREE
ROUND TWO
ROUND ONE
FINAL BATTLE
YOU POURED THE WATER FROM YOUR BOTTLE INTO YOUR BOWL, DIDN'T YOU?

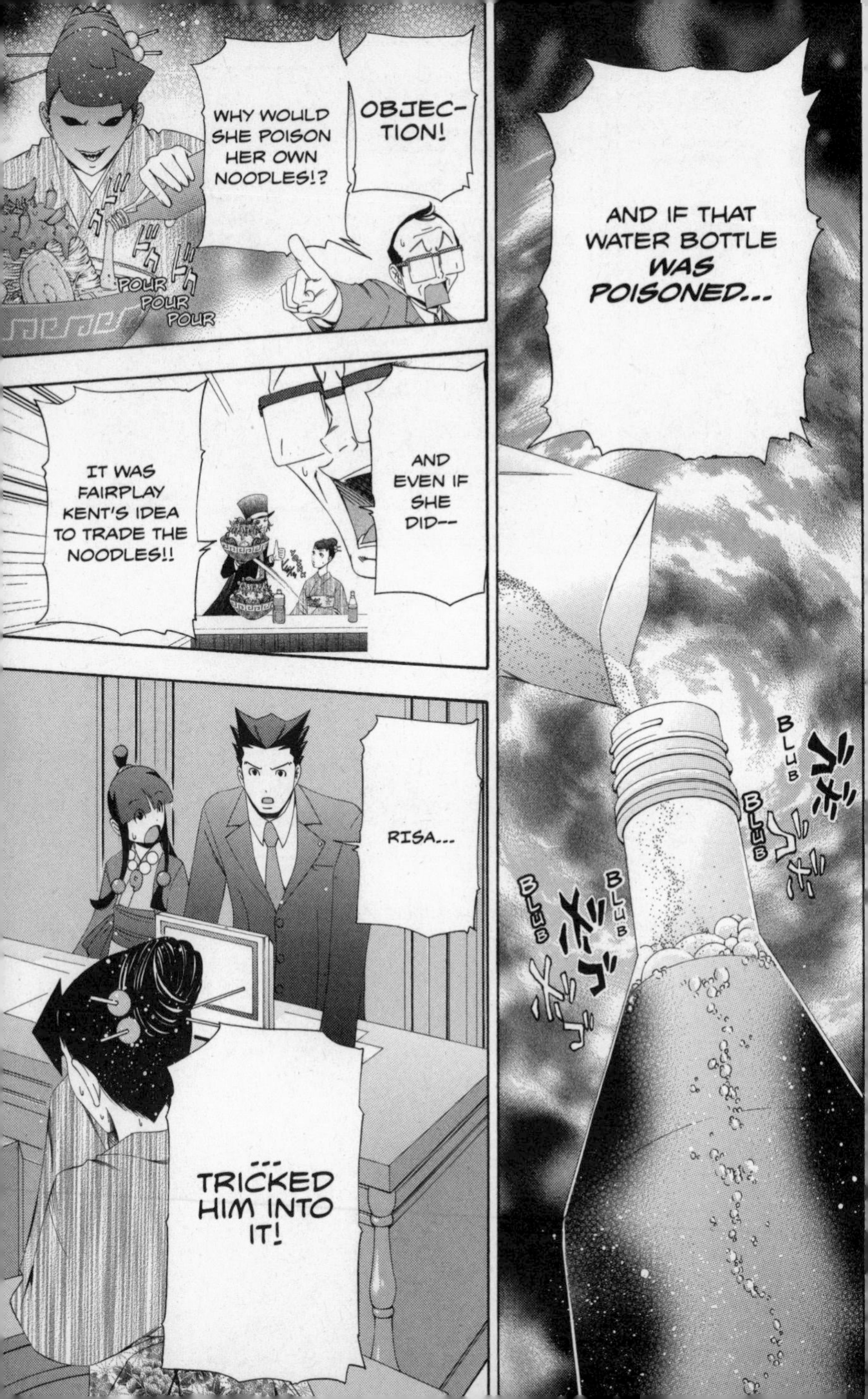
AND IF THAT WATER BOTTLE *WAS* *POISONED...*
BLUB
BLUB
BLUB
BLUB
OBJECTION!
WHY WOULD SHE POISON HER OWN NOODLES!?
POUR POUR POUR
AND EVEN IF SHE DID--
IT WAS FAIRPLAY KENT'S IDEA TO TRADE THE NOODLES!!
RISA...
...TRICKED HIM INTO IT!

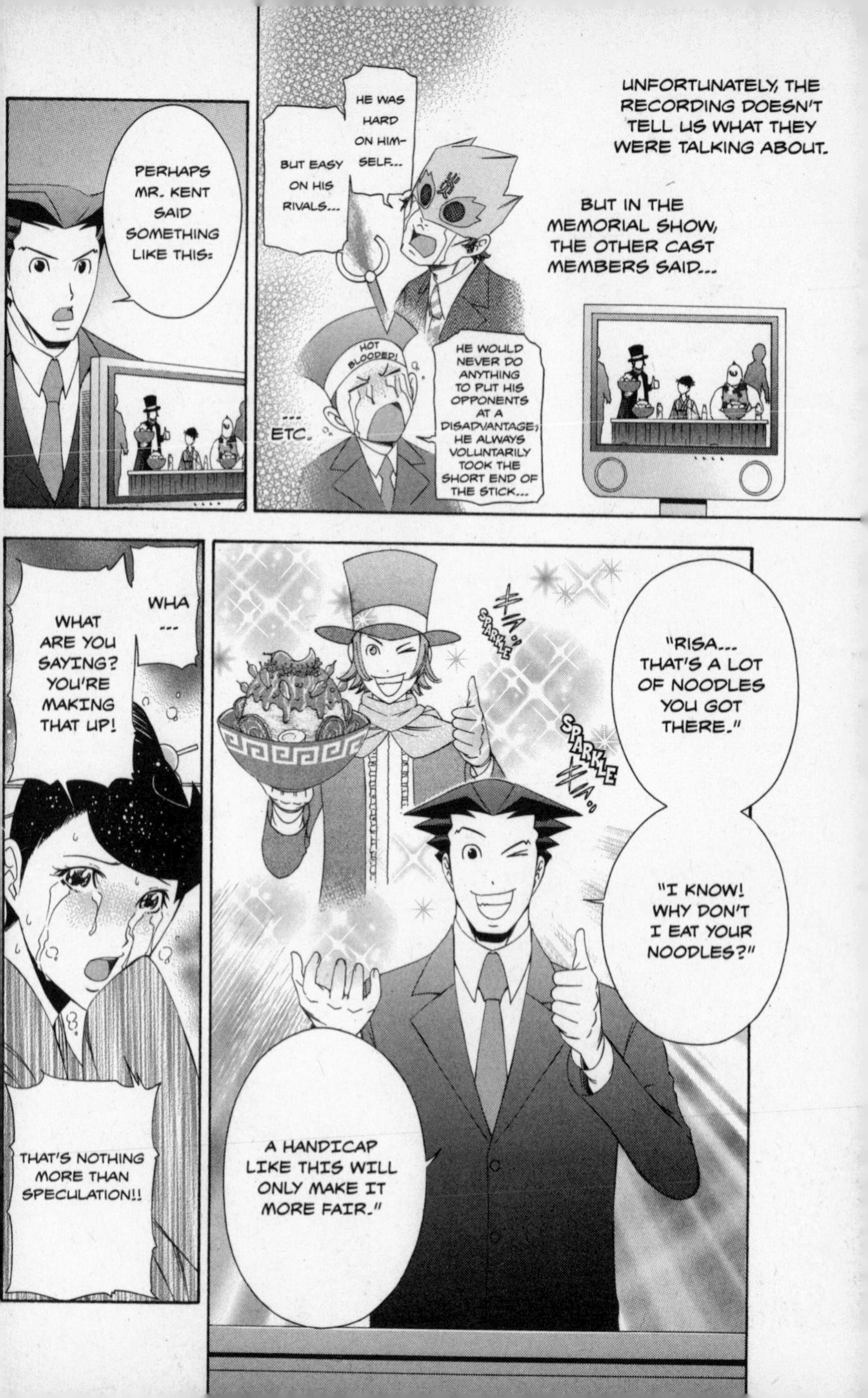
UNFORTUNATELY, THE RECORDING DOESN'T TELL US WHAT THEY WERE TALKING ABOUT.
BUT IN THE MEMORIAL SHOW, THE OTHER CAST MEMBERS SAID...
HE WAS HARD ON HIM-SELF...
BUT EASY ON HIS RIVALS...
HOT BLOODED!
HE WOULD NEVER DO ANYTHING TO PUT HIS OPPONENTS AT A DISADVANTAGE; HE ALWAYS VOLUNTARILY TOOK THE SHORT END OF THE STICK...
...ETC.
PERHAPS MR. KENT SAID SOMETHING LIKE THIS:
"RISA... THAT'S A LOT OF NOODLES YOU GOT THERE."
SPARKLE
SPARKLE
"I KNOW! WHY DON'T I EAT YOUR NOODLES?"
A HANDICAP LIKE THIS WILL ONLY MAKE IT MORE FAIR."
WHA...
WHAT ARE YOU SAYING? YOU'RE MAKING THAT UP!
THAT'S NOTHING MORE THAN SPECULATION!!

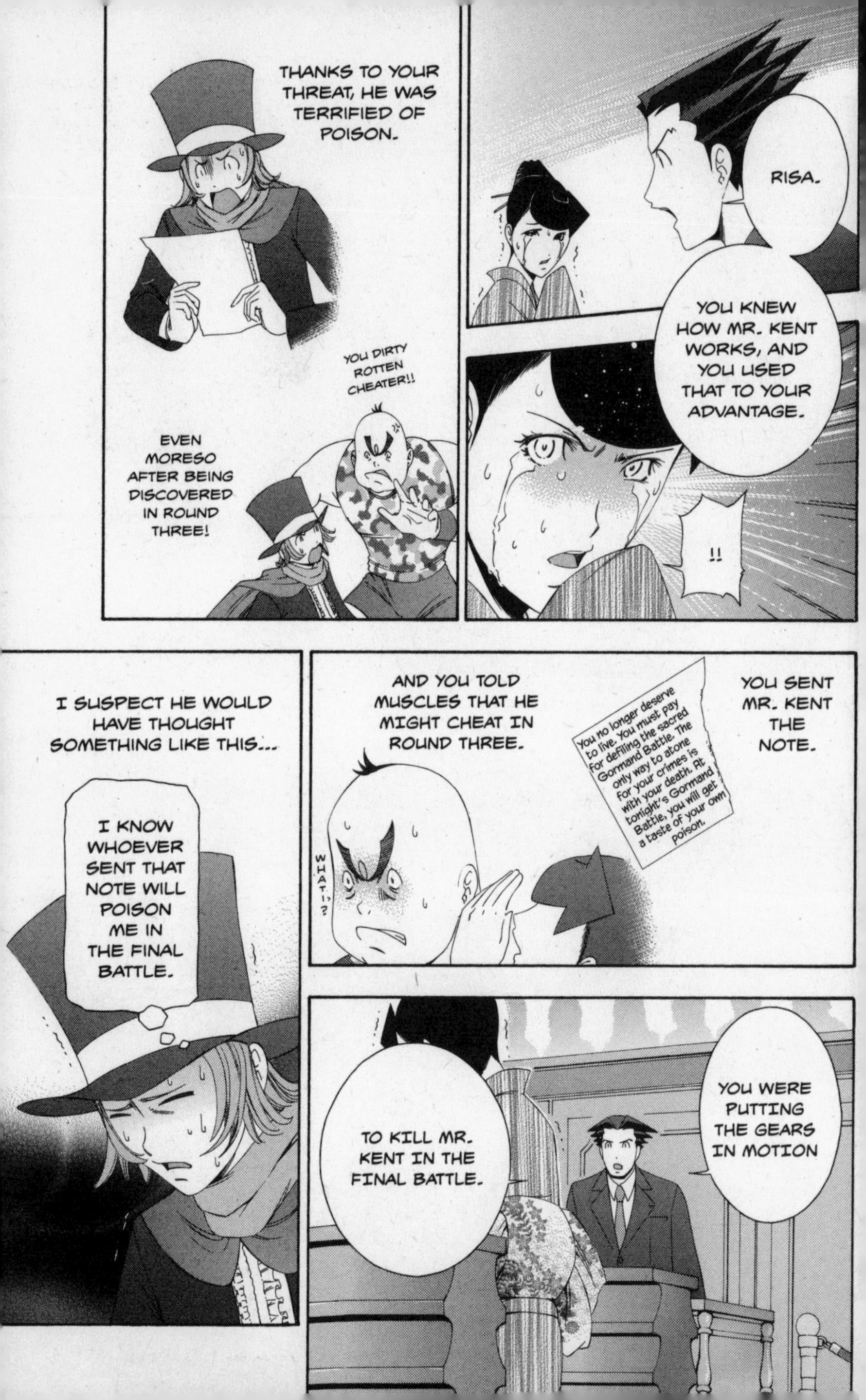
RISA.
YOU KNEW HOW MR. KENT WORKS, AND YOU USED THAT TO YOUR ADVANTAGE.
!!
THANKS TO YOUR THREAT, HE WAS TERRIFIED OF POISON.
YOU DIRTY ROTTEN CHEATER!!
EVEN MORESO AFTER BEING DISCOVERED IN ROUND THREE!
YOU SENT MR. KENT THE NOTE.
You no longer deserve to live. You must pay for defiling the sacred Gormand Battle. The only way to atone for your crimes is with your death. At tonight's Gormand Battle, you will get a taste of your own poison.
AND YOU TOLD MUSCLES THAT HE MIGHT CHEAT IN ROUND THREE.
WHAT!?
YOU WERE PUTTING THE GEARS IN MOTION
TO KILL MR. KENT IN THE FINAL BATTLE.
I SUSPECT HE WOULD HAVE THOUGHT SOMETHING LIKE THIS...
I KNOW WHOEVER SENT THAT NOTE WILL POISON ME IN THE FINAL BATTLE.

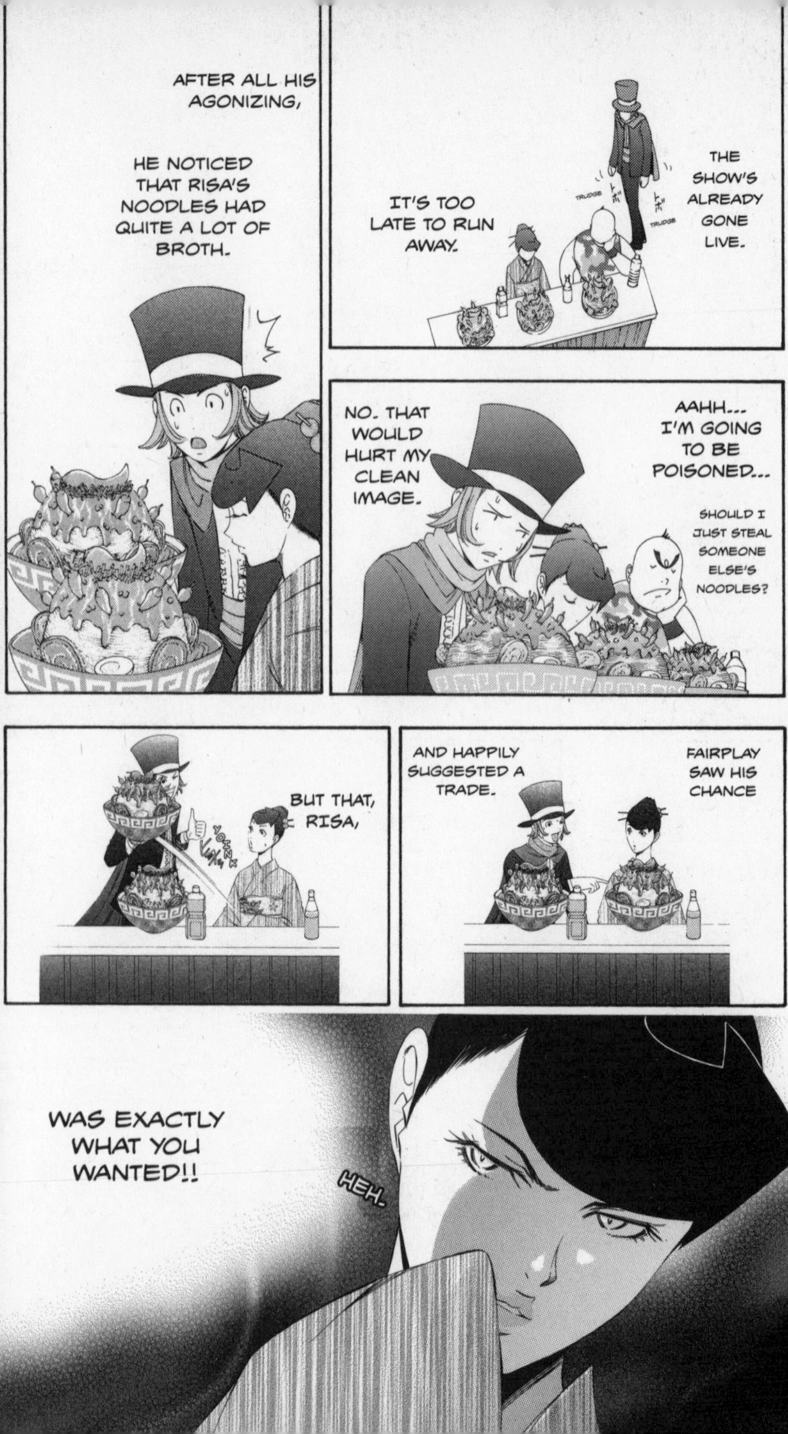
THE SHOW'S ALREADY GONE LIVE.
TRUDGE
TRUDGE
IT'S TOO LATE TO RUN AWAY.
AAHH... I'M GOING TO BE POISONED...
SHOULD I JUST STEAL SOMEONE ELSE'S NOODLES?
NO. THAT WOULD HURT MY CLEAN IMAGE.
AFTER ALL HIS AGONIZING,
HE NOTICED THAT RISA'S NOODLES HAD QUITE A LOT OF BROTH.
FAIRPLAY SAW HIS CHANCE
AND HAPPILY SUGGESTED A TRADE.
BUT THAT, RISA,
YOINK
WAS EXACTLY WHAT YOU WANTED!!
HEH.

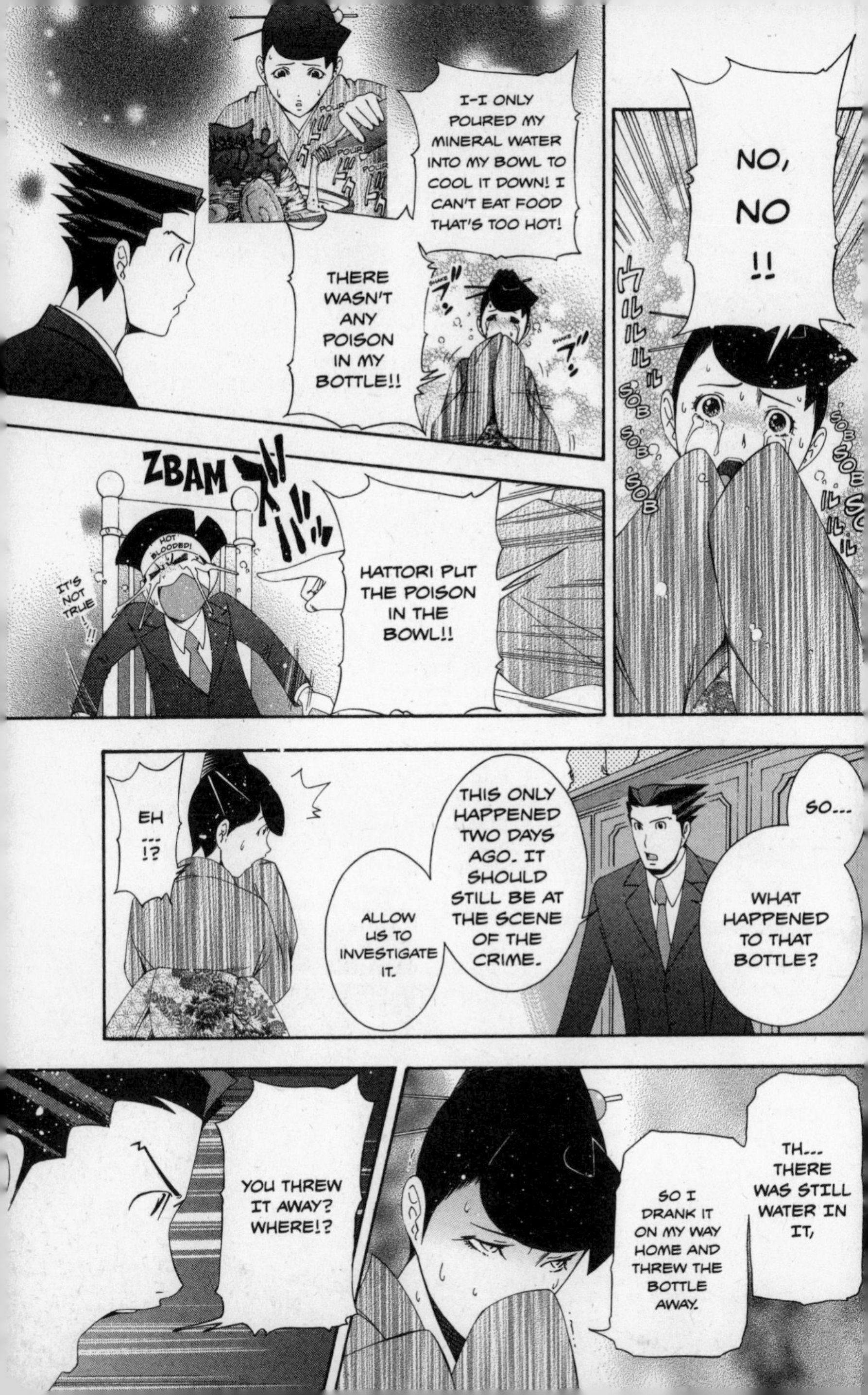
NO, NO!!
SOB SOB SOB
SOB SOB
I-I ONLY POURED MY MINERAL WATER INTO MY BOWL TO COOL IT DOWN! I CAN'T EAT FOOD THAT'S TOO HOT!
POUR POUR POUR
THERE WASN'T ANY POISON IN MY BOTTLE!!
HATTORI PUT THE POISON IN THE BOWL!!
ZBAM
HOT BLOODED!
IT'S NOT TRUE!!
SO... WHAT HAPPENED TO THAT BOTTLE?
THIS ONLY HAPPENED TWO DAYS AGO. IT SHOULD STILL BE AT THE SCENE OF THE CRIME.
ALLOW US TO INVESTIGATE IT.
EH...!?
TH... THERE WAS STILL WATER IN IT,
SO I DRANK IT ON MY WAY HOME AND THREW THE BOTTLE AWAY.
YOU THREW IT AWAY? WHERE!?

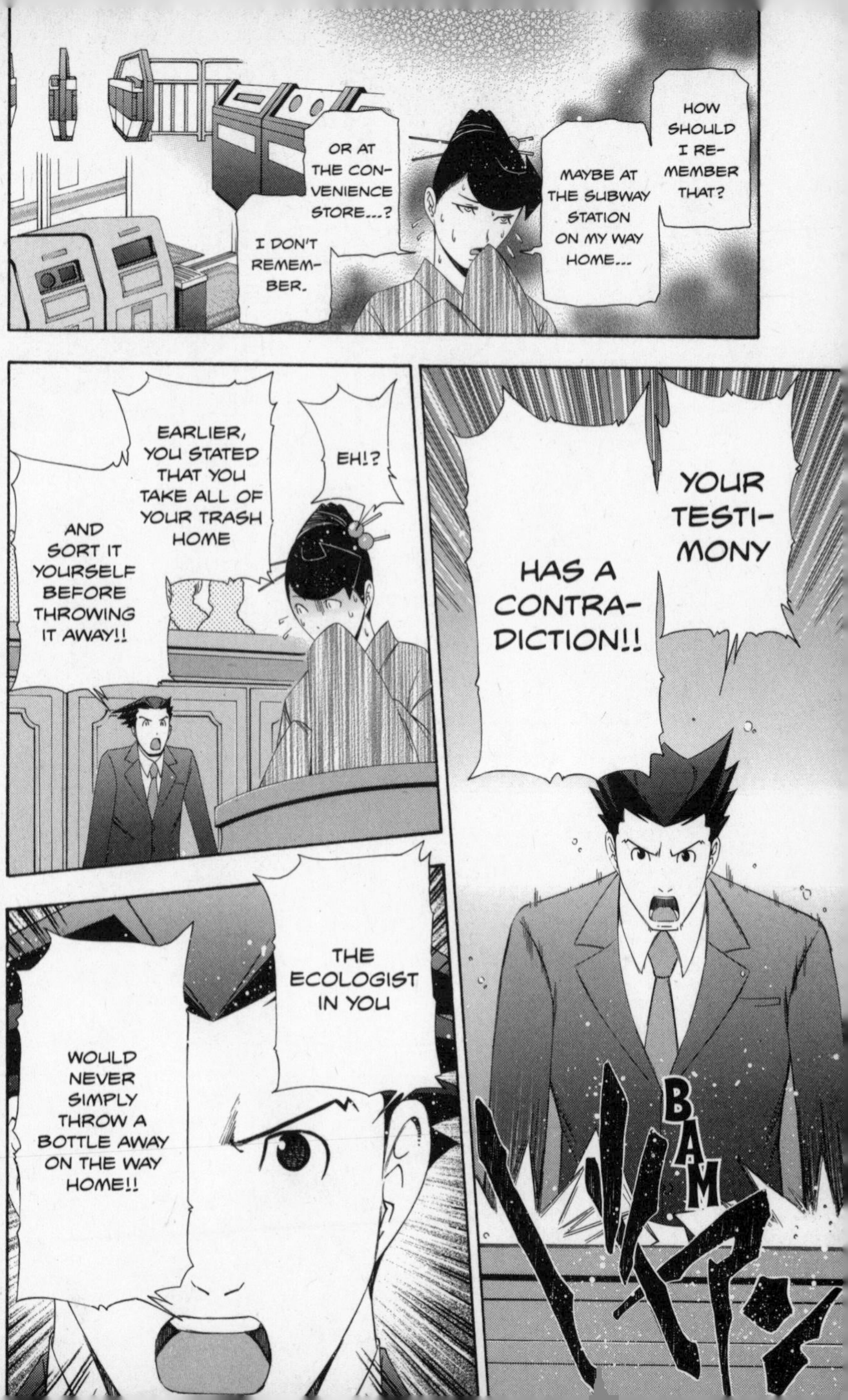
HOW SHOULD I REMEMBER THAT?
MAYBE AT THE SUBWAY STATION ON MY WAY HOME...
OR AT THE CONVENIENCE STORE...?
I DON'T REMEMBER.
YOUR TESTIMONY
HAS A CONTRADICTION!!
BAM
EH!?
EARLIER, YOU STATED THAT YOU TAKE ALL OF YOUR TRASH HOME
AND SORT IT YOURSELF BEFORE THROWING IT AWAY!!
THE ECOLOGIST IN YOU
WOULD NEVER SIMPLY THROW A BOTTLE AWAY ON THE WAY HOME!!

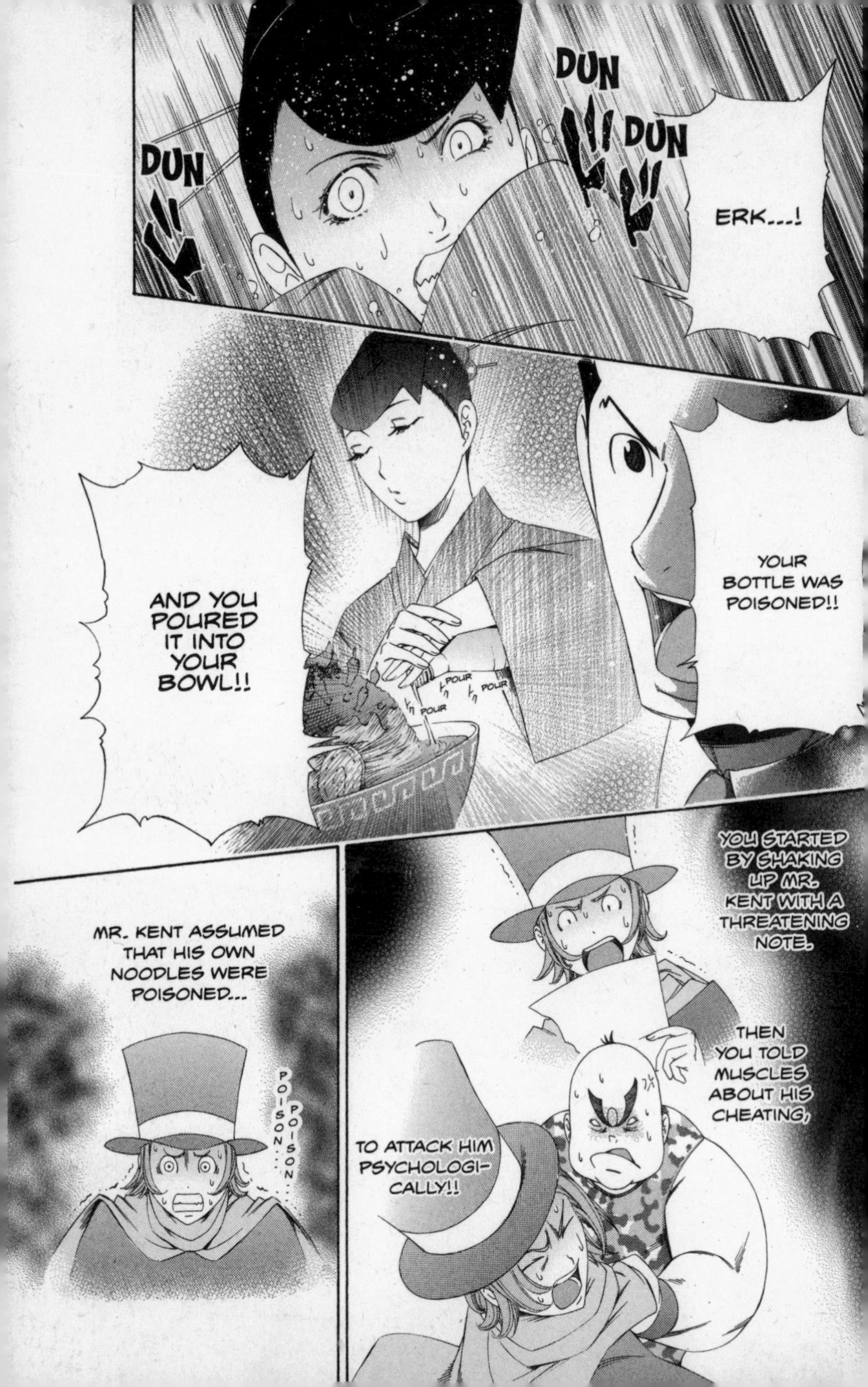
ERK...!
DUN
DUN
DUN
YOUR BOTTLE WAS POISONED!!
AND YOU POURED IT INTO YOUR BOWL!!
POUR
POUR
POUR
YOU STARTED BY SHAKING UP MR. KENT WITH A THREATENING NOTE.
THEN YOU TOLD MUSCLES ABOUT HIS CHEATING,
TO ATTACK HIM PSYCHOLOGI-CALLY!!
MR. KENT ASSUMED THAT HIS OWN NOODLES WERE POISONED...
POISON... POISON...

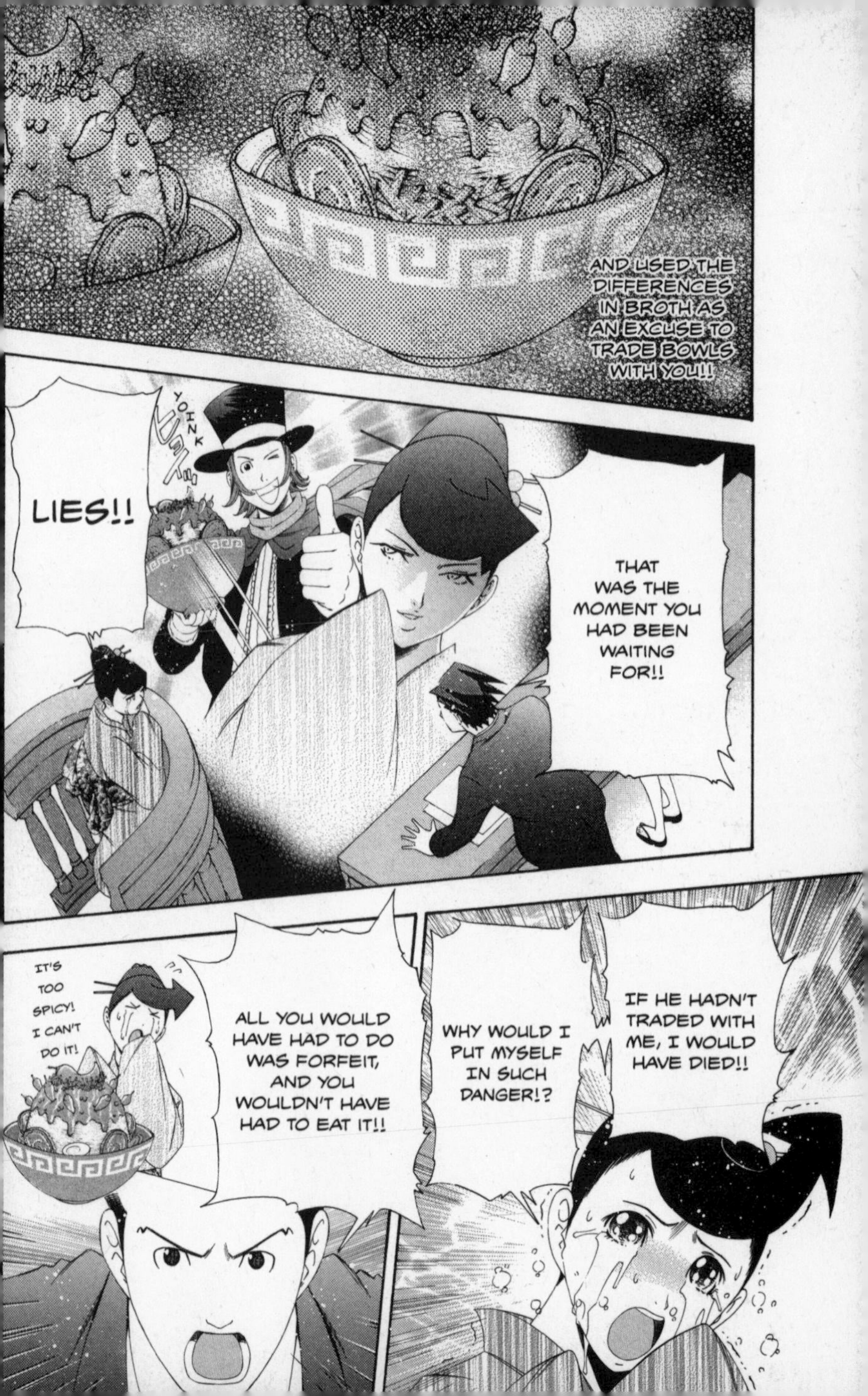
AND USED THE DIFFERENCES IN BROTH AS AN EXCUSE TO TRADE BOWLS WITH YOU!!
THAT WAS THE MOMENT YOU HAD BEEN WAITING FOR!!
YOINK
LIES!!
IF HE HADN'T TRADED WITH ME, I WOULD HAVE DIED!!
WHY WOULD I PUT MYSELF IN SUCH DANGER!?
ALL YOU WOULD HAVE HAD TO DO WAS FORFEIT, AND YOU WOULDN'T HAVE HAD TO EAT IT!!
IT'S TOO SPICY! I CAN'T DO IT!

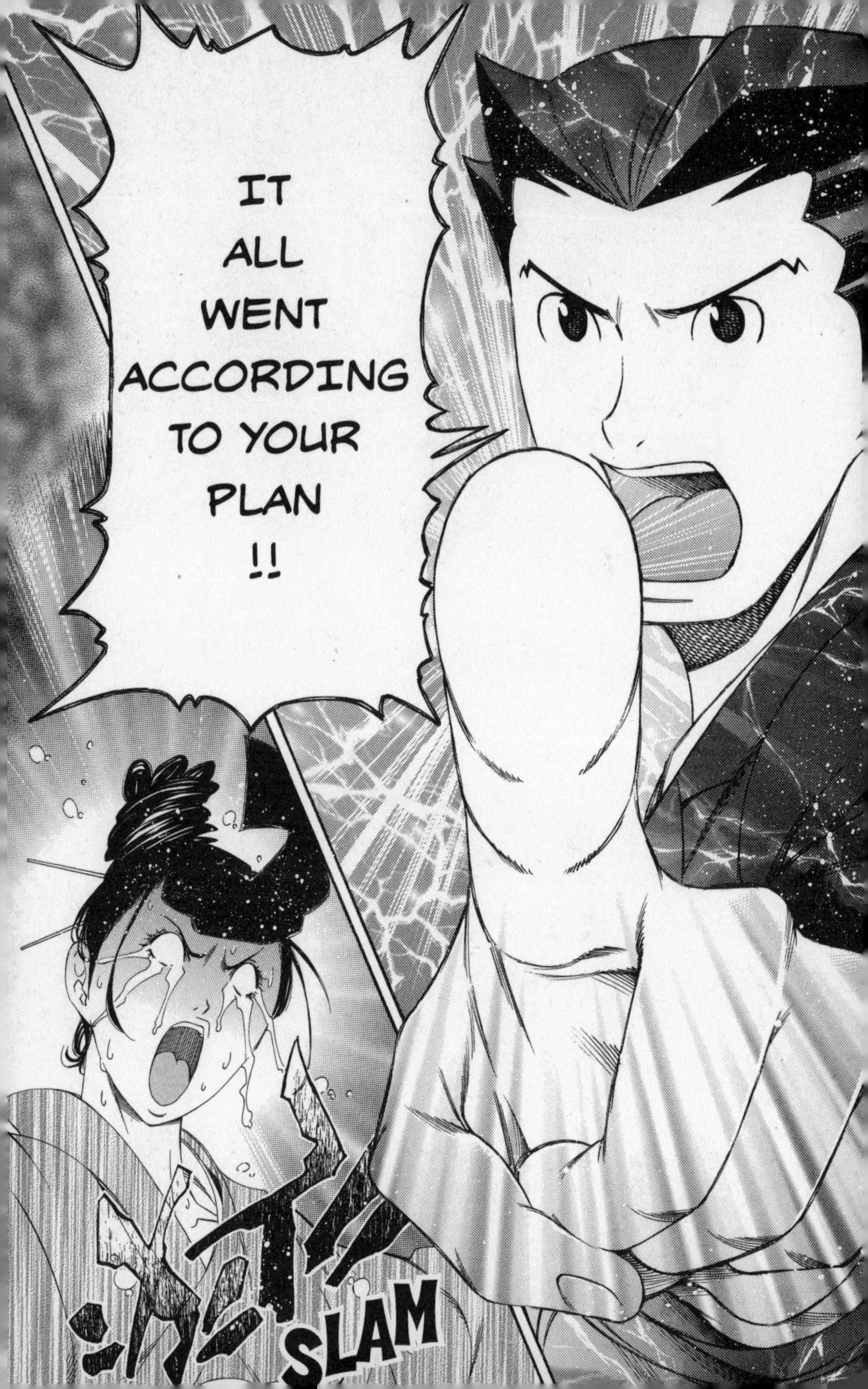
IT ALL WENT ACCORDING TO YOUR PLAN !!
SLAM

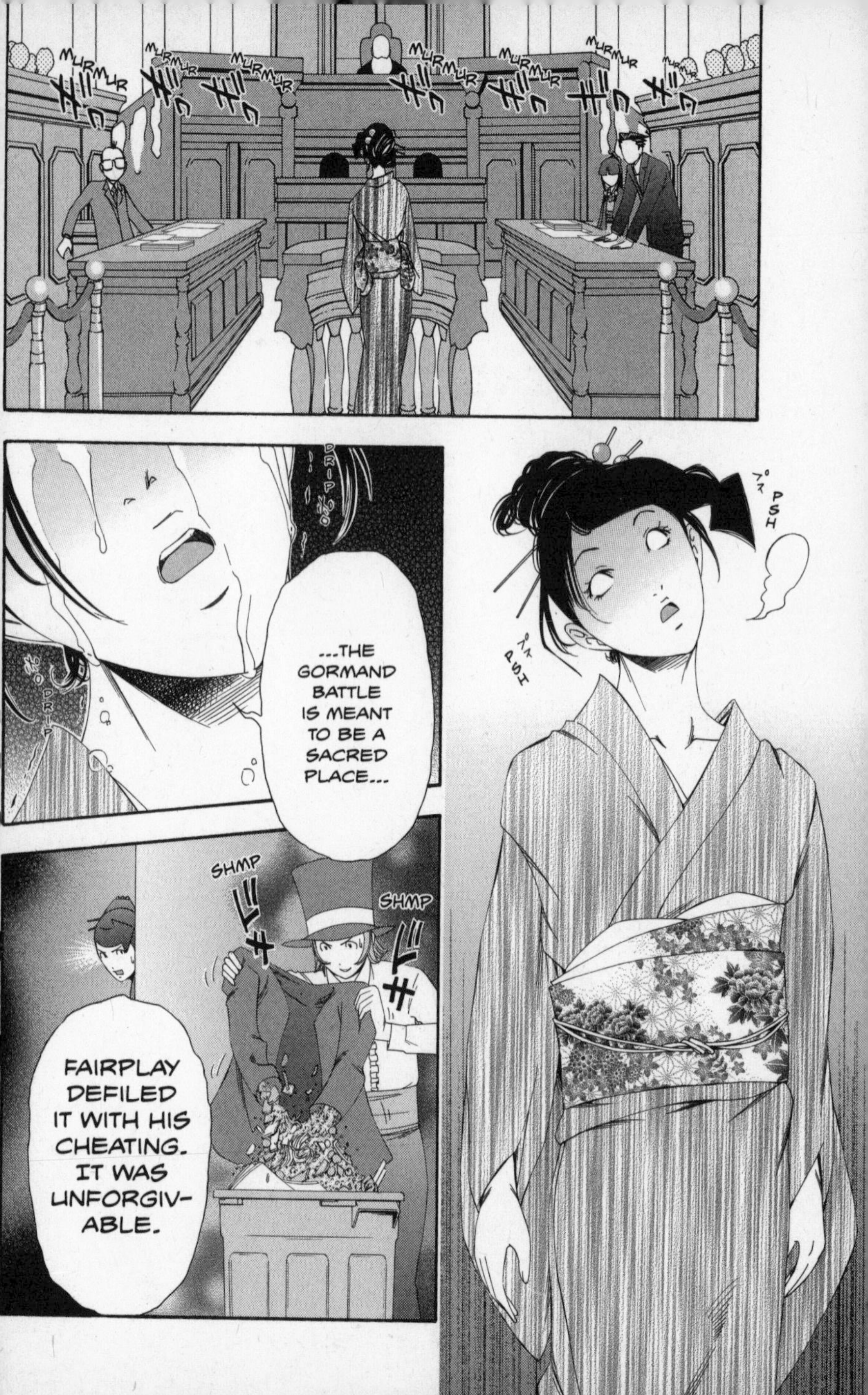
MURMUR
MURMUR
MURMUR
MURMUR
MURMUR
MURMUR
MURMUR
MURMUR
PSH
PSH
DRIP
DRIP
...THE GORMAND BATTLE IS MEANT TO BE A SACRED PLACE...
SHMP
SHMP
FAIRPLAY DEFILED IT WITH HIS CHEATING. IT WAS UNFORGIV-ABLE.

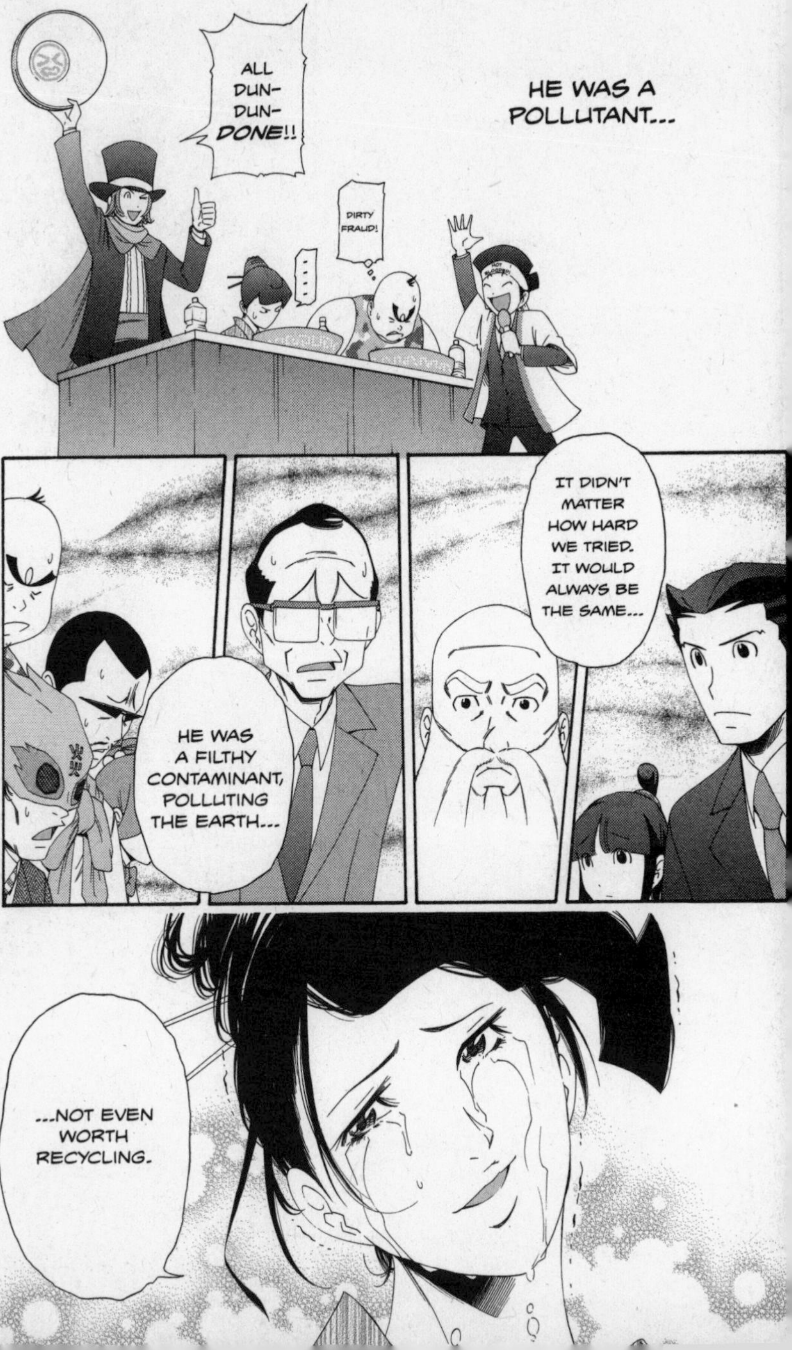
HE WAS A POLLUTANT...
ALL DUN-DUN-DONE!!
DIRTY FRAUD!
...
IT DIDN'T MATTER HOW HARD WE TRIED. IT WOULD ALWAYS BE THE SAME...
HE WAS A FILTHY CONTAMINANT, POLLUTING THE EARTH...
...NOT EVEN WORTH RECYCLING.

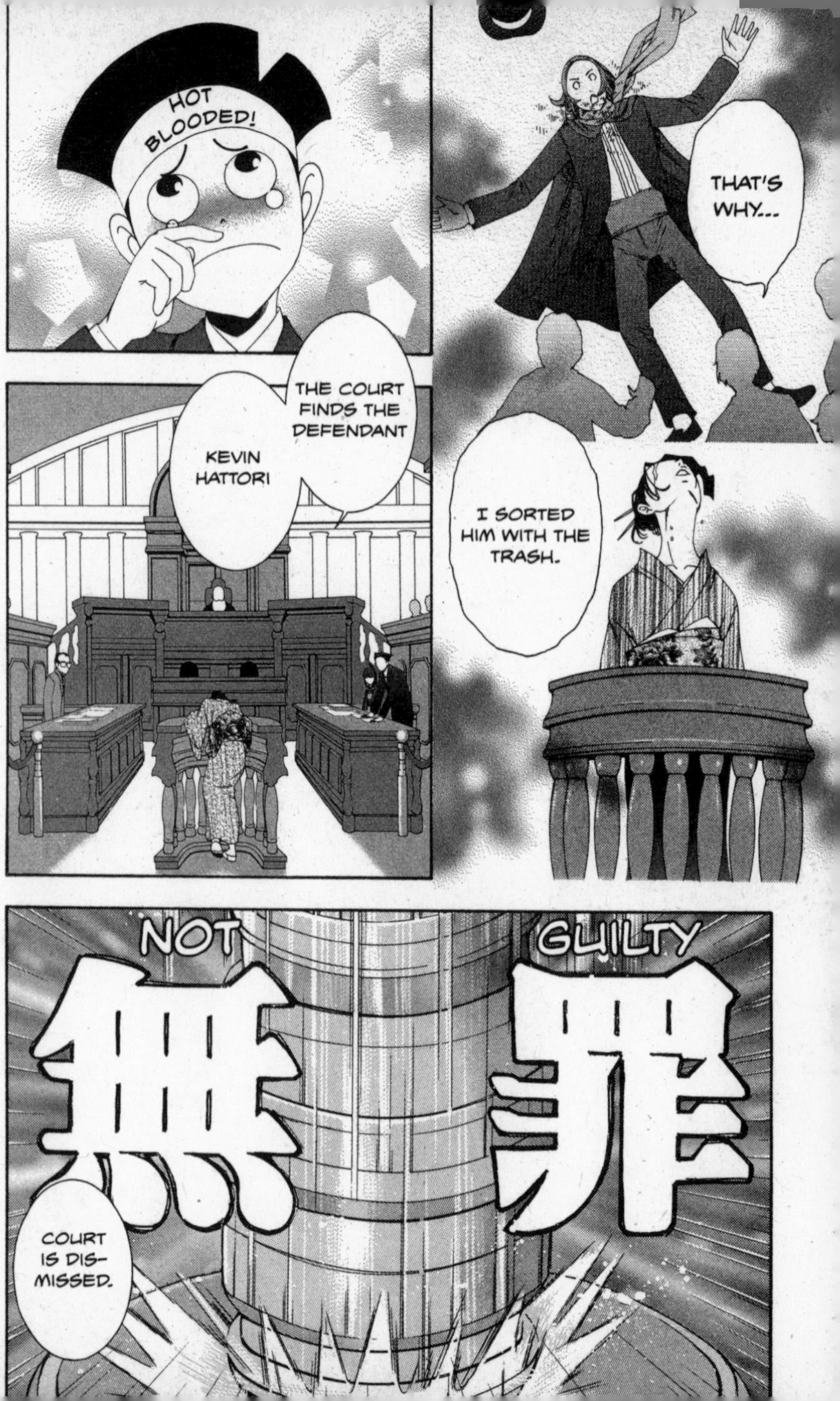
THAT'S WHY...
HOT BLOODED!
I SORTED HIM WITH THE TRASH.
THE COURT FINDS THE DEFENDANT
KEVIN HATTORI
NOT GUILTY
無罪
COURT IS DIS-MISSED.

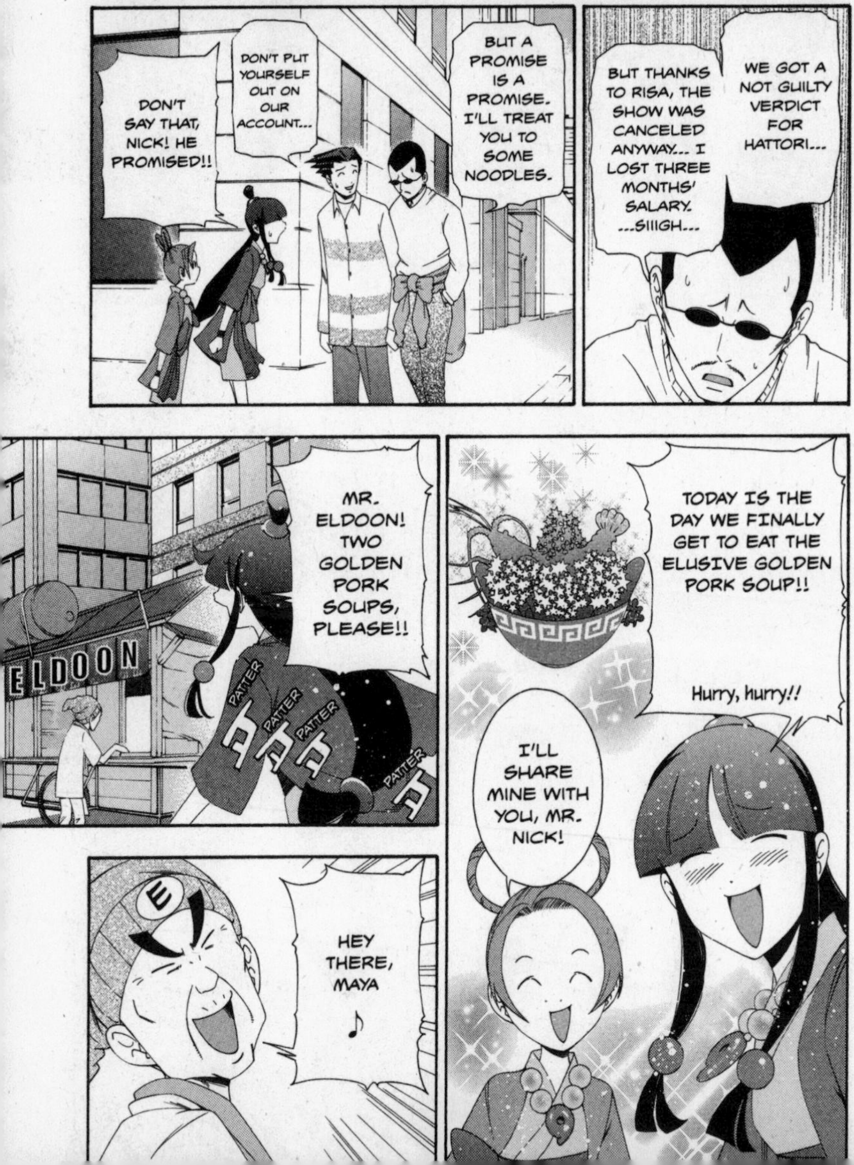
WE GOT A NOT GUILTY VERDICT FOR HATTORI...
BUT THANKS TO RISA, THE SHOW WAS CANCELED ANYWAY... I LOST THREE MONTHS' SALARY. ...SIIIGH...
BUT A PROMISE IS A PROMISE. I'LL TREAT YOU TO SOME NOODLES.
DON'T PUT YOURSELF OUT ON OUR ACCOUNT...
DON'T SAY THAT, NICK! HE PROMISED!!
TODAY IS THE DAY WE FINALLY GET TO EAT THE ELUSIVE GOLDEN PORK SOUP!!
Hurry, hurry!!
I'LL SHARE MINE WITH YOU, MR. NICK!
MR. ELDOON! TWO GOLDEN PORK SOUPS, PLEASE!!
PATTER
PATTER
PATTER
PATTER
ELDOON
HEY THERE, MAYA ♪

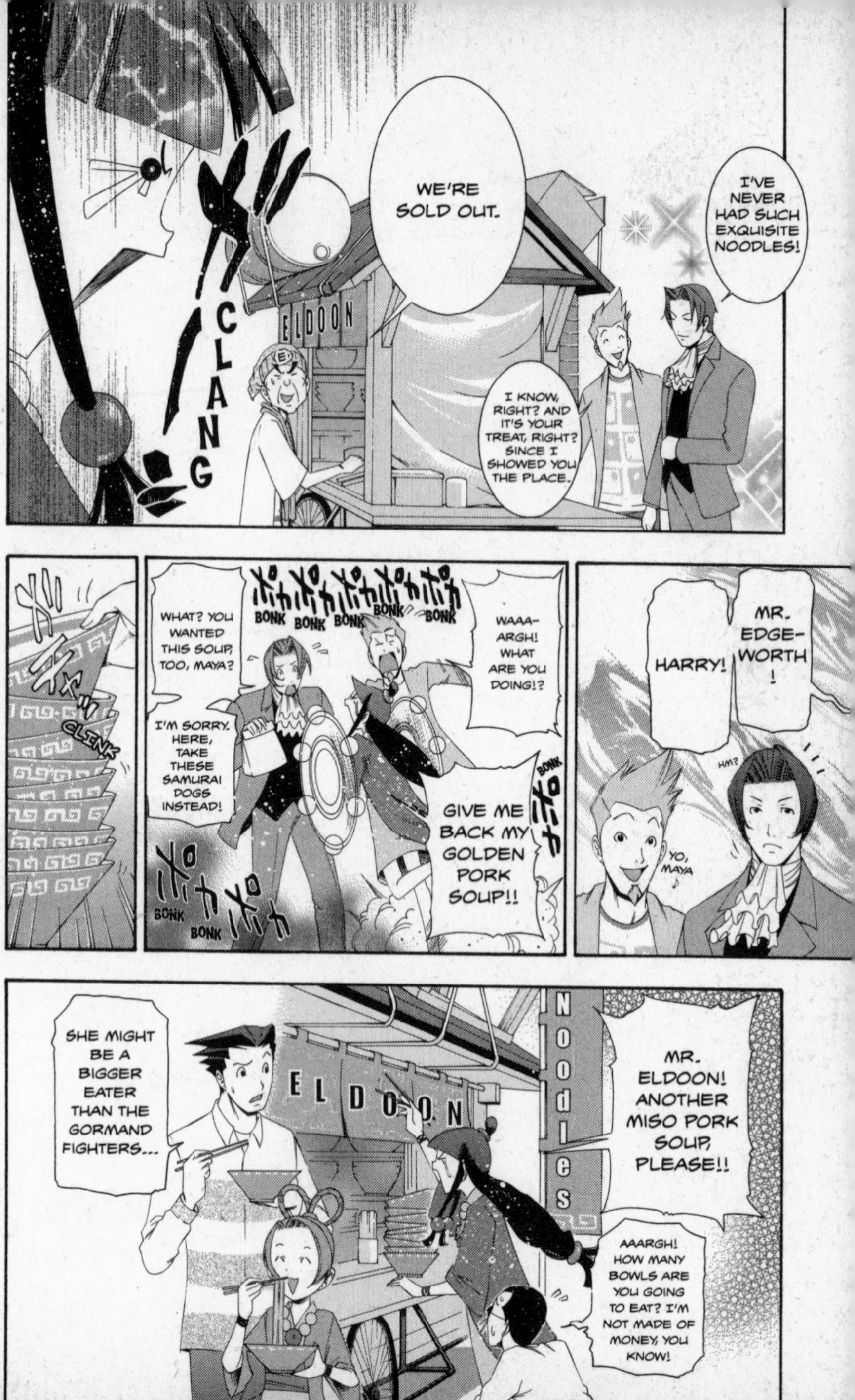
I'VE NEVER HAD SUCH EXQUISITE NOODLES!
I KNOW, RIGHT? AND IT'S YOUR TREAT, RIGHT? SINCE I SHOWED YOU THE PLACE.
WE'RE SOLD OUT.
ELDOON
CLANG
MR. EDGE-WORTH!
HARRY!
HM?
YO, MAYA ♪
WAAA-ARGH! WHAT ARE YOU DOING!?
BONK BONK BONK BONK BONK
WHAT? YOU WANTED THIS SOUP, TOO, MAYA?
I'M SORRY. HERE, TAKE THESE SAMURAI DOGS INSTEAD!
BONK
GIVE ME BACK MY GOLDEN PORK SOUP!!
BONK BONK
CLINK
MR. ELDOON! ANOTHER MISO PORK SOUP, PLEASE!!
Noodles
ELDOON
SHE MIGHT BE A BIGGER EATER THAN THE GORMAND FIGHTERS...
AAARGH! HOW MANY BOWLS ARE YOU GOING TO EAT? I'M NOT MADE OF MONEY, YOU KNOW!

Phoenix Wright
Ace Attorney™

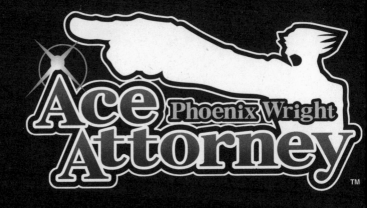

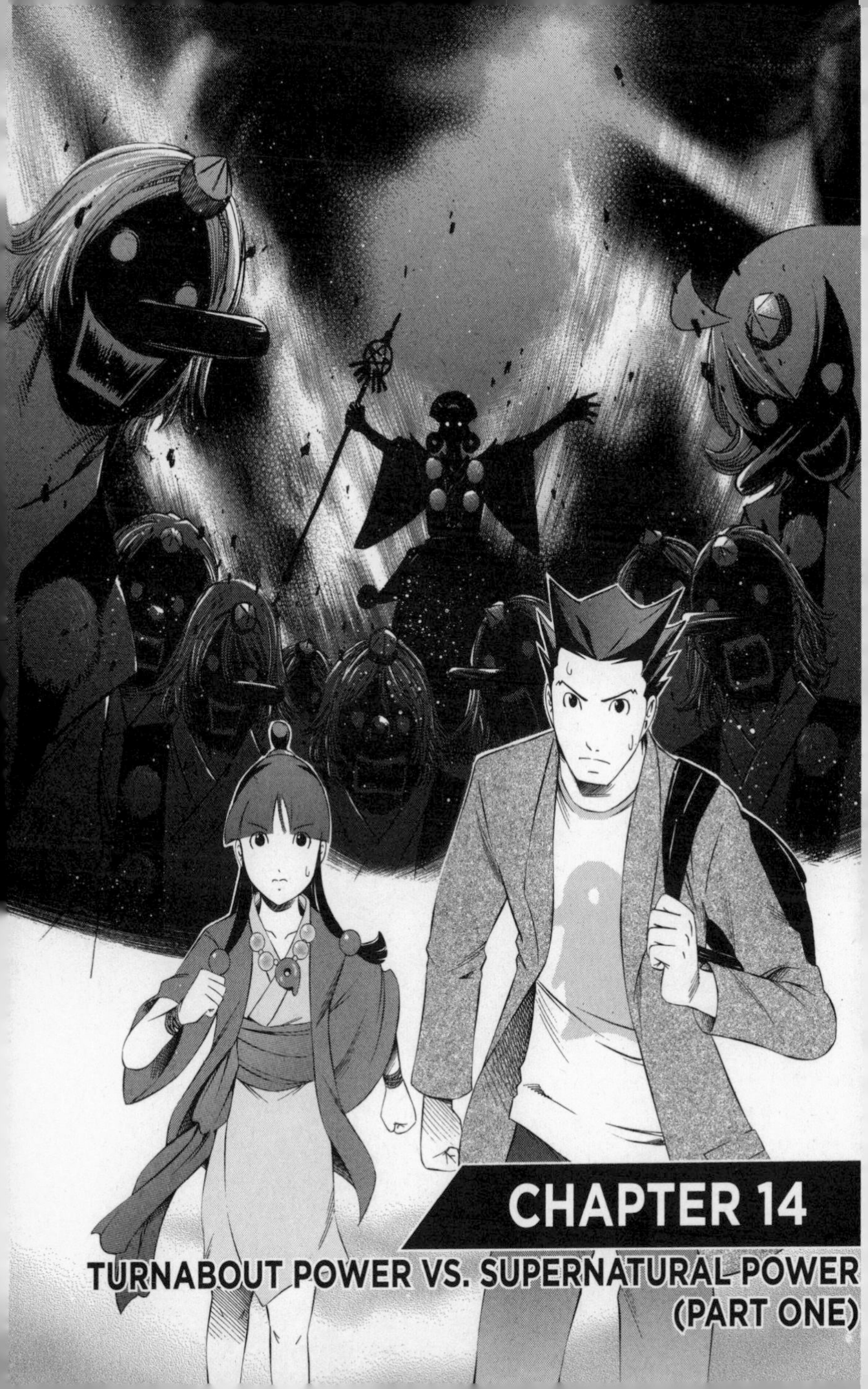
CHAPTER 14
TURNABOUT POWER VS. SUPERNATURAL POWER
(PART ONE)

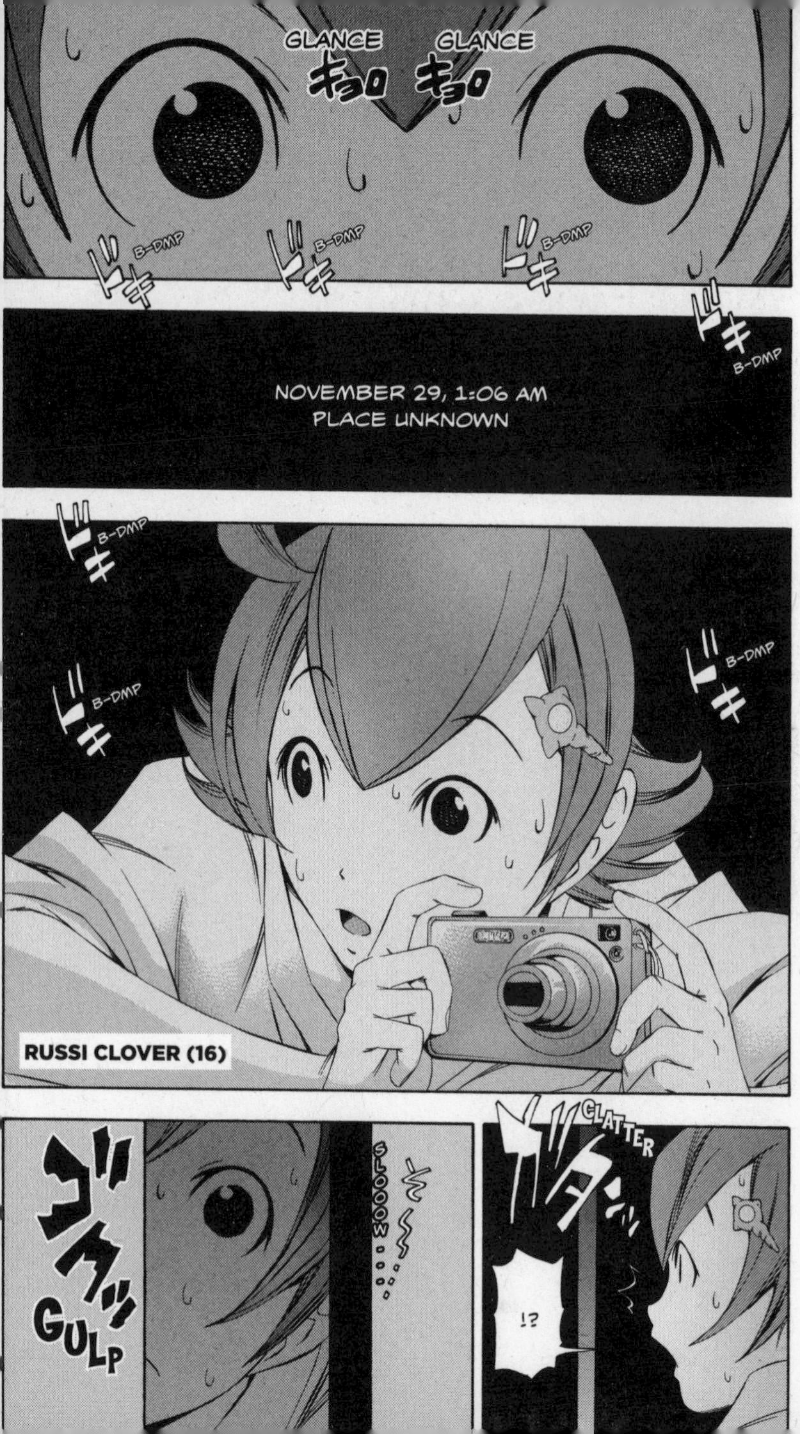

GLANCE GLANCE
キョロ キョロ
B-DMP
ドキ
B-DMP
ドキ
B-DMP
ドキ
B-DMP
ドキ
NOVEMBER 29, 1:06 AM
PLACE UNKNOWN
B-DMP
ドキ
B-DMP
ドキ
B-DMP
ドキ
RUSSI CLOVER (16)
CLATTER
ガタン
!?
SLOOOW
GULP

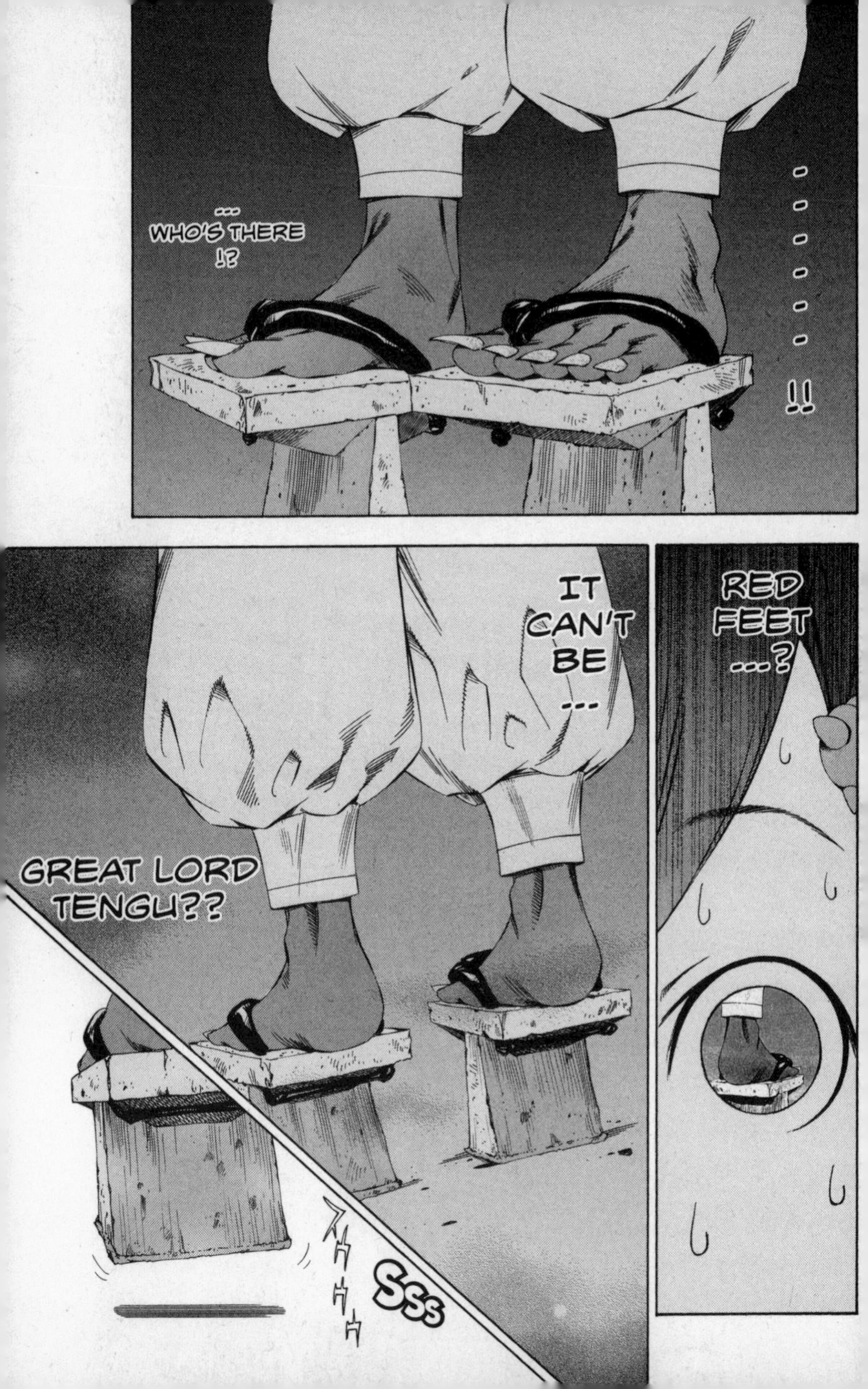

.... !!
... WHO'S THERE !?
RED FEET ...?
IT CAN'T BE ...
GREAT LORD TENGU??
スゥゥゥ
Sss

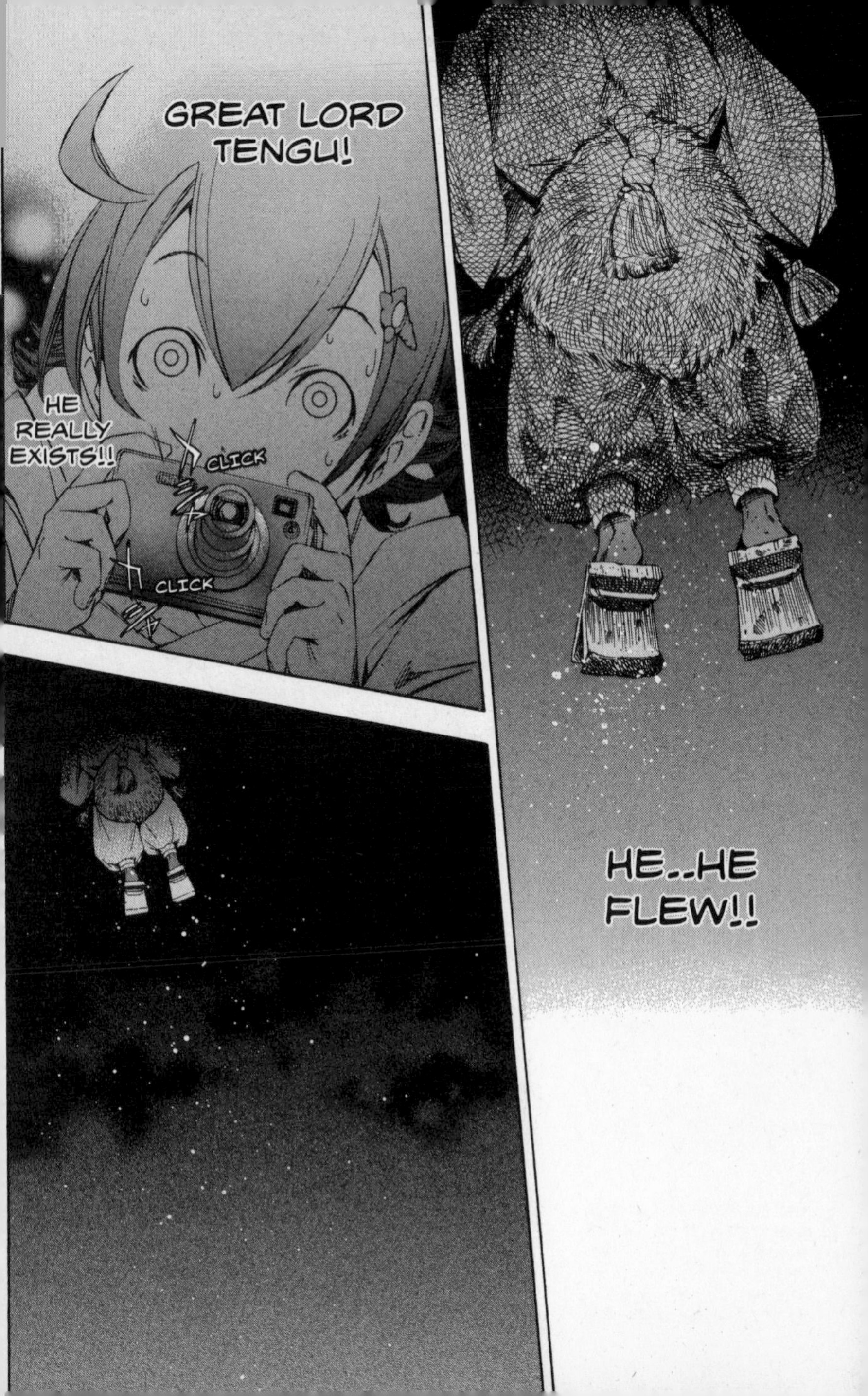
HE..HE FLEW!!
GREAT LORD TENGU!
HE REALLY EXISTS!!
CLICK
CLICK

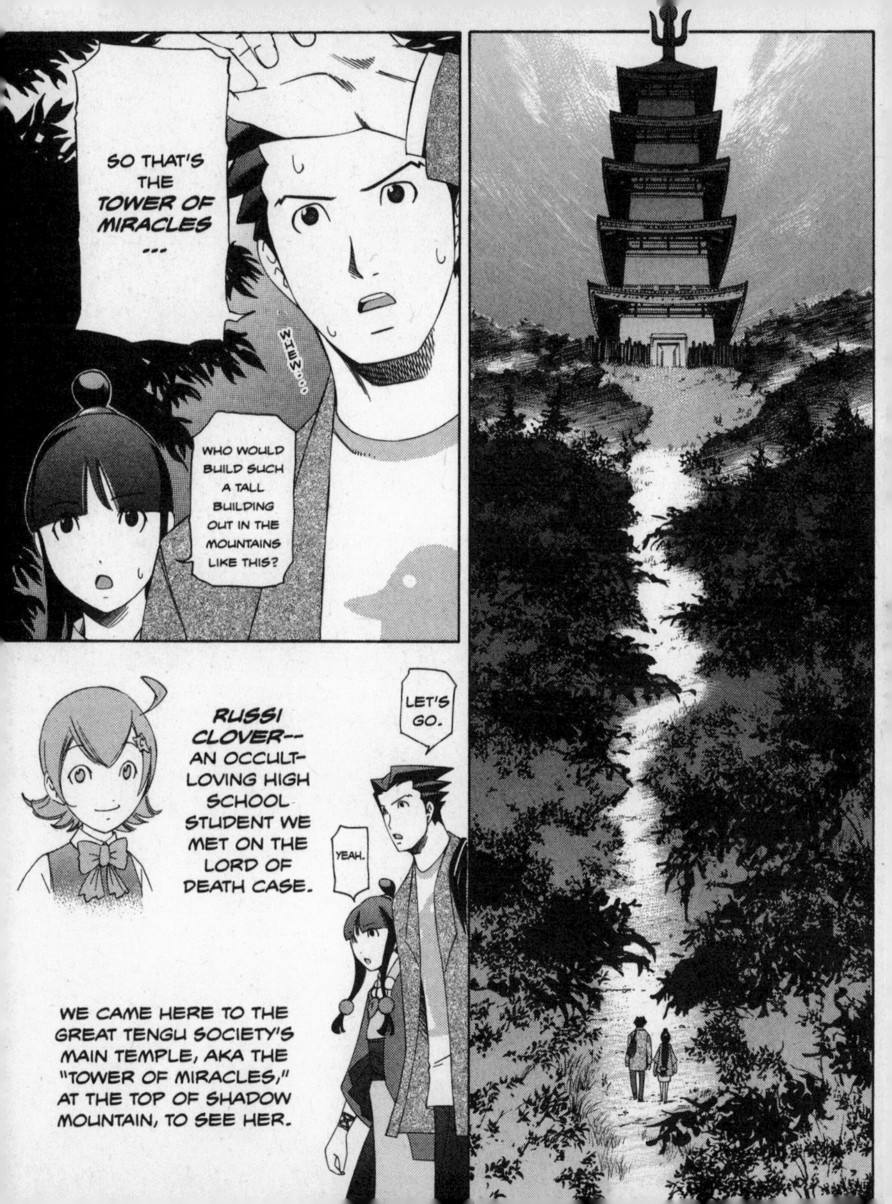
SO THAT'S THE *TOWER OF MIRACLES* ...
WHEW...
WHO WOULD BUILD SUCH A TALL BUILDING OUT IN THE MOUNTAINS LIKE THIS?
LET'S GO.
YEAH.
RUSSI CLOVER-- AN OCCULT-LOVING HIGH SCHOOL STUDENT WE MET ON THE LORD OF DEATH CASE.
WE CAME HERE TO THE GREAT TENGU SOCIETY'S MAIN TEMPLE, AKA THE "TOWER OF MIRACLES," AT THE TOP OF SHADOW MOUNTAIN, TO SEE HER.

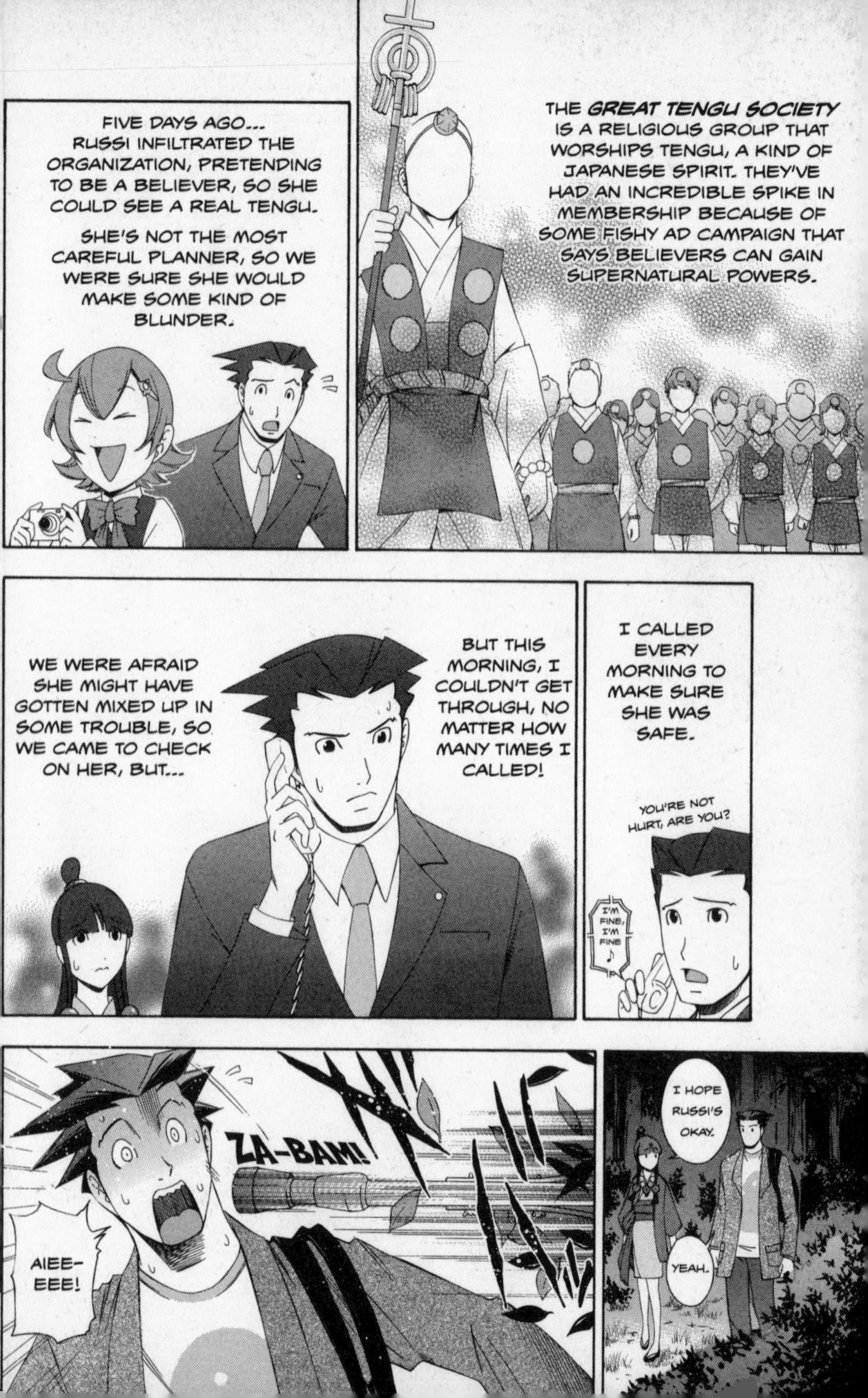
THE *GREAT TENGU SOCIETY* IS A RELIGIOUS GROUP THAT WORSHIPS TENGU, A KIND OF JAPANESE SPIRIT. THEY'VE HAD AN INCREDIBLE SPIKE IN MEMBERSHIP BECAUSE OF SOME FISHY AD CAMPAIGN THAT SAYS BELIEVERS CAN GAIN SUPERNATURAL POWERS.
FIVE DAYS AGO... RUSSI INFILTRATED THE ORGANIZATION, PRETENDING TO BE A BELIEVER, SO SHE COULD SEE A REAL TENGU.
SHE'S NOT THE MOST CAREFUL PLANNER, SO WE WERE SURE SHE WOULD MAKE SOME KIND OF BLUNDER.
I CALLED EVERY MORNING TO MAKE SURE SHE WAS SAFE.
YOU'RE NOT HURT, ARE YOU?
I'M FINE, I'M FINE ♪
BUT THIS MORNING, I COULDN'T GET THROUGH, NO MATTER HOW MANY TIMES I CALLED!
WE WERE AFRAID SHE MIGHT HAVE GOTTEN MIXED UP IN SOME TROUBLE, SO WE CAME TO CHECK ON HER, BUT...
I HOPE RUSSI'S OKAY.
YEAH.
ZA-BAM!
AIEE-EEE!

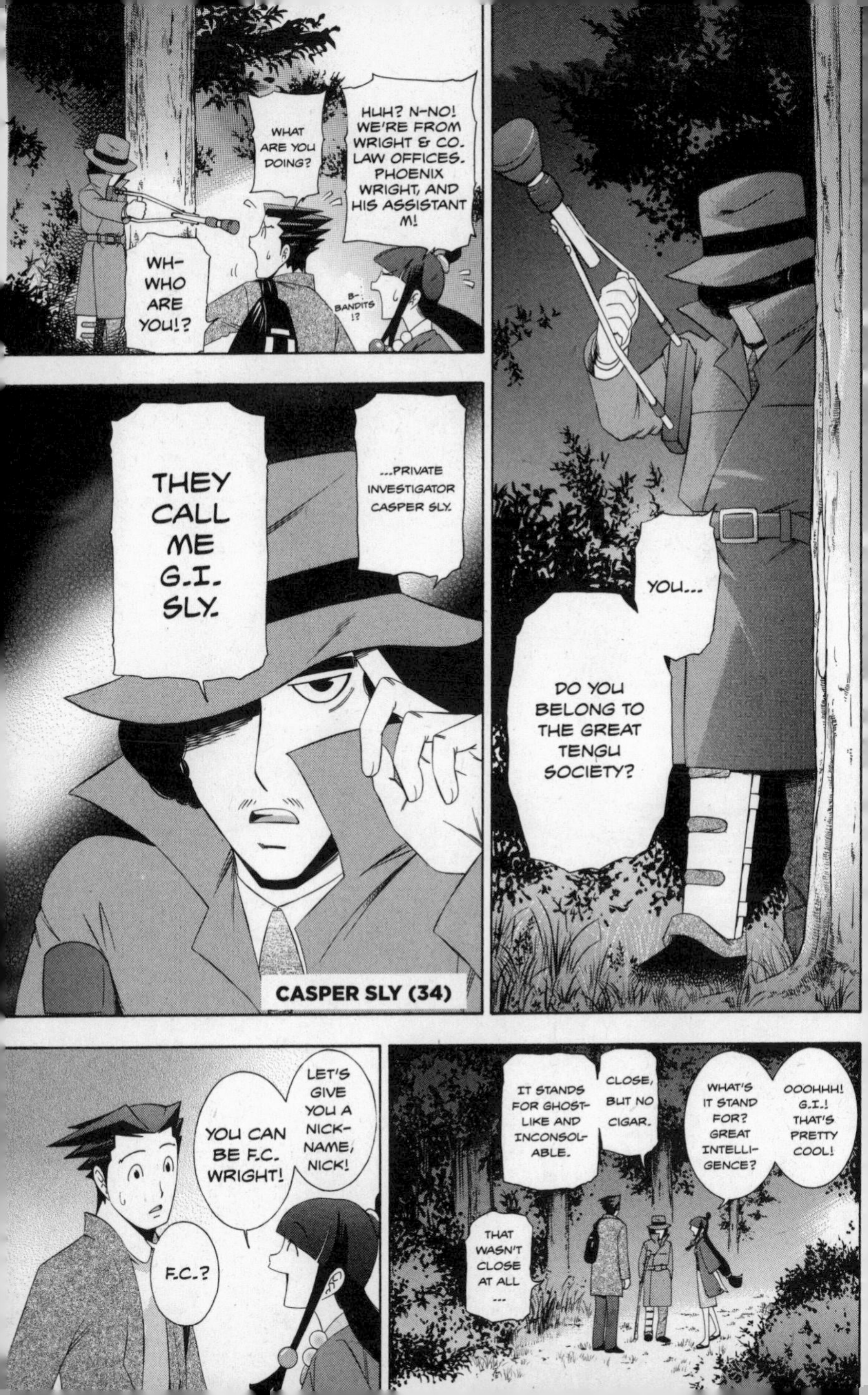
YOU...
DO YOU BELONG TO THE GREAT TENGU SOCIETY?
HUH? N-NO! WE'RE FROM WRIGHT & CO. LAW OFFICES. PHOENIX WRIGHT, AND HIS ASSISTANT M!
WHAT ARE YOU DOING?
B-BANDITS!?
WH-WHO ARE YOU!?
...PRIVATE INVESTIGATOR CASPER SLY.
THEY CALL ME G.I. SLY.
CASPER SLY (34)
OOOHHH! G.I.! THAT'S PRETTY COOL!
WHAT'S IT STAND FOR? GREAT INTELLIGENCE?
CLOSE, BUT NO CIGAR.
IT STANDS FOR GHOST-LIKE AND INCONSOLABLE.
THAT WASN'T CLOSE AT ALL...
LET'S GIVE YOU A NICKNAME, NICK!
YOU CAN BE F.C. WRIGHT!
F.C.?

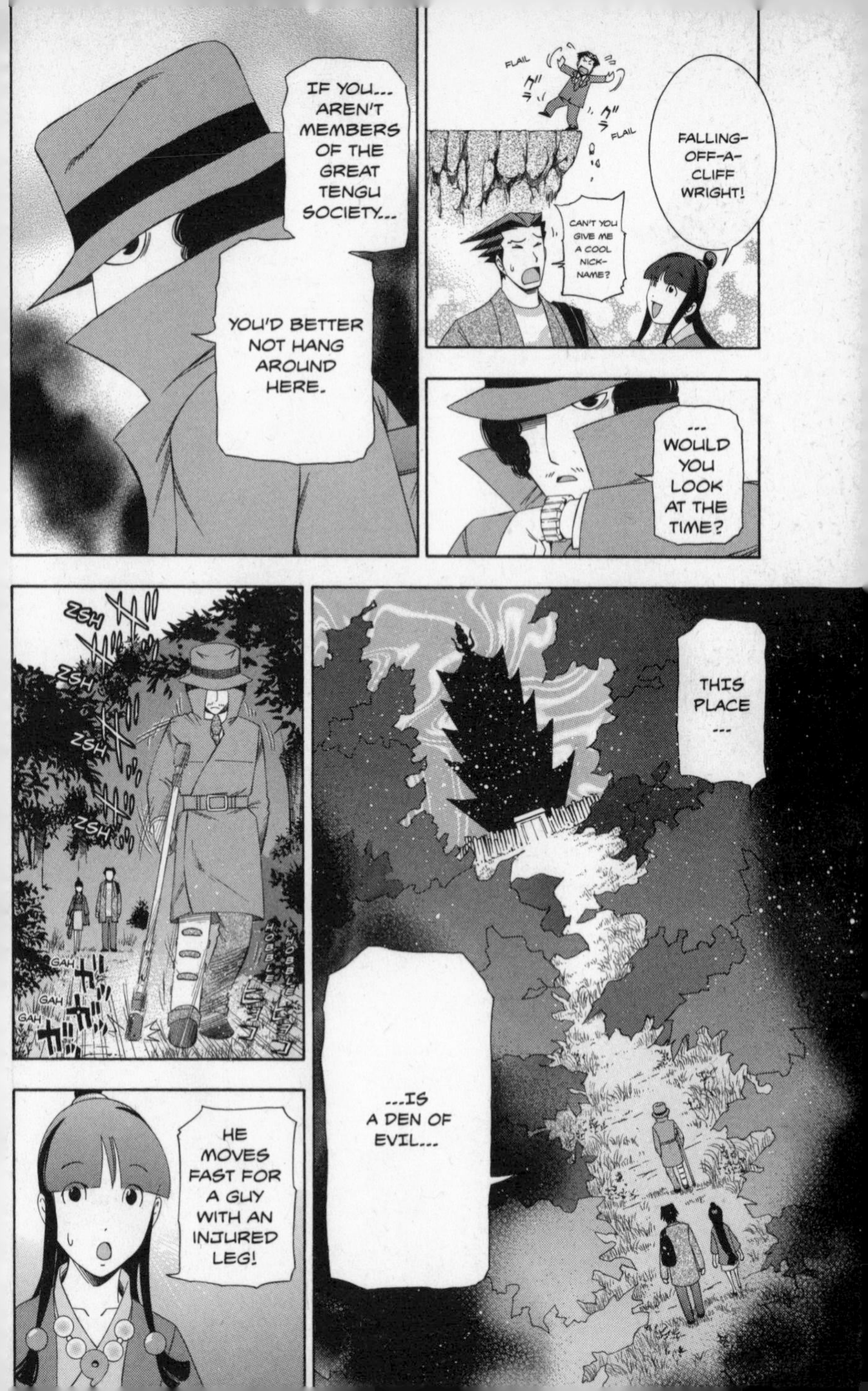
FLAIL
FLAIL
FALLING-OFF-A-CLIFF WRIGHT!
CAN'T YOU GIVE ME A COOL NICK-NAME?
...WOULD YOU LOOK AT THE TIME?
IF YOU... AREN'T MEMBERS OF THE GREAT TENGU SOCIETY...
YOU'D BETTER NOT HANG AROUND HERE.
THIS PLACE...
...IS A DEN OF EVIL...
ZSH
ZSH
ZSH
ZSH
HOBBLE
HOBBLE
GAH
GAH
GAH
HE MOVES FAST FOR A GUY WITH AN INJURED LEG!

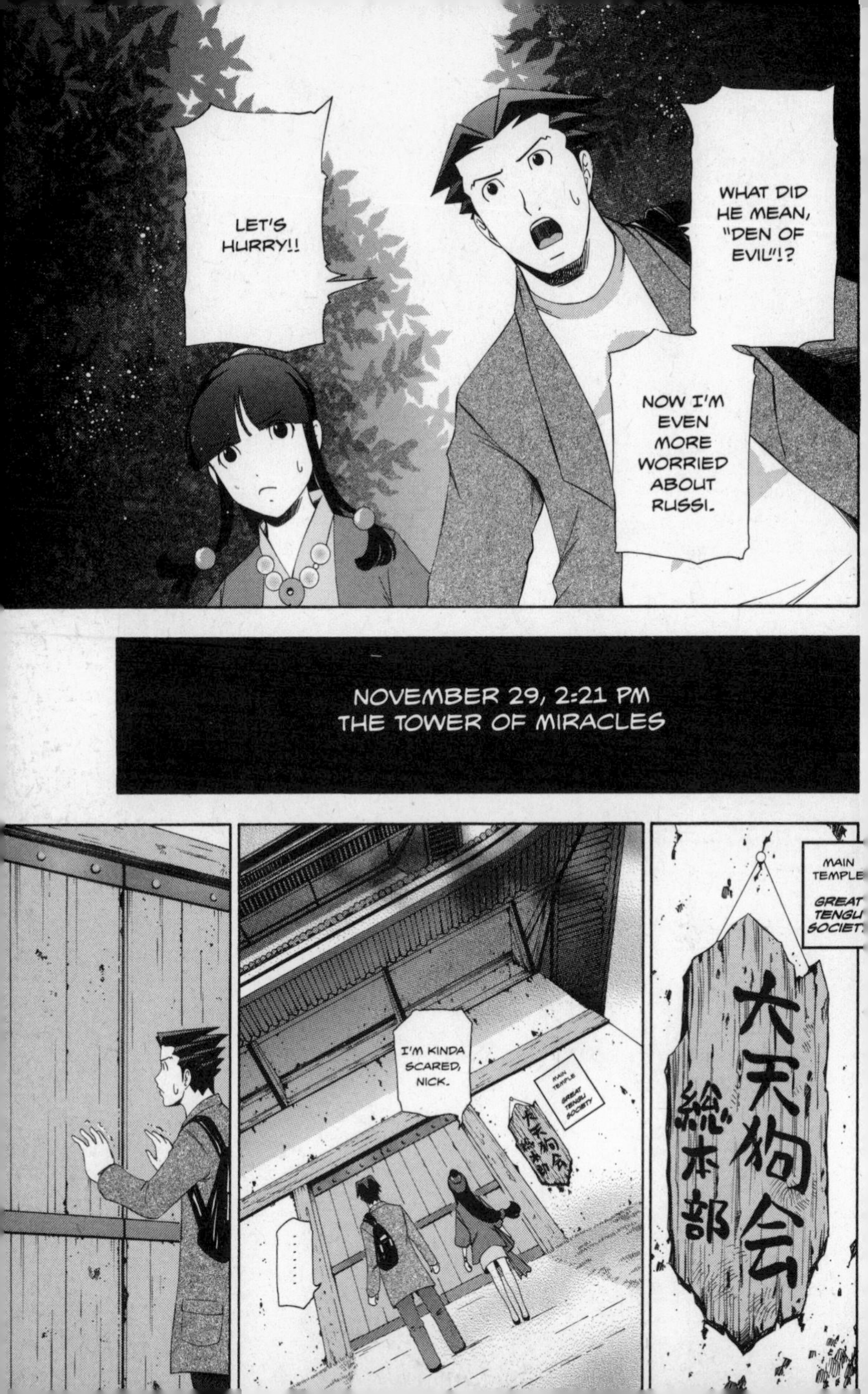
WHAT DID HE MEAN, "DEN OF EVIL"!?
NOW I'M EVEN MORE WORRIED ABOUT RUSSI.
LET'S HURRY!!
NOVEMBER 29, 2:21 PM
THE TOWER OF MIRACLES
MAIN TEMPLE
GREAT TENGU SOCIET
大天狗会
総本部
I'M KINDA SCARED, NICK.
MAIN TEMPLE
GREAT TENGU SOCIETY
...

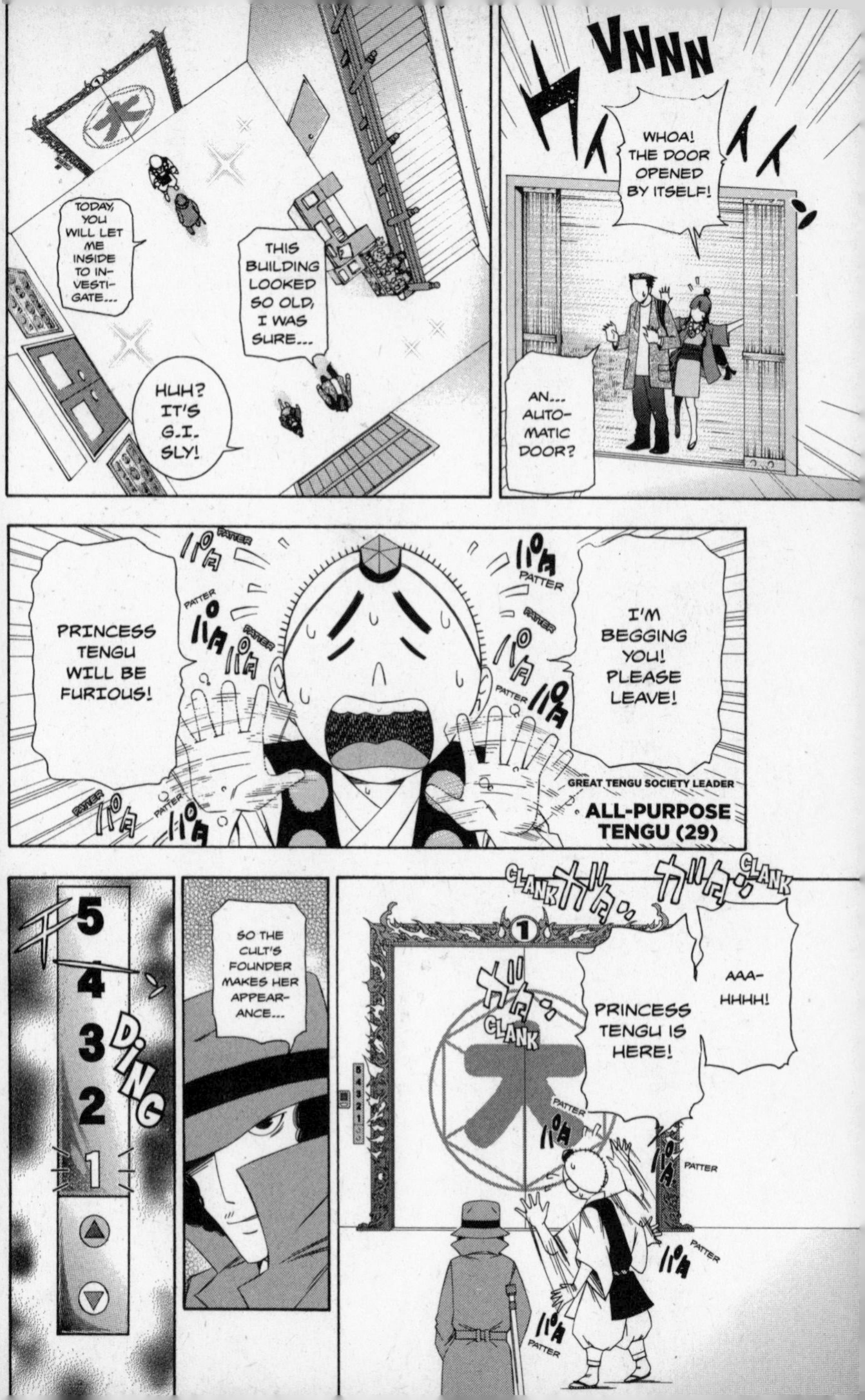
VNNN
WHOA! THE DOOR OPENED BY ITSELF!
AN... AUTO-MATIC DOOR?
THIS BUILDING LOOKED SO OLD, I WAS SURE...
TODAY, YOU WILL LET ME INSIDE TO IN-VESTI-GATE...
HUH? IT'S G.I. SLY!
PATTER
I'M BEGGING YOU! PLEASE LEAVE!
PRINCESS TENGU WILL BE FURIOUS!
GREAT TENGU SOCIETY LEADER
ALL-PURPOSE TENGU (29)
CLANK
CLANK
AAA-HHHH!
PRINCESS TENGU IS HERE!
CLANK
PATTER
SO THE CULT'S FOUNDER MAKES HER APPEAR-ANCE...
5
4
3
DING
2
1

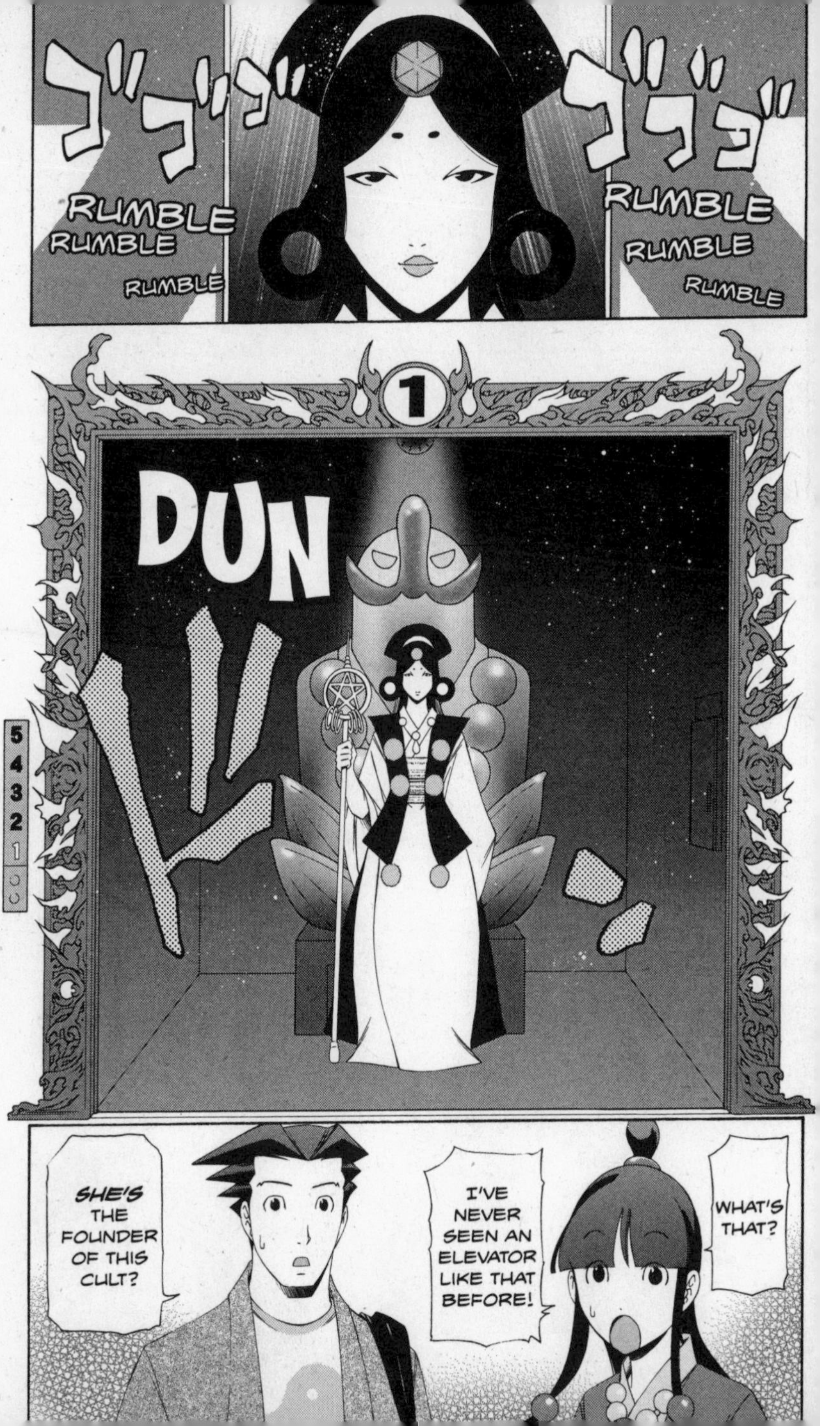
RUMBLE
RUMBLE
RUMBLE
RUMBLE
RUMBLE
RUMBLE
1
DUN
5
4
3
2
1
WHAT'S THAT?
I'VE NEVER SEEN AN ELEVATOR LIKE THAT BEFORE!
SHE'S THE FOUNDER OF THIS CULT?

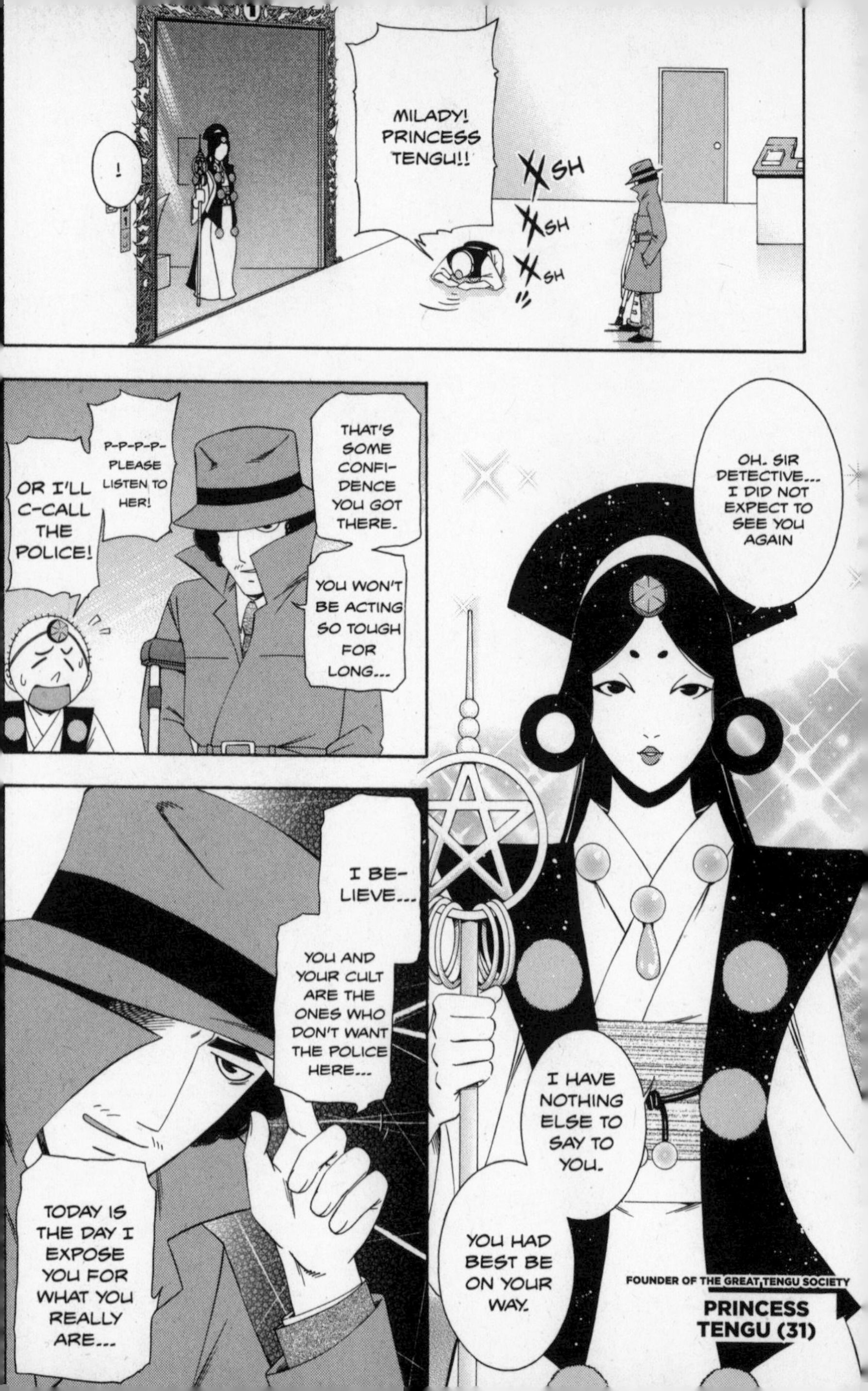
MILADY! PRINCESS TENGU!!
SH
SH
SH
!
OH. SIR DETECTIVE... I DID NOT EXPECT TO SEE YOU AGAIN
I HAVE NOTHING ELSE TO SAY TO YOU.
YOU HAD BEST BE ON YOUR WAY.
FOUNDER OF THE GREAT TENGU SOCIETY
PRINCESS TENGU (31)
THAT'S SOME CONFIDENCE YOU GOT THERE.
YOU WON'T BE ACTING SO TOUGH FOR LONG...
P-P-P-P-PLEASE LISTEN TO HER!
OR I'LL C-CALL THE POLICE!
I BELIEVE...
YOU AND YOUR CULT ARE THE ONES WHO DON'T WANT THE POLICE HERE...
TODAY IS THE DAY I EXPOSE YOU FOR WHAT YOU REALLY ARE...

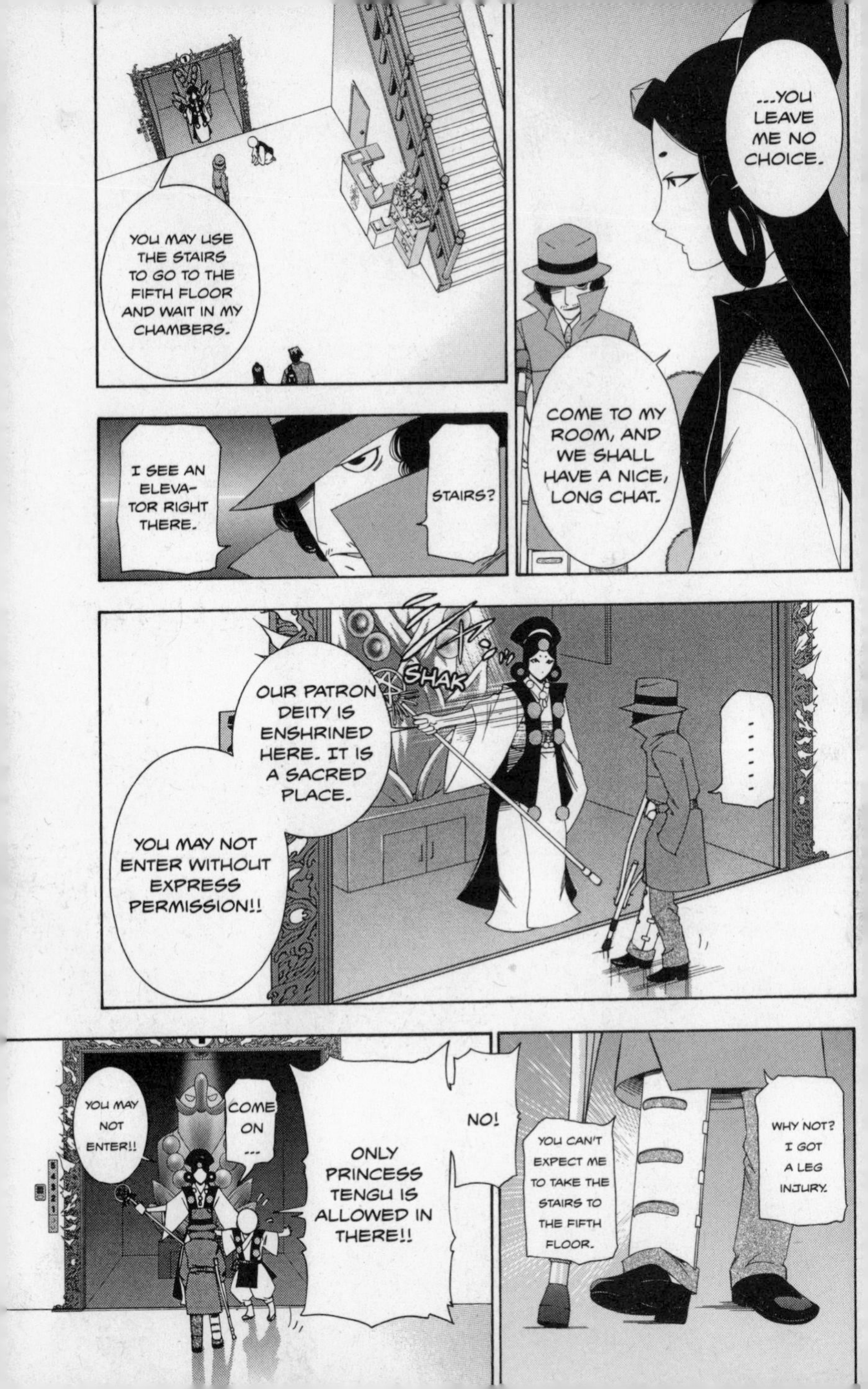
...YOU LEAVE ME NO CHOICE.
COME TO MY ROOM, AND WE SHALL HAVE A NICE, LONG CHAT.
YOU MAY USE THE STAIRS TO GO TO THE FIFTH FLOOR AND WAIT IN MY CHAMBERS.
STAIRS?
I SEE AN ELEVATOR RIGHT THERE.
......
SHAK
OUR PATRON DEITY IS ENSHRINED HERE. IT IS A SACRED PLACE.
YOU MAY NOT ENTER WITHOUT EXPRESS PERMISSION!!
WHY NOT? I GOT A LEG INJURY.
YOU CAN'T EXPECT ME TO TAKE THE STAIRS TO THE FIFTH FLOOR.
NO!
ONLY PRINCESS TENGU IS ALLOWED IN THERE!!
COME ON ---
YOU MAY NOT ENTER!!

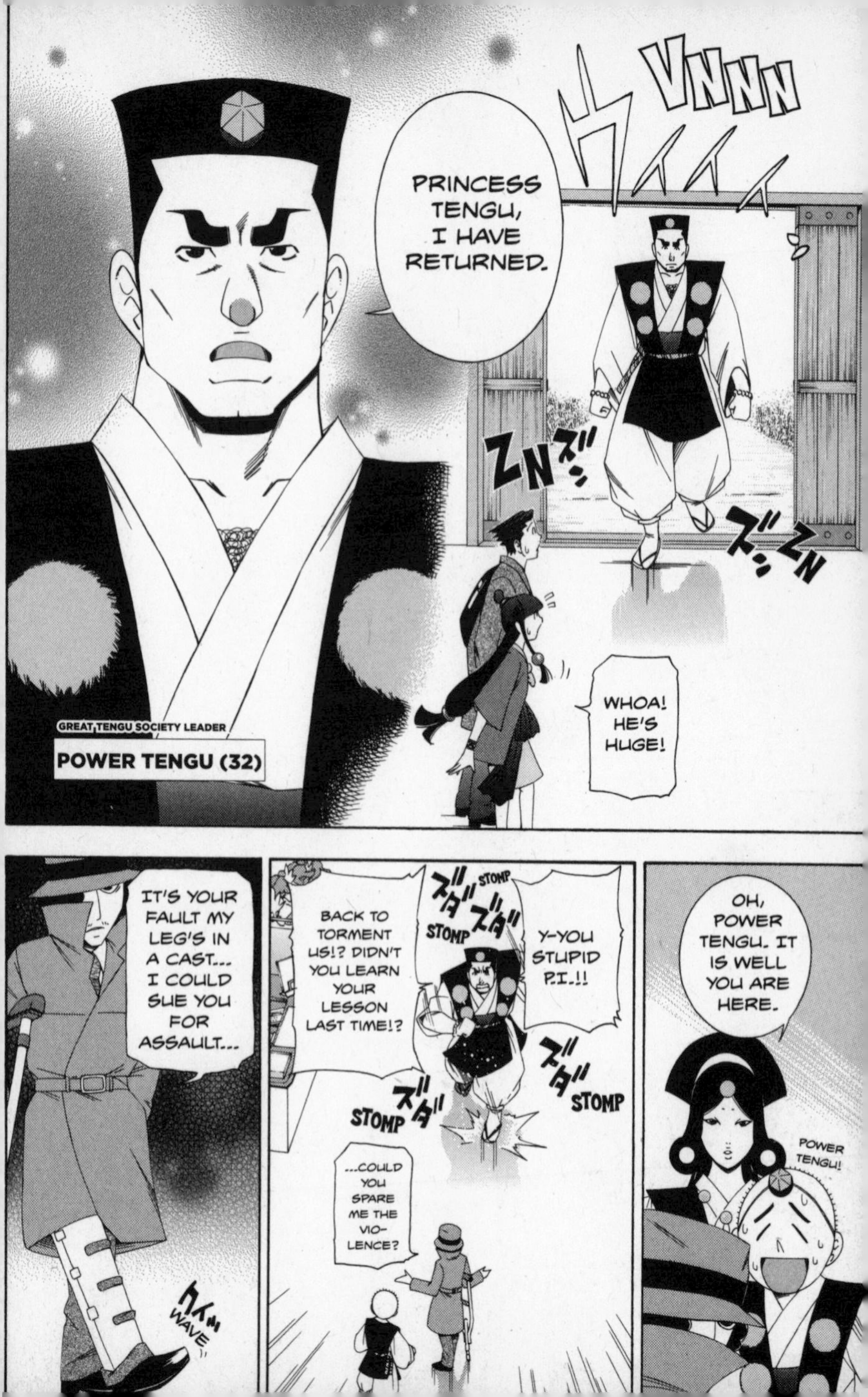
VNNN
PRINCESS TENGU, I HAVE RETURNED.
ZN
ZN
WHOA! HE'S HUGE!
GREAT TENGU SOCIETY LEADER
POWER TENGU (32)
OH, POWER TENGU. IT IS WELL YOU ARE HERE.
POWER TENGU!
Y-YOU STUPID P.I.!!
STOMP
BACK TO TORMENT US!? DIDN'T YOU LEARN YOUR LESSON LAST TIME!?
STOMP
STOMP
STOMP
...COULD YOU SPARE ME THE VIO-LENCE?
IT'S YOUR FAULT MY LEG'S IN A CAST... I COULD SUE YOU FOR ASSAULT...
WAVE

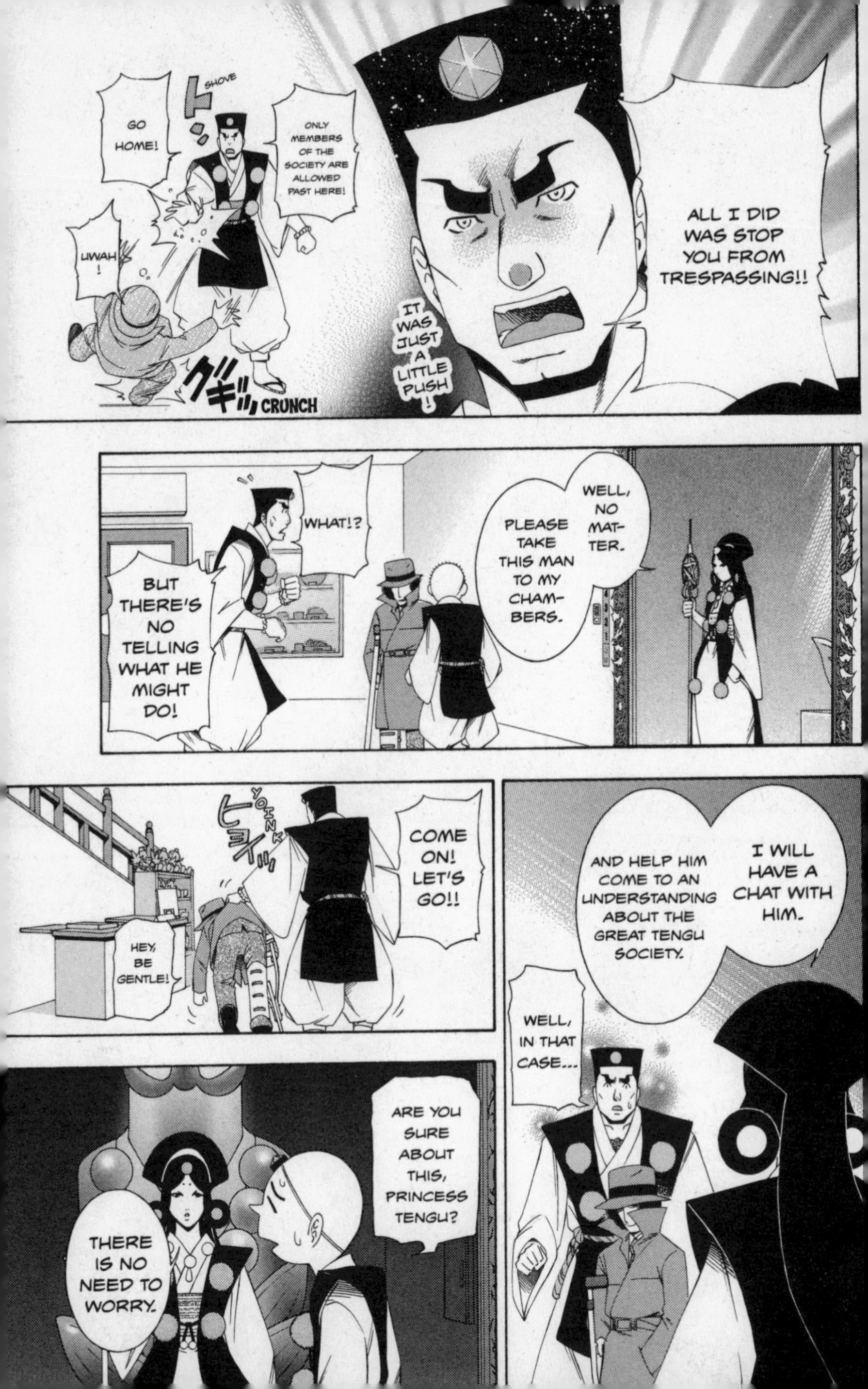
ALL I DID WAS STOP YOU FROM TRESPASSING!!
IT WAS JUST A LITTLE PUSH!
SHOVE
ONLY MEMBERS OF THE SOCIETY ARE ALLOWED PAST HERE!
GO HOME!
UWAH!
CRUNCH
WELL, NO MATTER.
PLEASE TAKE THIS MAN TO MY CHAMBERS.
WHAT!?
BUT THERE'S NO TELLING WHAT HE MIGHT DO!
I WILL HAVE A CHAT WITH HIM.
AND HELP HIM COME TO AN UNDERSTANDING ABOUT THE GREAT TENGU SOCIETY.
WELL, IN THAT CASE...
COME ON! LET'S GO!!
YOINK
HEY, BE GENTLE!
ARE YOU SURE ABOUT THIS, PRINCESS TENGU?
THERE IS NO NEED TO WORRY.

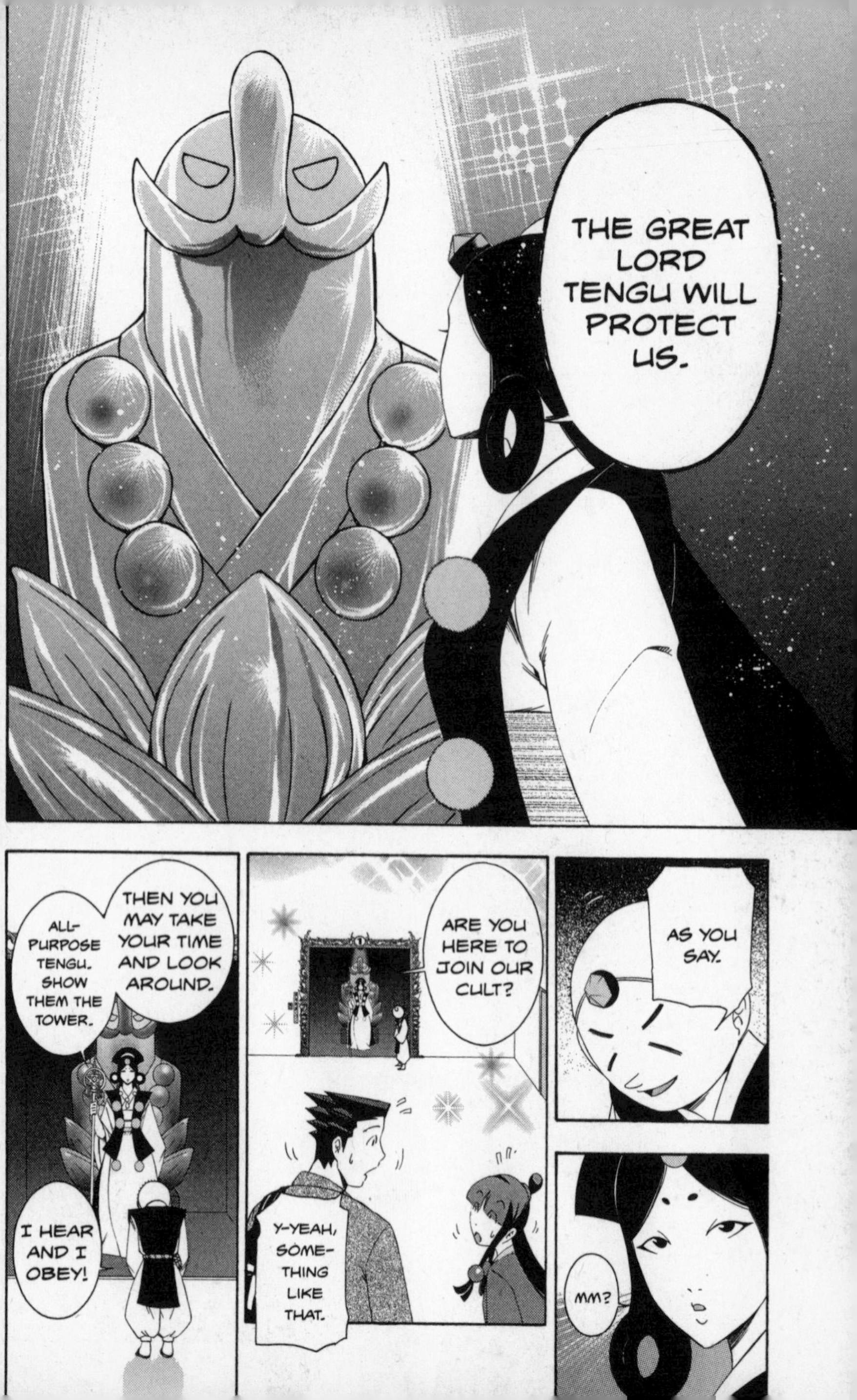
THE GREAT LORD TENGU WILL PROTECT US.
AS YOU SAY.
MM?
ARE YOU HERE TO JOIN OUR CULT?
Y-YEAH, SOME-THING LIKE THAT.
THEN YOU MAY TAKE YOUR TIME AND LOOK AROUND.
ALL-PURPOSE TENGU. SHOW THEM THE TOWER.
I HEAR AND I OBEY!

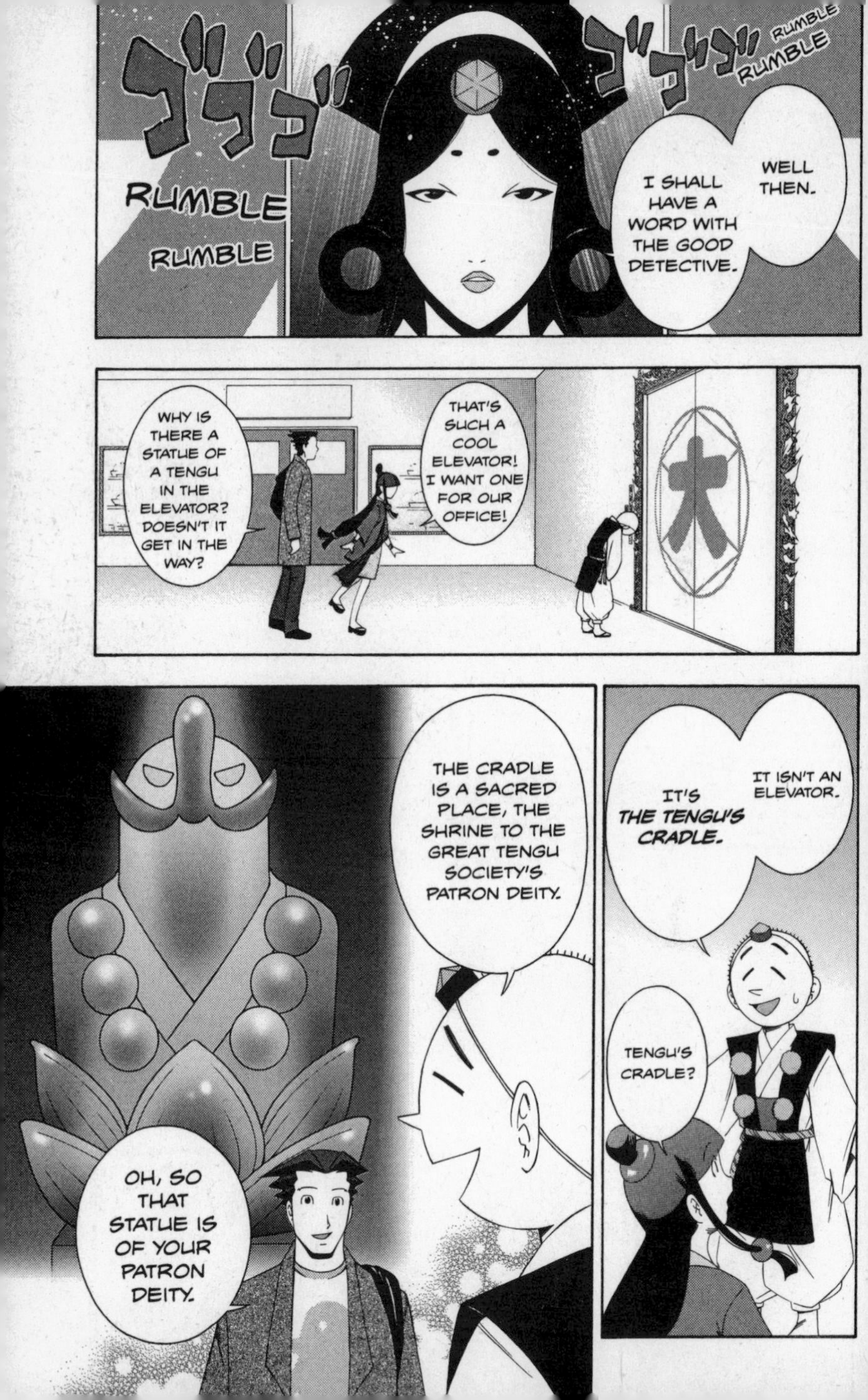

ゴゴゴ
RUMBLE RUMBLE
WELL THEN.
I SHALL HAVE A WORD WITH THE GOOD DETECTIVE.
ゴゴゴ
RUMBLE
RUMBLE
THAT'S SUCH A COOL ELEVATOR! I WANT ONE FOR OUR OFFICE!
WHY IS THERE A STATUE OF A TENGU IN THE ELEVATOR? DOESN'T IT GET IN THE WAY?
IT ISN'T AN ELEVATOR.
IT'S *THE TENGU'S CRADLE.*
TENGU'S CRADLE?
THE CRADLE IS A SACRED PLACE, THE SHRINE TO THE GREAT TENGU SOCIETY'S PATRON DEITY.
OH, SO THAT STATUE IS OF YOUR PATRON DEITY.

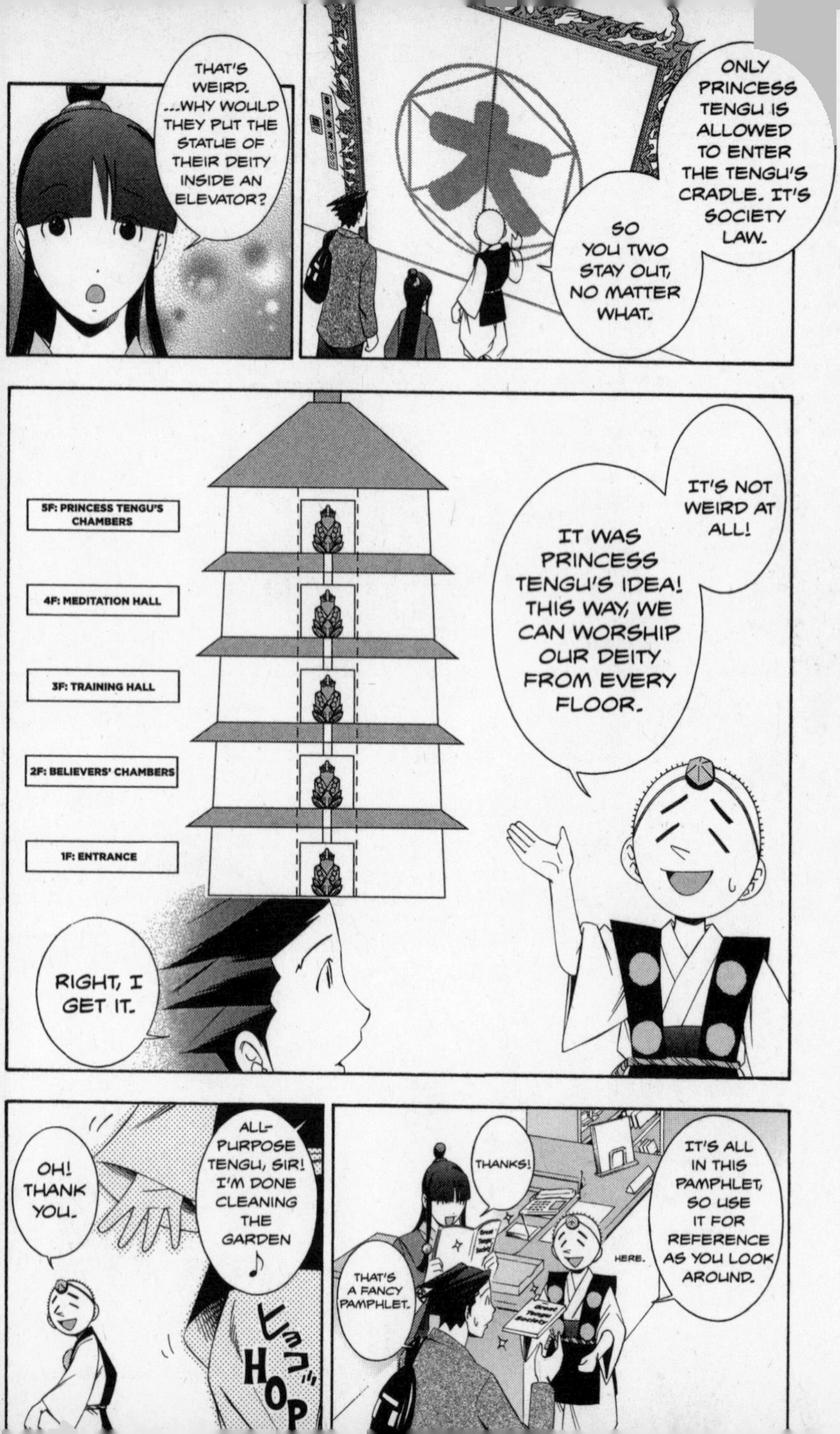
ONLY PRINCESS TENGU IS ALLOWED TO ENTER THE TENGU'S CRADLE. IT'S SOCIETY LAW.
SO YOU TWO STAY OUT, NO MATTER WHAT.
THAT'S WEIRD. ...WHY WOULD THEY PUT THE STATUE OF THEIR DEITY INSIDE AN ELEVATOR?
IT'S NOT WEIRD AT ALL!
IT WAS PRINCESS TENGU'S IDEA! THIS WAY, WE CAN WORSHIP OUR DEITY FROM EVERY FLOOR.
5F: PRINCESS TENGU'S CHAMBERS
4F: MEDITATION HALL
3F: TRAINING HALL
2F: BELIEVERS' CHAMBERS
1F: ENTRANCE
RIGHT, I GET IT.
IT'S ALL IN THIS PAMPHLET, SO USE IT FOR REFERENCE AS YOU LOOK AROUND.
HERE.
THANKS!
THAT'S A FANCY PAMPHLET.
ALL-PURPOSE TENGU, SIR! I'M DONE CLEANING THE GARDEN ♪
OH! THANK YOU.
HOP

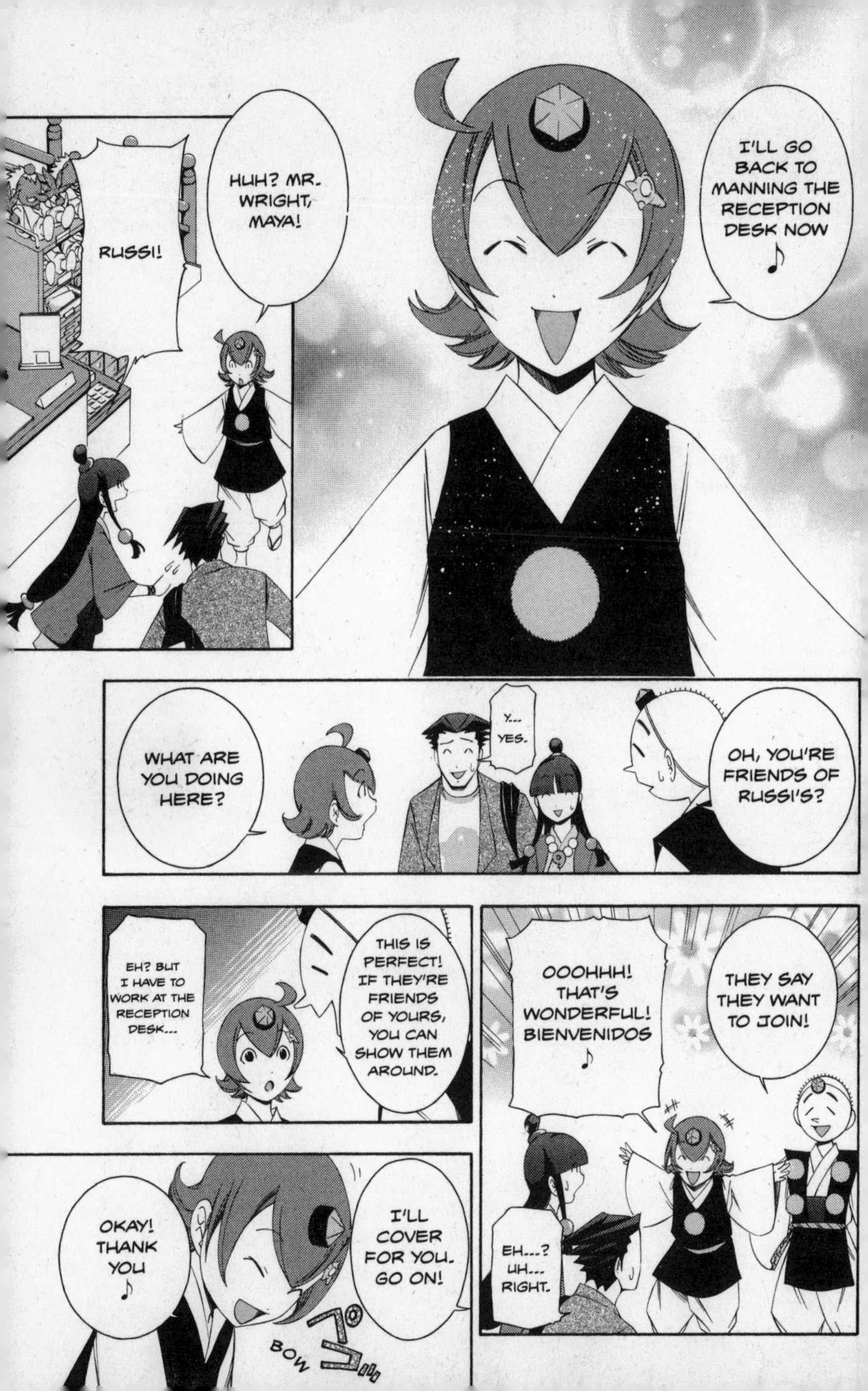

I'LL GO BACK TO MANNING THE RECEPTION DESK NOW ♪
HUH? MR. WRIGHT, MAYA!
RUSSI!
OH, YOU'RE FRIENDS OF RUSSI'S?
Y... YES.
WHAT ARE YOU DOING HERE?
THEY SAY THEY WANT TO JOIN!
OOOHHH! THAT'S WONDERFUL! BIENVENIDOS ♪
EH...? UH... RIGHT.
THIS IS PERFECT! IF THEY'RE FRIENDS OF YOURS, YOU CAN SHOW THEM AROUND.
EH? BUT I HAVE TO WORK AT THE RECEPTION DESK...
I'LL COVER FOR YOU. GO ON!
OKAY! THANK YOU ♪
BOW

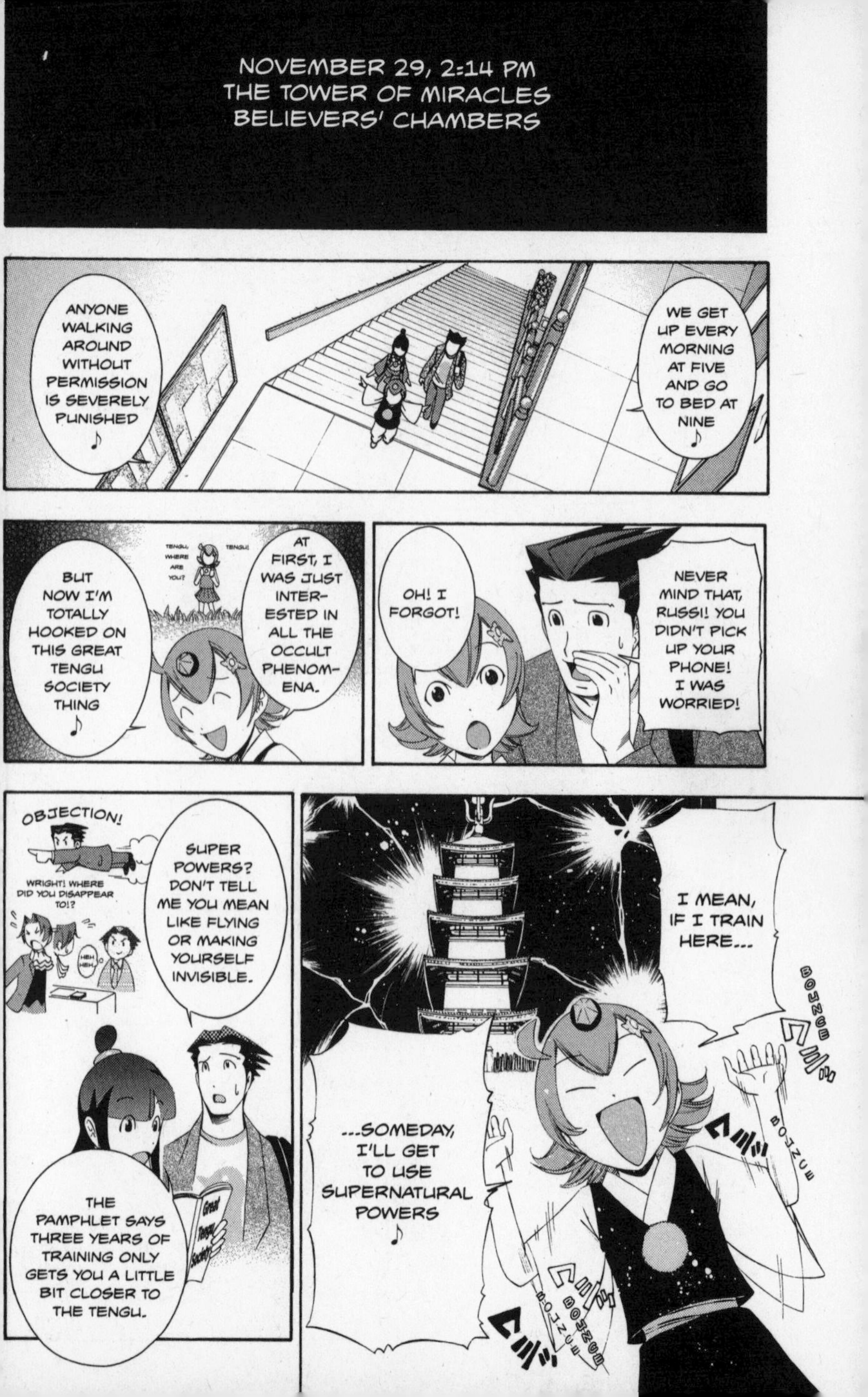
NOVEMBER 29, 2:14 PM
THE TOWER OF MIRACLES
BELIEVERS' CHAMBERS
WE GET UP EVERY MORNING AT FIVE AND GO TO BED AT NINE ♪
ANYONE WALKING AROUND WITHOUT PERMISSION IS SEVERELY PUNISHED ♪
NEVER MIND THAT, RUSSI! YOU DIDN'T PICK UP YOUR PHONE! I WAS WORRIED!
OH! I FORGOT!
AT FIRST, I WAS JUST INTERESTED IN ALL THE OCCULT PHENOMENA.
TENGU!
TENGU, WHERE ARE YOU?
BUT NOW I'M TOTALLY HOOKED ON THIS GREAT TENGU SOCIETY THING ♪
I MEAN, IF I TRAIN HERE...
BOUNCE
...SOMEDAY, I'LL GET TO USE SUPERNATURAL POWERS ♪
BOUNCE
SUPER POWERS? DON'T TELL ME YOU MEAN LIKE FLYING OR MAKING YOURSELF INVISIBLE.
OBJECTION!
WRIGHT! WHERE DID YOU DISAPPEAR TO!?
HEH HEH
Great Tengu Society
THE PAMPHLET SAYS THREE YEARS OF TRAINING ONLY GETS YOU A LITTLE BIT CLOSER TO THE TENGU.

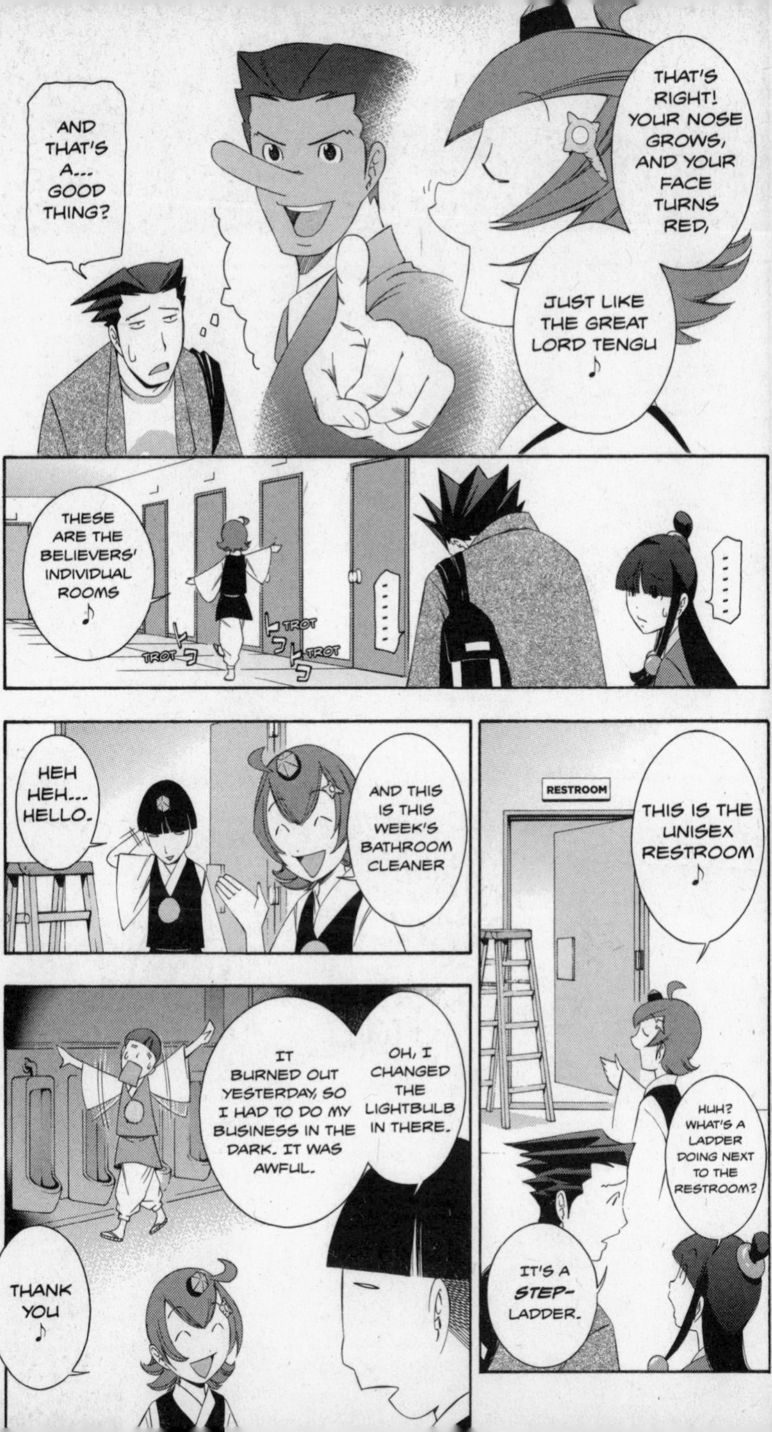
THAT'S RIGHT! YOUR NOSE GROWS, AND YOUR FACE TURNS RED,
JUST LIKE THE GREAT LORD TENGU ♪
AND THAT'S A... GOOD THING?
......
......
THESE ARE THE BELIEVERS' INDIVIDUAL ROOMS ♪
TROT
TROT
TROT
RESTROOM
THIS IS THE UNISEX RESTROOM ♪
HUH? WHAT'S A LADDER DOING NEXT TO THE RESTROOM?
IT'S A STEP-LADDER.
AND THIS IS THIS WEEK'S BATHROOM CLEANER
HEH HEH... HELLO.
OH, I CHANGED THE LIGHTBULB IN THERE.
IT BURNED OUT YESTERDAY, SO I HAD TO DO MY BUSINESS IN THE DARK. IT WAS AWFUL.
THANK YOU ♪

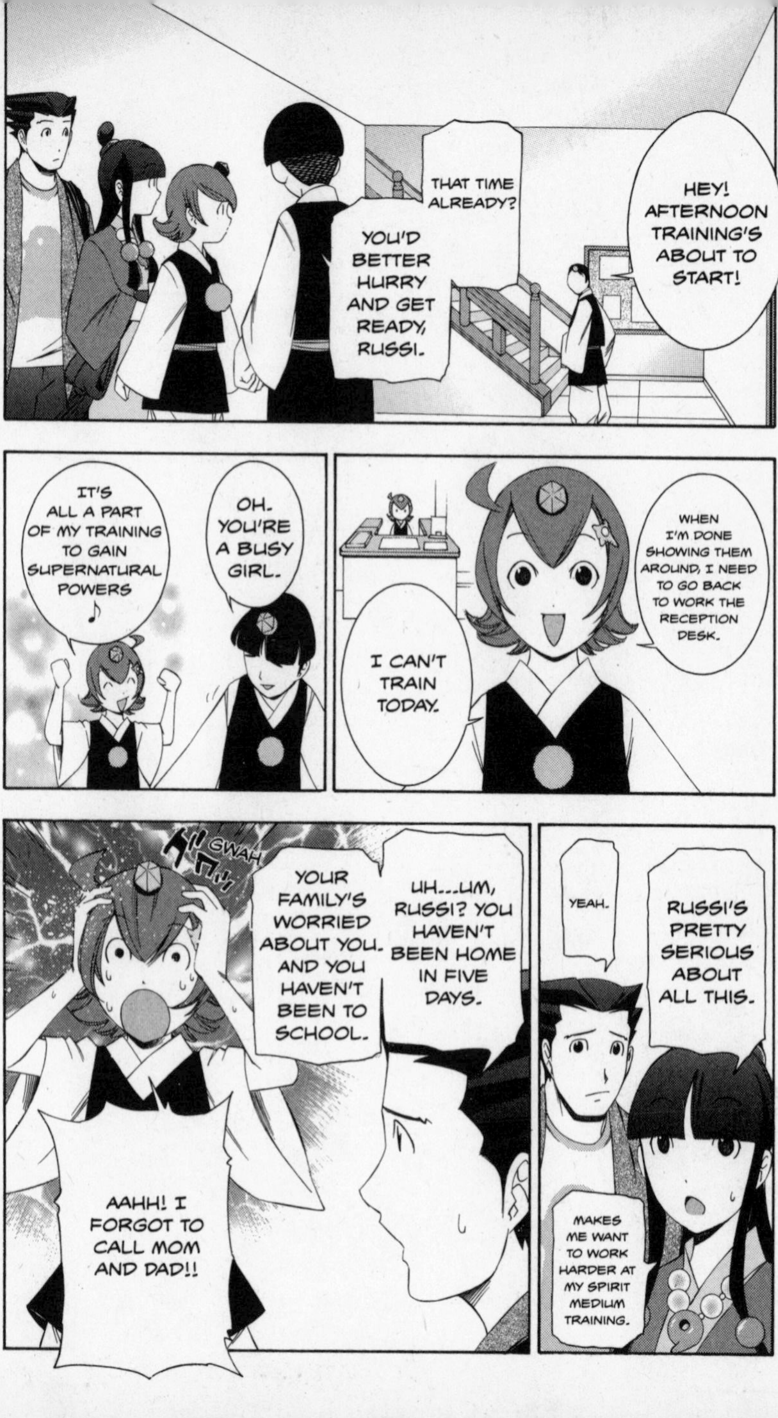
HEY! AFTERNOON TRAINING'S ABOUT TO START!
THAT TIME ALREADY?
YOU'D BETTER HURRY AND GET READY, RUSSI.
WHEN I'M DONE SHOWING THEM AROUND, I NEED TO GO BACK TO WORK THE RECEPTION DESK.
I CAN'T TRAIN TODAY.
OH. YOU'RE A BUSY GIRL.
IT'S ALL A PART OF MY TRAINING TO GAIN SUPERNATURAL POWERS ♪
RUSSI'S PRETTY SERIOUS ABOUT ALL THIS.
YEAH.
MAKES ME WANT TO WORK HARDER AT MY SPIRIT MEDIUM TRAINING.
UH...UM, RUSSI? YOU HAVEN'T BEEN HOME IN FIVE DAYS.
YOUR FAMILY'S WORRIED ABOUT YOU. AND YOU HAVEN'T BEEN TO SCHOOL.
GWAH
AAHH! I FORGOT TO CALL MOM AND DAD!!

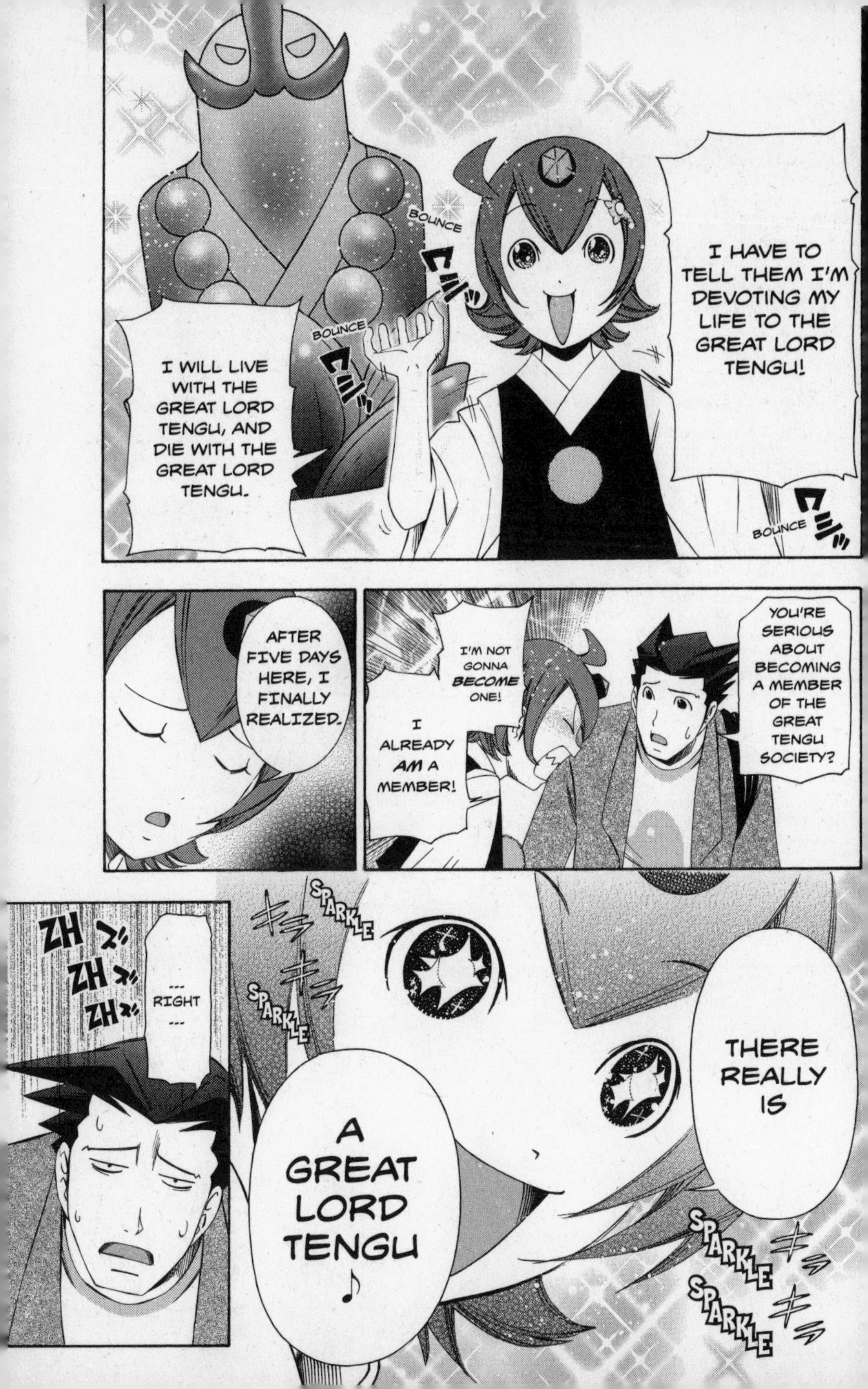
I HAVE TO TELL THEM I'M DEVOTING MY LIFE TO THE GREAT LORD TENGU!
BOUNCE
BOUNCE
BOUNCE
I WILL LIVE WITH THE GREAT LORD TENGU, AND DIE WITH THE GREAT LORD TENGU.
YOU'RE SERIOUS ABOUT BECOMING A MEMBER OF THE GREAT TENGU SOCIETY?
I'M NOT GONNA *BECOME* ONE!
I ALREADY *AM* A MEMBER!
AFTER FIVE DAYS HERE, I FINALLY REALIZED.
SPARKLE
SPARKLE
THERE REALLY IS
A GREAT LORD TENGU ♪
SPARKLE
SPARKLE
... RIGHT ...
ZH
ZH
ZH

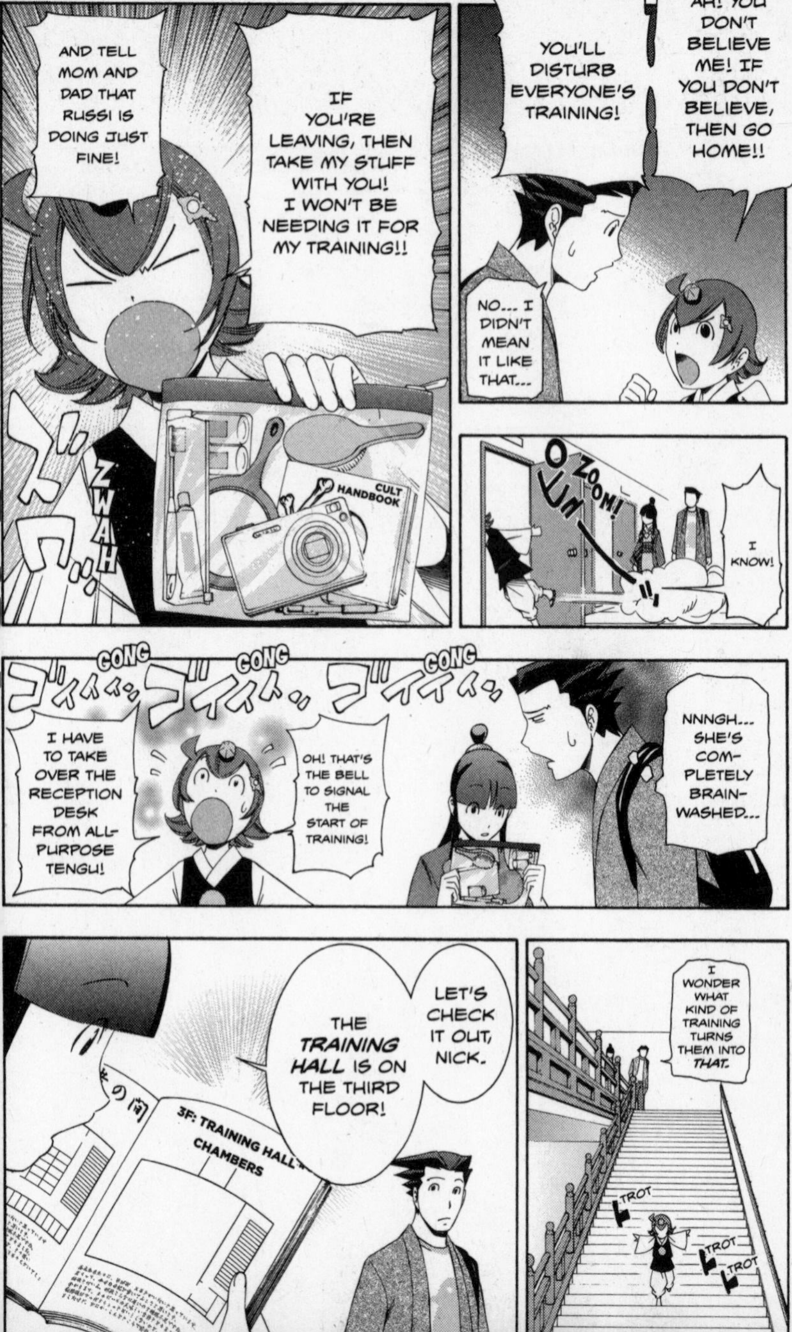
AH! YOU DON'T BELIEVE ME! IF YOU DON'T BELIEVE, THEN GO HOME!!
YOU'LL DISTURB EVERYONE'S TRAINING!
NO... I DIDN'T MEAN IT LIKE THAT...
ZOOM!
I KNOW!
IF YOU'RE LEAVING, THEN TAKE MY STUFF WITH YOU! I WON'T BE NEEDING IT FOR MY TRAINING!!
AND TELL MOM AND DAD THAT RUSSI IS DOING JUST FINE!
ZWAH
CULT HANDBOOK
GONG
GONG
GONG
NNNGH... SHE'S COM-PLETELY BRAIN-WASHED...
OH! THAT'S THE BELL TO SIGNAL THE START OF TRAINING!
I HAVE TO TAKE OVER THE RECEPTION DESK FROM ALL-PURPOSE TENGU!
I WONDER WHAT KIND OF TRAINING TURNS THEM INTO *THAT.*
TROT
TROT
TROT
LET'S CHECK IT OUT, NICK.
THE *TRAINING HALL* IS ON THE THIRD FLOOR!
3F: TRAINING HALL CHAMBERS

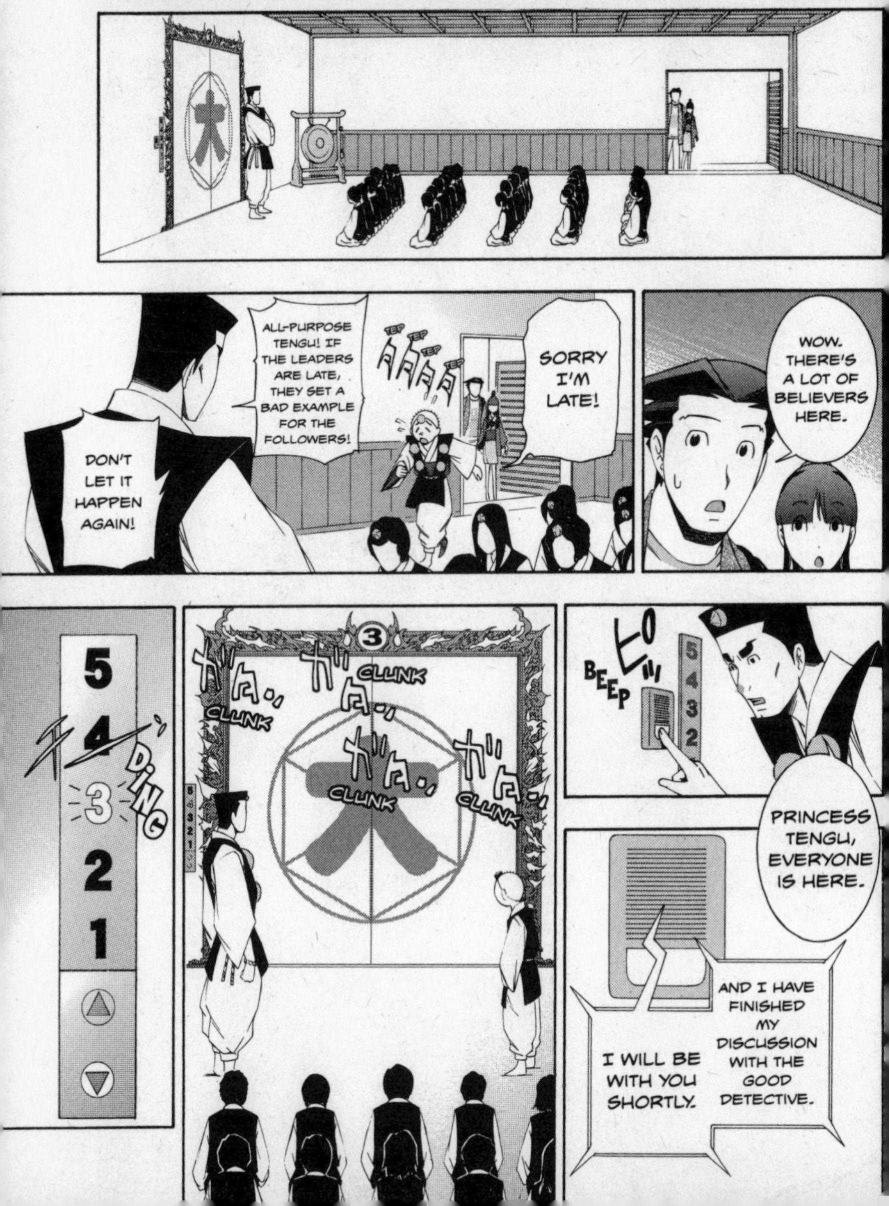
WOW. THERE'S A LOT OF BELIEVERS HERE.
SORRY I'M LATE!
TEP TEP TEP TEP
ALL-PURPOSE TENGU! IF THE LEADERS ARE LATE, THEY SET A BAD EXAMPLE FOR THE FOLLOWERS!
DON'T LET IT HAPPEN AGAIN!
BEEP
PRINCESS TENGU, EVERYONE IS HERE.
AND I HAVE FINISHED MY DISCUSSION WITH THE GOOD DETECTIVE.
I WILL BE WITH YOU SHORTLY.
CLUNK
CLUNK
CLUNK
CLUNK
5
4
3
2
1
DING

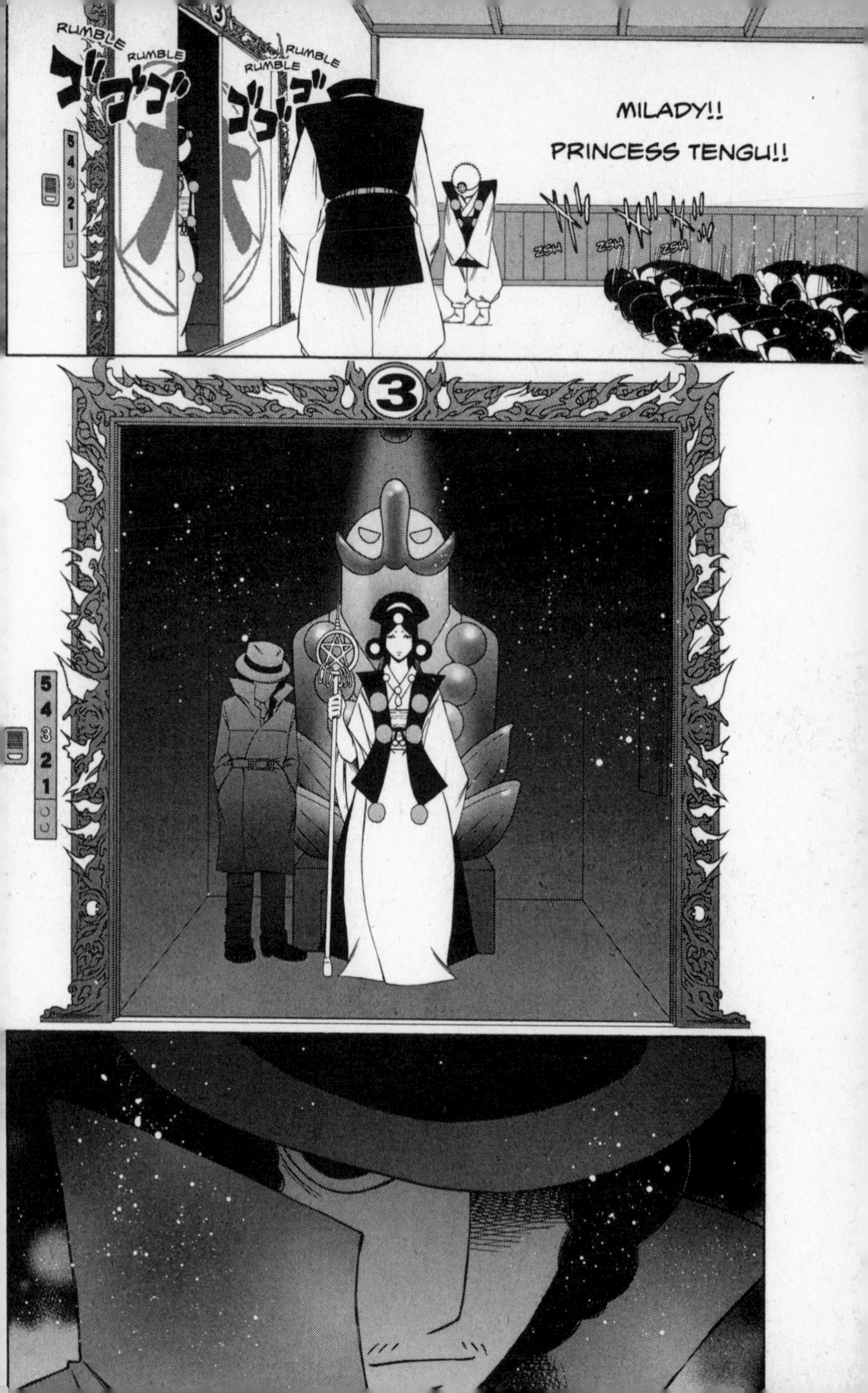

MILADY!!
PRINCESS TENGU!!
ZSH
ZSH
ZSH
RUMBLE RUMBLE
ゴゴゴ
RUMBLE RUMBLE
ゴゴゴ

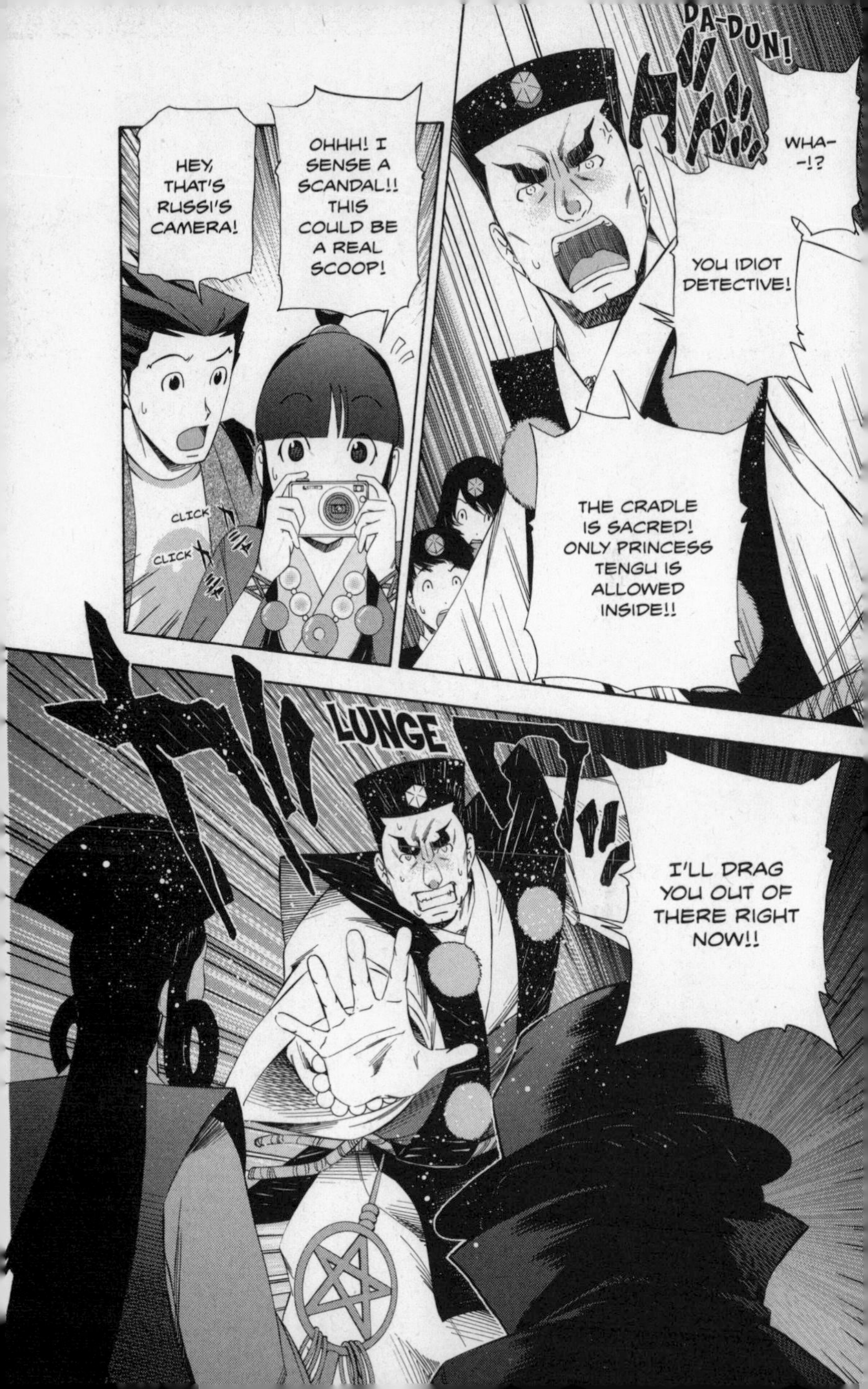
DA-DUN!
WHA- -!?
YOU IDIOT DETECTIVE!
THE CRADLE IS SACRED! ONLY PRINCESS TENGU IS ALLOWED INSIDE!!
OHHH! I SENSE A SCANDAL!! THIS COULD BE A REAL SCOOP!
HEY, THAT'S RUSSI'S CAMERA!
CLICK
CLICK
LUNGE
I'LL DRAG YOU OUT OF THERE RIGHT NOW!!

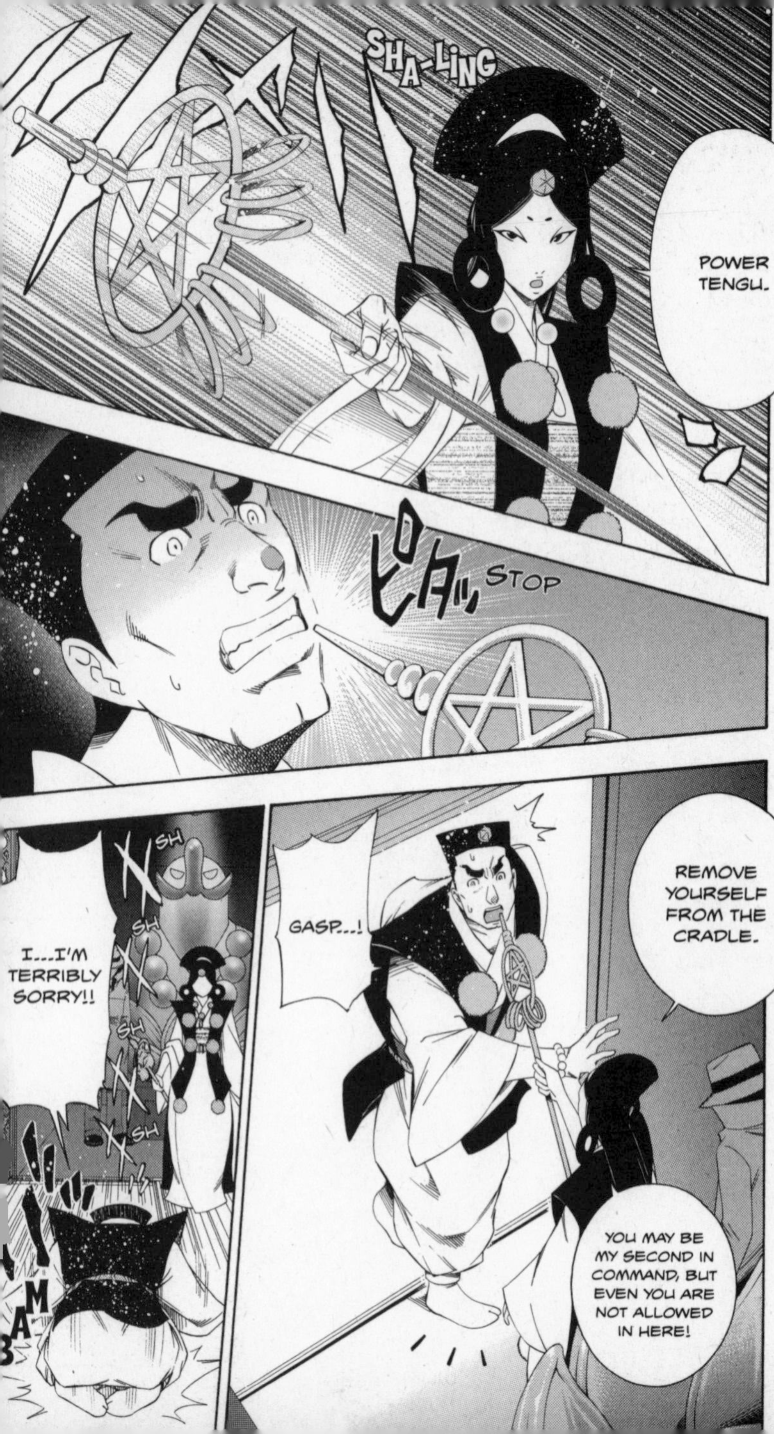
SHA-LING
POWER TENGU.
STOP
REMOVE YOURSELF FROM THE CRADLE.
GASP...!
YOU MAY BE MY SECOND IN COMMAND, BUT EVEN YOU ARE NOT ALLOWED IN HERE!
SH
SH
SH
SH
I...I'M TERRIBLY SORRY!!
BAM

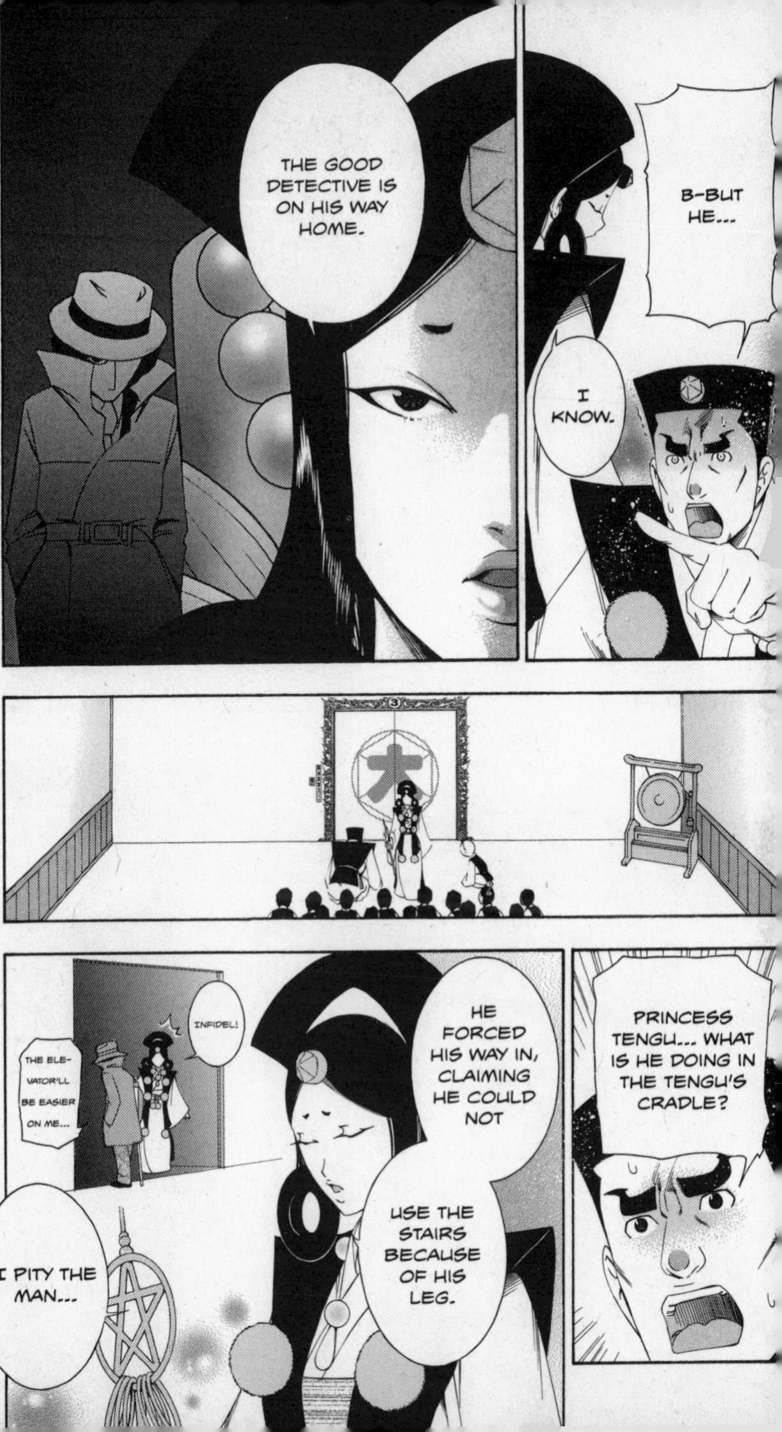
B-BUT HE...
I KNOW.
THE GOOD DETECTIVE IS ON HIS WAY HOME.
PRINCESS TENGU... WHAT IS HE DOING IN THE TENGU'S CRADLE?
HE FORCED HIS WAY IN, CLAIMING HE COULD NOT
USE THE STAIRS BECAUSE OF HIS LEG.
INFIDEL!
THE ELE-VATOR'LL BE EASIER ON ME...
I PITY THE MAN...

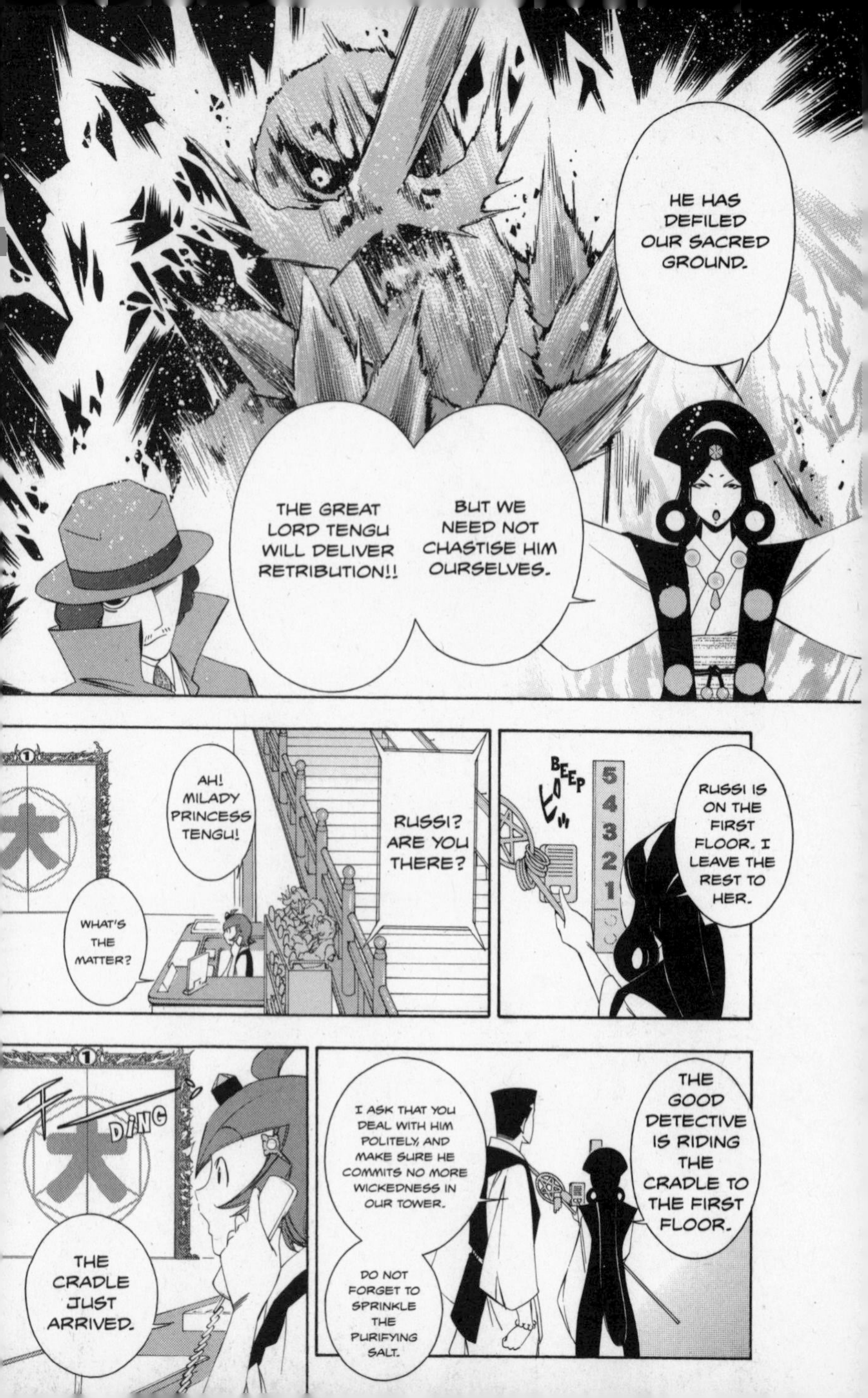
HE HAS DEFILED OUR SACRED GROUND.
BUT WE NEED NOT CHASTISE HIM OURSELVES.
THE GREAT LORD TENGU WILL DELIVER RETRIBUTION!!
BEEP
RUSSI IS ON THE FIRST FLOOR. I LEAVE THE REST TO HER.
RUSSI? ARE YOU THERE?
AH! MILADY PRINCESS TENGU!
WHAT'S THE MATTER?
THE GOOD DETECTIVE IS RIDING THE CRADLE TO THE FIRST FLOOR.
I ASK THAT YOU DEAL WITH HIM POLITELY, AND MAKE SURE HE COMMITS NO MORE WICKEDNESS IN OUR TOWER.
DO NOT FORGET TO SPRINKLE THE PURIFYING SALT.
DING
THE CRADLE JUST ARRIVED.

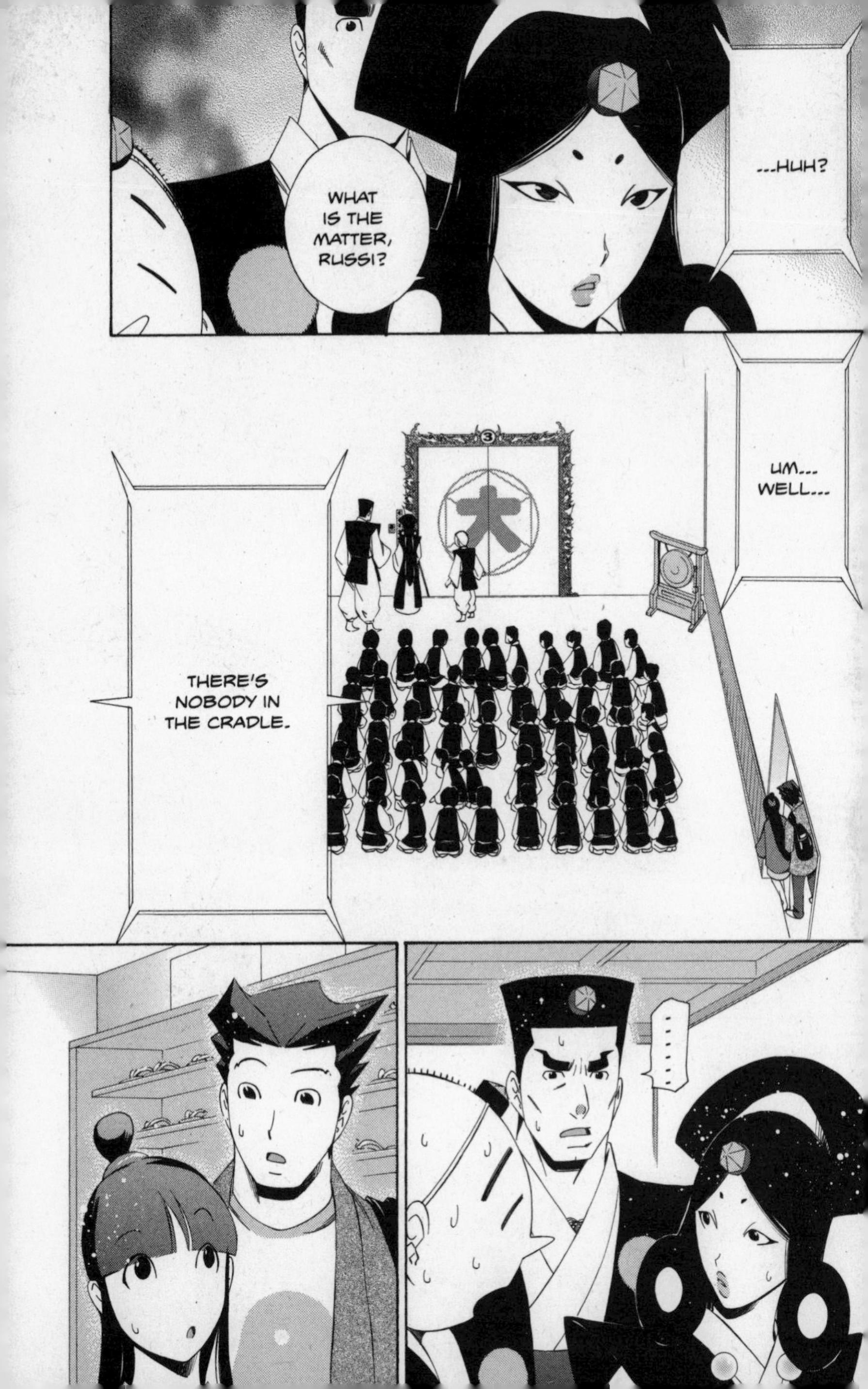
...HUH?
WHAT IS THE MATTER, RUSSI?
UM... WELL...
THERE'S NOBODY IN THE CRADLE.
......

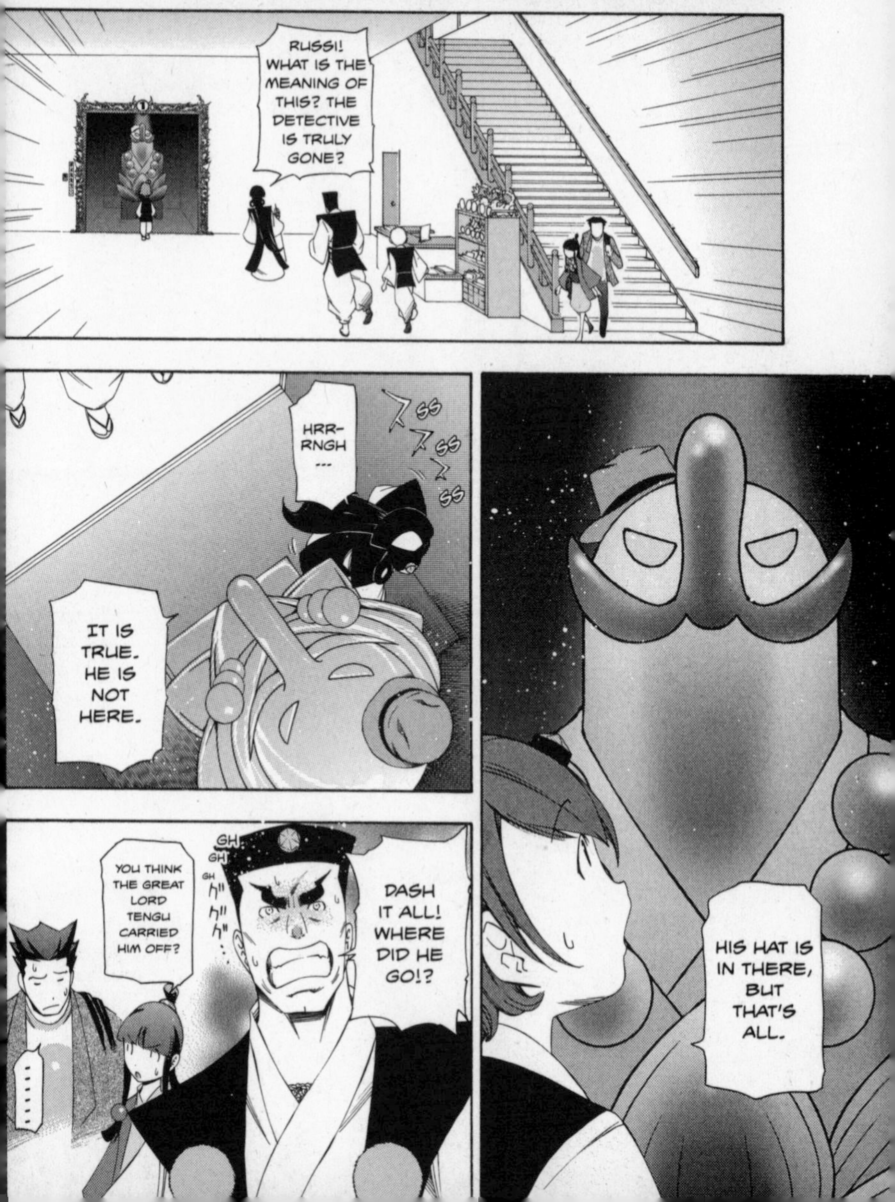
RUSSI! WHAT IS THE MEANING OF THIS? THE DETECTIVE IS TRULY GONE?
HIS HAT IS IN THERE, BUT THAT'S ALL.
HRR-RNGH ---
IT IS TRUE. HE IS NOT HERE.
DASH IT ALL! WHERE DID HE GO!?
GH GH GH
YOU THINK THE GREAT LORD TENGU CARRIED HIM OFF?
......

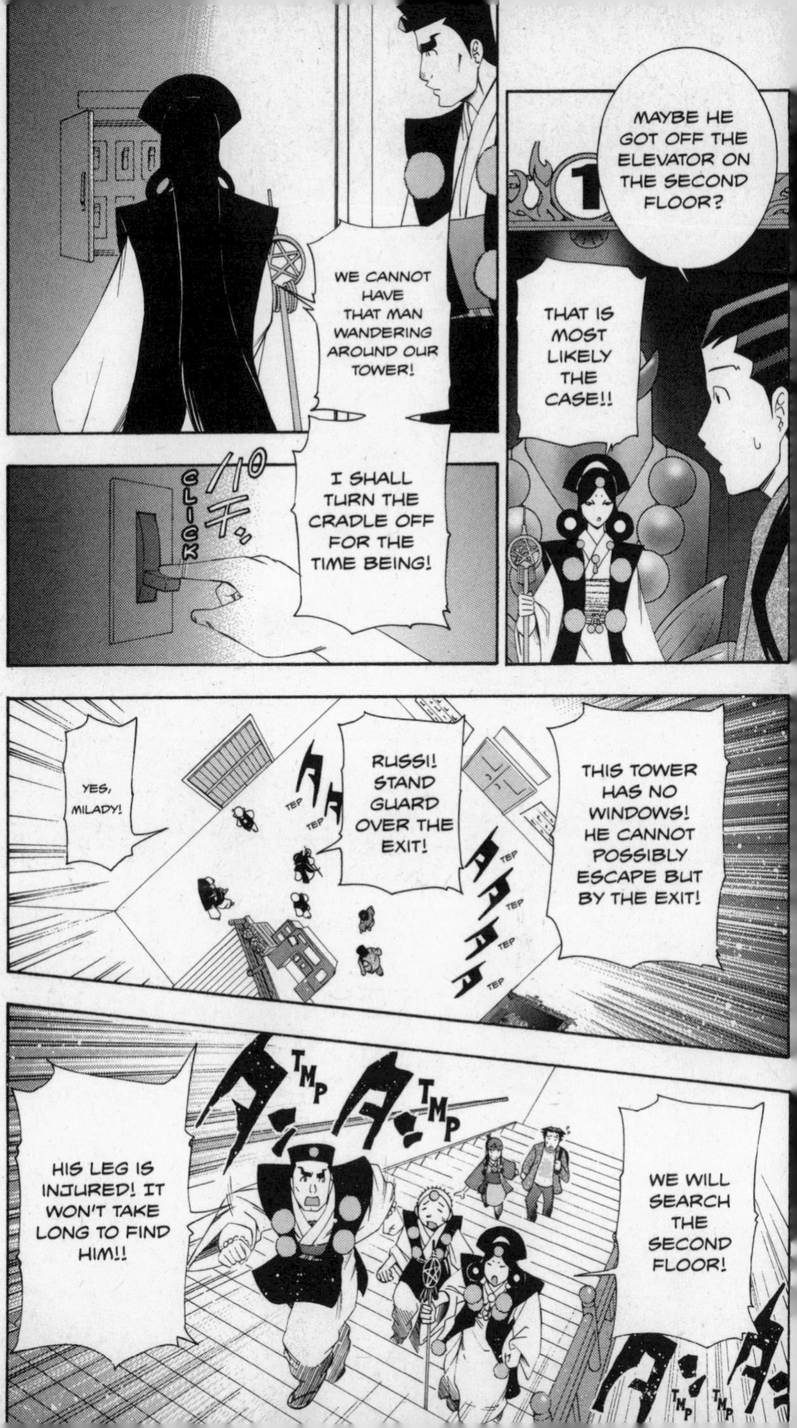
MAYBE HE GOT OFF THE ELEVATOR ON THE SECOND FLOOR?
THAT IS MOST LIKELY THE CASE!!
WE CANNOT HAVE THAT MAN WANDERING AROUND OUR TOWER!
CLICK
I SHALL TURN THE CRADLE OFF FOR THE TIME BEING!
THIS TOWER HAS NO WINDOWS! HE CANNOT POSSIBLY ESCAPE BUT BY THE EXIT!
TEP TEP TEP TEP
RUSSI! STAND GUARD OVER THE EXIT!
TEP TEP
YES, MILADY!
TMP TMP
WE WILL SEARCH THE SECOND FLOOR!
TMP TMP
HIS LEG IS INJURED! IT WON'T TAKE LONG TO FIND HIM!!

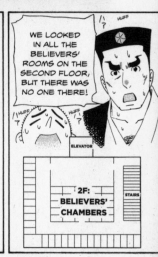

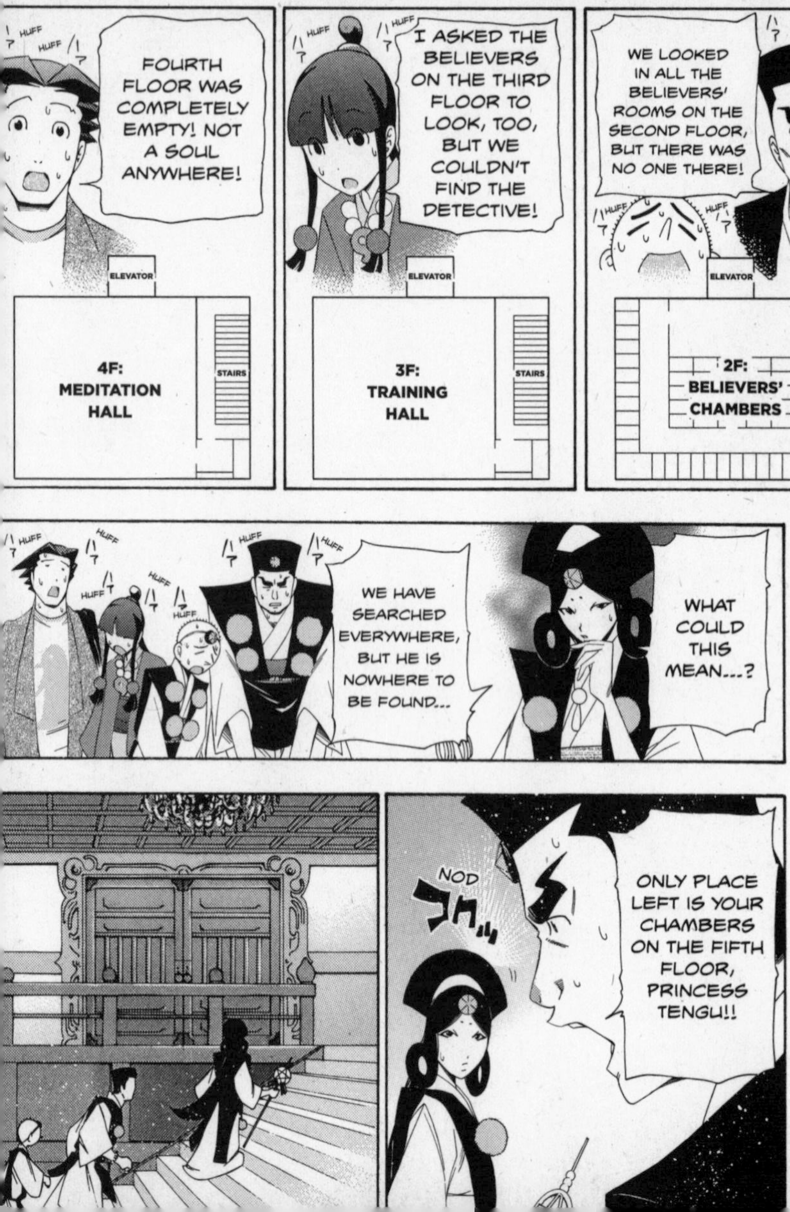
HUFF
WE LOOKED IN ALL THE BELIEVERS' ROOMS ON THE SECOND FLOOR, BUT THERE WAS NO ONE THERE!
HUFF
HUFF
ELEVATOR
2F: BELIEVERS' CHAMBERS
STAIRS
HUFF
HUFF
I ASKED THE BELIEVERS ON THE THIRD FLOOR TO LOOK, TOO, BUT WE COULDN'T FIND THE DETECTIVE!
ELEVATOR
3F: TRAINING HALL
STAIRS
HUFF
HUFF
FOURTH FLOOR WAS COMPLETELY EMPTY! NOT A SOUL ANYWHERE!
ELEVATOR
4F: MEDITATION HALL
STAIRS
WHAT COULD THIS MEAN...?
WE HAVE SEARCHED EVERYWHERE, BUT HE IS NOWHERE TO BE FOUND...
HUFF
HUFF
HUFF
HUFF
HUFF
HUFF
HUFF
ONLY PLACE LEFT IS YOUR CHAMBERS ON THE FIFTH FLOOR, PRINCESS TENGU!!
NOD

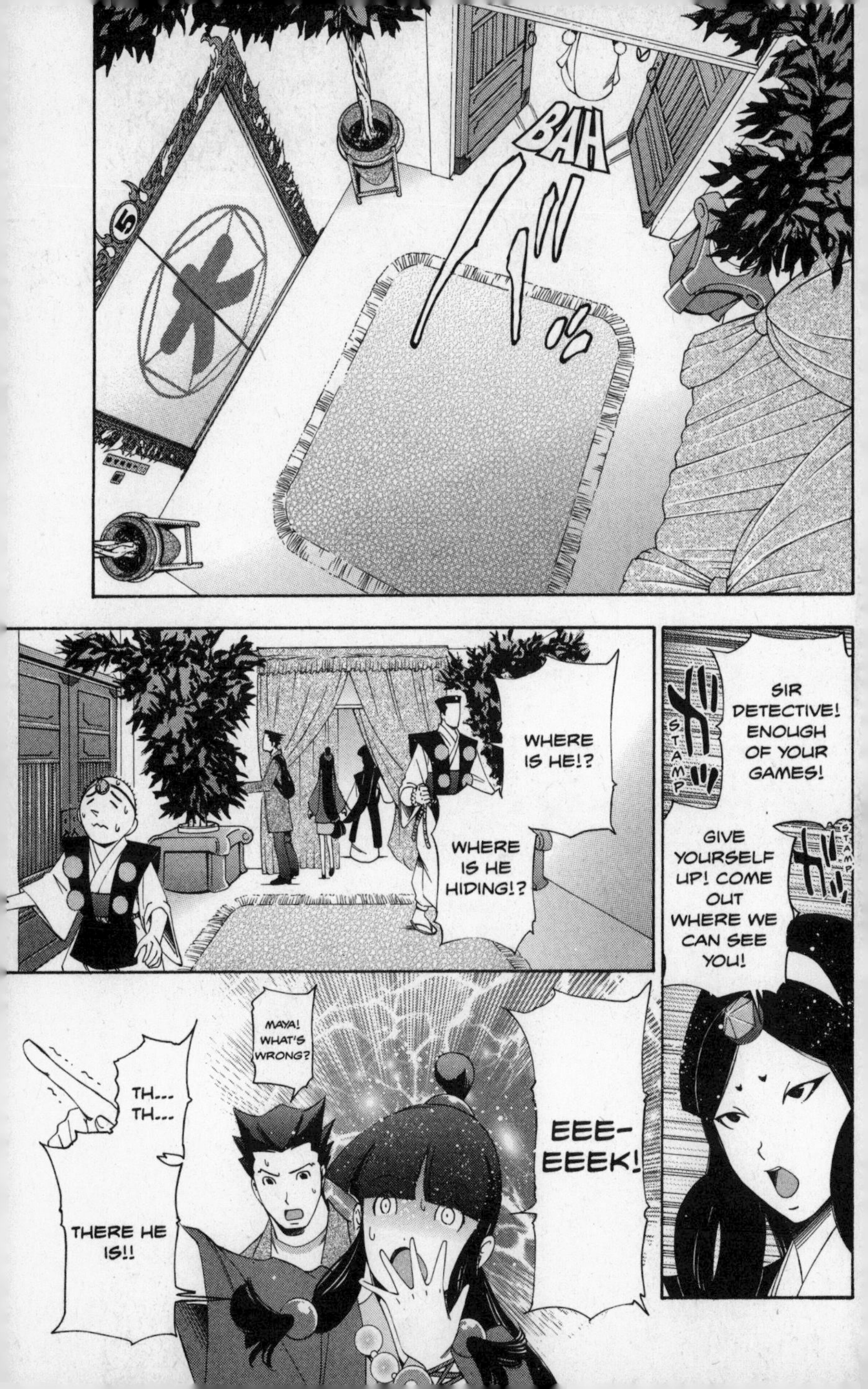
BAH
STAMP
SIR DETECTIVE! ENOUGH OF YOUR GAMES!
STAMP
GIVE YOURSELF UP! COME OUT WHERE WE CAN SEE YOU!
WHERE IS HE!?
WHERE IS HE HIDING!?
EEE-EEEK!
MAYA! WHAT'S WRONG?
TH... TH...
THERE HE IS!!

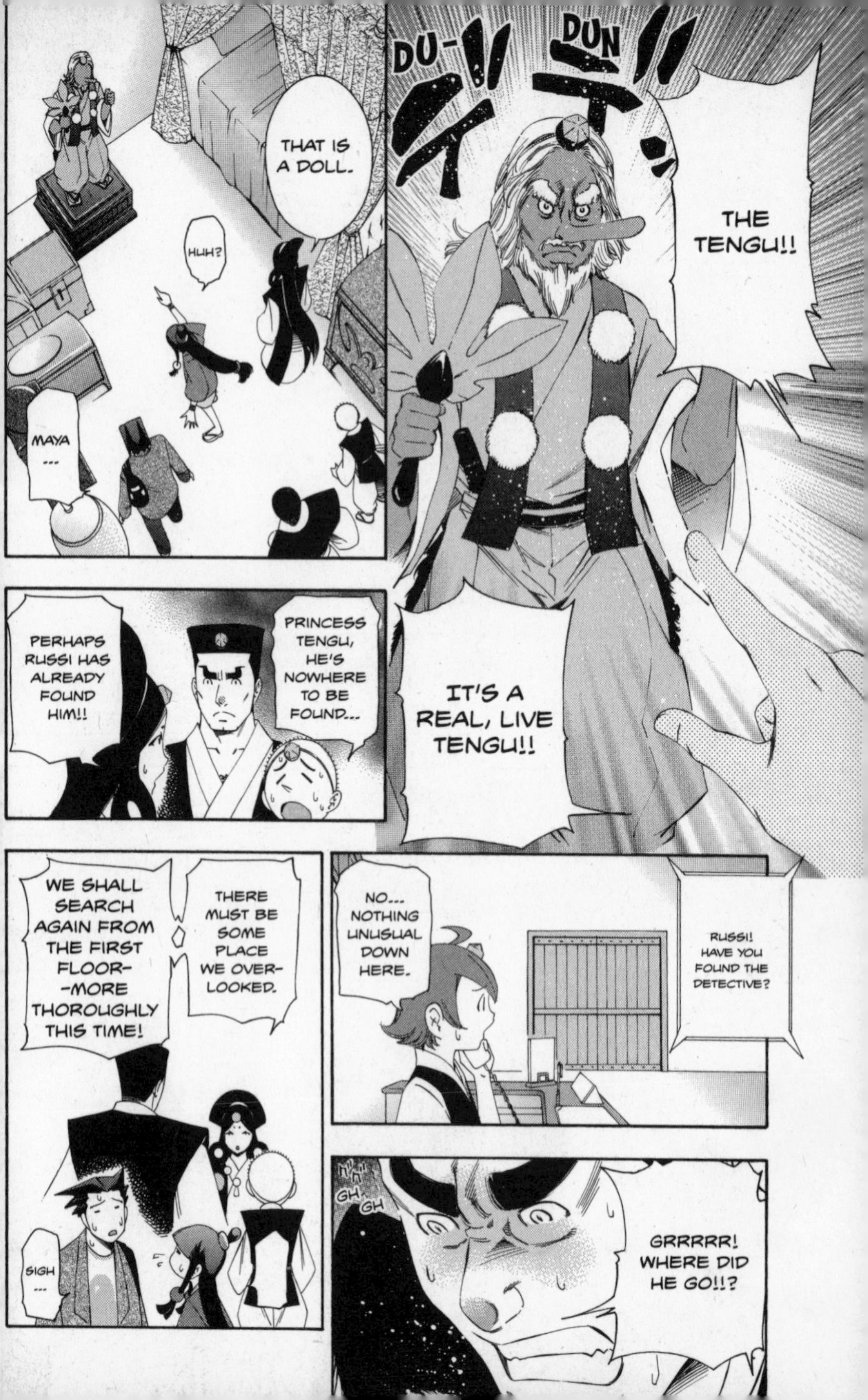
DU-DUN
THE TENGU!!
IT'S A REAL, LIVE TENGU!!
THAT IS A DOLL.
HUH?
MAYA...
PRINCESS TENGU, HE'S NOWHERE TO BE FOUND...
PERHAPS RUSSI HAS ALREADY FOUND HIM!!
RUSSI! HAVE YOU FOUND THE DETECTIVE?
NO... NOTHING UNUSUAL DOWN HERE.
GH GH
GRRRRR! WHERE DID HE GO!!?
THERE MUST BE SOME PLACE WE OVER-LOOKED.
WE SHALL SEARCH AGAIN FROM THE FIRST FLOOR--MORE THOROUGHLY THIS TIME!
SIGH...

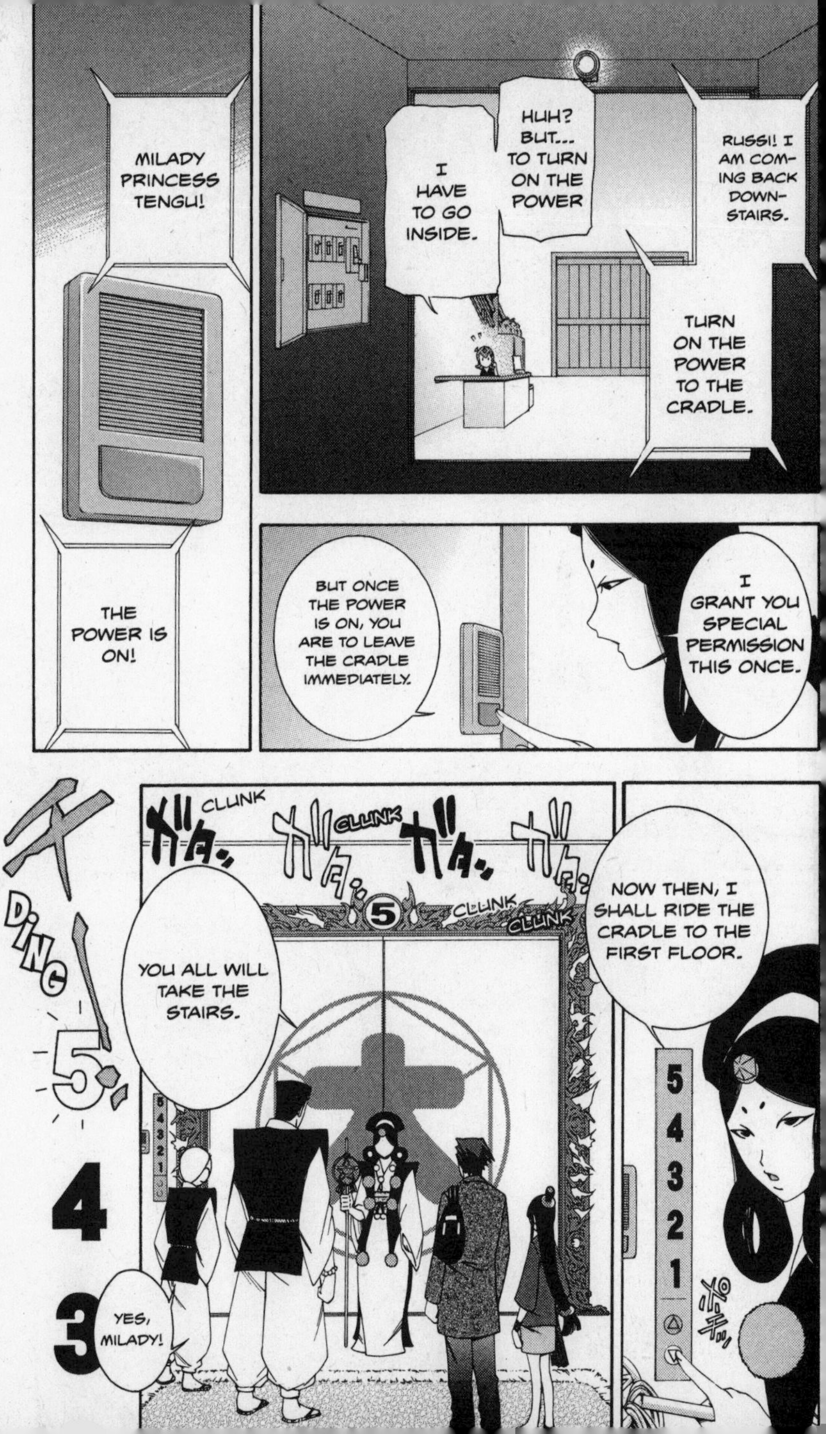
RUSSI! I AM COMING BACK DOWNSTAIRS.
TURN ON THE POWER TO THE CRADLE.
HUH? BUT... TO TURN ON THE POWER
I HAVE TO GO INSIDE.
I GRANT YOU SPECIAL PERMISSION THIS ONCE.
BUT ONCE THE POWER IS ON, YOU ARE TO LEAVE THE CRADLE IMMEDIATELY.
MILADY PRINCESS TENGU!
THE POWER IS ON!
NOW THEN, I SHALL RIDE THE CRADLE TO THE FIRST FLOOR.
CLUNK
CLUNK
CLUNK
CLUNK
YOU ALL WILL TAKE THE STAIRS.
DING
5
4
3
YES, MILADY!

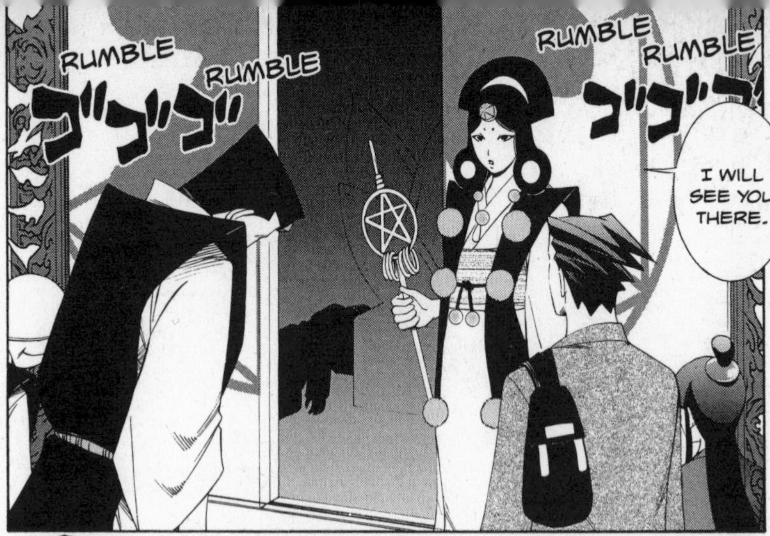
RUMBLE
RUMBLE
ゴゴゴ
I WILL SEE YOU THERE.
RUMBLE
RUMBLE
ゴゴゴ

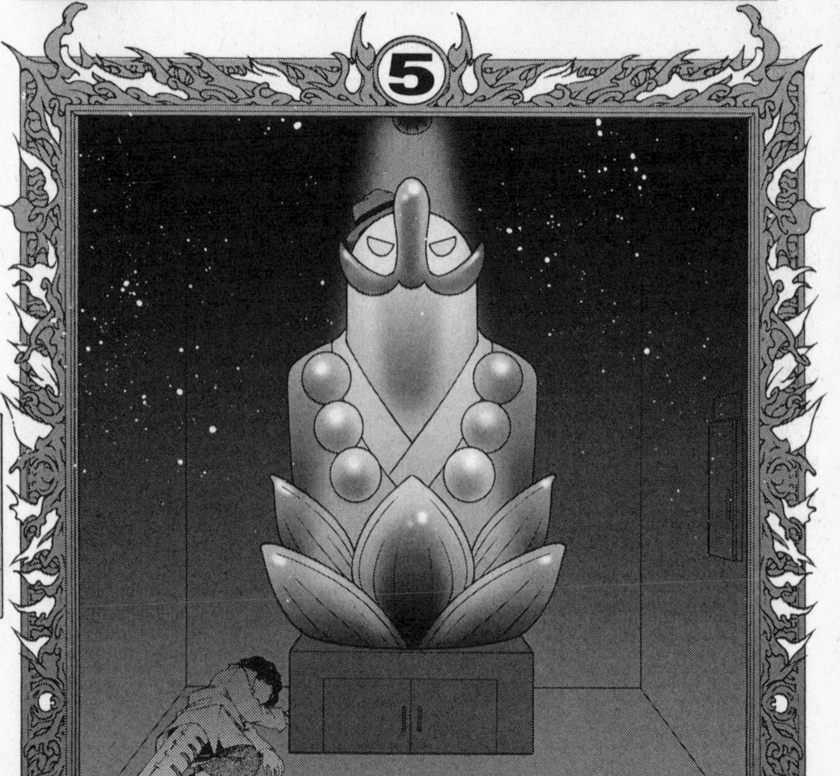
5

5
4
3
2
1

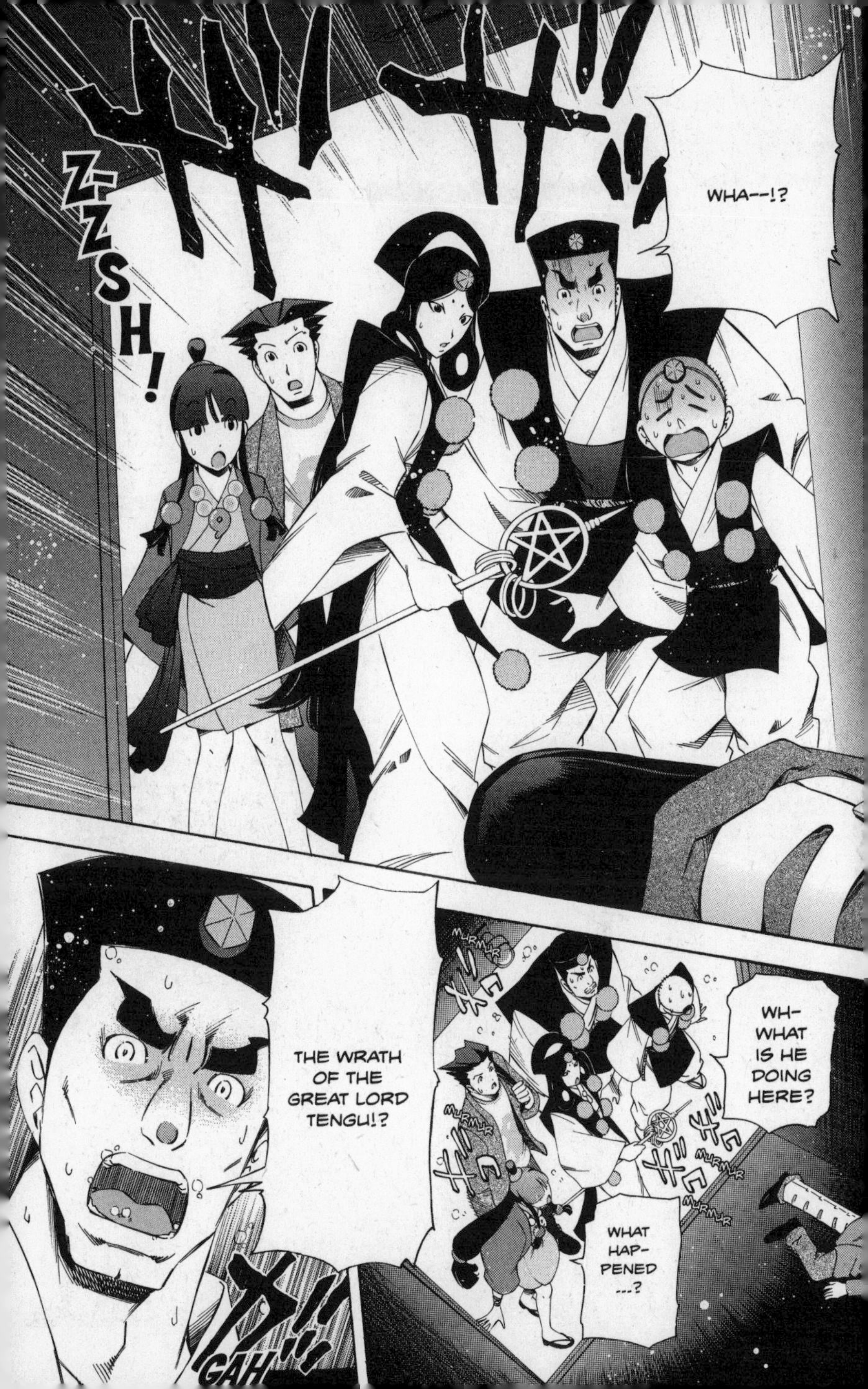
WHA--!?
Z-ZSH!
WH-WHAT IS HE DOING HERE?
MURMUR
MURMUR
MURMUR
MURMUR
WHAT HAP-PENED ...?
THE WRATH OF THE GREAT LORD TENGU!?
GAH

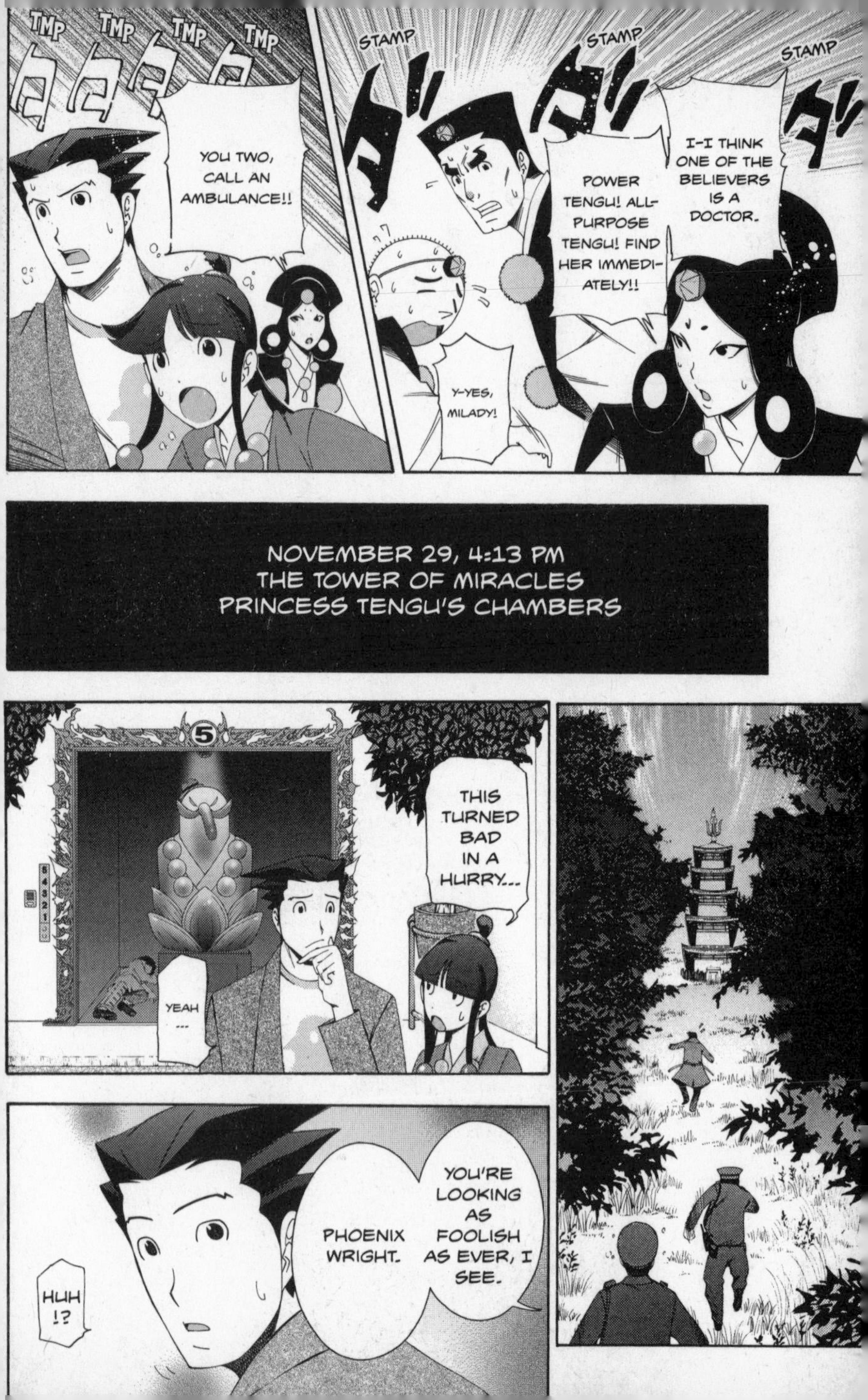
STAMP
STAMP
STAMP
I-I THINK ONE OF THE BELIEVERS IS A DOCTOR.
POWER TENGU! ALL-PURPOSE TENGU! FIND HER IMMEDIATELY!!
Y-YES, MILADY!
TMP
TMP
TMP
TMP
YOU TWO, CALL AN AMBULANCE!!
NOVEMBER 29, 4:13 PM
THE TOWER OF MIRACLES
PRINCESS TENGU'S CHAMBERS
THIS TURNED BAD IN A HURRY...
YEAH ...
YOU'RE LOOKING AS FOOLISH AS EVER, I SEE.
PHOENIX WRIGHT.
HUH !?

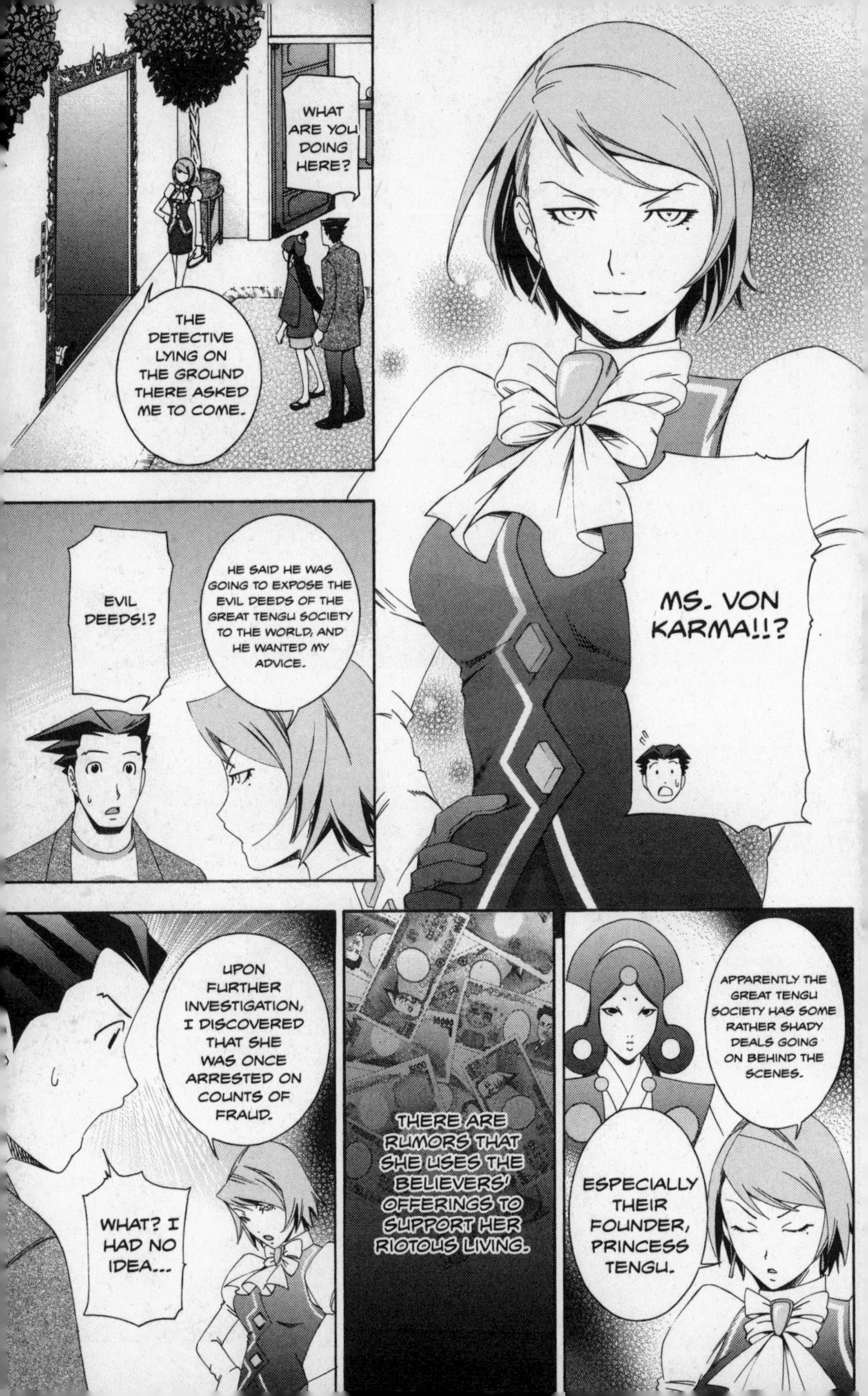
MS. VON KARMA!!?
WHAT ARE YOU DOING HERE?
THE DETECTIVE LYING ON THE GROUND THERE ASKED ME TO COME.
HE SAID HE WAS GOING TO EXPOSE THE EVIL DEEDS OF THE GREAT TENGU SOCIETY TO THE WORLD, AND HE WANTED MY ADVICE.
EVIL DEEDS!?
APPARENTLY THE GREAT TENGU SOCIETY HAS SOME RATHER SHADY DEALS GOING ON BEHIND THE SCENES.
ESPECIALLY THEIR FOUNDER, PRINCESS TENGU.
THERE ARE RUMORS THAT SHE USES THE BELIEVERS' OFFERINGS TO SUPPORT HER RIOTOUS LIVING.
UPON FURTHER INVESTIGATION, I DISCOVERED THAT SHE WAS ONCE ARRESTED ON COUNTS OF FRAUD.
WHAT? I HAD NO IDEA...

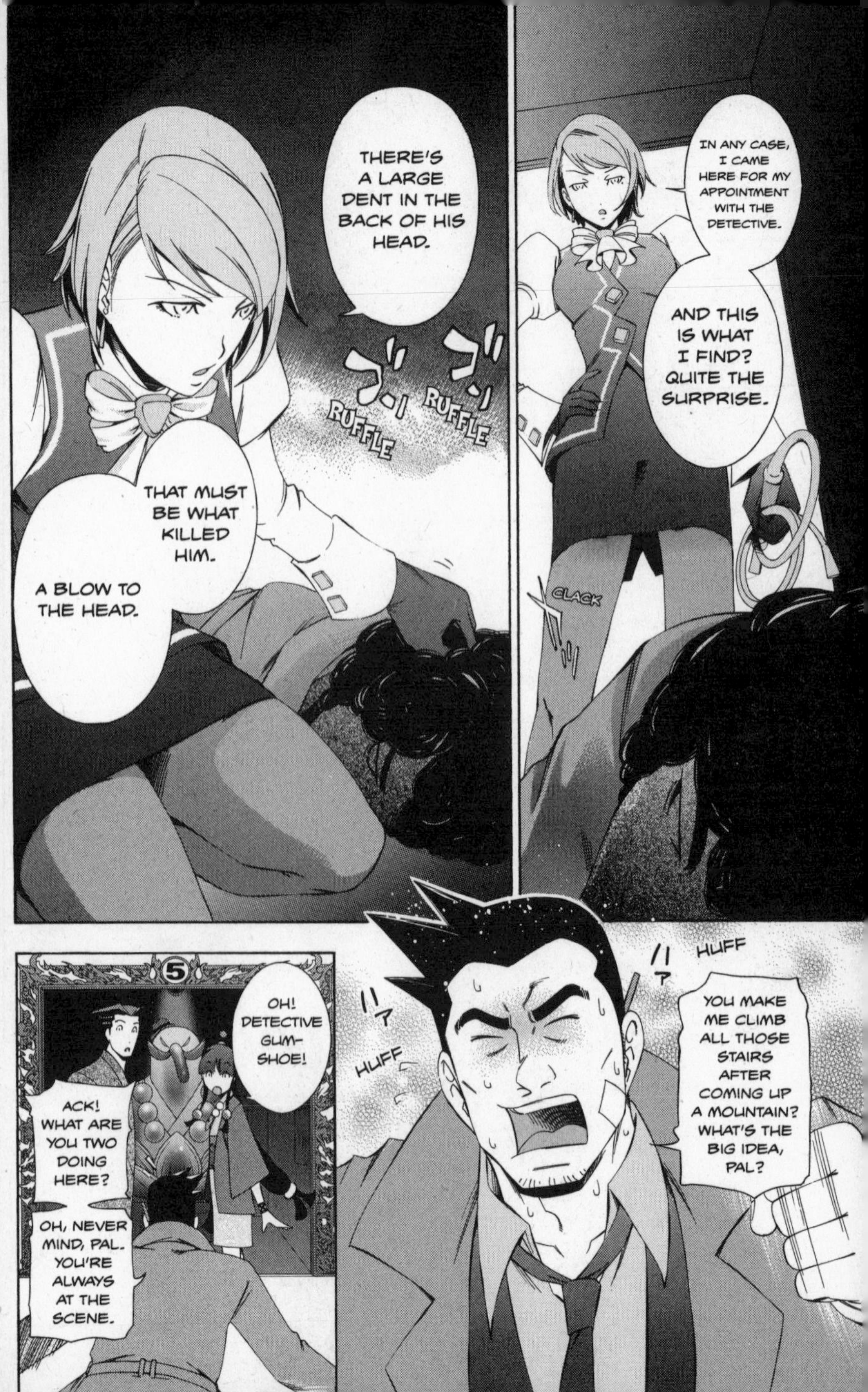
IN ANY CASE, I CAME HERE FOR MY APPOINTMENT WITH THE DETECTIVE.
AND THIS IS WHAT I FIND? QUITE THE SURPRISE.
CLACK
THERE'S A LARGE DENT IN THE BACK OF HIS HEAD.
RUFFLE
RUFFLE
THAT MUST BE WHAT KILLED HIM.
A BLOW TO THE HEAD.
HUFF
HUFF
YOU MAKE ME CLIMB ALL THOSE STAIRS AFTER COMING UP A MOUNTAIN? WHAT'S THE BIG IDEA, PAL?
5
OH! DETECTIVE GUM-SHOE!
ACK! WHAT ARE YOU TWO DOING HERE?
OH, NEVER MIND, PAL. YOU'RE ALWAYS AT THE SCENE.

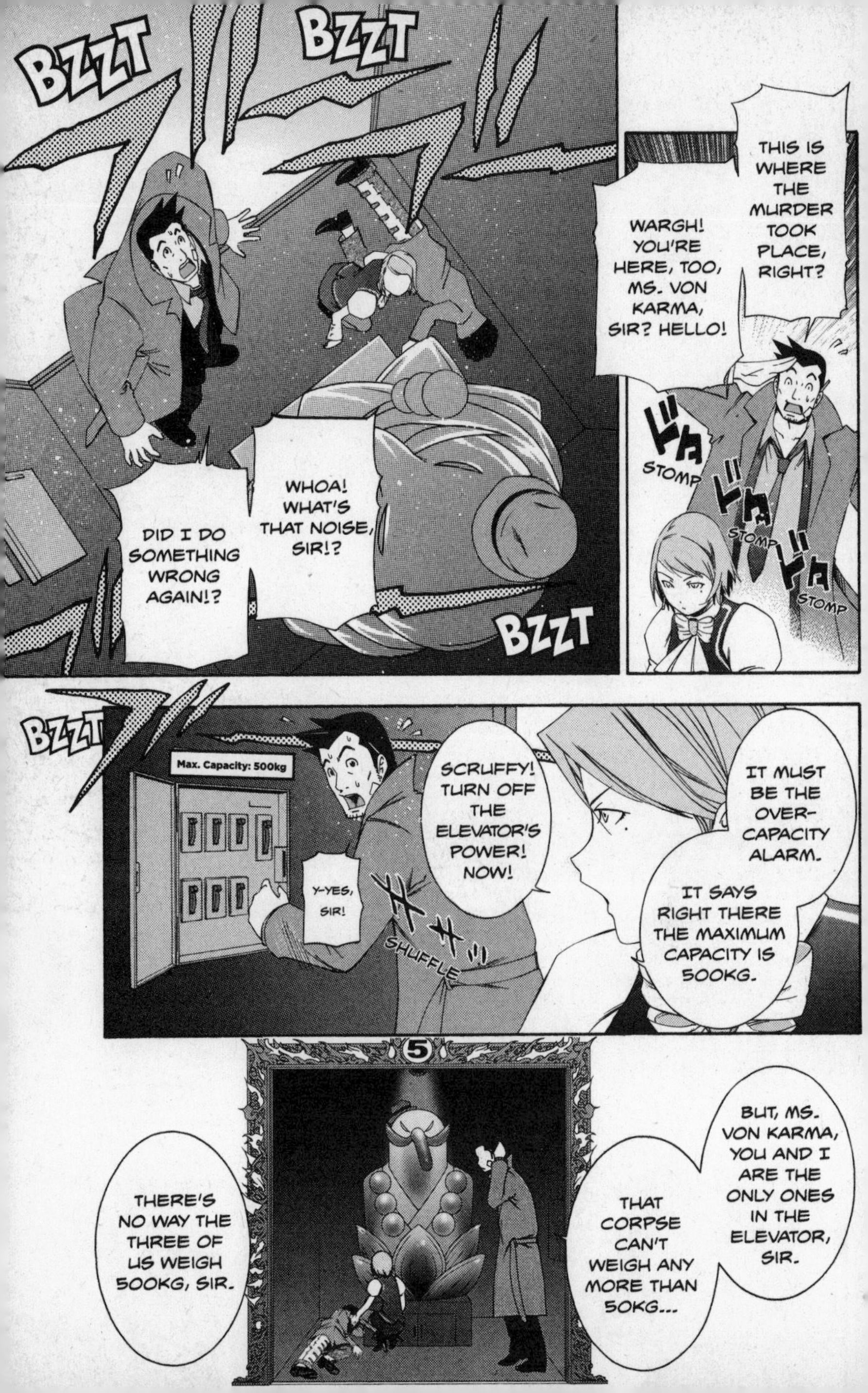
THIS IS WHERE THE MURDER TOOK PLACE, RIGHT?
WARGH! YOU'RE HERE, TOO, MS. VON KARMA, SIR? HELLO!
ドカ STOMP
ドカ STOMP
ドカ STOMP
BZZT
BZZT
WHOA! WHAT'S THAT NOISE, SIR!?
DID I DO SOMETHING WRONG AGAIN!?
BZZT
IT MUST BE THE OVER-CAPACITY ALARM.
IT SAYS RIGHT THERE THE MAXIMUM CAPACITY IS 500KG.
SCRUFFY! TURN OFF THE ELEVATOR'S POWER! NOW!
Y-YES, SIR!
SHUFFLE
Max. Capacity: 500kg
BZZT
5
BUT, MS. VON KARMA, YOU AND I ARE THE ONLY ONES IN THE ELEVATOR, SIR.
THAT CORPSE CAN'T WEIGH ANY MORE THAN 50KG...
THERE'S NO WAY THE THREE OF US WEIGH 500KG, SIR.

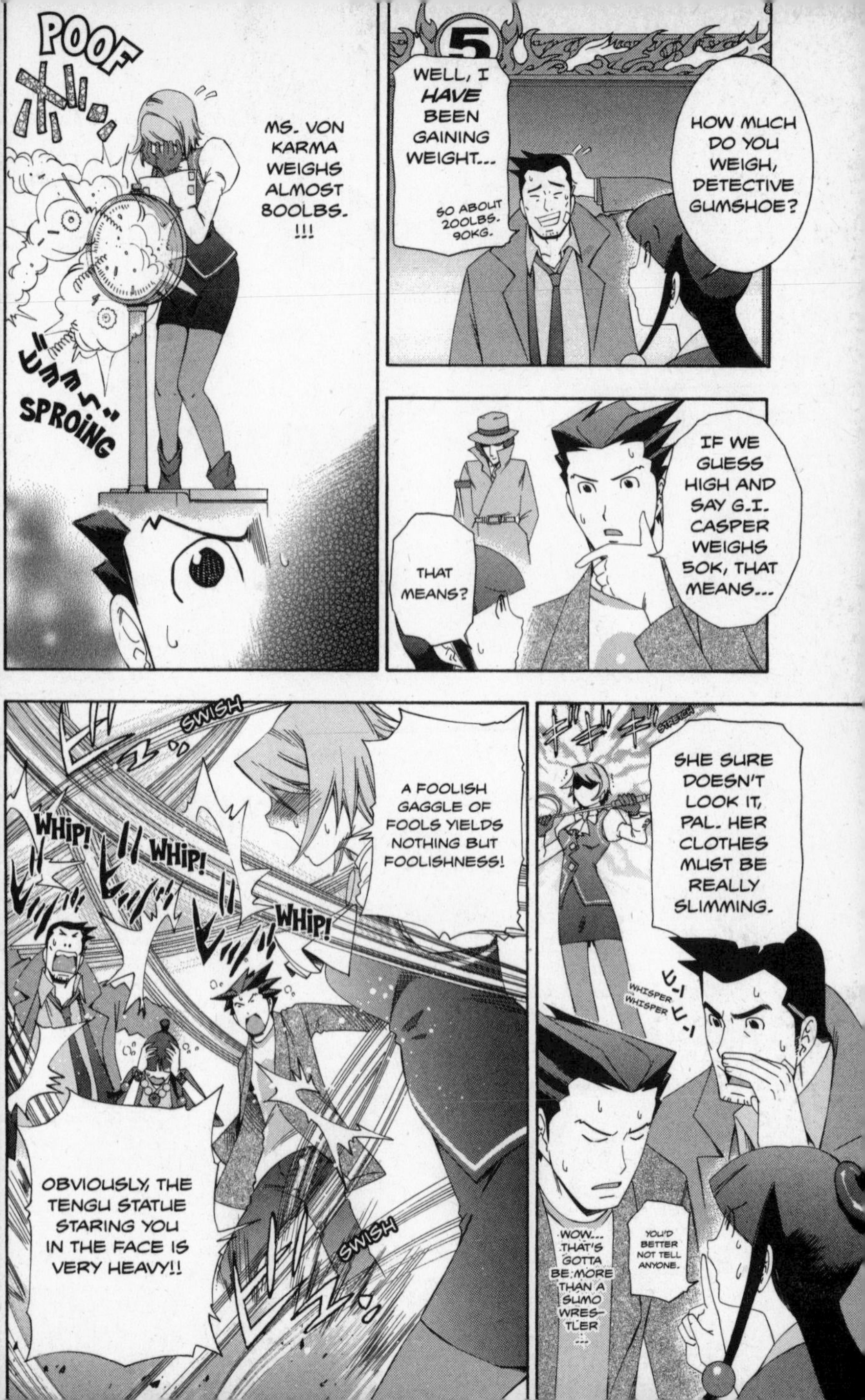
5
HOW MUCH DO YOU WEIGH, DETECTIVE GUMSHOE?
WELL, I HAVE BEEN GAINING WEIGHT...
SO ABOUT 200LBS. 90KG.
IF WE GUESS HIGH AND SAY G.I. CASPER WEIGHS 50K, THAT MEANS...
THAT MEANS?
POOF
MS. VON KARMA WEIGHS ALMOST 800LBS. !!!
SPROING
STRETCH
SHE SURE DOESN'T LOOK IT, PAL. HER CLOTHES MUST BE REALLY SLIMMING.
WHISPER WHISPER
YOU'D BETTER NOT TELL ANYONE.
WOW... THAT'S GOTTA BE MORE THAN A SUMO WRES-TLER ...
SWISH
A FOOLISH GAGGLE OF FOOLS YIELDS NOTHING BUT FOOLISHNESS!
WHIP!
WHIP!
WHIP!
OBVIOUSLY, THE TENGU STATUE STARING YOU IN THE FACE IS VERY HEAVY!!
SWISH

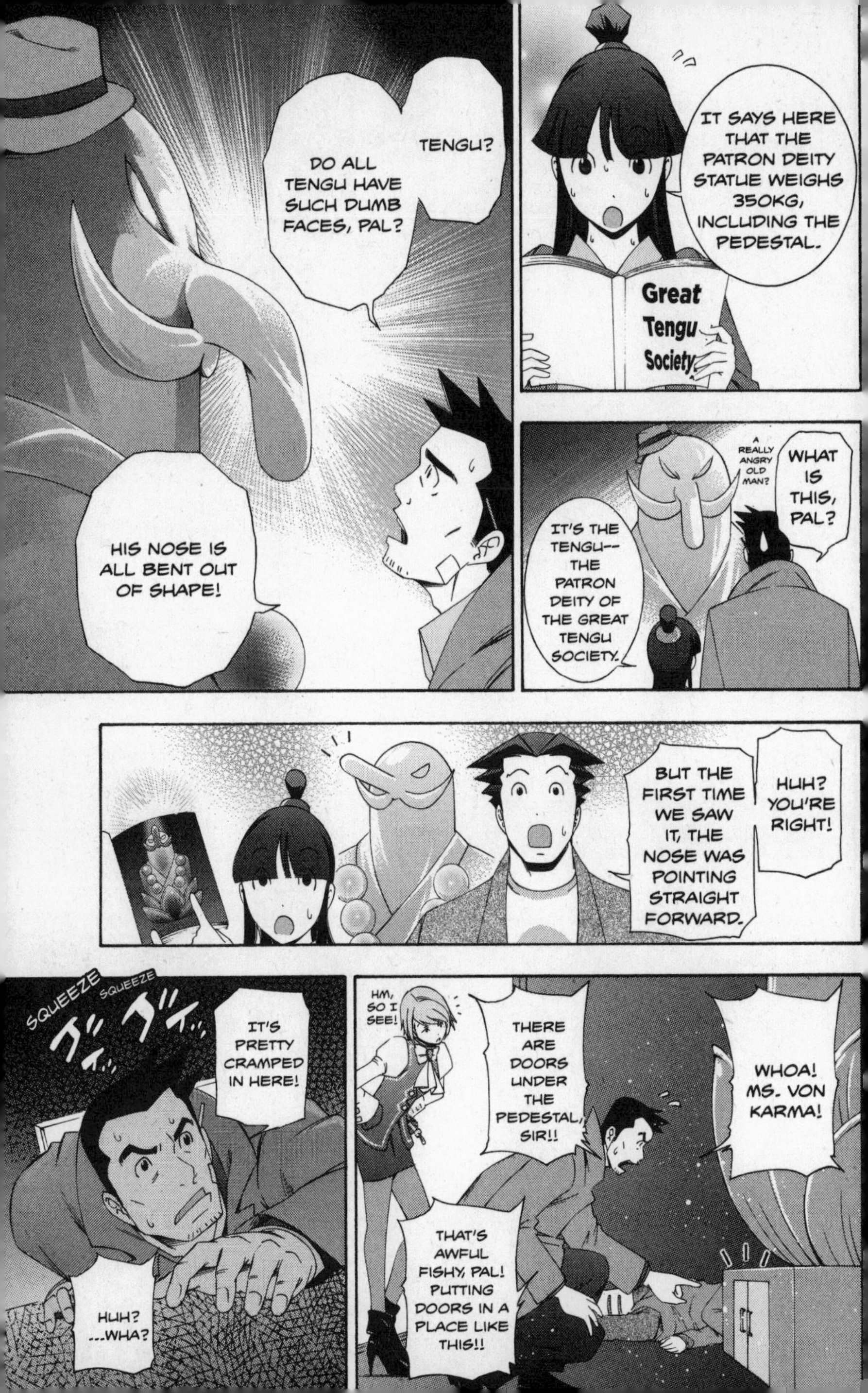
IT SAYS HERE THAT THE PATRON DEITY STATUE WEIGHS 350KG, INCLUDING THE PEDESTAL.
Great Tengu Society
WHAT IS THIS, PAL?
A REALLY ANGRY OLD MAN?
IT'S THE TENGU-- THE PATRON DEITY OF THE GREAT TENGU SOCIETY.
TENGU?
DO ALL TENGU HAVE SUCH DUMB FACES, PAL?
HIS NOSE IS ALL BENT OUT OF SHAPE!
HUH? YOU'RE RIGHT!
BUT THE FIRST TIME WE SAW IT, THE NOSE WAS POINTING STRAIGHT FORWARD.
WHOA! MS. VON KARMA!
THERE ARE DOORS UNDER THE PEDESTAL, SIR!!
HM, SO I SEE!
THAT'S AWFUL FISHY, PAL! PUTTING DOORS IN A PLACE LIKE THIS!!
SQUEEZE
SQUEEZE
IT'S PRETTY CRAMPED IN HERE!
HUH? ...WHA?

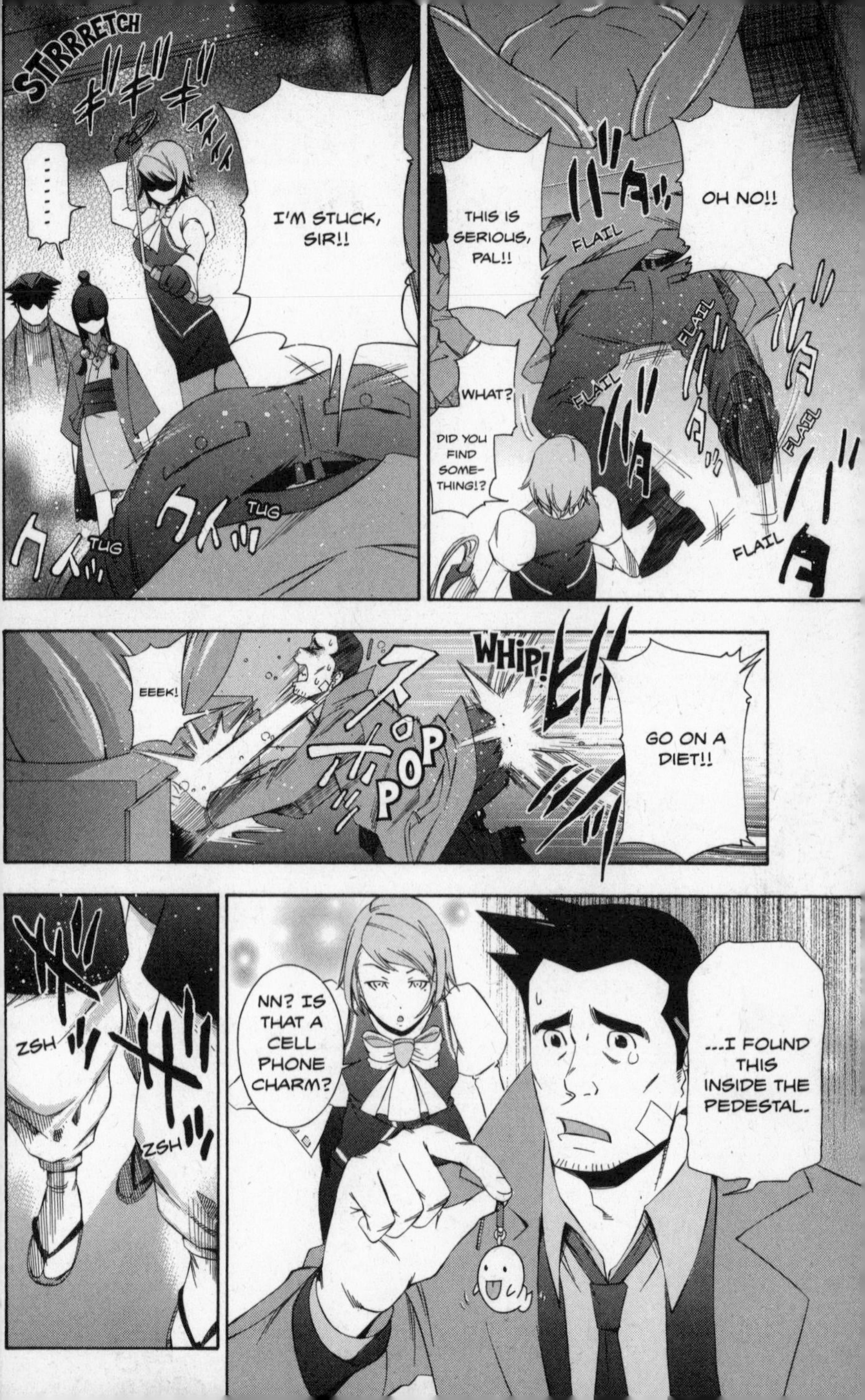
OH NO!!
THIS IS SERIOUS, PAL!!
FLAIL
FLAIL
FLAIL
FLAIL
FLAIL
WHAT?
DID YOU FIND SOME-THING!?
STRRRETCH
I'M STUCK, SIR!!
......
TUG
TUG
GO ON A DIET!!
WHIP!
POP
EEEK!
...I FOUND THIS INSIDE THE PEDESTAL.
NN? IS THAT A CELL PHONE CHARM?
ZSH
ZSH

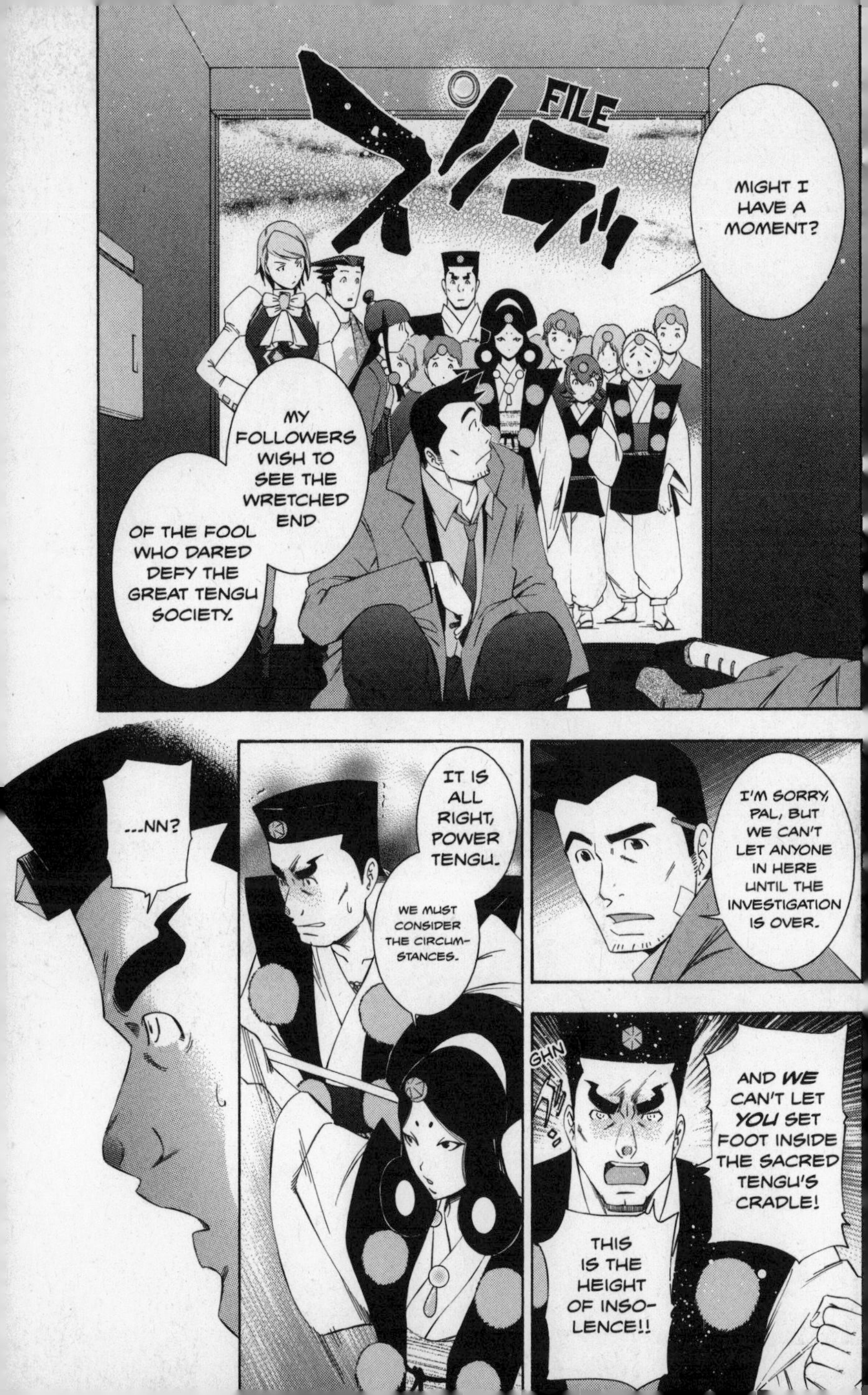
FILE
MIGHT I HAVE A MOMENT?
MY FOLLOWERS WISH TO SEE THE WRETCHED END
OF THE FOOL WHO DARED DEFY THE GREAT TENGU SOCIETY.
I'M SORRY, PAL, BUT WE CAN'T LET ANYONE IN HERE UNTIL THE INVESTIGATION IS OVER.
GHN
AND WE CAN'T LET YOU SET FOOT INSIDE THE SACRED TENGU'S CRADLE!
THIS IS THE HEIGHT OF INSO-LENCE!!
IT IS ALL RIGHT, POWER TENGU.
WE MUST CONSIDER THE CIRCUM-STANCES.
...NN?

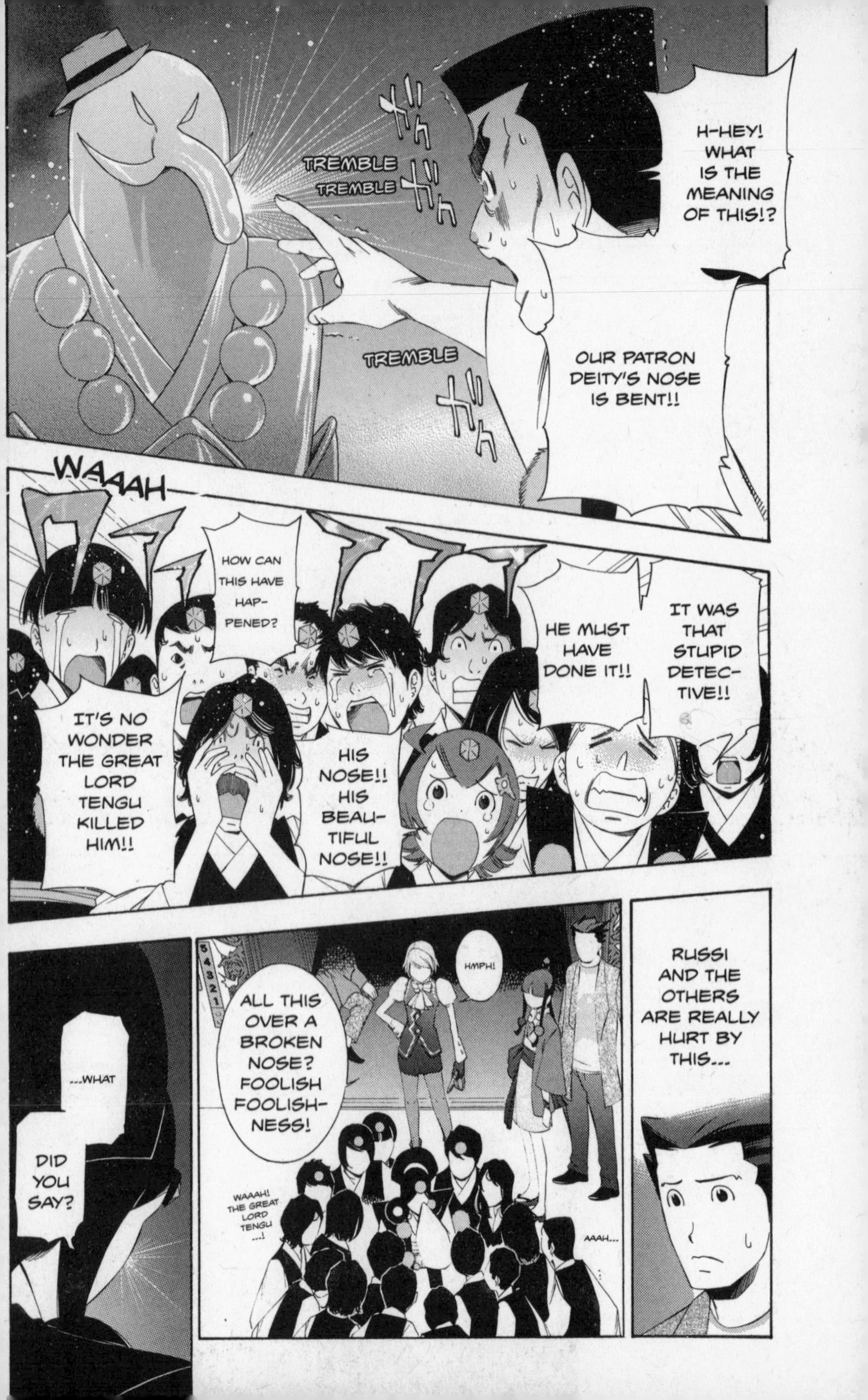
H-HEY! WHAT IS THE MEANING OF THIS!?
TREMBLE
TREMBLE
OUR PATRON DEITY'S NOSE IS BENT!!
TREMBLE
WAAAH
IT WAS THAT STUPID DETEC-TIVE!!
HE MUST HAVE DONE IT!!
HOW CAN THIS HAVE HAP-PENED?
HIS NOSE!! HIS BEAU-TIFUL NOSE!!
IT'S NO WONDER THE GREAT LORD TENGU KILLED HIM!!
RUSSI AND THE OTHERS ARE REALLY HURT BY THIS...
HMPH!
ALL THIS OVER A BROKEN NOSE? FOOLISH FOOLISH-NESS!
WAAAH! THE GREAT LORD TENGU ...!
AAAH...
...WHAT
DID YOU SAY?

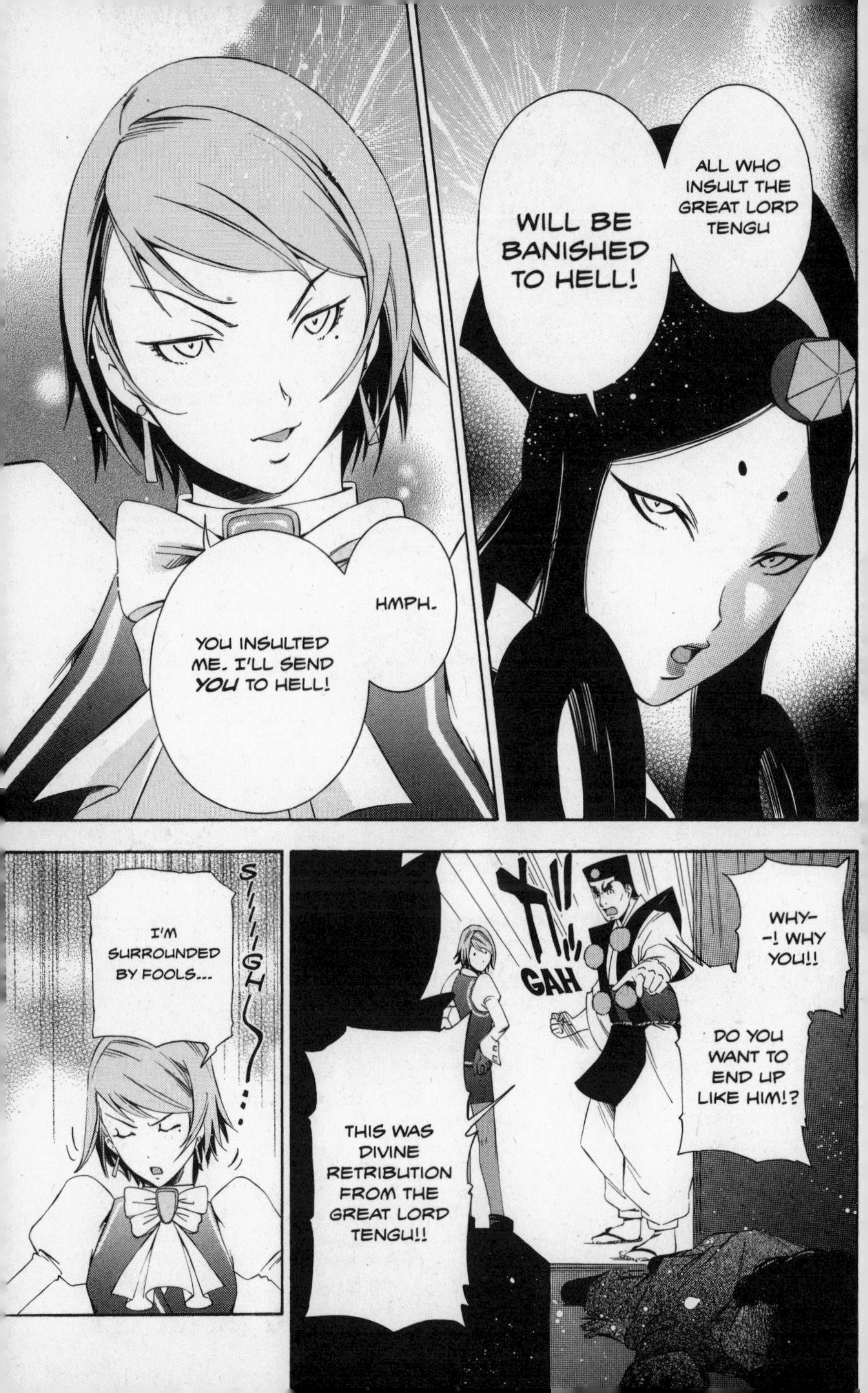
ALL WHO INSULT THE GREAT LORD TENGU
WILL BE BANISHED TO HELL!
HMPH.
YOU INSULTED ME. I'LL SEND YOU TO HELL!
WHY- -! WHY YOU!!
GAH
DO YOU WANT TO END UP LIKE HIM!?
THIS WAS DIVINE RETRIBUTION FROM THE GREAT LORD TENGU!!
SIIIGH...
I'M SURROUNDED BY FOOLS...

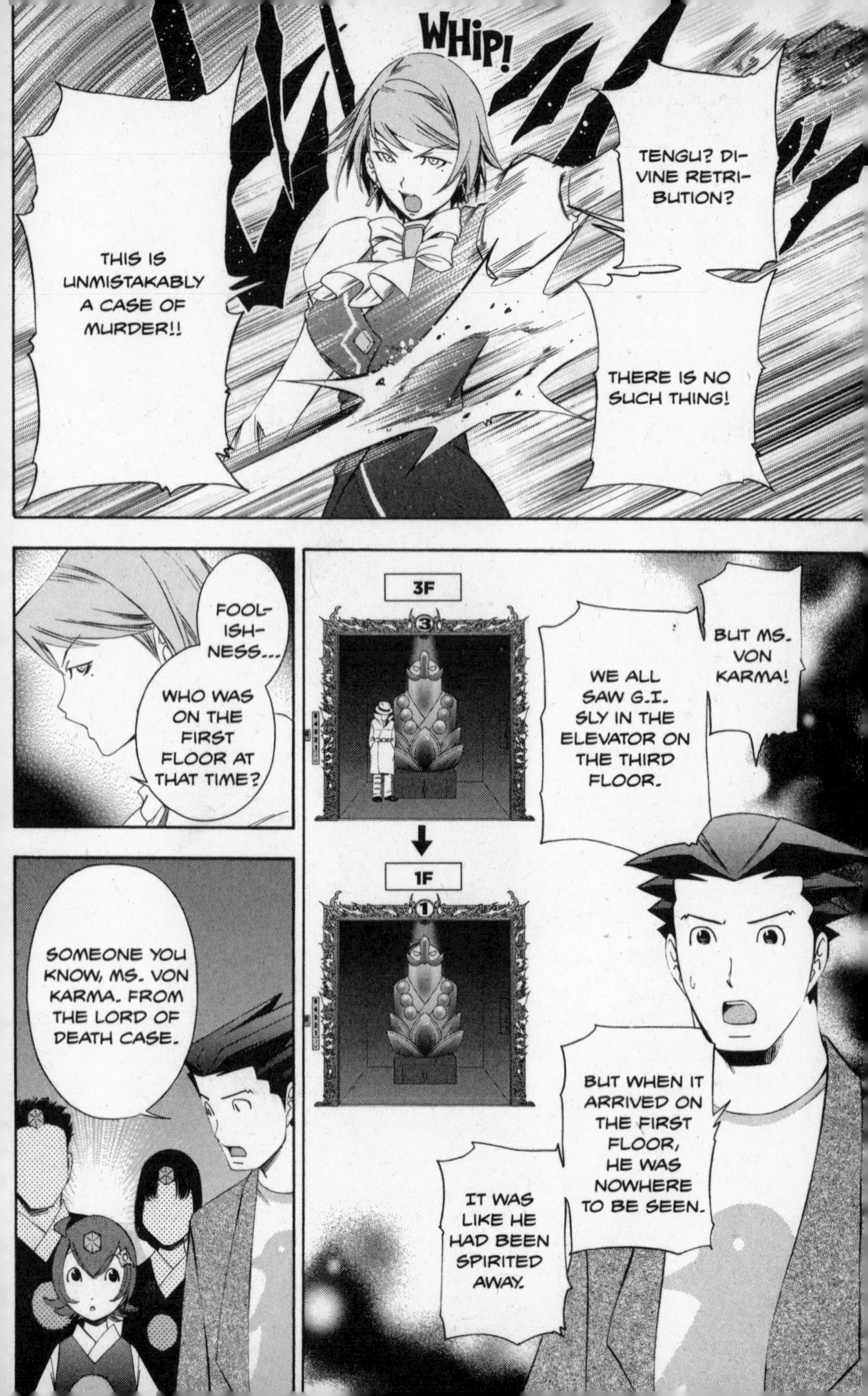
WHIP!
TENGU? DI-VINE RETRI-BUTION?
THERE IS NO SUCH THING!
THIS IS UNMISTAKABLY A CASE OF MURDER!!
BUT MS. VON KARMA!
WE ALL SAW G.I. SLY IN THE ELEVATOR ON THE THIRD FLOOR.
3F
1F
BUT WHEN IT ARRIVED ON THE FIRST FLOOR, HE WAS NOWHERE TO BE SEEN.
IT WAS LIKE HE HAD BEEN SPIRITED AWAY.
FOOL-ISH-NESS...
WHO WAS ON THE FIRST FLOOR AT THAT TIME?
SOMEONE YOU KNOW, MS. VON KARMA. FROM THE LORD OF DEATH CASE.

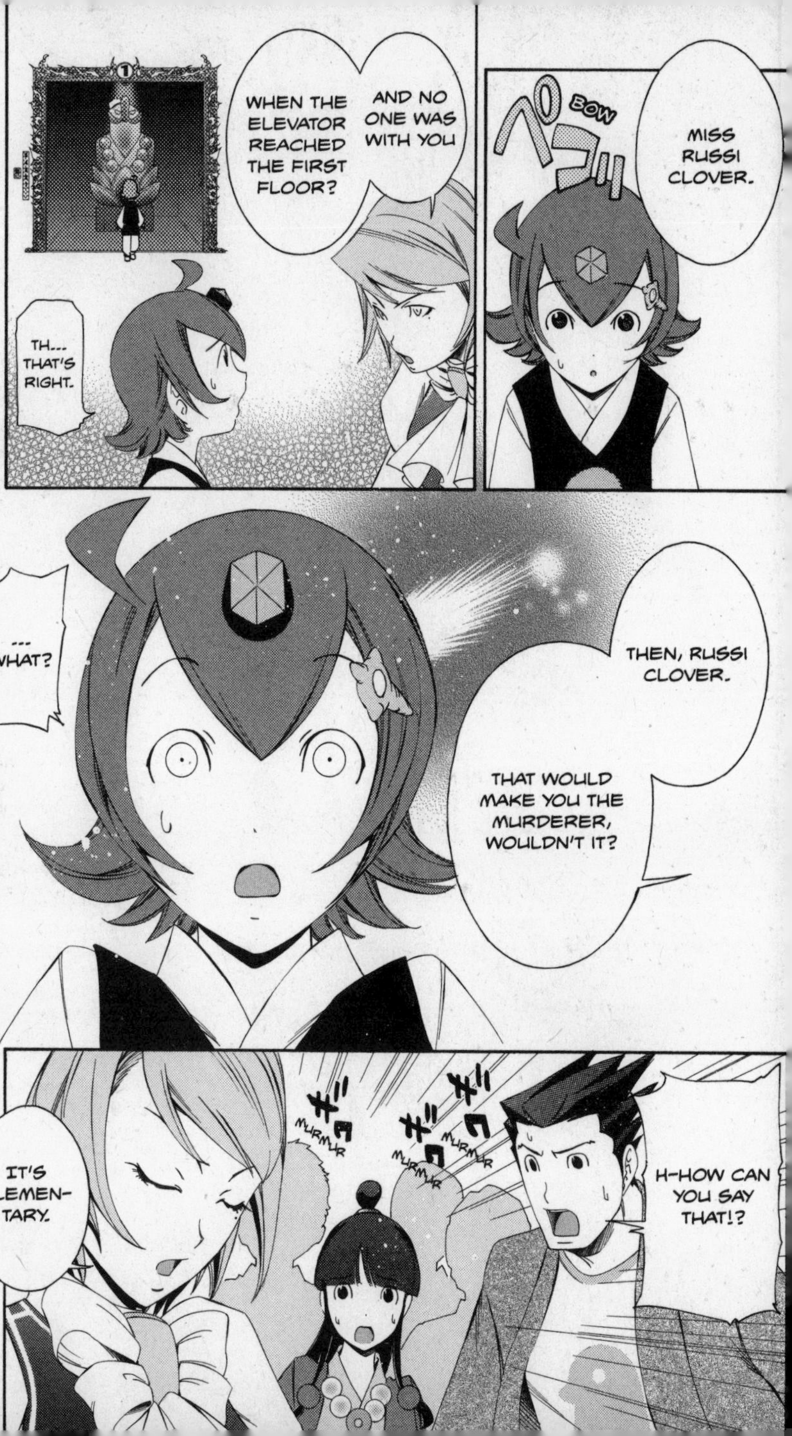
BOW
MISS RUSSI CLOVER.
AND NO ONE WAS WITH YOU
WHEN THE ELEVATOR REACHED THE FIRST FLOOR?
TH... THAT'S RIGHT.
THEN, RUSSI CLOVER.
THAT WOULD MAKE YOU THE MURDERER, WOULDN'T IT?
...WHAT?
H-HOW CAN YOU SAY THAT!?
MURMUR
MURMUR
MURMUR
IT'S ELEMENTARY.

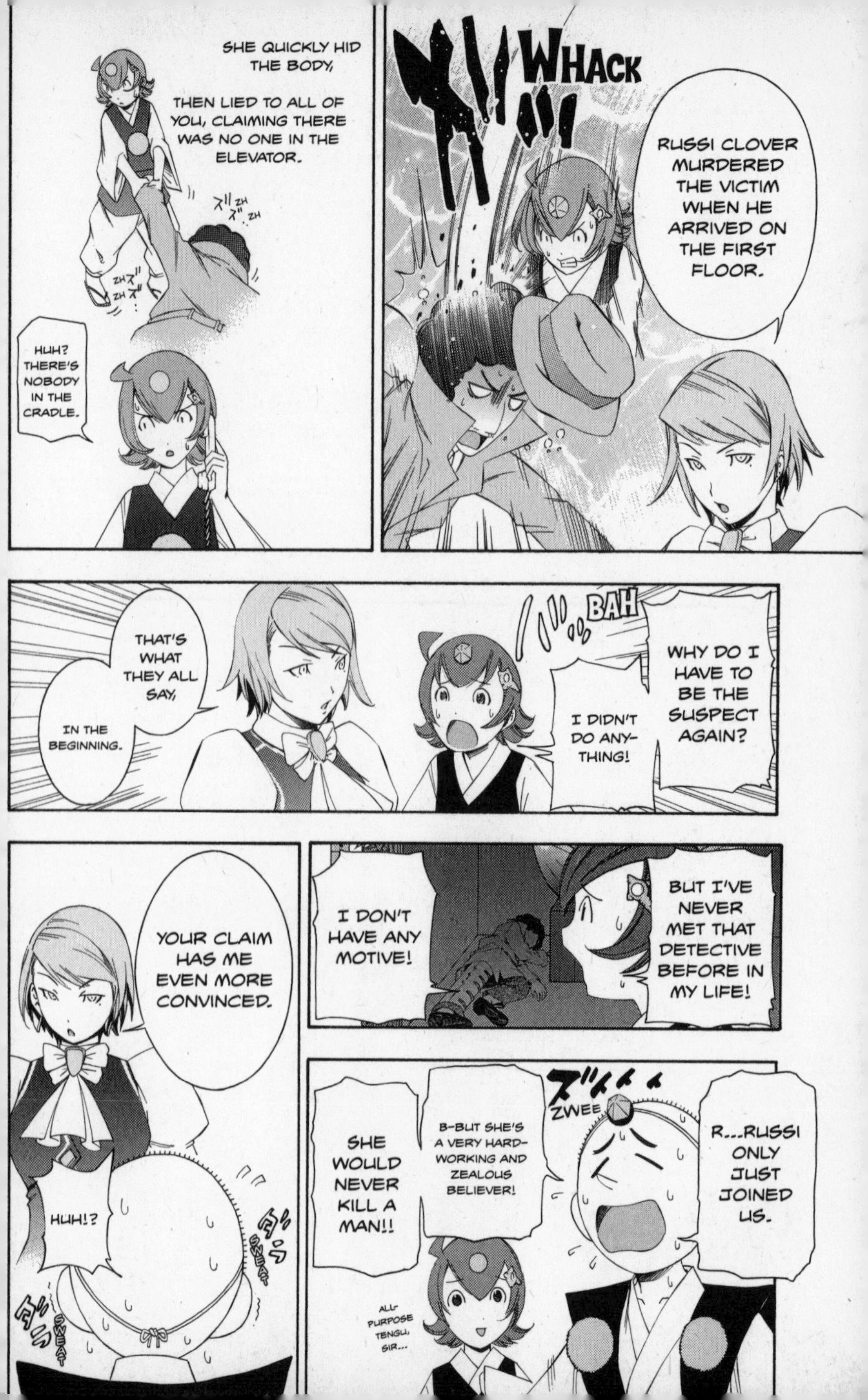
WHACK
RUSSI CLOVER MURDERED THE VICTIM WHEN HE ARRIVED ON THE FIRST FLOOR.
SHE QUICKLY HID THE BODY,
THEN LIED TO ALL OF YOU, CLAIMING THERE WAS NO ONE IN THE ELEVATOR.
ZH ZH
ZH ZH
HUH? THERE'S NOBODY IN THE CRADLE.
BAH
WHY DO I HAVE TO BE THE SUSPECT AGAIN?
I DIDN'T DO ANYTHING!
THAT'S WHAT THEY ALL SAY,
IN THE BEGINNING.
BUT I'VE NEVER MET THAT DETECTIVE BEFORE IN MY LIFE!
I DON'T HAVE ANY MOTIVE!
ZWEE
R...RUSSI ONLY JUST JOINED US.
B-BUT SHE'S A VERY HARD-WORKING AND ZEALOUS BELIEVER!
SHE WOULD NEVER KILL A MAN!!
ALL-PURPOSE TENGU, SIR...
YOUR CLAIM HAS ME EVEN MORE CONVINCED.
HUH!?
SWEAT
SWEAT

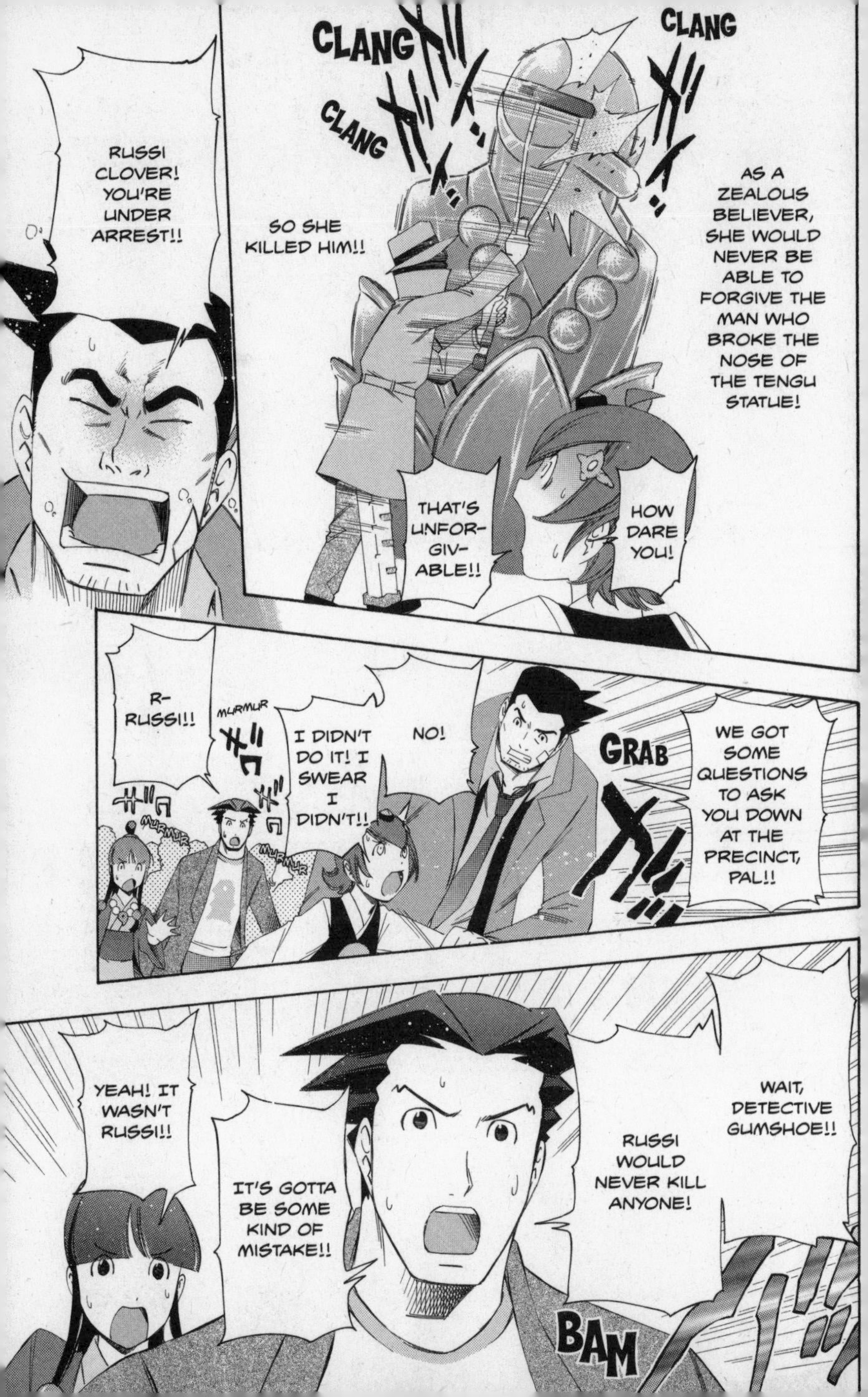
CLANG
CLANG
CLANG
AS A ZEALOUS BELIEVER, SHE WOULD NEVER BE ABLE TO FORGIVE THE MAN WHO BROKE THE NOSE OF THE TENGU STATUE!
SO SHE KILLED HIM!!
HOW DARE YOU!
THAT'S UNFORGIVABLE!!
RUSSI CLOVER! YOU'RE UNDER ARREST!!
WE GOT SOME QUESTIONS TO ASK YOU DOWN AT THE PRECINCT, PAL!!
GRAB
NO!
I DIDN'T DO IT! I SWEAR I DIDN'T!!
MURMUR
MURMUR
MURMUR
R-RUSSI!!
WAIT, DETECTIVE GUMSHOE!!
RUSSI WOULD NEVER KILL ANYONE!
IT'S GOTTA BE SOME KIND OF MISTAKE!!
YEAH! IT WASN'T RUSSI!!
BAM

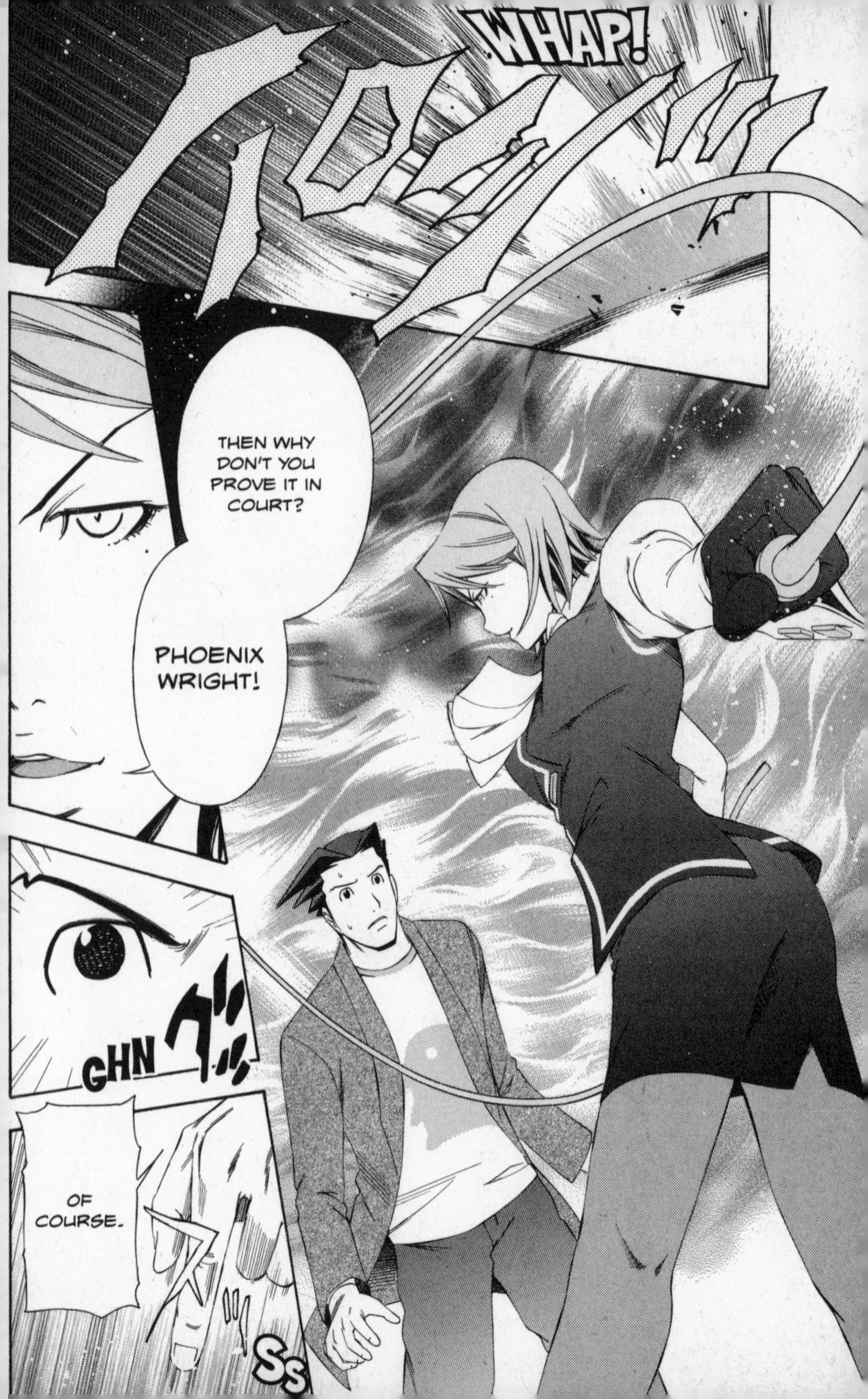
WHAP!
THEN WHY DON'T YOU PROVE IT IN COURT?
PHOENIX WRIGHT!
GHN
OF COURSE.
Ss

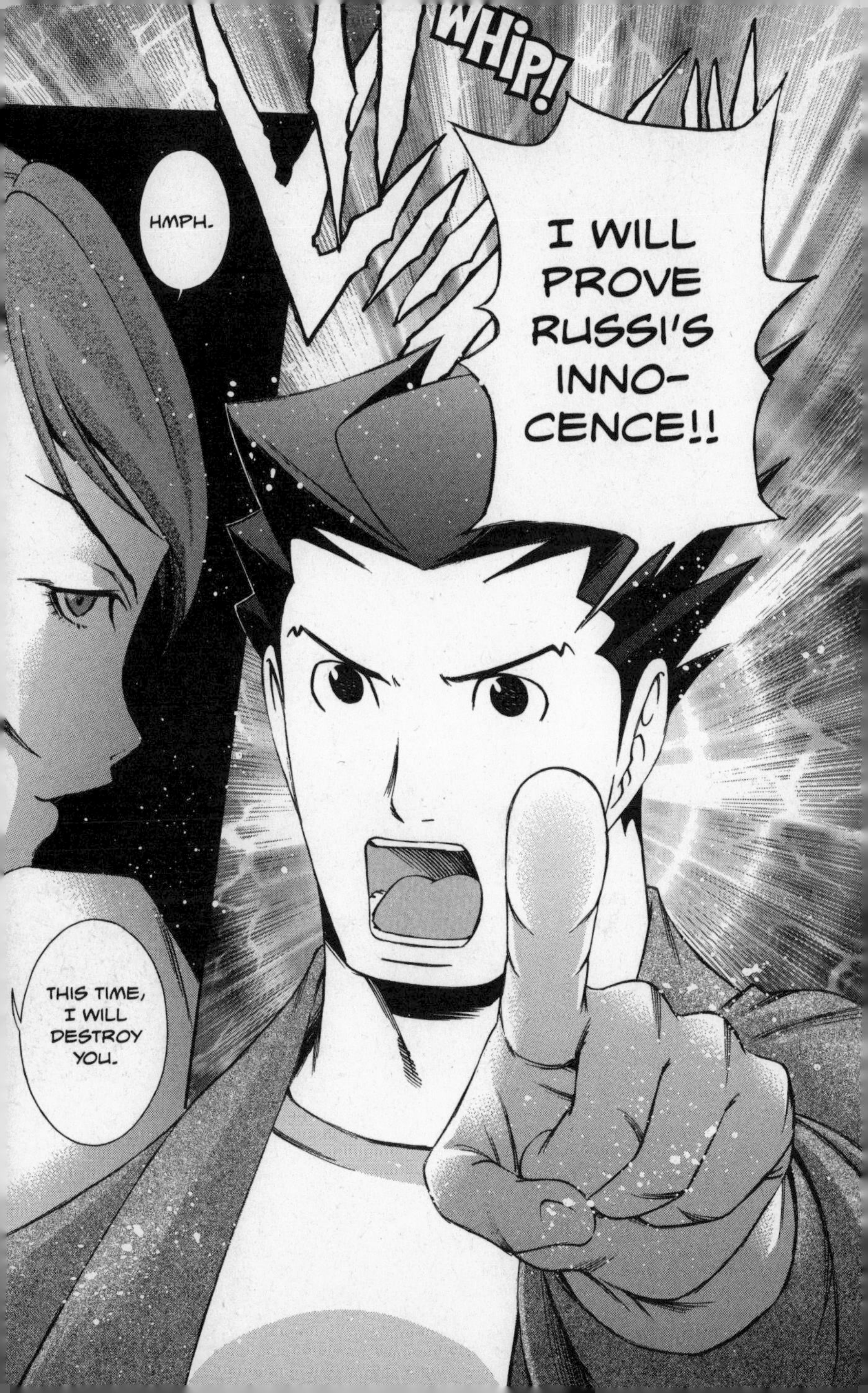
WHIP!
I WILL PROVE RUSSI'S INNO-CENCE!!
HMPH.
THIS TIME, I WILL DESTROY YOU.

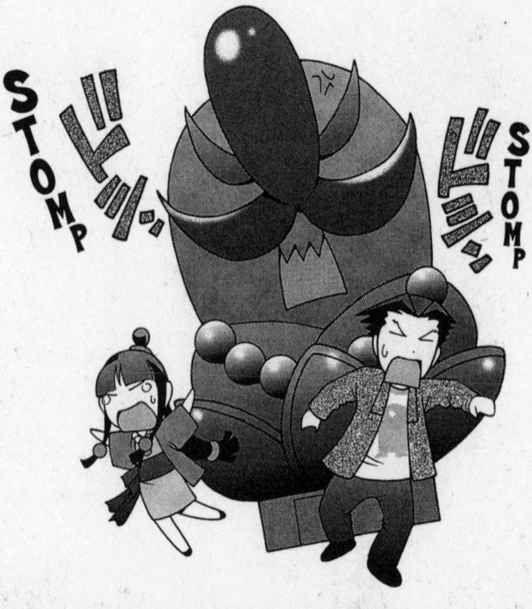
STOMP
STOMP

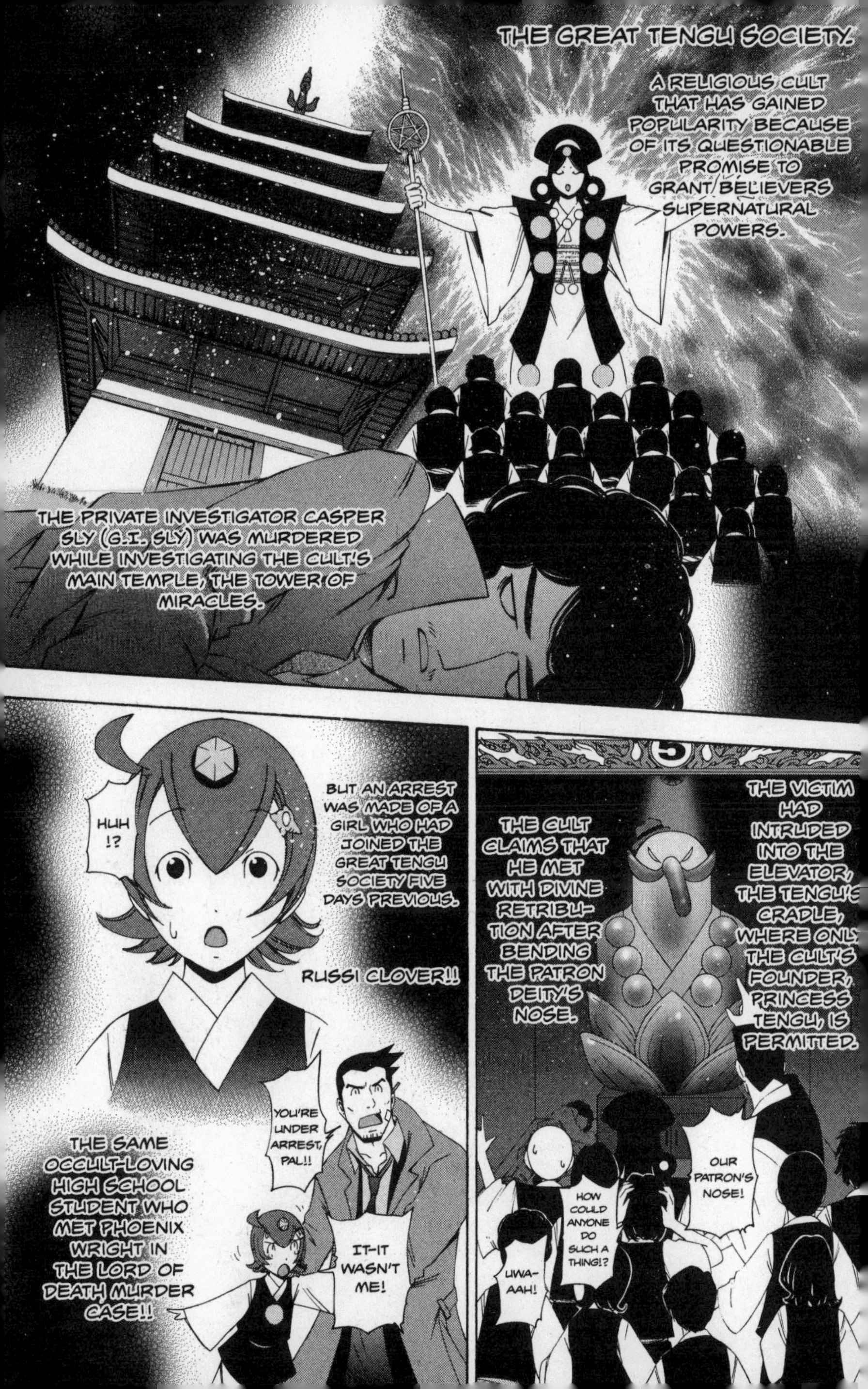
THE GREAT TENGU SOCIETY.
A RELIGIOUS CULT THAT HAS GAINED POPULARITY BECAUSE OF ITS QUESTIONABLE PROMISE TO GRANT BELIEVERS SUPERNATURAL POWERS.
THE PRIVATE INVESTIGATOR CASPER SLY (G.I. SLY) WAS MURDERED WHILE INVESTIGATING THE CULT'S MAIN TEMPLE, THE TOWER OF MIRACLES.
5
THE VICTIM HAD INTRUDED INTO THE ELEVATOR, THE TENGU'S CRADLE, WHERE ONLY THE CULT'S FOUNDER, PRINCESS TENGU, IS PERMITTED.
THE CULT CLAIMS THAT HE MET WITH DIVINE RETRIBUTION AFTER BENDING THE PATRON DEITY'S NOSE.
OUR PATRON'S NOSE!
HOW COULD ANYONE DO SUCH A THING!?
UWAAAH!
BUT AN ARREST WAS MADE OF A GIRL WHO HAD JOINED THE GREAT TENGU SOCIETY FIVE DAYS PREVIOUS.
HUH!?
RUSSI CLOVER!!
YOU'RE UNDER ARREST, PAL!!
IT-IT WASN'T ME!
THE SAME OCCULT-LOVING HIGH SCHOOL STUDENT WHO MET PHOENIX WRIGHT IN THE LORD OF DEATH MURDER CASE!!

CHAPTER 15

TURNABOUT POWER VS. SUPERNATURAL POWER (PART TWO)

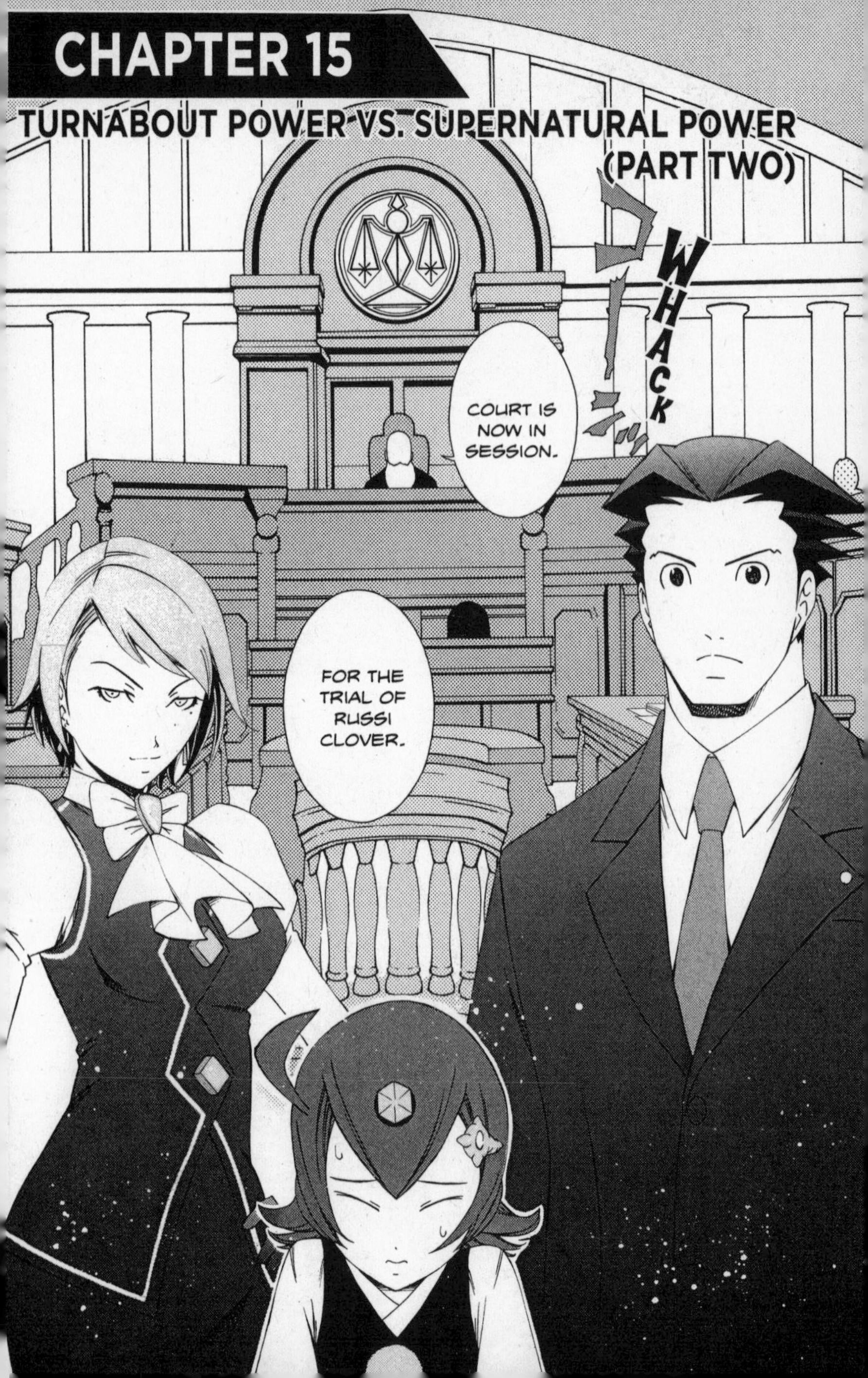
WHACK
COURT IS NOW IN SESSION.
FOR THE TRIAL OF RUSSI CLOVER.

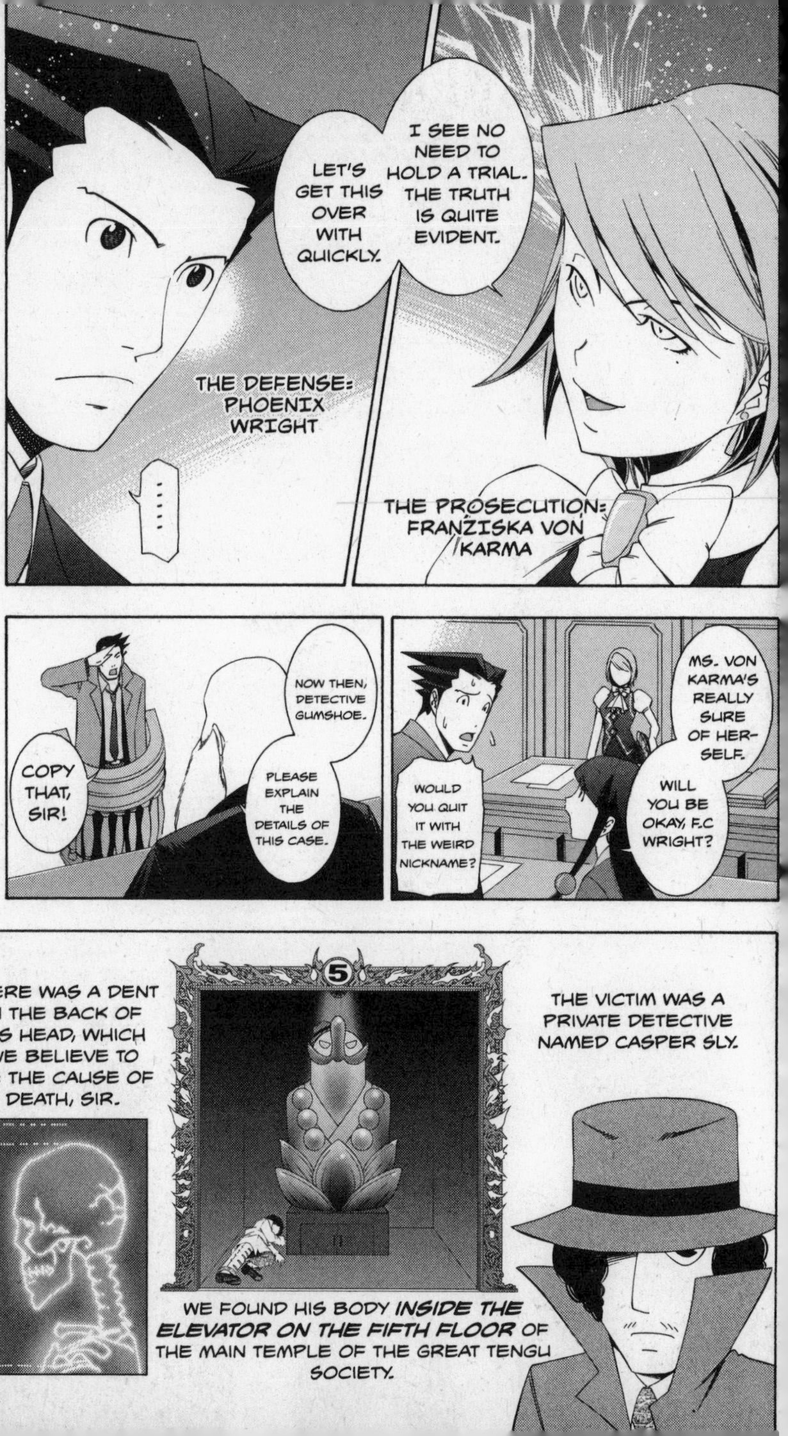
I SEE NO NEED TO HOLD A TRIAL. THE TRUTH IS QUITE EVIDENT.
LET'S GET THIS OVER WITH QUICKLY.
THE PROSECUTION: FRANZISKA VON KARMA
THE DEFENSE: PHOENIX WRIGHT
......
MS. VON KARMA'S REALLY SURE OF HER-SELF.
WILL YOU BE OKAY, F.C WRIGHT?
WOULD YOU QUIT IT WITH THE WEIRD NICKNAME?
NOW THEN, DETECTIVE GUMSHOE.
PLEASE EXPLAIN THE DETAILS OF THIS CASE.
COPY THAT, SIR!
THE VICTIM WAS A PRIVATE DETECTIVE NAMED CASPER SLY.
5
THERE WAS A DENT IN THE BACK OF HIS HEAD, WHICH WE BELIEVE TO BE THE CAUSE OF DEATH, SIR.
WE FOUND HIS BODY ***INSIDE THE ELEVATOR ON THE FIFTH FLOOR*** OF THE MAIN TEMPLE OF THE GREAT TENGU SOCIETY.

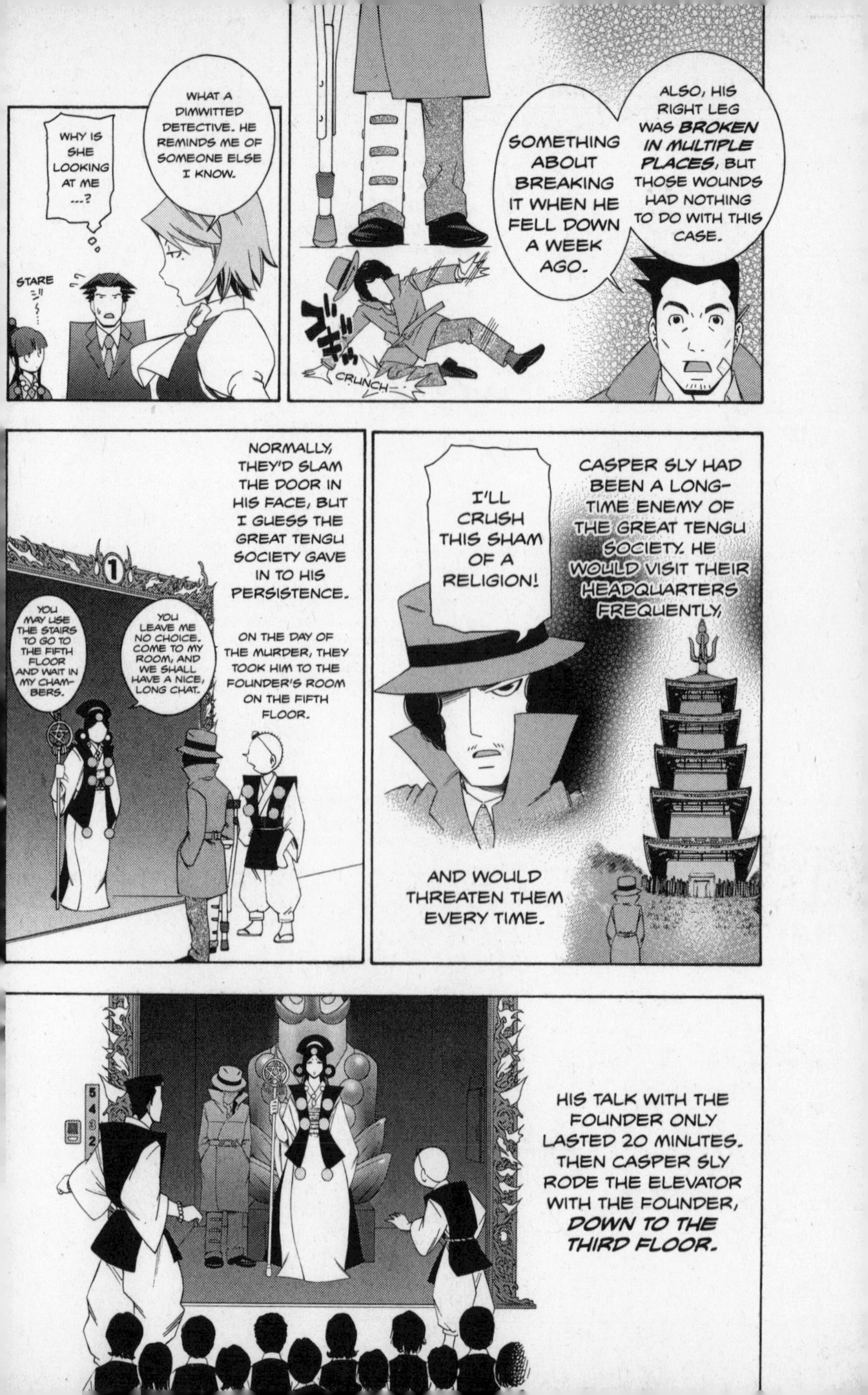
ALSO, HIS RIGHT LEG WAS ***BROKEN IN MULTIPLE PLACES***, BUT THOSE WOUNDS HAD NOTHING TO DO WITH THIS CASE.
SOMETHING ABOUT BREAKING IT WHEN HE FELL DOWN A WEEK AGO.
CRUNCH
WHAT A DIMWITTED DETECTIVE. HE REMINDS ME OF SOMEONE ELSE I KNOW.
WHY IS SHE LOOKING AT ME ...?
STARE
CASPER SLY HAD BEEN A LONG-TIME ENEMY OF THE GREAT TENGU SOCIETY. HE WOULD VISIT THEIR HEADQUARTERS FREQUENTLY,
I'LL CRUSH THIS SHAM OF A RELIGION!
AND WOULD THREATEN THEM EVERY TIME.
NORMALLY, THEY'D SLAM THE DOOR IN HIS FACE, BUT I GUESS THE GREAT TENGU SOCIETY GAVE IN TO HIS PERSISTENCE.
YOU LEAVE ME NO CHOICE. COME TO MY ROOM, AND WE SHALL HAVE A NICE, LONG CHAT.
YOU MAY USE THE STAIRS TO GO TO THE FIFTH FLOOR AND WAIT IN MY CHAMBERS.
ON THE DAY OF THE MURDER, THEY TOOK HIM TO THE FOUNDER'S ROOM ON THE FIFTH FLOOR.
HIS TALK WITH THE FOUNDER ONLY LASTED 20 MINUTES. THEN CASPER SLY RODE THE ELEVATOR WITH THE FOUNDER, ***DOWN TO THE THIRD FLOOR.***

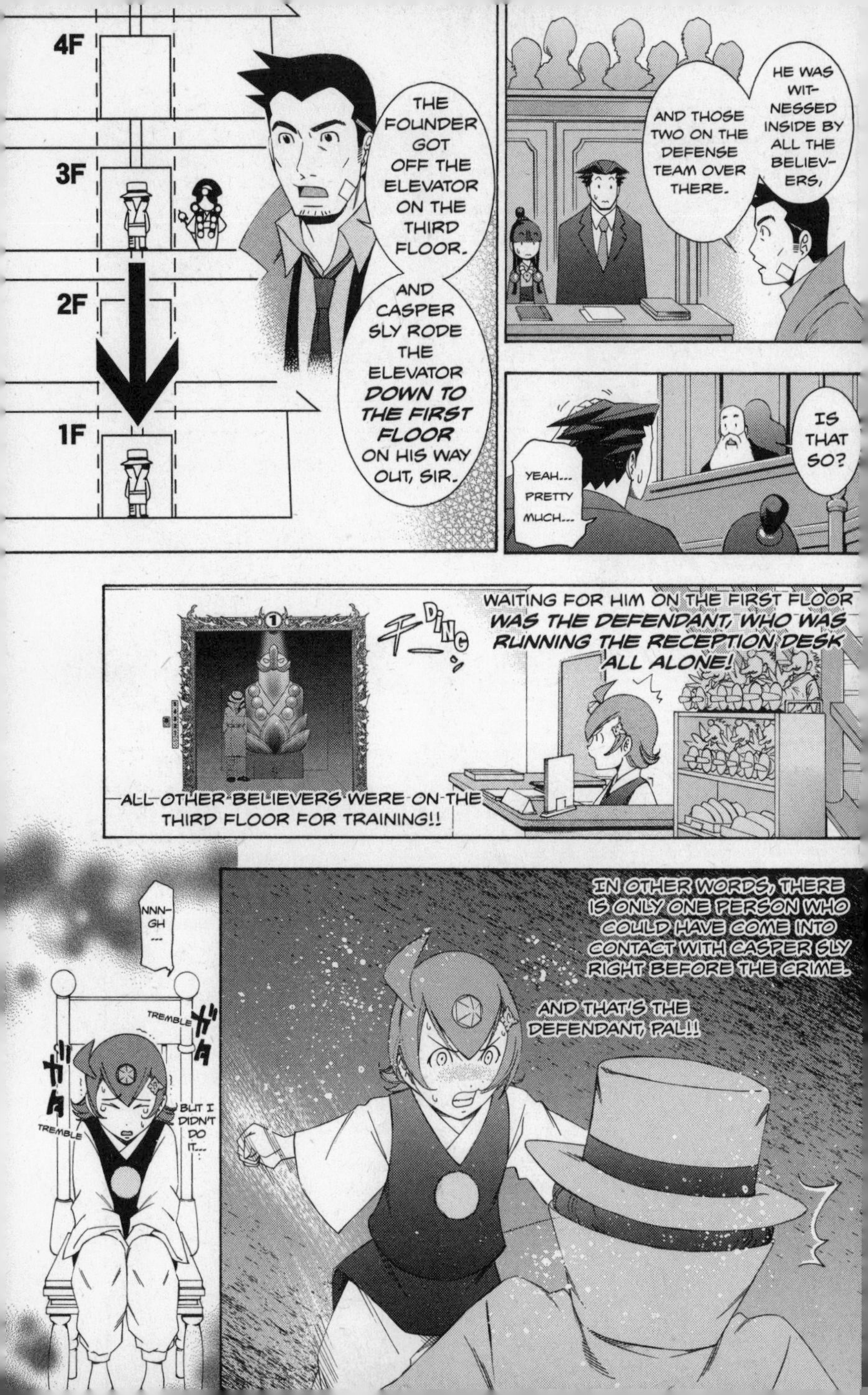
HE WAS WITNESSED INSIDE BY ALL THE BELIEVERS,
AND THOSE TWO ON THE DEFENSE TEAM OVER THERE.
IS THAT SO?
YEAH... PRETTY MUCH...
THE FOUNDER GOT OFF THE ELEVATOR ON THE THIRD FLOOR.
AND CASPER SLY RODE THE ELEVATOR ***DOWN TO THE FIRST FLOOR*** ON HIS WAY OUT, SIR.
4F
3F
2F
1F
WAITING FOR HIM ON THE FIRST FLOOR ***WAS THE DEFENDANT, WHO WAS RUNNING THE RECEPTION DESK ALL ALONE!***
DING
ALL OTHER BELIEVERS WERE ON THE THIRD FLOOR FOR TRAINING!!
IN OTHER WORDS, THERE IS ONLY ONE PERSON WHO COULD HAVE COME INTO CONTACT WITH CASPER SLY RIGHT BEFORE THE CRIME.
AND THAT'S THE DEFENDANT, PAL!!
NNN-GH ---
TREMBLE
BUT I DIDN'T DO IT...
TREMBLE

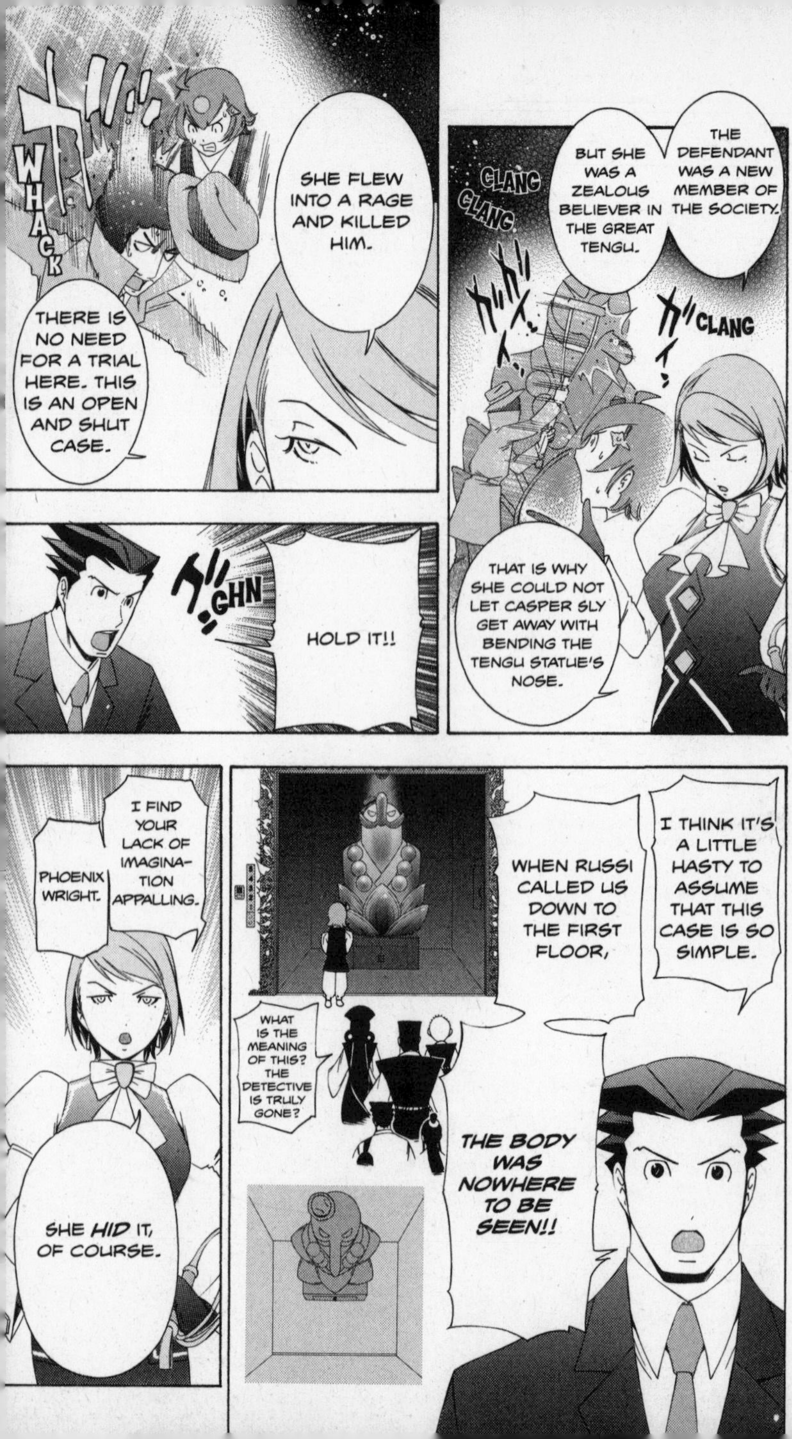
THE DEFENDANT WAS A NEW MEMBER OF THE SOCIETY.
BUT SHE WAS A ZEALOUS BELIEVER IN THE GREAT TENGU.
CLANG
CLANG
CLANG
THAT IS WHY SHE COULD NOT LET CASPER SLY GET AWAY WITH BENDING THE TENGU STATUE'S NOSE.
SHE FLEW INTO A RAGE AND KILLED HIM.
WHACK
THERE IS NO NEED FOR A TRIAL HERE. THIS IS AN OPEN AND SHUT CASE.
HOLD IT!!
GHN
I THINK IT'S A LITTLE HASTY TO ASSUME THAT THIS CASE IS SO SIMPLE.
WHEN RUSSI CALLED US DOWN TO THE FIRST FLOOR,
WHAT IS THE MEANING OF THIS? THE DETECTIVE IS TRULY GONE?
THE BODY WAS NOWHERE TO BE SEEN!!
I FIND YOUR LACK OF IMAGINATION APPALLING.
PHOENIX WRIGHT.
SHE *HID* IT, OF COURSE.

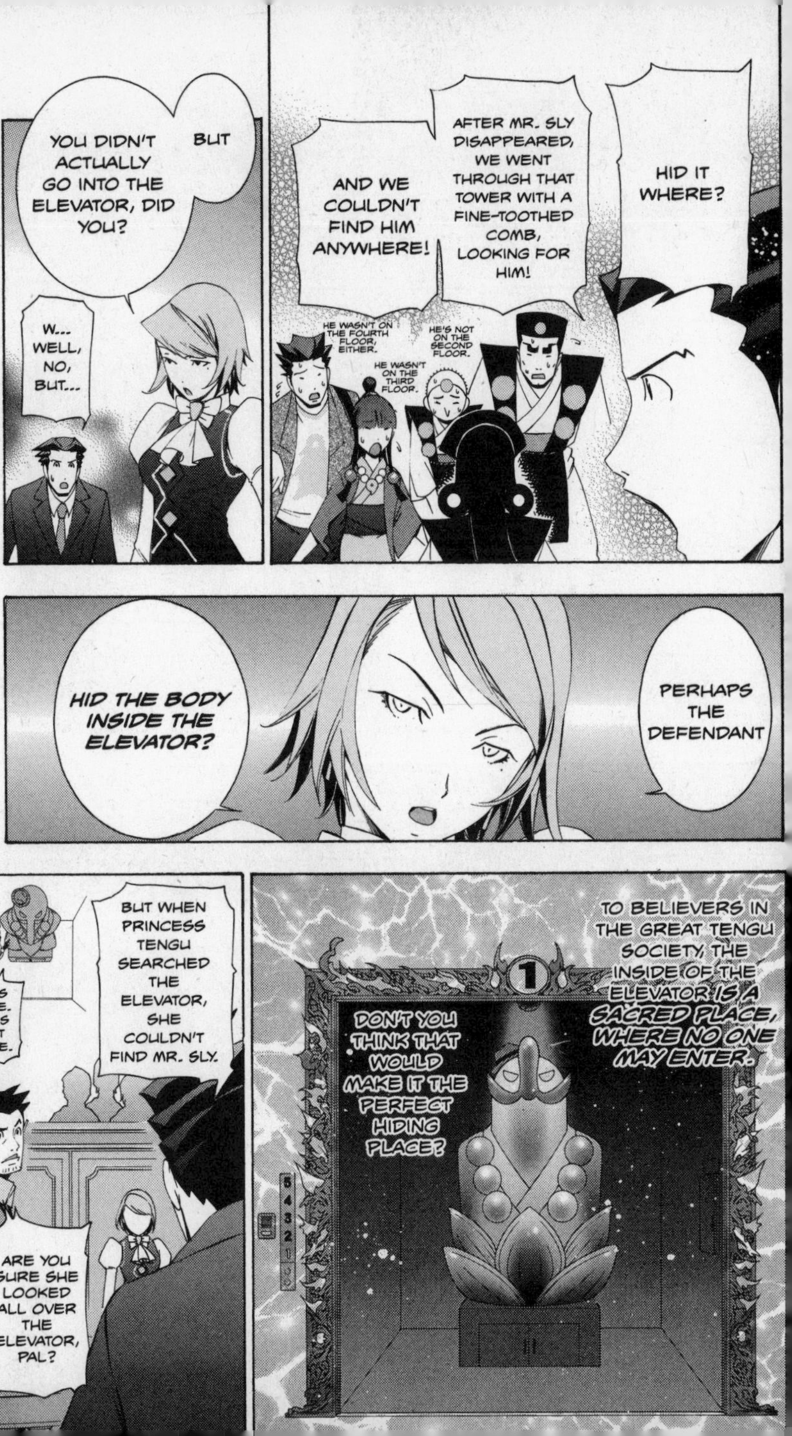
HID IT WHERE?
AFTER MR. SLY DISAPPEARED, WE WENT THROUGH THAT TOWER WITH A FINE-TOOTHED COMB, LOOKING FOR HIM!
AND WE COULDN'T FIND HIM ANYWHERE!
HE'S NOT ON THE SECOND FLOOR.
HE WASN'T ON THE THIRD FLOOR.
HE WASN'T ON THE FOURTH FLOOR, EITHER.
BUT
YOU DIDN'T ACTUALLY GO INTO THE ELEVATOR, DID YOU?
W... WELL, NO, BUT...
PERHAPS THE DEFENDANT
HID THE BODY INSIDE THE ELEVATOR?
TO BELIEVERS IN THE GREAT TENGU SOCIETY, THE INSIDE OF THE ELEVATOR IS A SACRED PLACE, WHERE NO ONE MAY ENTER.
DON'T YOU THINK THAT WOULD MAKE IT THE PERFECT HIDING PLACE?
BUT WHEN PRINCESS TENGU SEARCHED THE ELEVATOR, SHE COULDN'T FIND MR. SLY.
IT IS TRUE. HE IS NOT HERE.
ARE YOU SURE SHE LOOKED ALL OVER THE ELEVATOR, PAL?

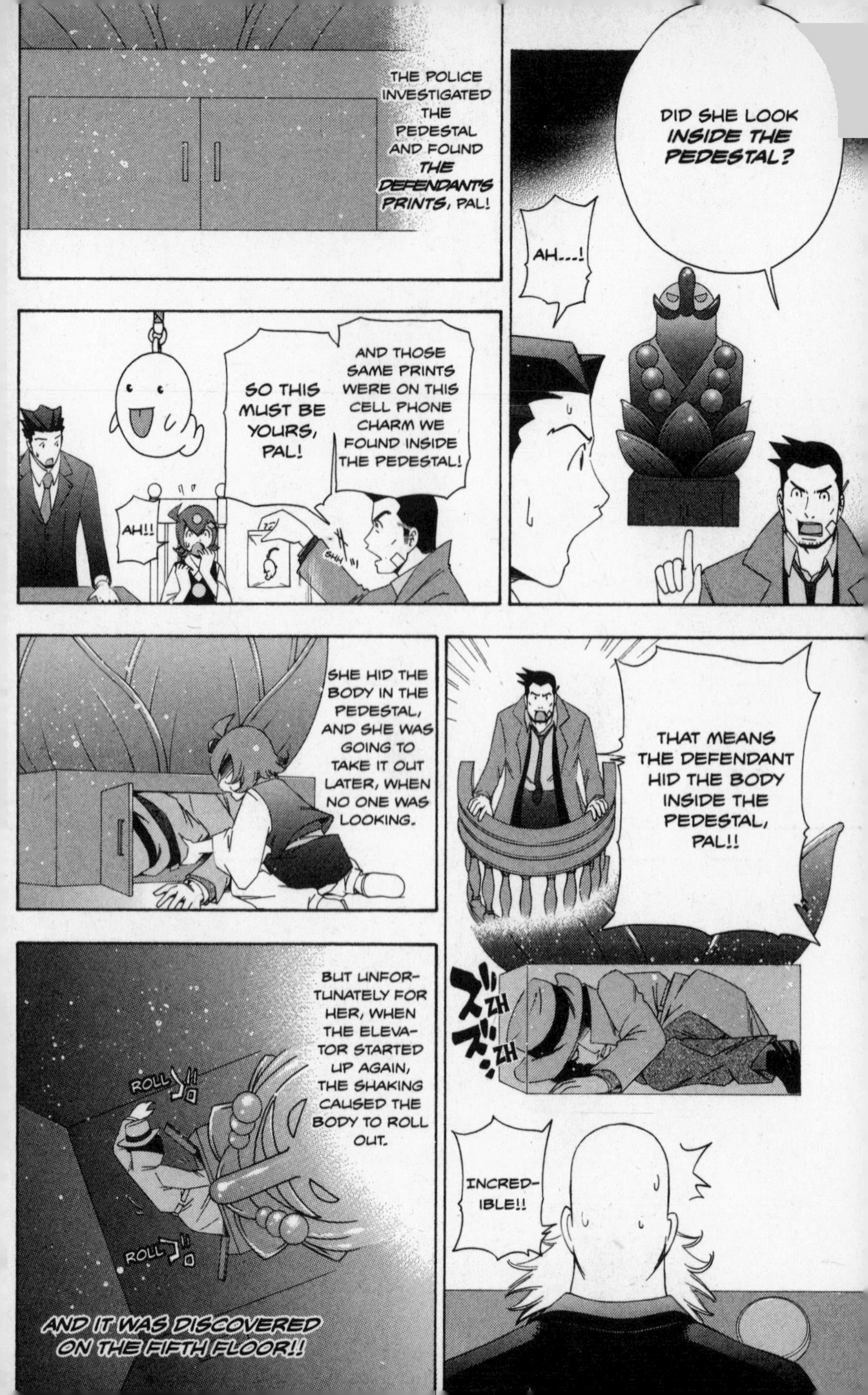

DID SHE LOOK INSIDE THE PEDESTAL?
AH...!
THE POLICE INVESTIGATED THE PEDESTAL AND FOUND THE DEFENDANT'S PRINTS, PAL!
AND THOSE SAME PRINTS WERE ON THIS CELL PHONE CHARM WE FOUND INSIDE THE PEDESTAL!
SO THIS MUST BE YOURS, PAL!
SHH
AH!!
THAT MEANS THE DEFENDANT HID THE BODY INSIDE THE PEDESTAL, PAL!!
ZH
ZH
SHE HID THE BODY IN THE PEDESTAL, AND SHE WAS GOING TO TAKE IT OUT LATER, WHEN NO ONE WAS LOOKING.
BUT UNFORTUNATELY FOR HER, WHEN THE ELEVATOR STARTED UP AGAIN, THE SHAKING CAUSED THE BODY TO ROLL OUT.
ROLL
ROLL
AND IT WAS DISCOVERED ON THE FIFTH FLOOR!!
INCREDIBLE!!

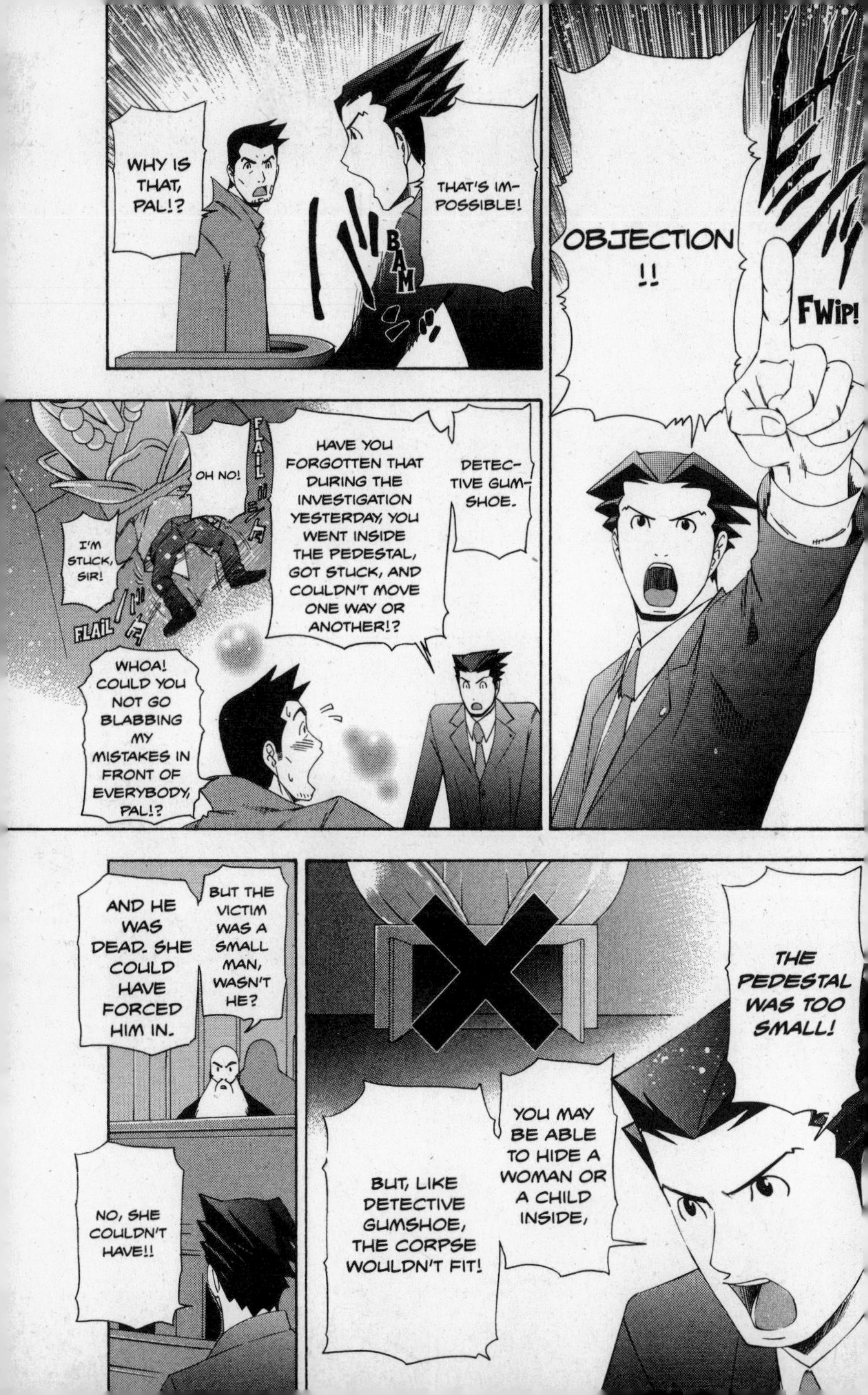
OBJECTION!!
FWIP!
THAT'S IMPOSSIBLE!
BAM
WHY IS THAT, PAL!?
DETECTIVE GUMSHOE.
HAVE YOU FORGOTTEN THAT DURING THE INVESTIGATION YESTERDAY, YOU WENT INSIDE THE PEDESTAL, GOT STUCK, AND COULDN'T MOVE ONE WAY OR ANOTHER!?
OH NO!
FLAIL
I'M STUCK, SIR!
FLAIL
WHOA! COULD YOU NOT GO BLABBING MY MISTAKES IN FRONT OF EVERYBODY, PAL!?
THE PEDESTAL WAS TOO SMALL!
YOU MAY BE ABLE TO HIDE A WOMAN OR A CHILD INSIDE,
BUT, LIKE DETECTIVE GUMSHOE, THE CORPSE WOULDN'T FIT!
BUT THE VICTIM WAS A SMALL MAN, WASN'T HE?
AND HE WAS DEAD. SHE COULD HAVE FORCED HIM IN.
NO, SHE COULDN'T HAVE!!

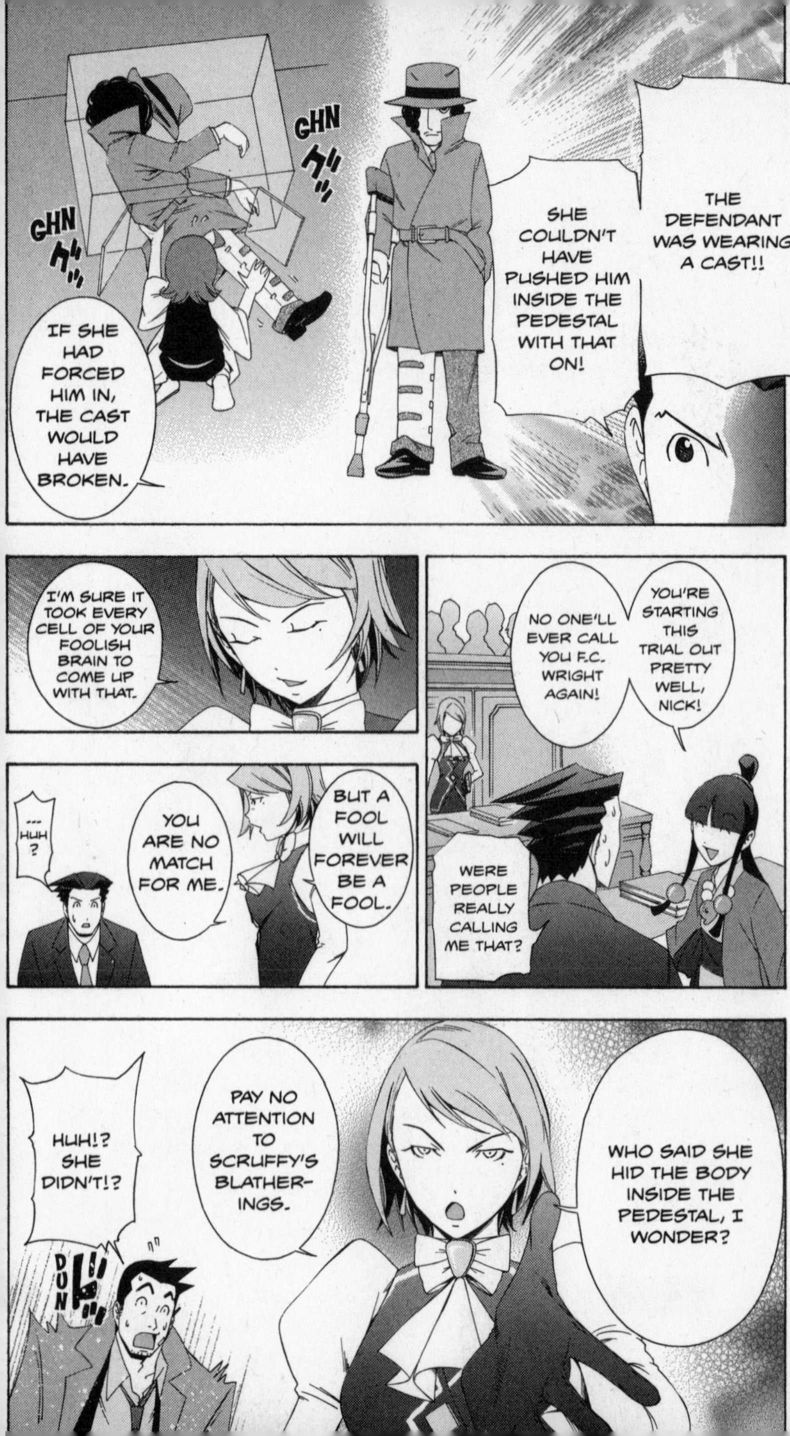
THE DEFENDANT WAS WEARING A CAST!!
SHE COULDN'T HAVE PUSHED HIM INSIDE THE PEDESTAL WITH THAT ON!
GHN
GHN
IF SHE HAD FORCED HIM IN, THE CAST WOULD HAVE BROKEN.
YOU'RE STARTING THIS TRIAL OUT PRETTY WELL, NICK!
NO ONE'LL EVER CALL YOU F.C. WRIGHT AGAIN!
WERE PEOPLE REALLY CALLING ME THAT?
I'M SURE IT TOOK EVERY CELL OF YOUR FOOLISH BRAIN TO COME UP WITH THAT.
BUT A FOOL WILL FOREVER BE A FOOL.
YOU ARE NO MATCH FOR ME.
...HUH?
WHO SAID SHE HID THE BODY INSIDE THE PEDESTAL, I WONDER?
PAY NO ATTENTION TO SCRUFFY'S BLATHERINGS.
HUH!? SHE DIDN'T!?
DUN

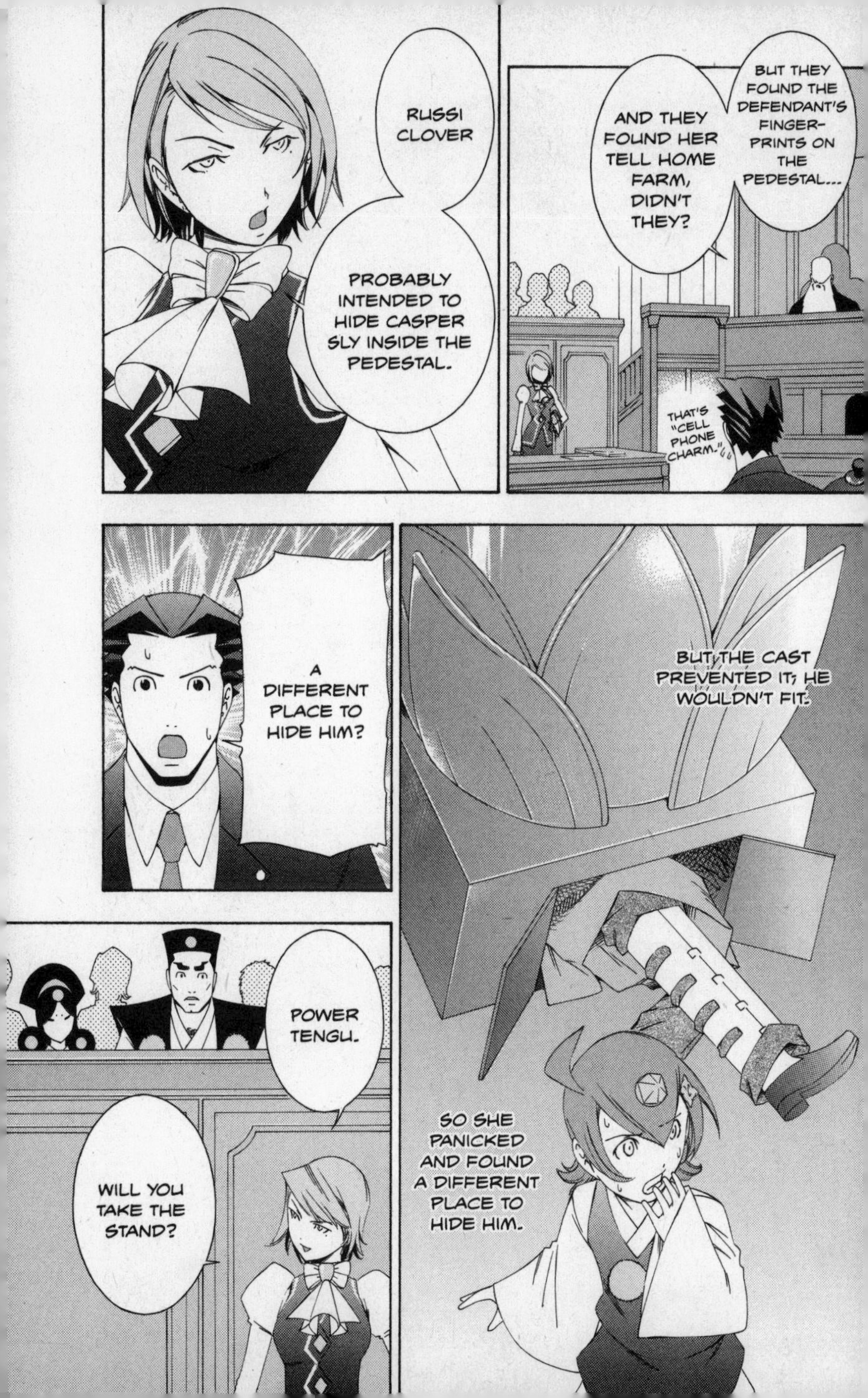
BUT THEY FOUND THE DEFENDANT'S FINGER-PRINTS ON THE PEDESTAL...
AND THEY FOUND HER TELL HOME FARM, DIDN'T THEY?
THAT'S "CELL PHONE CHARM."
RUSSI CLOVER
PROBABLY INTENDED TO HIDE CASPER SLY INSIDE THE PEDESTAL.
BUT THE CAST PREVENTED IT; HE WOULDN'T FIT.
SO SHE PANICKED AND FOUND A DIFFERENT PLACE TO HIDE HIM.
A DIFFERENT PLACE TO HIDE HIM?
POWER TENGU.
WILL YOU TAKE THE STAND?

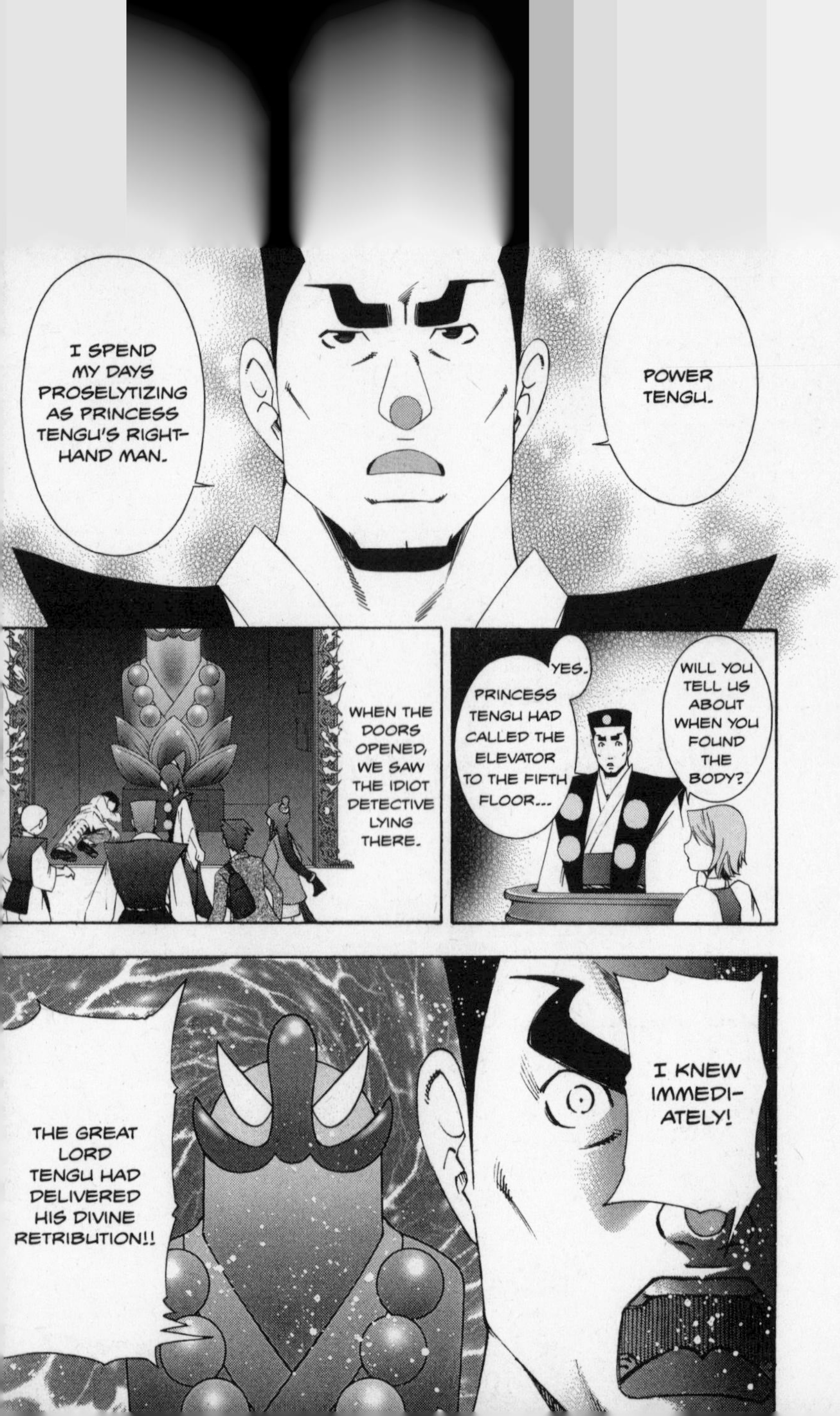
POWER TENGU.
I SPEND MY DAYS PROSELYTIZING AS PRINCESS TENGU'S RIGHT-HAND MAN.
WILL YOU TELL US ABOUT WHEN YOU FOUND THE BODY?
YES.
PRINCESS TENGU HAD CALLED THE ELEVATOR TO THE FIFTH FLOOR...
WHEN THE DOORS OPENED, WE SAW THE IDIOT DETECTIVE LYING THERE.
I KNEW IMMEDI-ATELY!
THE GREAT LORD TENGU HAD DELIVERED HIS DIVINE RETRIBUTION!!

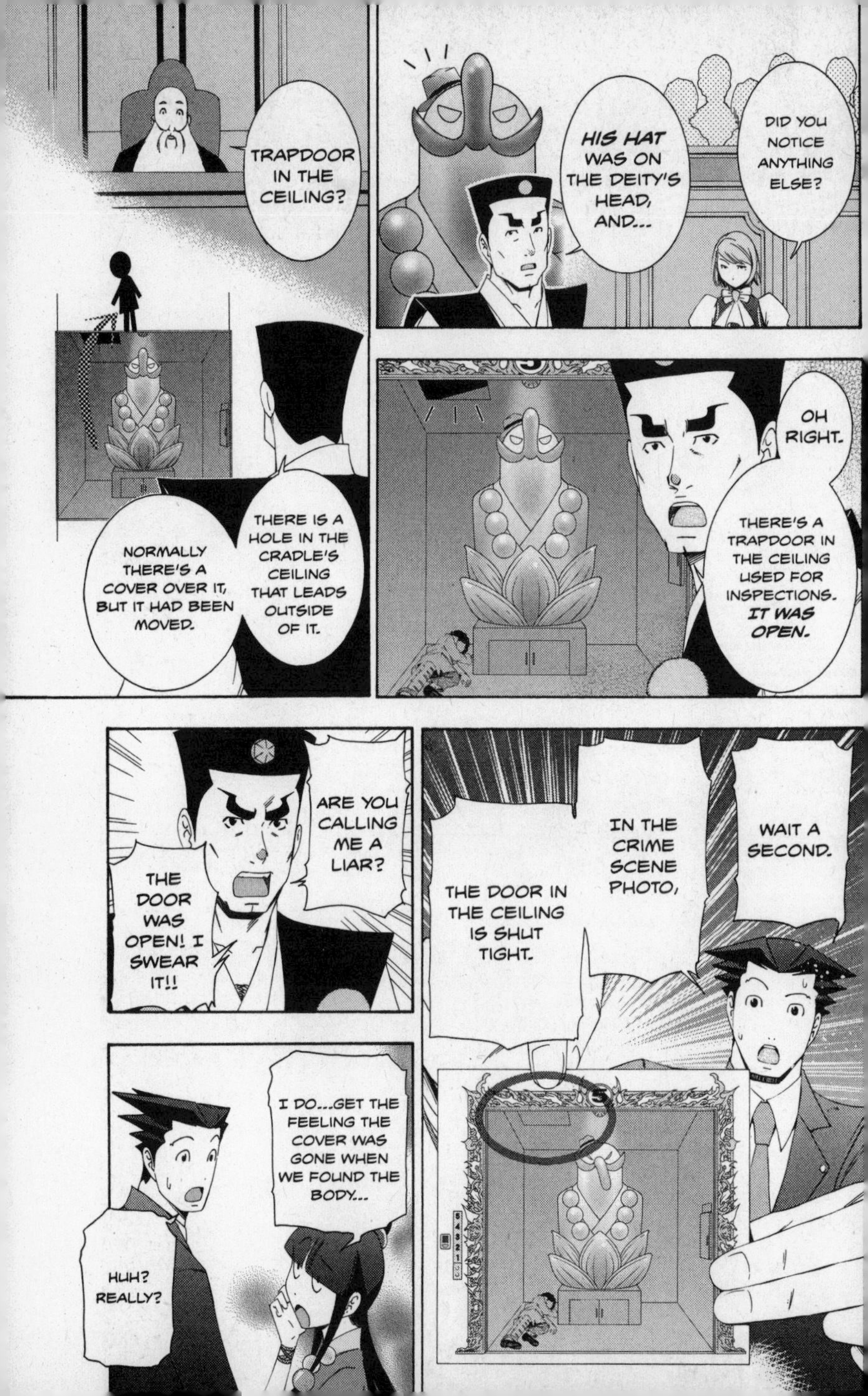
DID YOU NOTICE ANYTHING ELSE?
HIS HAT WAS ON THE DEITY'S HEAD, AND...
OH RIGHT.
THERE'S A TRAPDOOR IN THE CEILING USED FOR INSPECTIONS. IT WAS OPEN.
TRAPDOOR IN THE CEILING?
THERE IS A HOLE IN THE CRADLE'S CEILING THAT LEADS OUTSIDE OF IT.
NORMALLY THERE'S A COVER OVER IT, BUT IT HAD BEEN MOVED.
WAIT A SECOND.
IN THE CRIME SCENE PHOTO,
THE DOOR IN THE CEILING IS SHUT TIGHT.
ARE YOU CALLING ME A LIAR?
THE DOOR WAS OPEN! I SWEAR IT!!
I DO...GET THE FEELING THE COVER WAS GONE WHEN WE FOUND THE BODY...
HUH? REALLY?

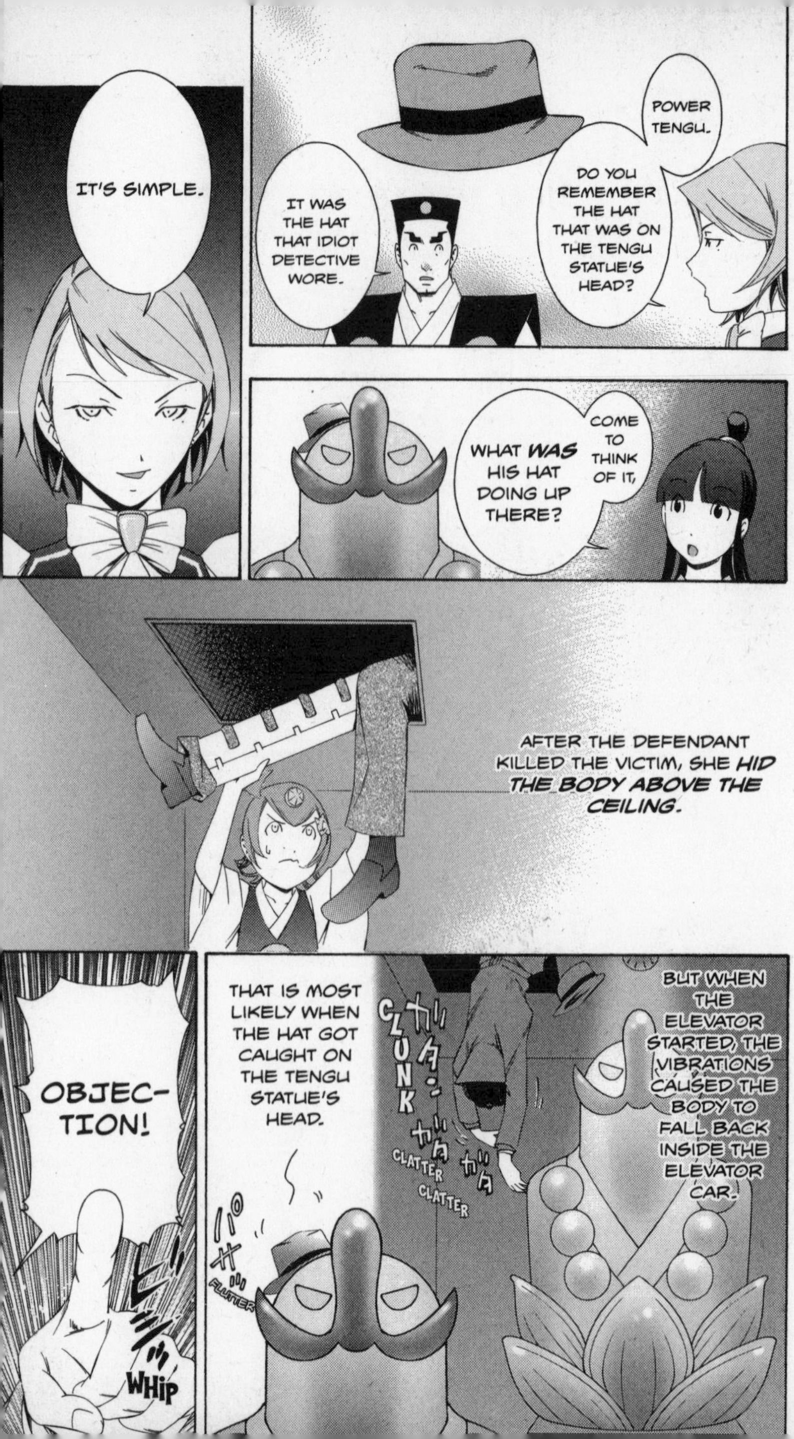
POWER TENGU.
DO YOU REMEMBER THE HAT THAT WAS ON THE TENGU STATUE'S HEAD?
IT WAS THE HAT THAT IDIOT DETECTIVE WORE.
COME TO THINK OF IT,
WHAT *WAS* HIS HAT DOING UP THERE?
IT'S SIMPLE.
AFTER THE DEFENDANT KILLED THE VICTIM, SHE *HID THE BODY ABOVE THE CEILING.*
BUT WHEN THE ELEVATOR STARTED, THE VIBRATIONS CAUSED THE BODY TO FALL BACK INSIDE THE ELEVATOR CAR.
CLUNK
CLATTER
CLATTER
THAT IS MOST LIKELY WHEN THE HAT GOT CAUGHT ON THE TENGU STATUE'S HEAD.
FLUTTER
OBJEC-TION!
WHIP

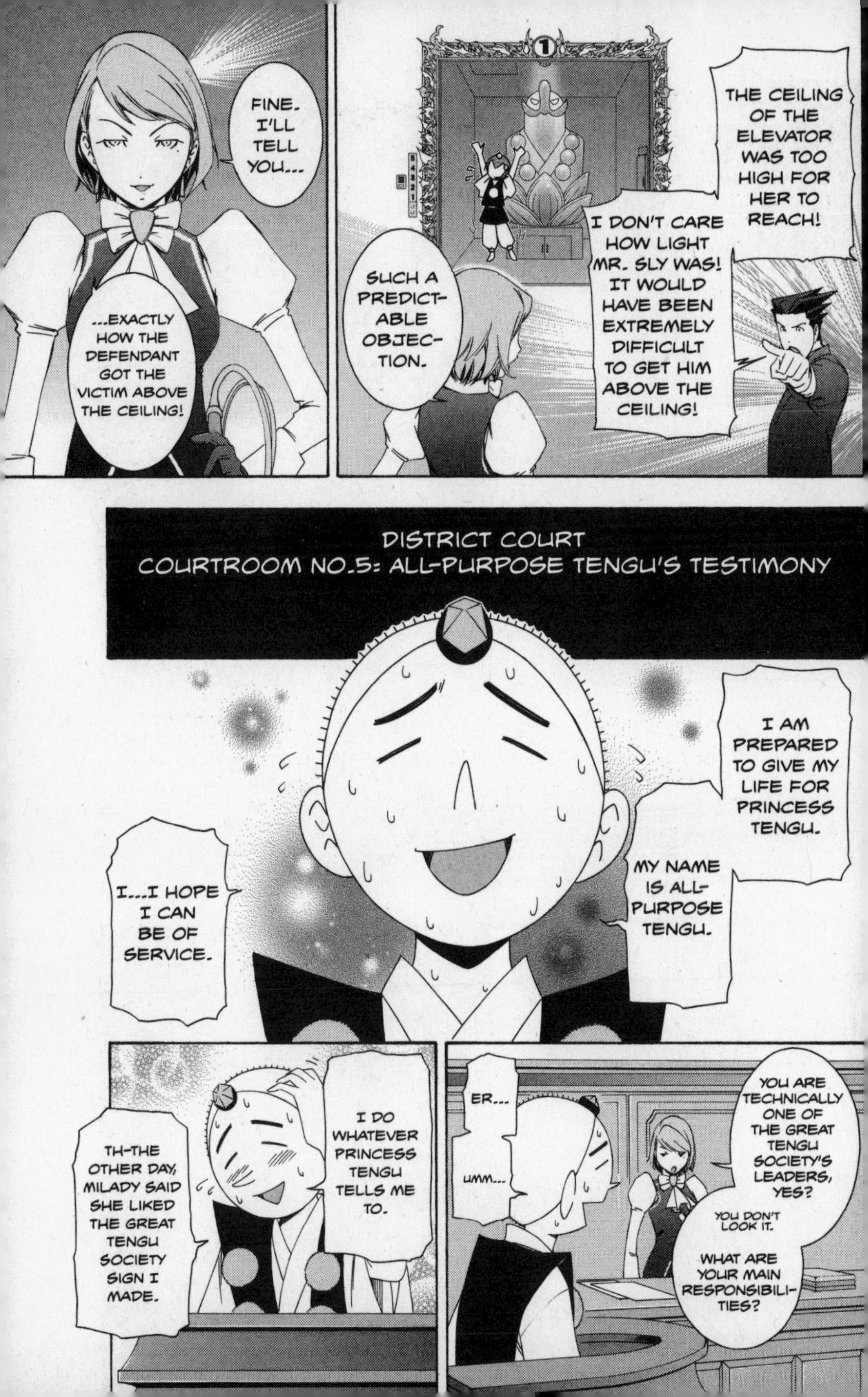
THE CEILING OF THE ELEVATOR WAS TOO HIGH FOR HER TO REACH!
I DON'T CARE HOW LIGHT MR. SLY WAS! IT WOULD HAVE BEEN EXTREMELY DIFFICULT TO GET HIM ABOVE THE CEILING!
SUCH A PREDICT-ABLE OBJEC-TION.
FINE. I'LL TELL YOU...
...EXACTLY HOW THE DEFENDANT GOT THE VICTIM ABOVE THE CEILING!
DISTRICT COURT
COURTROOM NO.5: ALL-PURPOSE TENGU'S TESTIMONY
I AM PREPARED TO GIVE MY LIFE FOR PRINCESS TENGU.
MY NAME IS ALL-PURPOSE TENGU.
I...I HOPE I CAN BE OF SERVICE.
YOU ARE TECHNICALLY ONE OF THE GREAT TENGU SOCIETY'S LEADERS, YES?
YOU DON'T LOOK IT.
WHAT ARE YOUR MAIN RESPONSIBILI-TIES?
ER...
UMM...
I DO WHATEVER PRINCESS TENGU TELLS ME TO.
TH-THE OTHER DAY, MILADY SAID SHE LIKED THE GREAT TENGU SOCIETY SIGN I MADE.

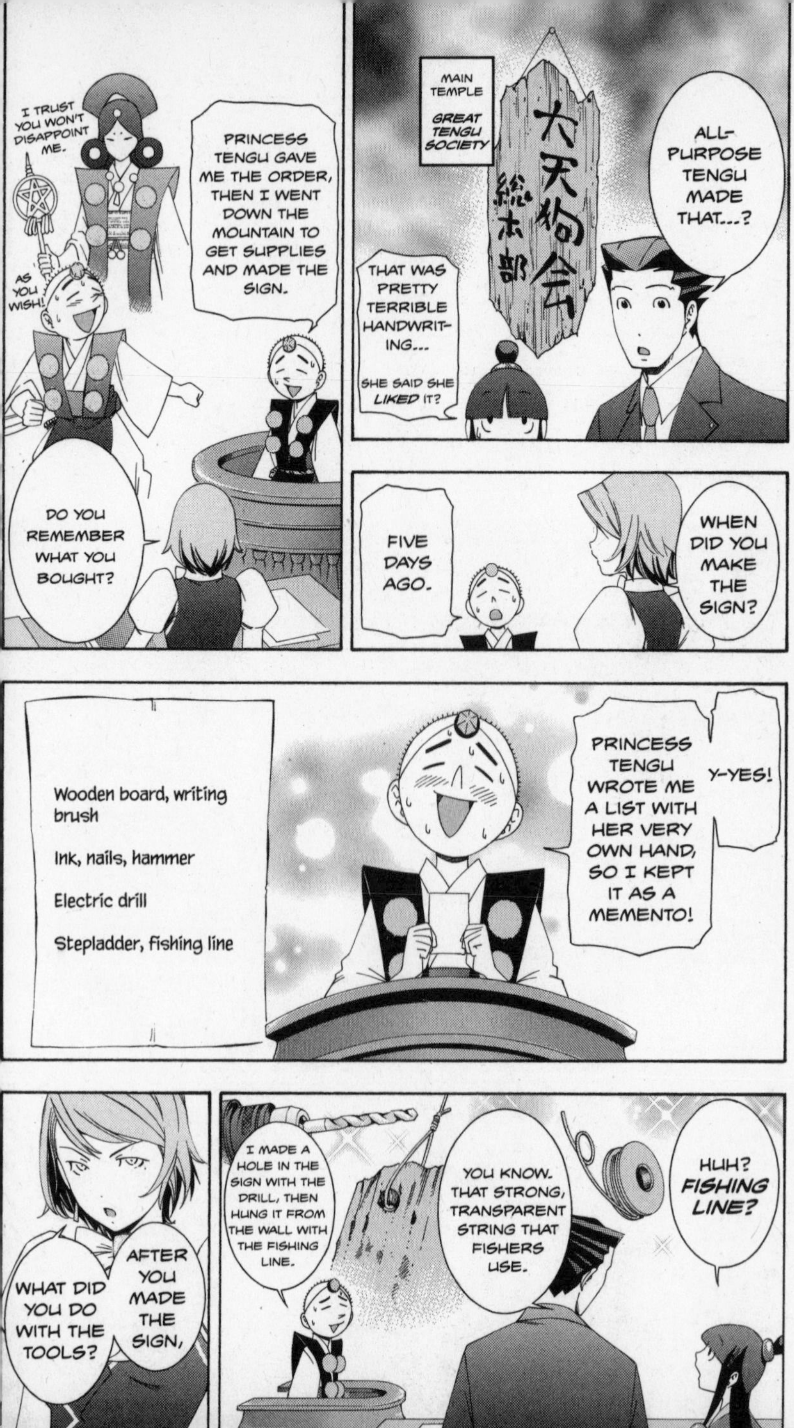
ALL-PURPOSE TENGU MADE THAT...?
大天狗会 総本部
MAIN TEMPLE
GREAT TENGU SOCIETY
THAT WAS PRETTY TERRIBLE HANDWRITING...
SHE SAID SHE *LIKED* IT?
WHEN DID YOU MAKE THE SIGN?
FIVE DAYS AGO.
PRINCESS TENGU GAVE ME THE ORDER, THEN I WENT DOWN THE MOUNTAIN TO GET SUPPLIES AND MADE THE SIGN.
I TRUST YOU WON'T DISAPPOINT ME.
AS YOU WISH!
DO YOU REMEMBER WHAT YOU BOUGHT?
Y-YES!
PRINCESS TENGU WROTE ME A LIST WITH HER VERY OWN HAND, SO I KEPT IT AS A MEMENTO!
Wooden board, writing brush
Ink, nails, hammer
Electric drill
Stepladder, fishing line
HUH? *FISHING LINE?*
YOU KNOW. THAT STRONG, TRANSPARENT STRING THAT FISHERS USE.
I MADE A HOLE IN THE SIGN WITH THE DRILL, THEN HUNG IT FROM THE WALL WITH THE FISHING LINE.
AFTER YOU MADE THE SIGN,
WHAT DID YOU DO WITH THE TOOLS?

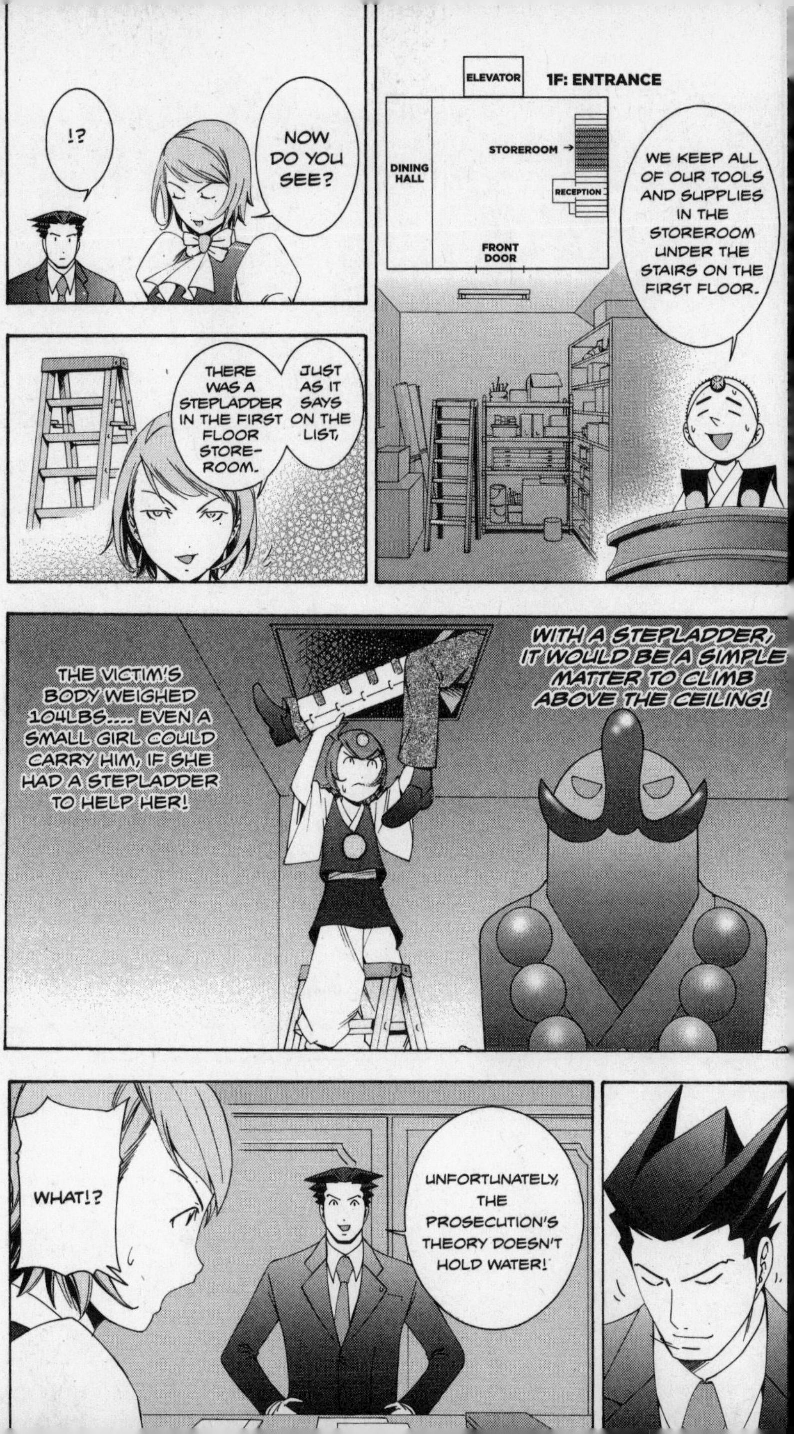
ELEVATOR
1F: ENTRANCE
STOREROOM
DINING HALL
RECEPTION
FRONT DOOR
WE KEEP ALL OF OUR TOOLS AND SUPPLIES IN THE STOREROOM UNDER THE STAIRS ON THE FIRST FLOOR.
NOW DO YOU SEE?
!?
JUST AS IT SAYS ON THE LIST,
THERE WAS A STEPLADDER IN THE FIRST FLOOR STORE-ROOM.
WITH A STEPLADDER, IT WOULD BE A SIMPLE MATTER TO CLIMB ABOVE THE CEILING!
THE VICTIM'S BODY WEIGHED 104LBS.... EVEN A SMALL GIRL COULD CARRY HIM, IF SHE HAD A STEPLADDER TO HELP HER!
UNFORTUNATELY, THE PROSECUTION'S THEORY DOESN'T HOLD WATER!
WHAT!?

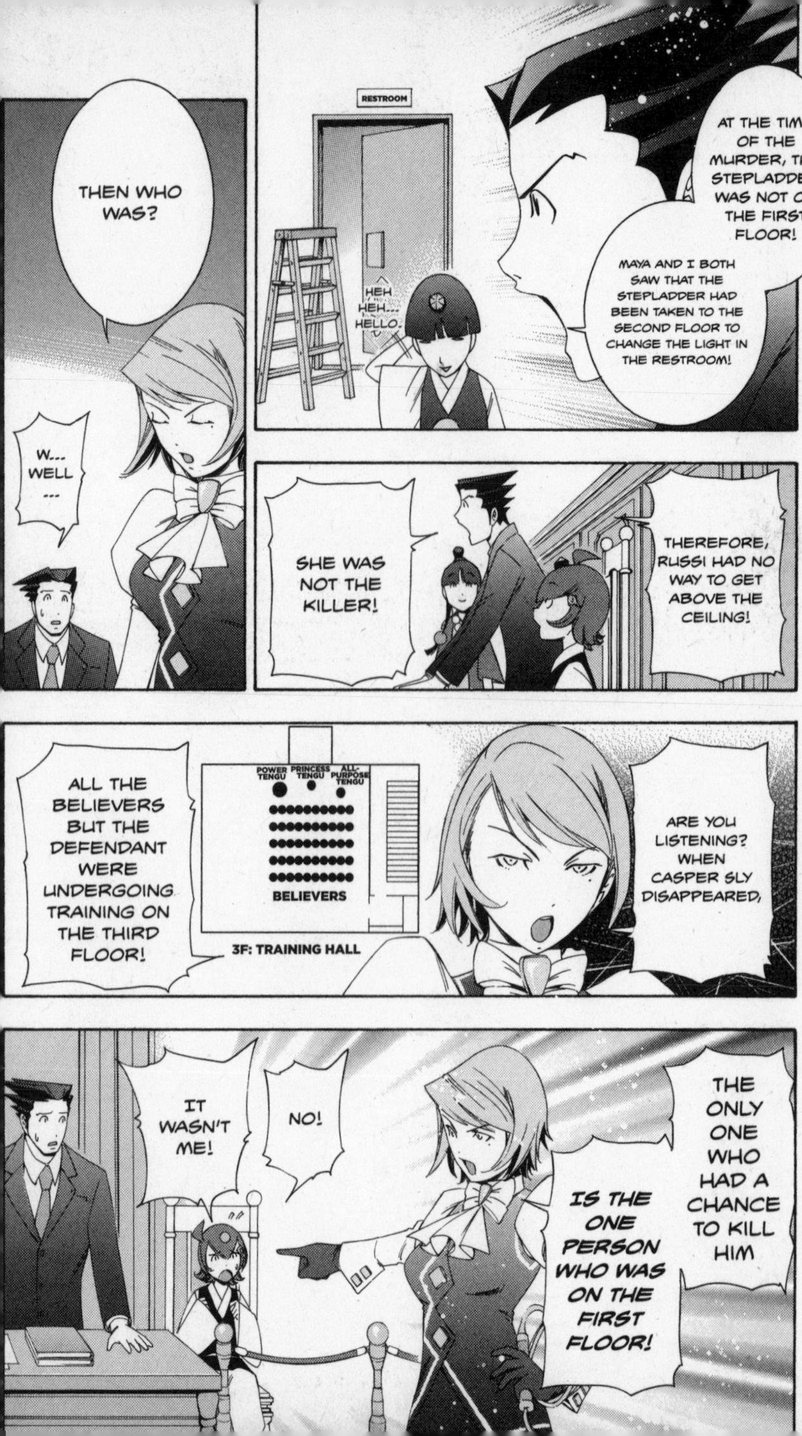
AT THE TIME OF THE MURDER, THE STEPLADDER WAS NOT ON THE FIRST FLOOR!
MAYA AND I BOTH SAW THAT THE STEPLADDER HAD BEEN TAKEN TO THE SECOND FLOOR TO CHANGE THE LIGHT IN THE RESTROOM!
RESTROOM
HEH HEH... HELLO.
THEREFORE, RUSSI HAD NO WAY TO GET ABOVE THE CEILING!
SHE WAS NOT THE KILLER!
THEN WHO WAS?
W... WELL ...
ARE YOU LISTENING? WHEN CASPER SLY DISAPPEARED,
POWER TENGU
PRINCESS TENGU
ALL-PURPOSE TENGU
BELIEVERS
3F: TRAINING HALL
ALL THE BELIEVERS BUT THE DEFENDANT WERE UNDERGOING TRAINING ON THE THIRD FLOOR!
THE ONLY ONE WHO HAD A CHANCE TO KILL HIM
IS THE ONE PERSON WHO WAS ON THE FIRST FLOOR!
NO!
IT WASN'T ME!

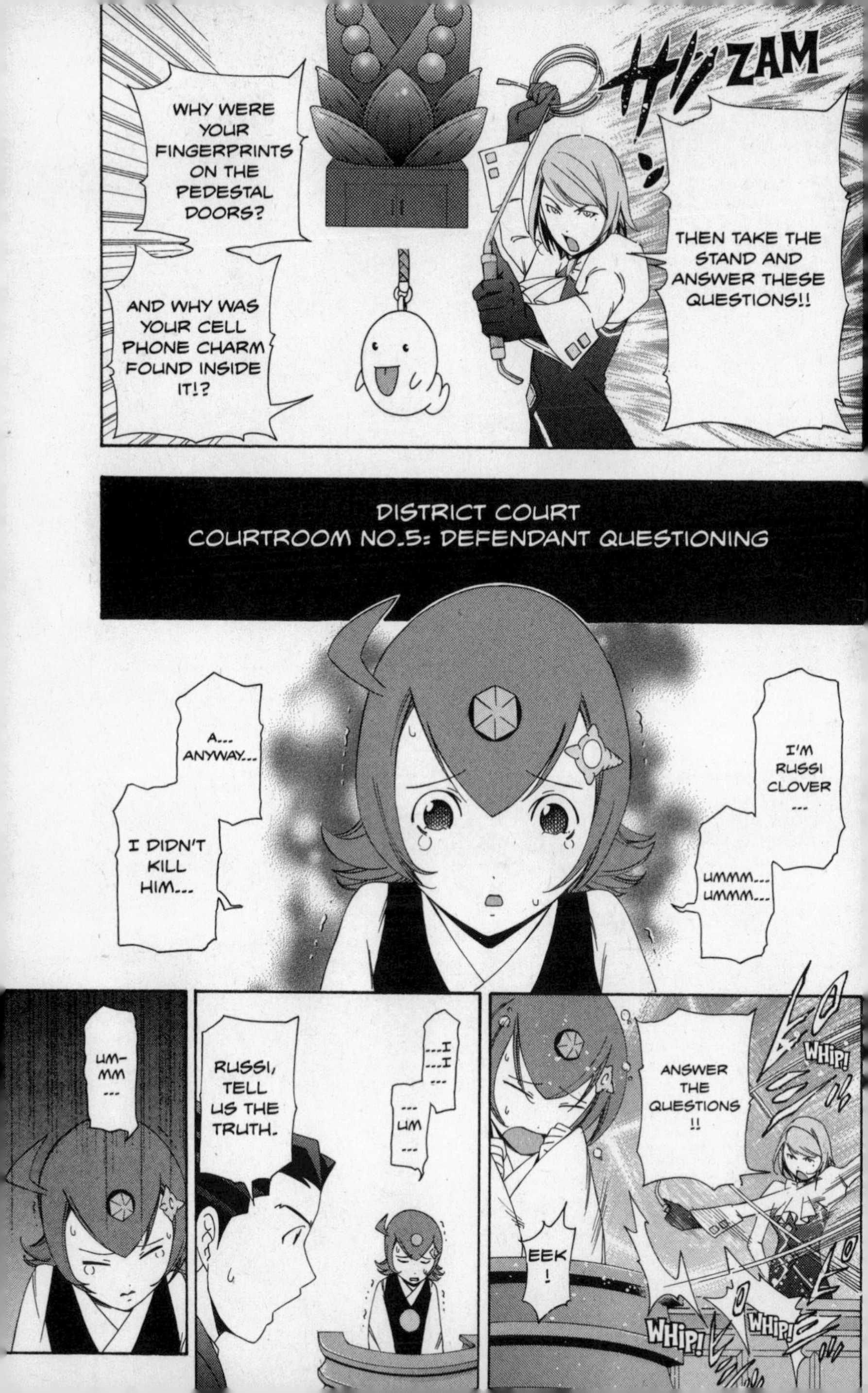
ZAM
THEN TAKE THE STAND AND ANSWER THESE QUESTIONS!!
WHY WERE YOUR FINGERPRINTS ON THE PEDESTAL DOORS?
AND WHY WAS YOUR CELL PHONE CHARM FOUND INSIDE IT!?
DISTRICT COURT
COURTROOM NO.5: DEFENDANT QUESTIONING
I'M RUSSI CLOVER ...
UMMM... UMMM...
A... ANYWAY...
I DIDN'T KILL HIM...
WHIP!
ANSWER THE QUESTIONS !!
EEK !
WHIP!
WHIP!
...I ...I ...
... UM ...
RUSSI, TELL US THE TRUTH.
UM-MM ...

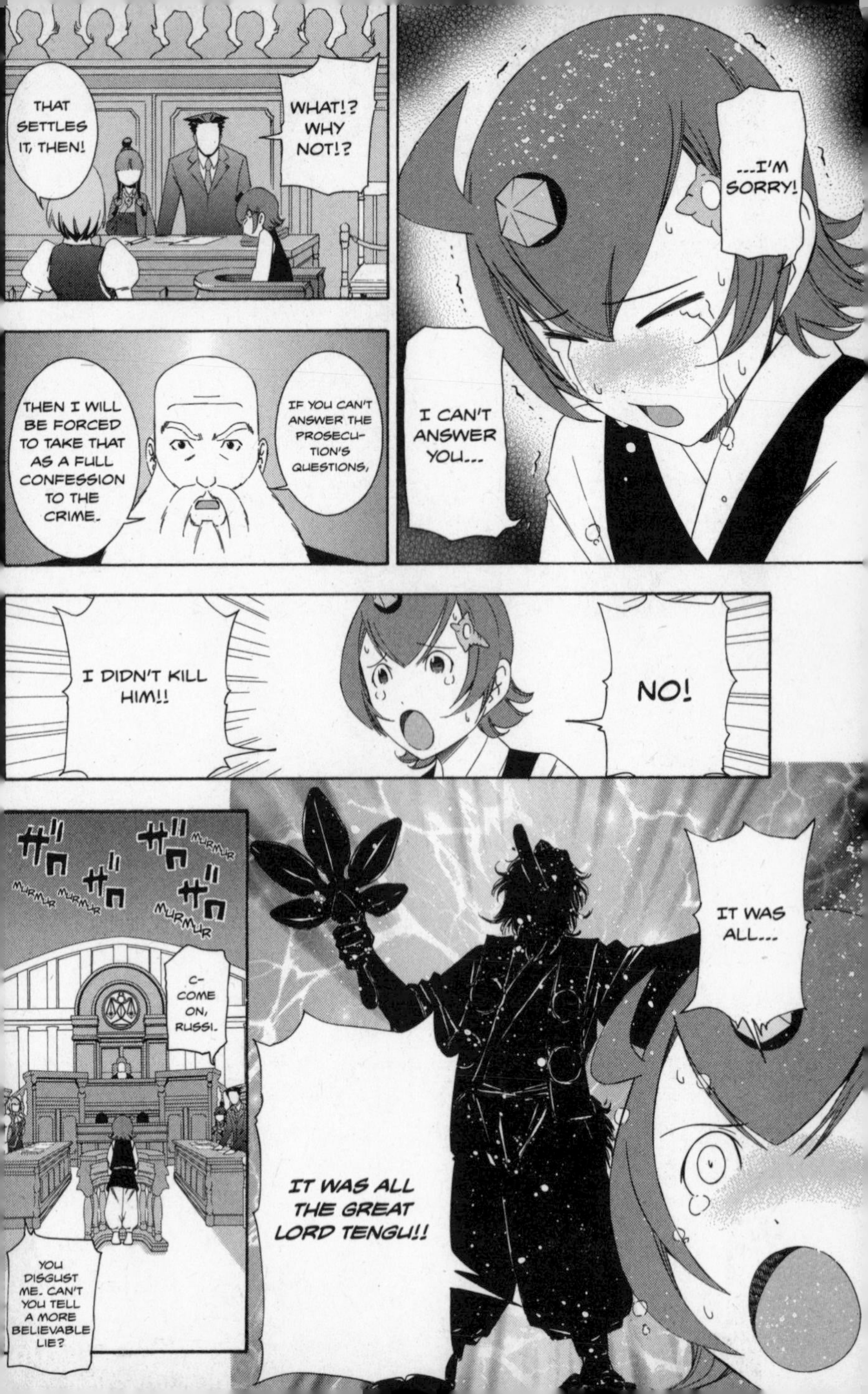
...I'M SORRY!
I CAN'T ANSWER YOU...
WHAT!? WHY NOT!?
THAT SETTLES IT, THEN!
IF YOU CAN'T ANSWER THE PROSECUTION'S QUESTIONS,
THEN I WILL BE FORCED TO TAKE THAT AS A FULL CONFESSION TO THE CRIME.
NO!
I DIDN'T KILL HIM!!
IT WAS ALL...
IT WAS ALL THE GREAT LORD TENGU!!
ザワ ザワ ザワ ザワ
MURMUR MURMUR MURMUR MURMUR
C-COME ON, RUSSI.
YOU DISGUST ME. CAN'T YOU TELL A MORE BELIEVABLE LIE?

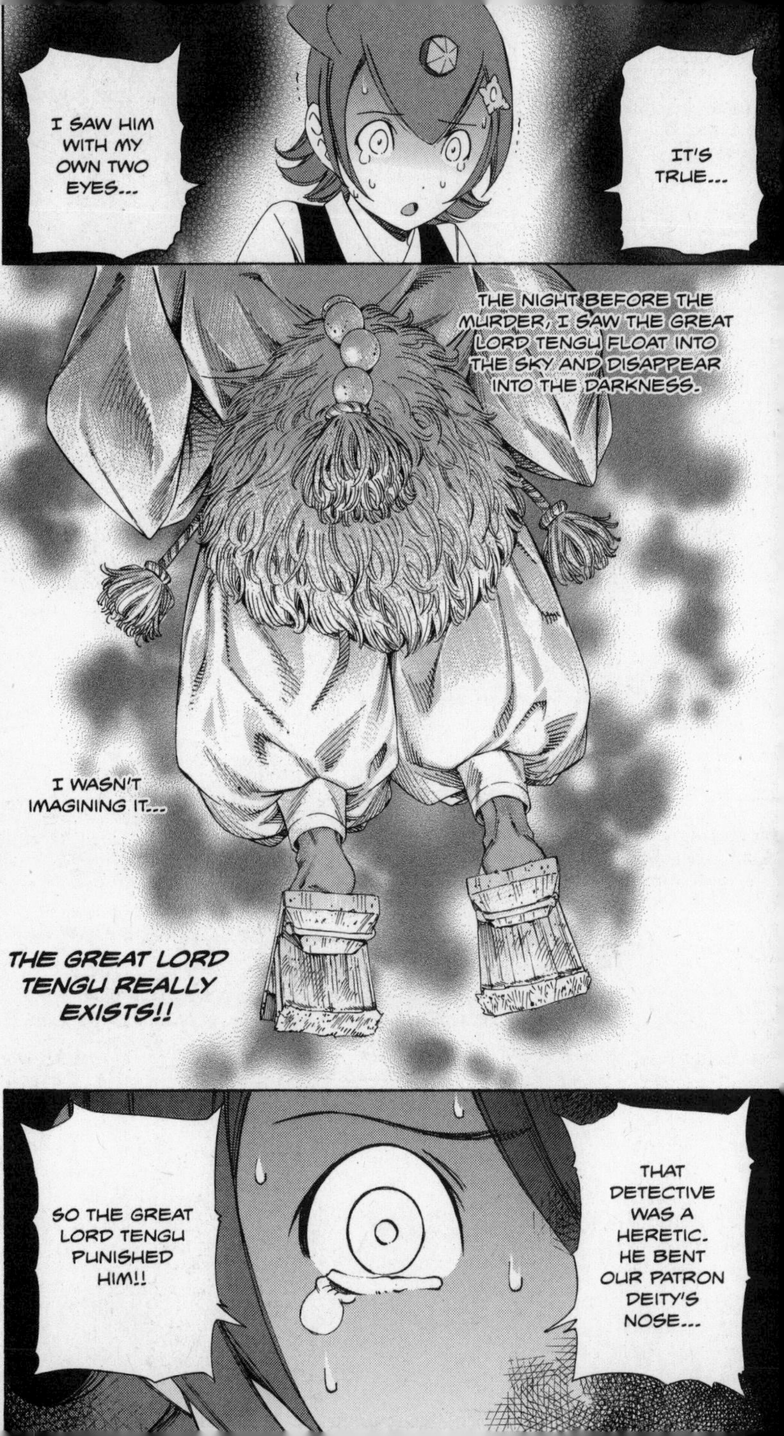
IT'S TRUE...
I SAW HIM WITH MY OWN TWO EYES...
THE NIGHT BEFORE THE MURDER, I SAW THE GREAT LORD TENGU FLOAT INTO THE SKY AND DISAPPEAR INTO THE DARKNESS.
I WASN'T IMAGINING IT...
THE GREAT LORD TENGU REALLY EXISTS!!
THAT DETECTIVE WAS A HERETIC. HE BENT OUR PATRON DEITY'S NOSE...
SO THE GREAT LORD TENGU PUNISHED HIM!!

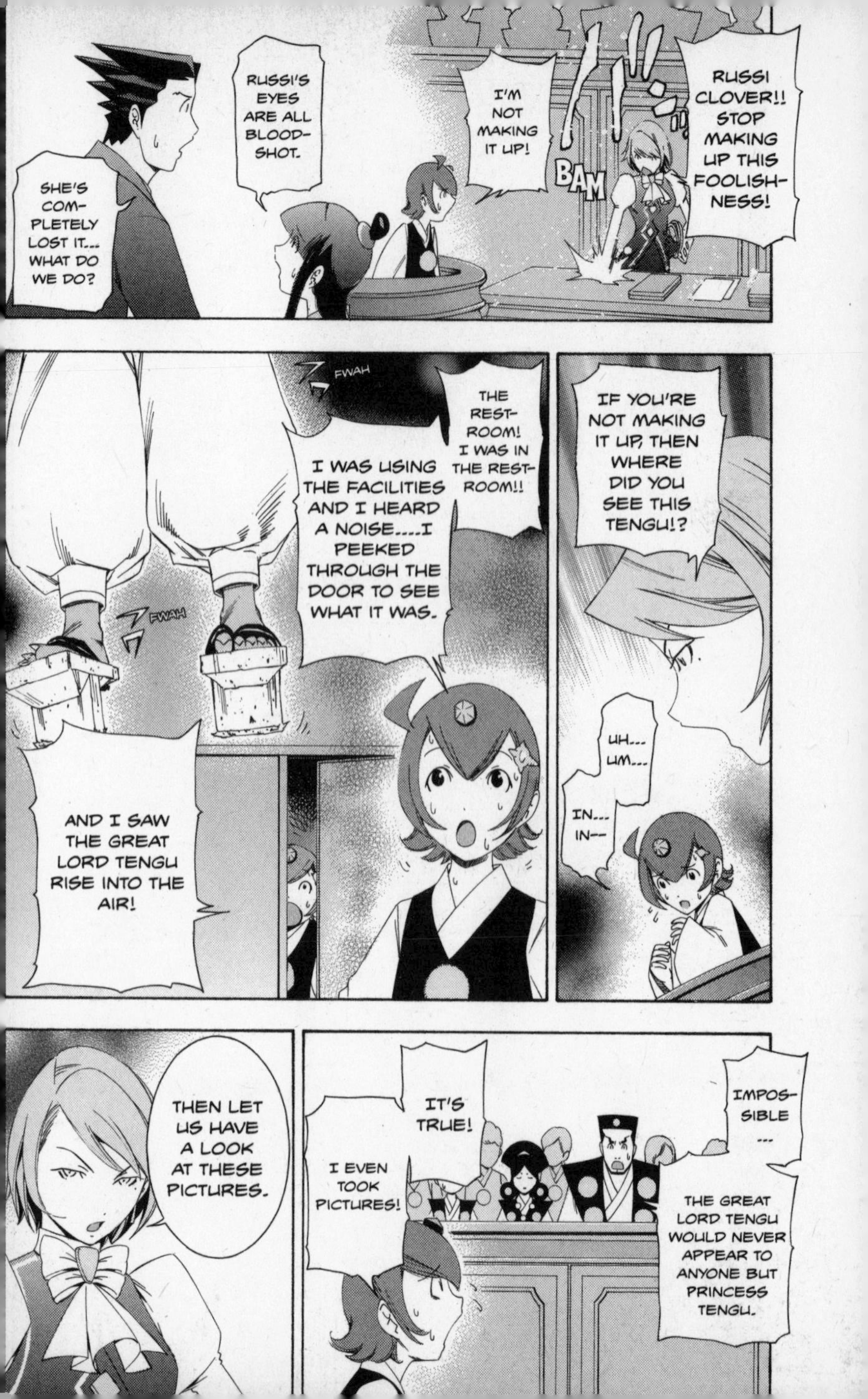
RUSSI CLOVER!! STOP MAKING UP THIS FOOLISH-NESS!
BAM
I'M NOT MAKING IT UP!
RUSSI'S EYES ARE ALL BLOOD-SHOT.
SHE'S COM-PLETELY LOST IT... WHAT DO WE DO?
IF YOU'RE NOT MAKING IT UP, THEN WHERE DID YOU SEE THIS TENGU!?
UH... UM...
IN... IN--
FWAH
THE REST-ROOM! I WAS IN THE REST-ROOM!!
I WAS USING THE FACILITIES AND I HEARD A NOISE....I PEEKED THROUGH THE DOOR TO SEE WHAT IT WAS.
FWAH
AND I SAW THE GREAT LORD TENGU RISE INTO THE AIR!
IMPOS-SIBLE ...
THE GREAT LORD TENGU WOULD NEVER APPEAR TO ANYONE BUT PRINCESS TENGU.
IT'S TRUE!
I EVEN TOOK PICTURES!
THEN LET US HAVE A LOOK AT THESE PICTURES.

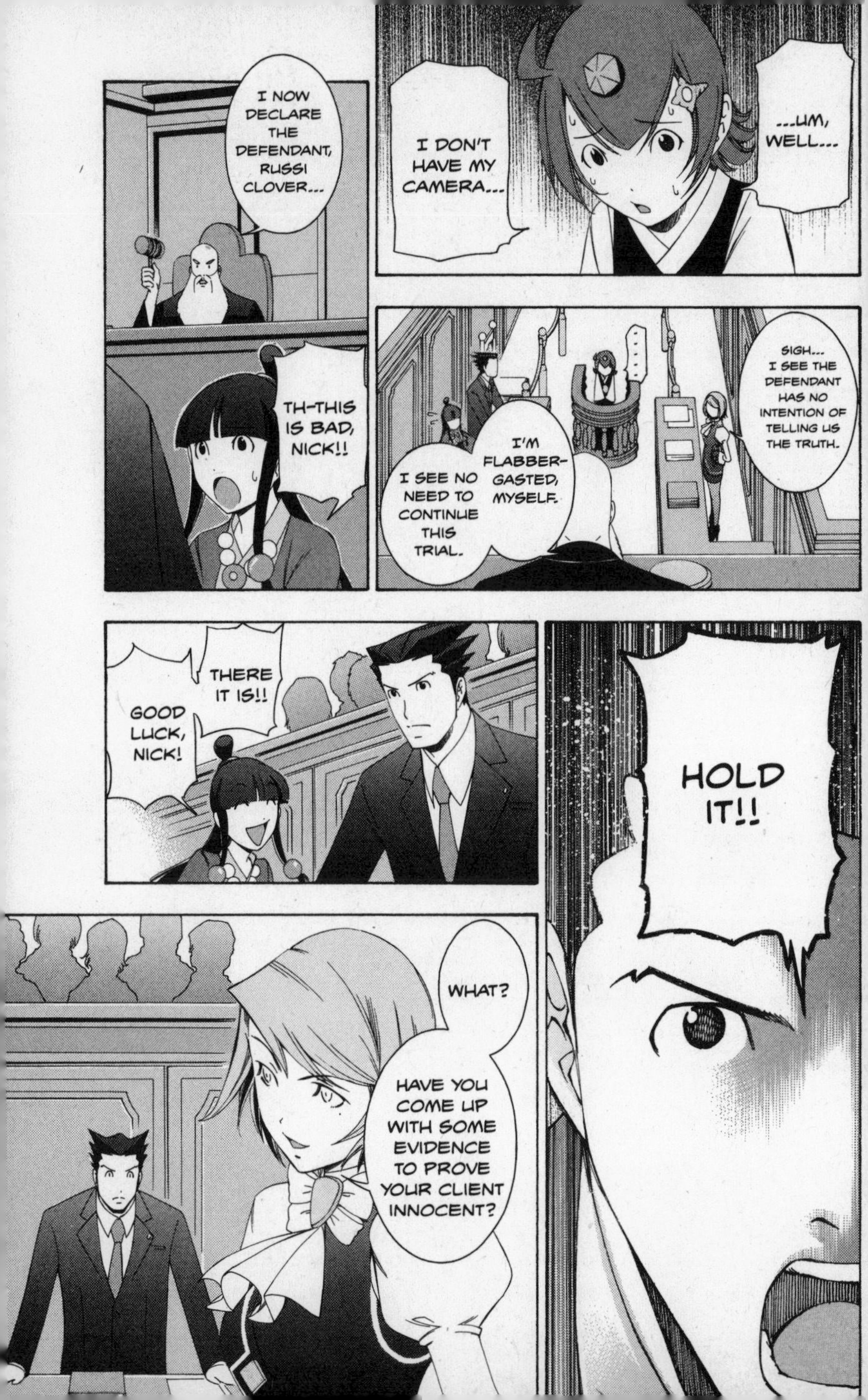
...UM, WELL...
I DON'T HAVE MY CAMERA...
I NOW DECLARE THE DEFENDANT, RUSSI CLOVER...
SIGH... I SEE THE DEFENDANT HAS NO INTENTION OF TELLING US THE TRUTH.
I'M FLABBERGASTED, MYSELF.
I SEE NO NEED TO CONTINUE THIS TRIAL.
TH-THIS IS BAD, NICK!!
HOLD IT!!
THERE IT IS!!
GOOD LUCK, NICK!
WHAT?
HAVE YOU COME UP WITH SOME EVIDENCE TO PROVE YOUR CLIENT INNOCENT?

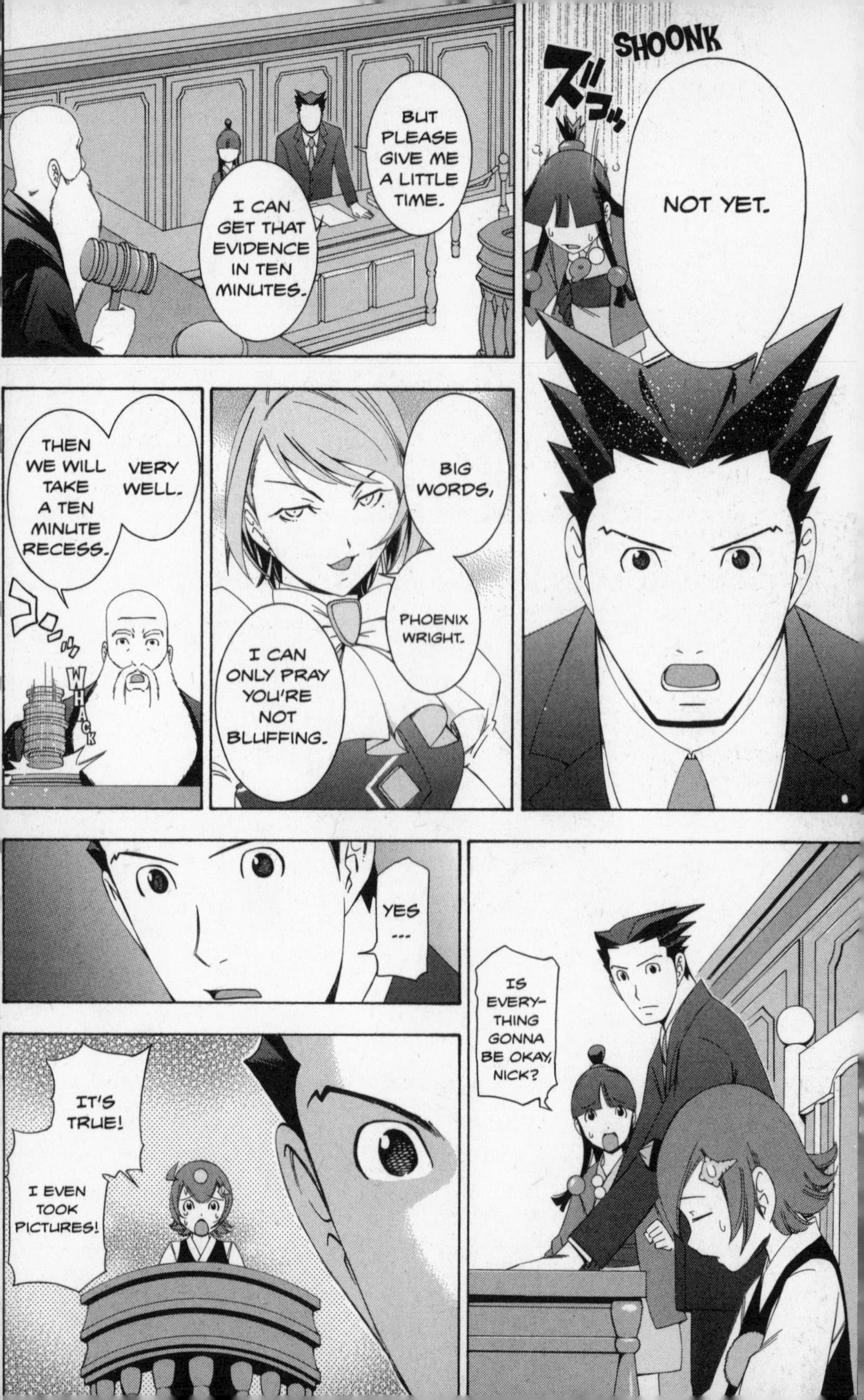
SHOONK
NOT YET.
BUT PLEASE GIVE ME A LITTLE TIME.
I CAN GET THAT EVIDENCE IN TEN MINUTES.
BIG WORDS,
PHOENIX WRIGHT.
I CAN ONLY PRAY YOU'RE NOT BLUFFING.
VERY WELL.
THEN WE WILL TAKE A TEN MINUTE RECESS.
WHACK
IS EVERY-THING GONNA BE OKAY, NICK?
YES ...
IT'S TRUE!
I EVEN TOOK PICTURES!

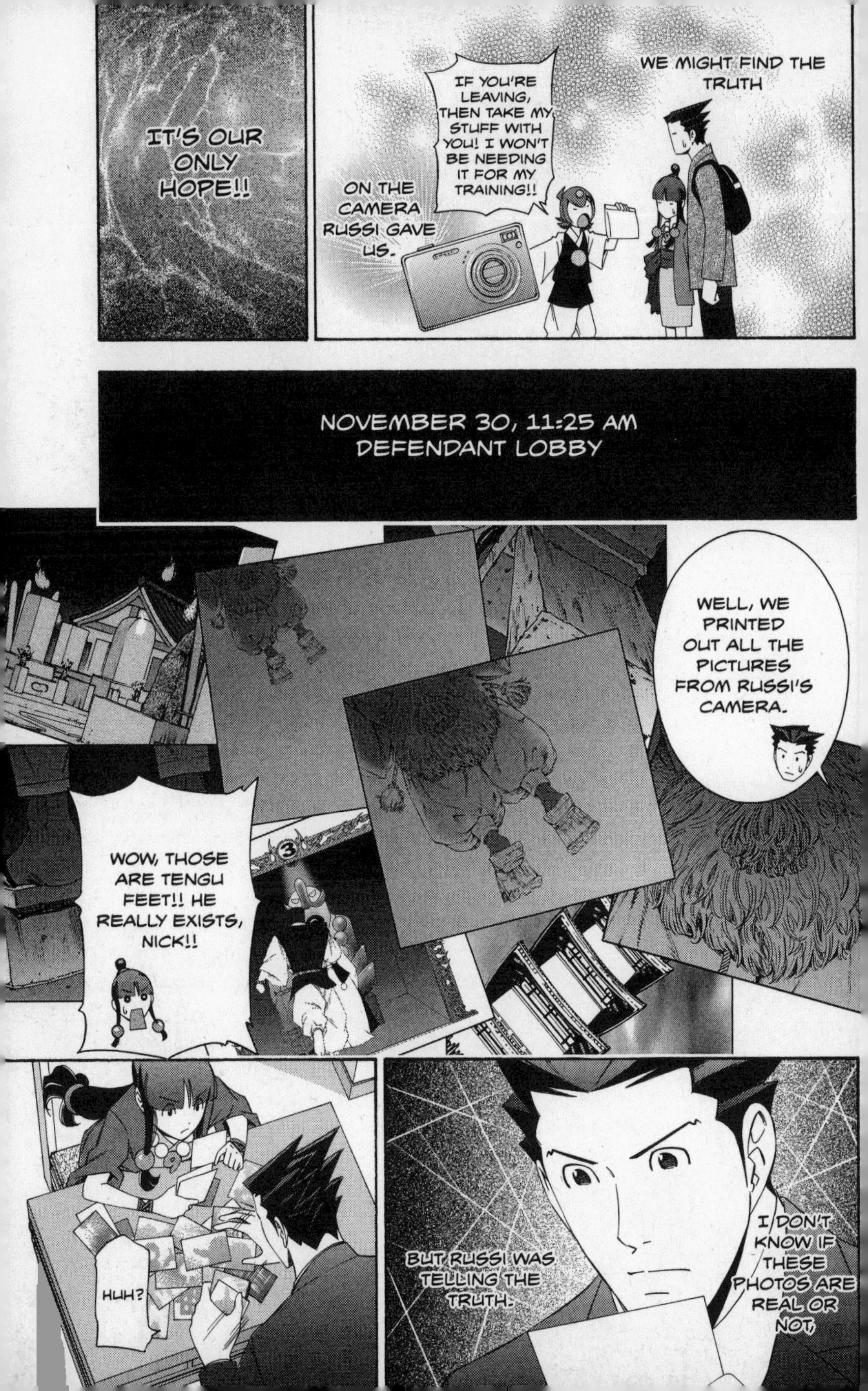
WE MIGHT FIND THE TRUTH
IF YOU'RE LEAVING, THEN TAKE MY STUFF WITH YOU! I WON'T BE NEEDING IT FOR MY TRAINING!!
ON THE CAMERA RUSSI GAVE US.
IT'S OUR ONLY HOPE!!
NOVEMBER 30, 11:25 AM
DEFENDANT LOBBY
WELL, WE PRINTED OUT ALL THE PICTURES FROM RUSSI'S CAMERA.
WOW, THOSE ARE TENGU FEET!! HE REALLY EXISTS, NICK!!
I DON'T KNOW IF THESE PHOTOS ARE REAL OR NOT,
BUT RUSSI WAS TELLING THE TRUTH.
HUH?

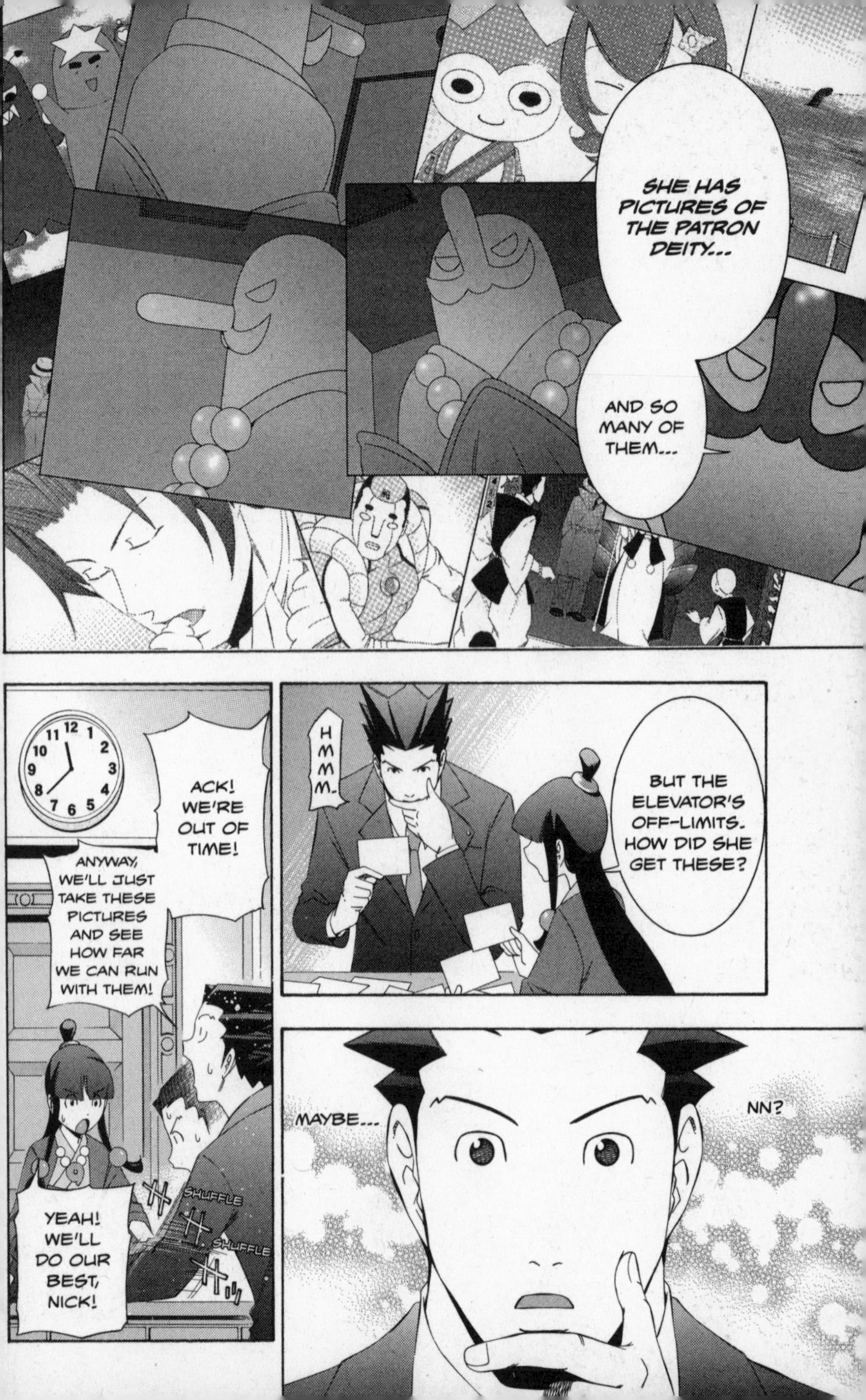
SHE HAS PICTURES OF THE PATRON DEITY...
AND SO MANY OF THEM...
BUT THE ELEVATOR'S OFF-LIMITS. HOW DID SHE GET THESE?
HMMM.
NN?
MAYBE...
ACK! WE'RE OUT OF TIME!
ANYWAY, WE'LL JUST TAKE THESE PICTURES AND SEE HOW FAR WE CAN RUN WITH THEM!
SHUFFLE
SHUFFLE
YEAH! WE'LL DO OUR BEST, NICK!

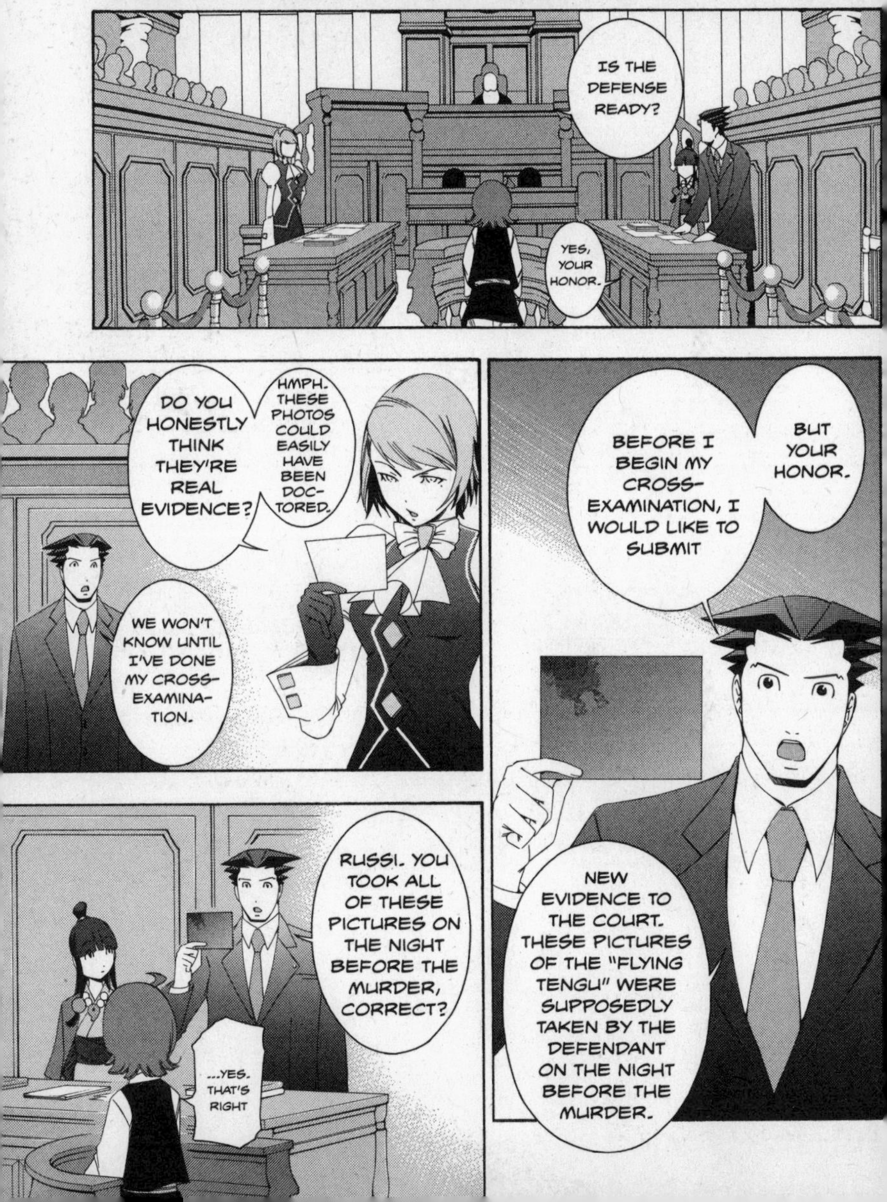
IS THE DEFENSE READY?
YES, YOUR HONOR.
BUT YOUR HONOR.
BEFORE I BEGIN MY CROSS-EXAMINATION, I WOULD LIKE TO SUBMIT
NEW EVIDENCE TO THE COURT. THESE PICTURES OF THE "FLYING TENGU" WERE SUPPOSEDLY TAKEN BY THE DEFENDANT ON THE NIGHT BEFORE THE MURDER.
HMPH. THESE PHOTOS COULD EASILY HAVE BEEN DOCTORED.
DO YOU HONESTLY THINK THEY'RE REAL EVIDENCE?
WE WON'T KNOW UNTIL I'VE DONE MY CROSS-EXAMINATION.
RUSSI. YOU TOOK ALL OF THESE PICTURES ON THE NIGHT BEFORE THE MURDER, CORRECT?
...YES. THAT'S RIGHT

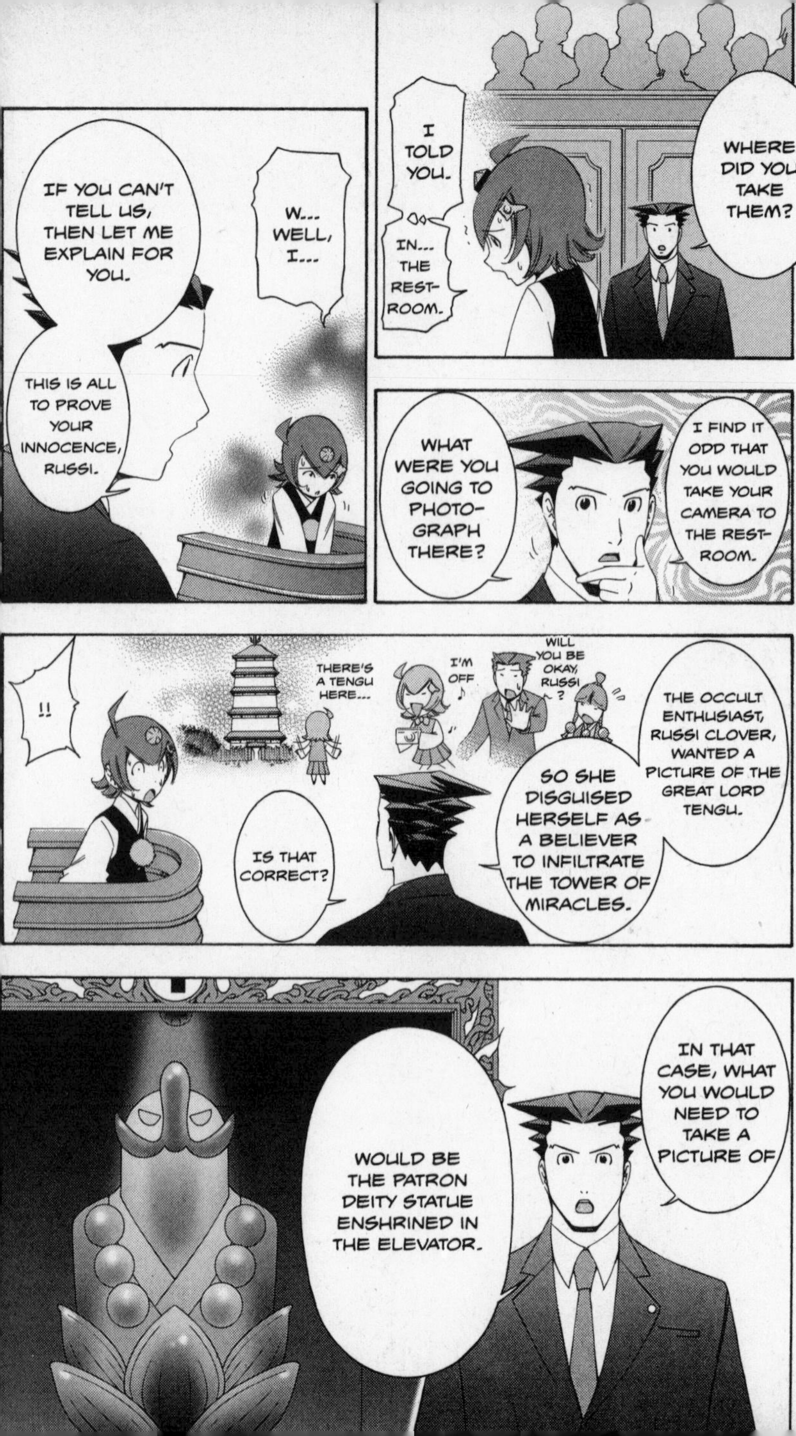
WHERE DID YOU TAKE THEM?
I TOLD YOU.
IN... THE REST-ROOM.
I FIND IT ODD THAT YOU WOULD TAKE YOUR CAMERA TO THE REST-ROOM.
WHAT WERE YOU GOING TO PHOTO-GRAPH THERE?
W... WELL, I...
IF YOU CAN'T TELL US, THEN LET ME EXPLAIN FOR YOU.
THIS IS ALL TO PROVE YOUR INNOCENCE, RUSSI.
THE OCCULT ENTHUSIAST, RUSSI CLOVER, WANTED A PICTURE OF THE GREAT LORD TENGU.
WILL YOU BE OKAY, RUSSI?
I'M OFF
THERE'S A TENGU HERE...
SO SHE DISGUISED HERSELF AS A BELIEVER TO INFILTRATE THE TOWER OF MIRACLES.
IS THAT CORRECT?
!!
IN THAT CASE, WHAT YOU WOULD NEED TO TAKE A PICTURE OF
WOULD BE THE PATRON DEITY STATUE ENSHRINED IN THE ELEVATOR.

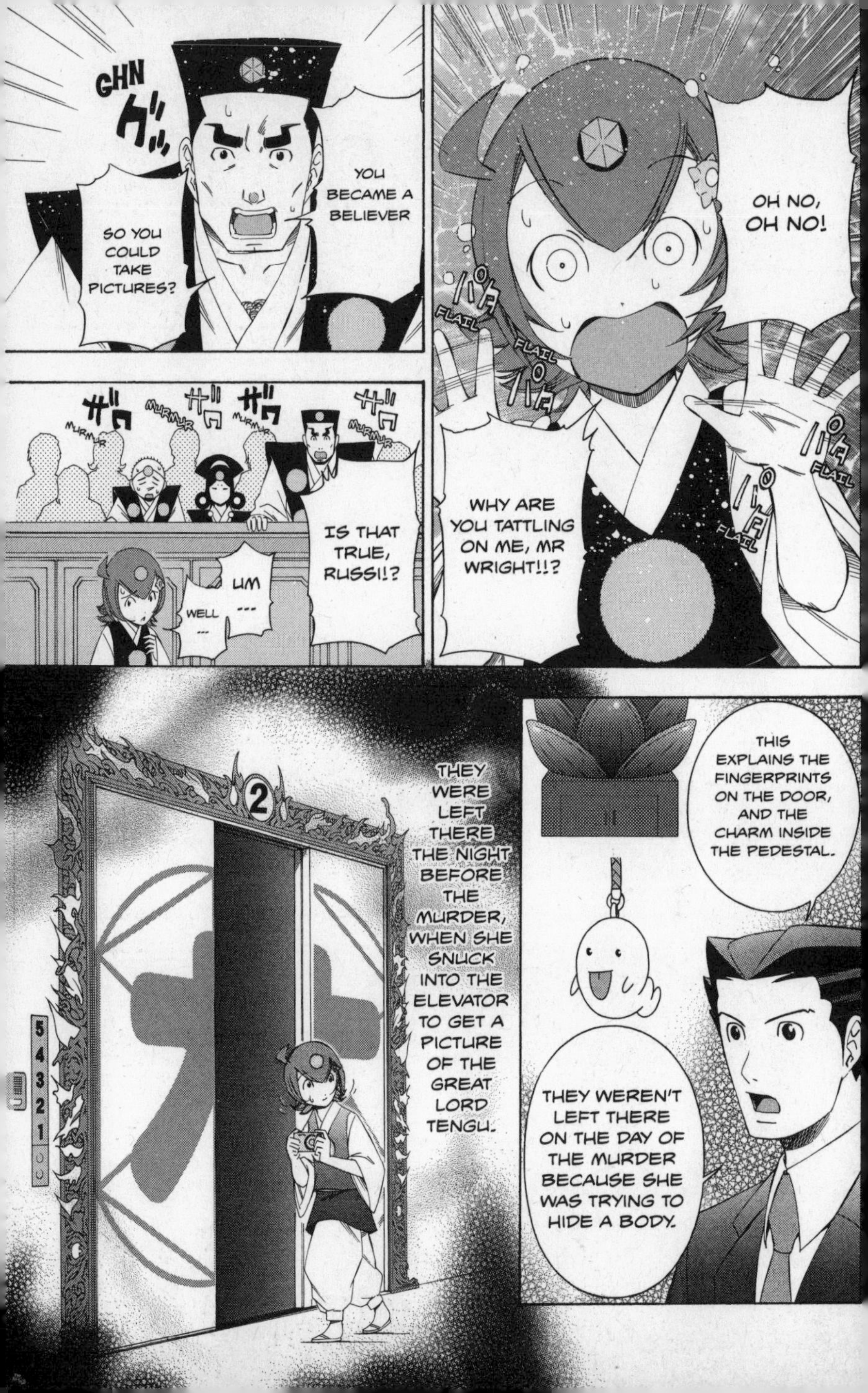
OH NO, OH NO!
パタ
FLAIL
FLAIL
パタ
パタ
FLAIL
パタ
FLAIL
WHY ARE YOU TATTLING ON ME, MR WRIGHT!!?
GHN
グッ
YOU BECAME A BELIEVER
SO YOU COULD TAKE PICTURES?
ザワ
MURMUR
ザワ
MURMUR
ザワ
MURMUR
ザワ
MURMUR
IS THAT TRUE, RUSSI!?
UM ---
WELL ---
THIS EXPLAINS THE FINGERPRINTS ON THE DOOR, AND THE CHARM INSIDE THE PEDESTAL.
THEY WEREN'T LEFT THERE ON THE DAY OF THE MURDER BECAUSE SHE WAS TRYING TO HIDE A BODY.
THEY WERE LEFT THERE THE NIGHT BEFORE THE MURDER, WHEN SHE SNUCK INTO THE ELEVATOR TO GET A PICTURE OF THE GREAT LORD TENGU.
2
5
4
3
2
1

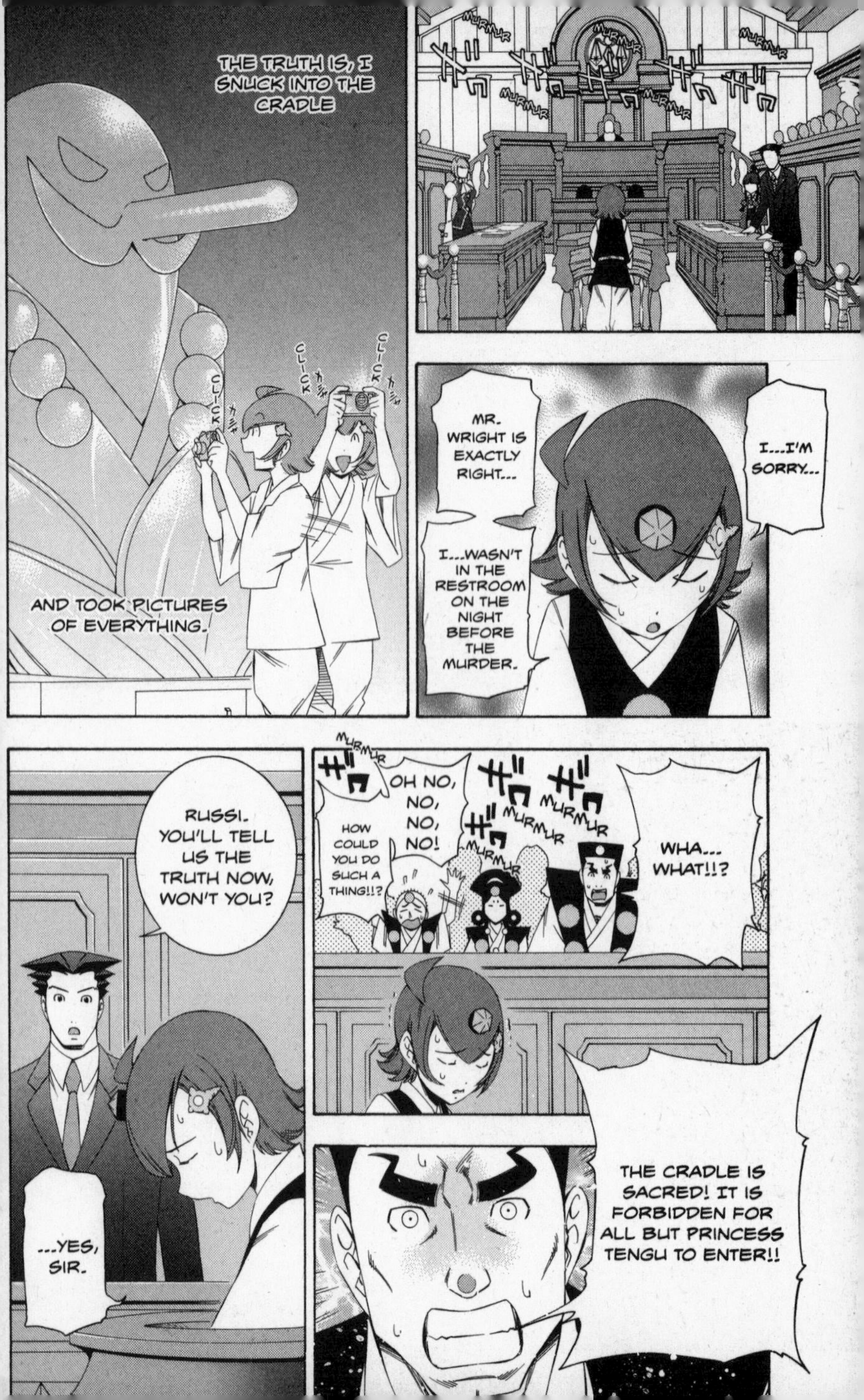
MURMUR
MURMUR
MURMUR
MURMUR
MURMUR
I...I'M SORRY...
MR. WRIGHT IS EXACTLY RIGHT...
I...WASN'T IN THE RESTROOM ON THE NIGHT BEFORE THE MURDER.
THE TRUTH IS, I SNUCK INTO THE CRADLE
CLICK
CLICK
AND TOOK PICTURES OF EVERYTHING.
WHA... WHAT!!?
MURMUR
MURMUR
MURMUR
OH NO, NO, NO, NO!
MURMUR
HOW COULD YOU DO SUCH A THING!!?
THE CRADLE IS SACRED! IT IS FORBIDDEN FOR ALL BUT PRINCESS TENGU TO ENTER!!
RUSSI. YOU'LL TELL US THE TRUTH NOW, WON'T YOU?
...YES, SIR.

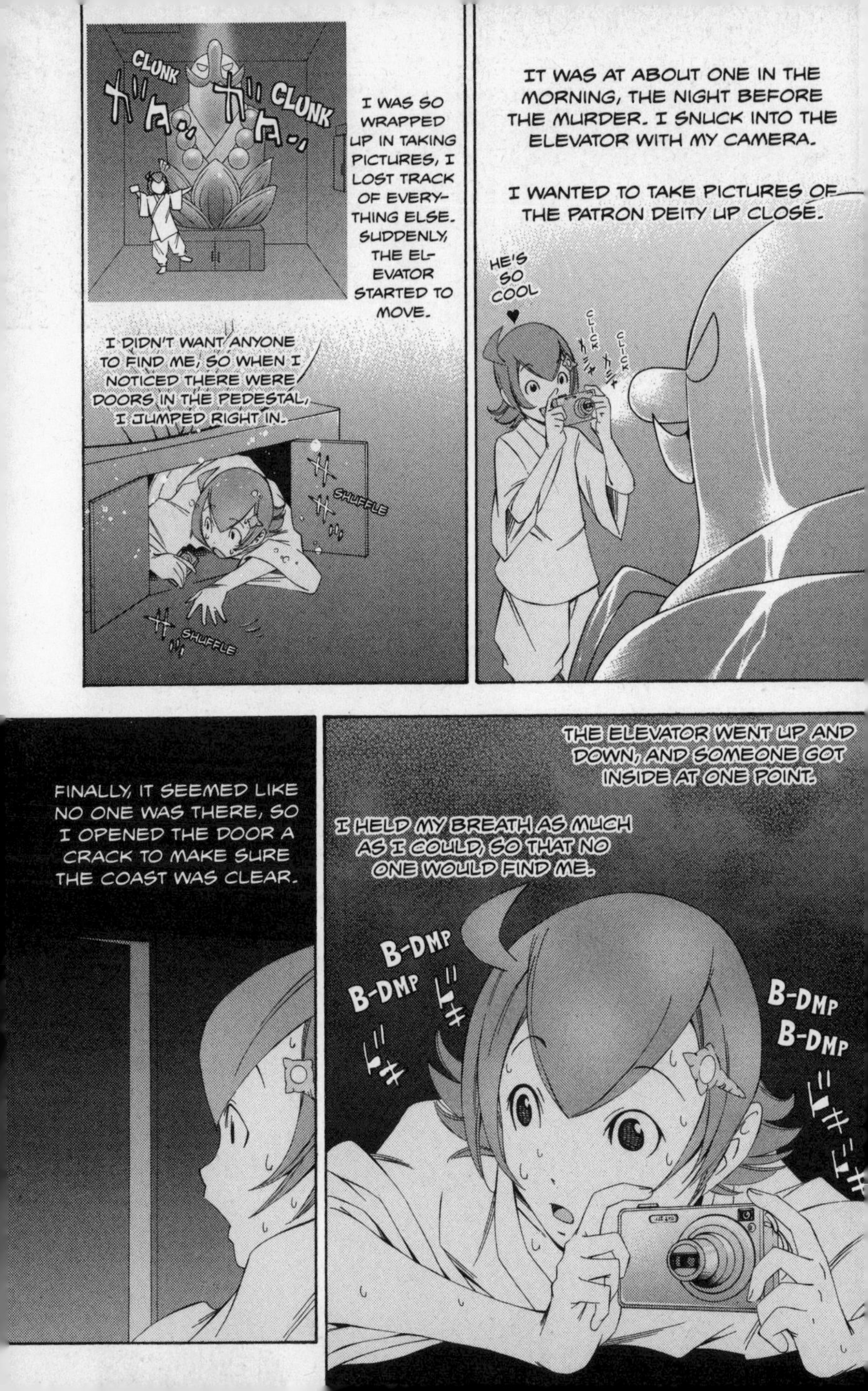
IT WAS AT ABOUT ONE IN THE MORNING, THE NIGHT BEFORE THE MURDER. I SNUCK INTO THE ELEVATOR WITH MY CAMERA.
I WANTED TO TAKE PICTURES OF THE PATRON DEITY UP CLOSE.
HE'S SO COOL ♥
CLICK
CLICK
CLUNK
CLUNK
I WAS SO WRAPPED UP IN TAKING PICTURES, I LOST TRACK OF EVERY-THING ELSE. SUDDENLY, THE EL-EVATOR STARTED TO MOVE.
I DIDN'T WANT ANYONE TO FIND ME, SO WHEN I NOTICED THERE WERE DOORS IN THE PEDESTAL, I JUMPED RIGHT IN.
SHUFFLE
SHUFFLE
THE ELEVATOR WENT UP AND DOWN, AND SOMEONE GOT INSIDE AT ONE POINT.
I HELD MY BREATH AS MUCH AS I COULD, SO THAT NO ONE WOULD FIND ME.
B-DMP
B-DMP
B-DMP
B-DMP
FINALLY, IT SEEMED LIKE NO ONE WAS THERE, SO I OPENED THE DOOR A CRACK TO MAKE SURE THE COAST WAS CLEAR.

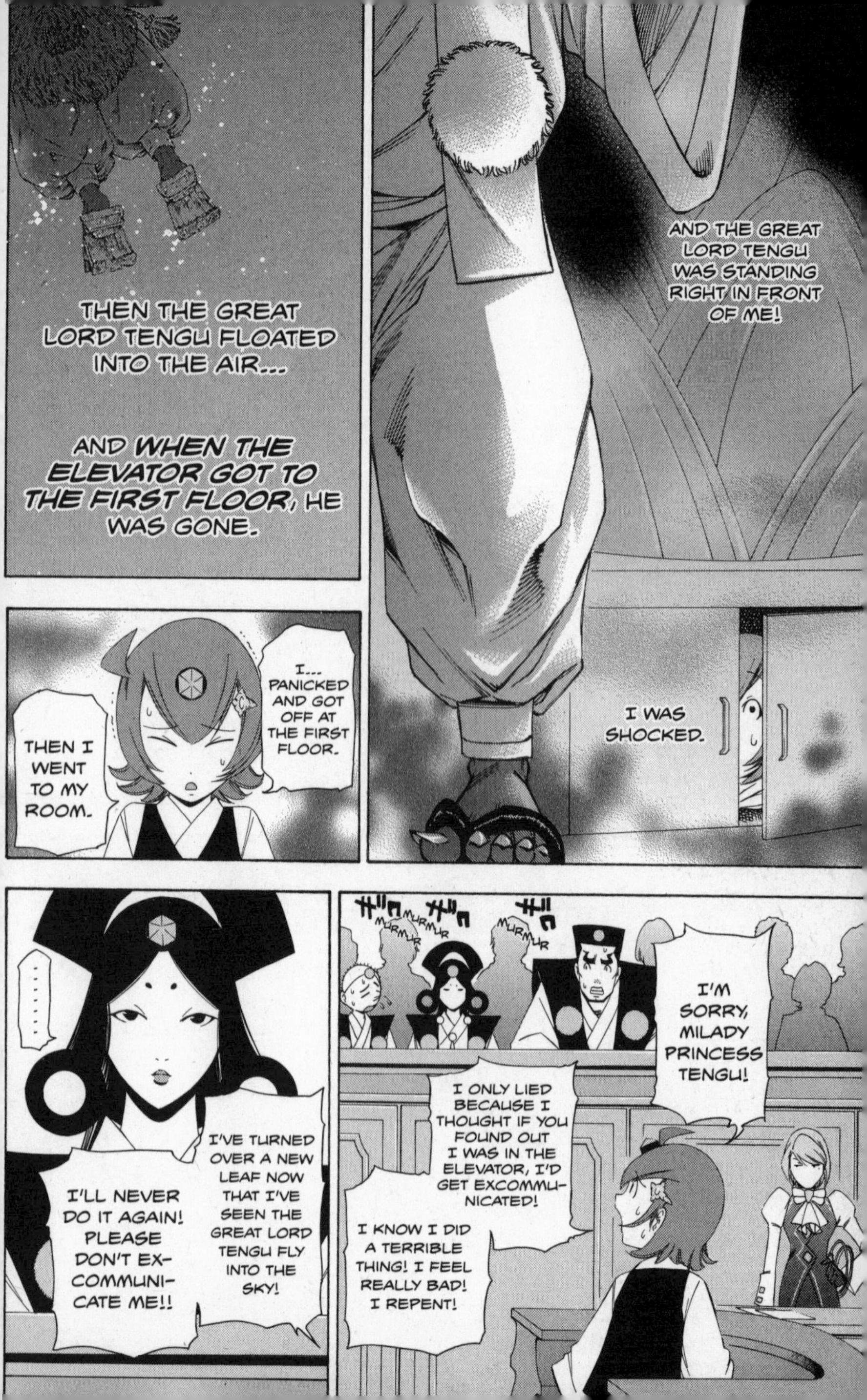
AND THE GREAT LORD TENGU WAS STANDING RIGHT IN FRONT OF ME!
I WAS SHOCKED.
THEN THE GREAT LORD TENGU FLOATED INTO THE AIR...
AND WHEN THE ELEVATOR GOT TO THE FIRST FLOOR, HE WAS GONE.
I... PANICKED AND GOT OFF AT THE FIRST FLOOR.
THEN I WENT TO MY ROOM.
MURMUR MURMUR
MURMUR
I'M SORRY, MILADY PRINCESS TENGU!
I ONLY LIED BECAUSE I THOUGHT IF YOU FOUND OUT I WAS IN THE ELEVATOR, I'D GET EXCOMMUNICATED!
I KNOW I DID A TERRIBLE THING! I FEEL REALLY BAD! I REPENT!
....
I'VE TURNED OVER A NEW LEAF NOW THAT I'VE SEEN THE GREAT LORD TENGU FLY INTO THE SKY!
I'LL NEVER DO IT AGAIN! PLEASE DON'T EXCOMMUNICATE ME!!

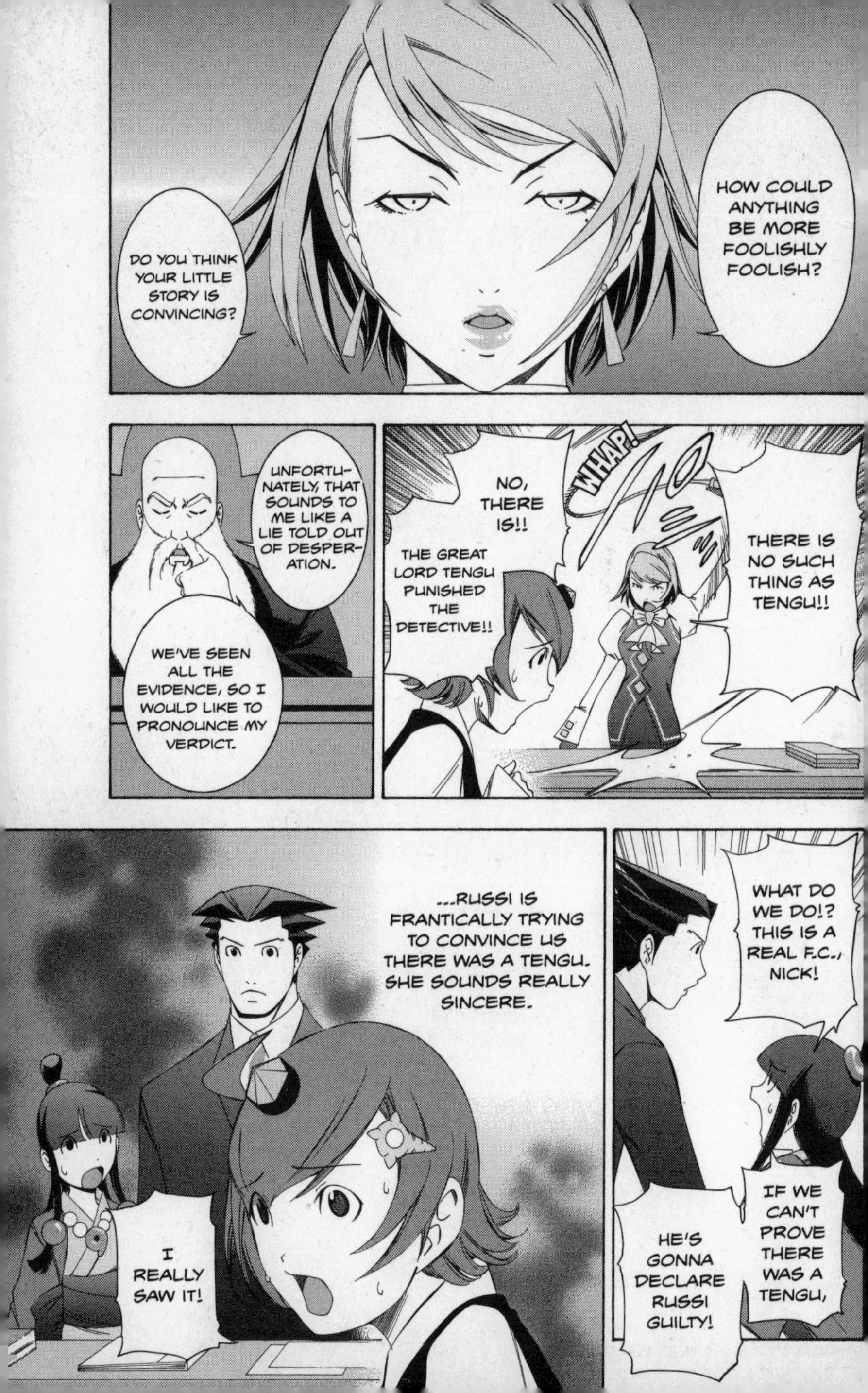
HOW COULD ANYTHING BE MORE FOOLISHLY FOOLISH?
DO YOU THINK YOUR LITTLE STORY IS CONVINCING?
WHAP!
THERE IS NO SUCH THING AS TENGU!!
NO, THERE IS!!
THE GREAT LORD TENGU PUNISHED THE DETECTIVE!!
UNFORTUNATELY, THAT SOUNDS TO ME LIKE A LIE TOLD OUT OF DESPERATION.
WE'VE SEEN ALL THE EVIDENCE, SO I WOULD LIKE TO PRONOUNCE MY VERDICT.
WHAT DO WE DO!? THIS IS A REAL F.C., NICK!
IF WE CAN'T PROVE THERE WAS A TENGU,
HE'S GONNA DECLARE RUSSI GUILTY!
...RUSSI IS FRANTICALLY TRYING TO CONVINCE US THERE WAS A TENGU. SHE SOUNDS REALLY SINCERE.
I REALLY SAW IT!

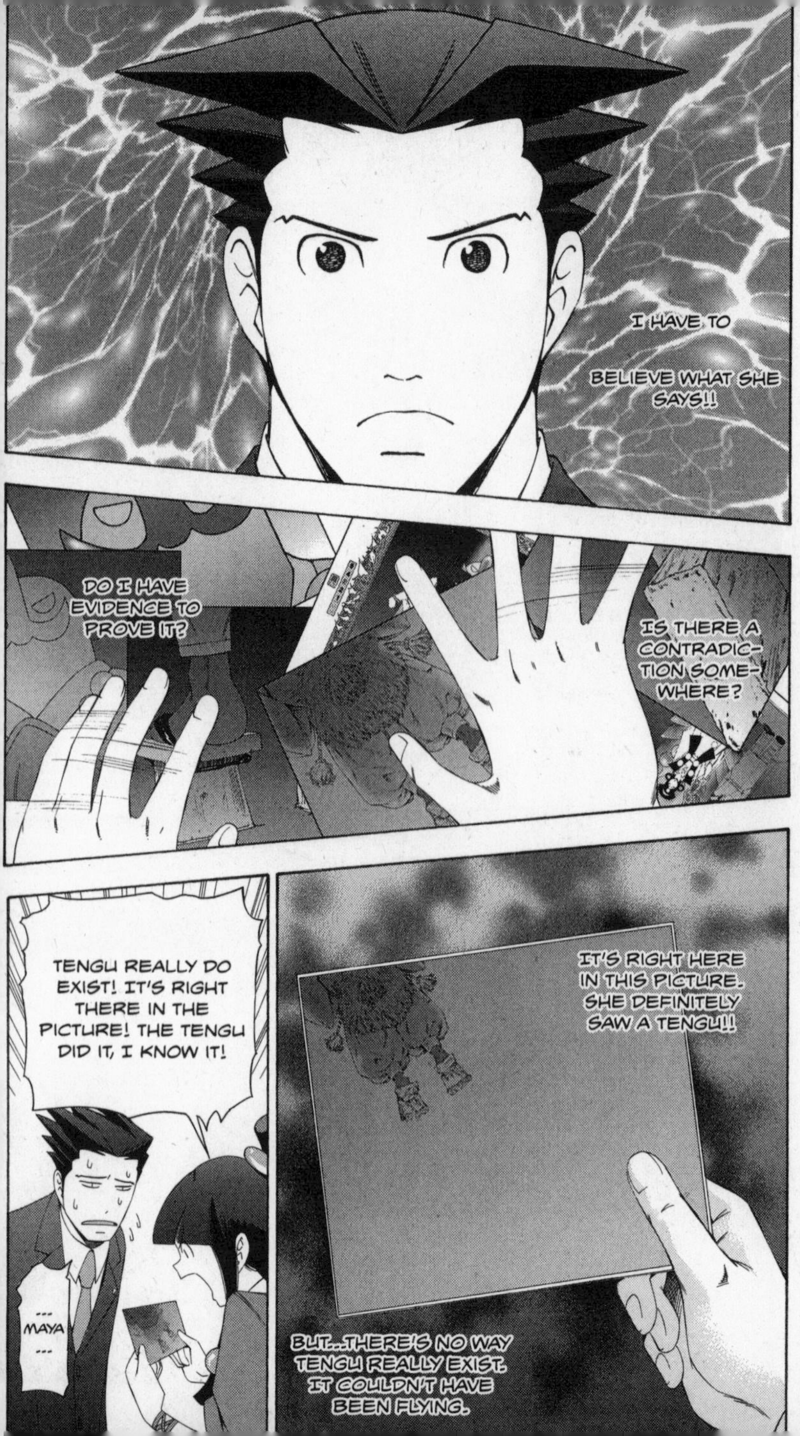
I HAVE TO
BELIEVE WHAT SHE SAYS!!
IS THERE A CONTRADIC-TION SOME-WHERE?
DO I HAVE EVIDENCE TO PROVE IT?
IT'S RIGHT HERE IN THIS PICTURE. SHE DEFINITELY SAW A TENGU!!
BUT...THERE'S NO WAY TENGU REALLY EXIST. IT COULDN'T HAVE BEEN FLYING.
TENGU REALLY DO EXIST! IT'S RIGHT THERE IN THE PICTURE! THE TENGU DID IT, I KNOW IT!
...MAYA...

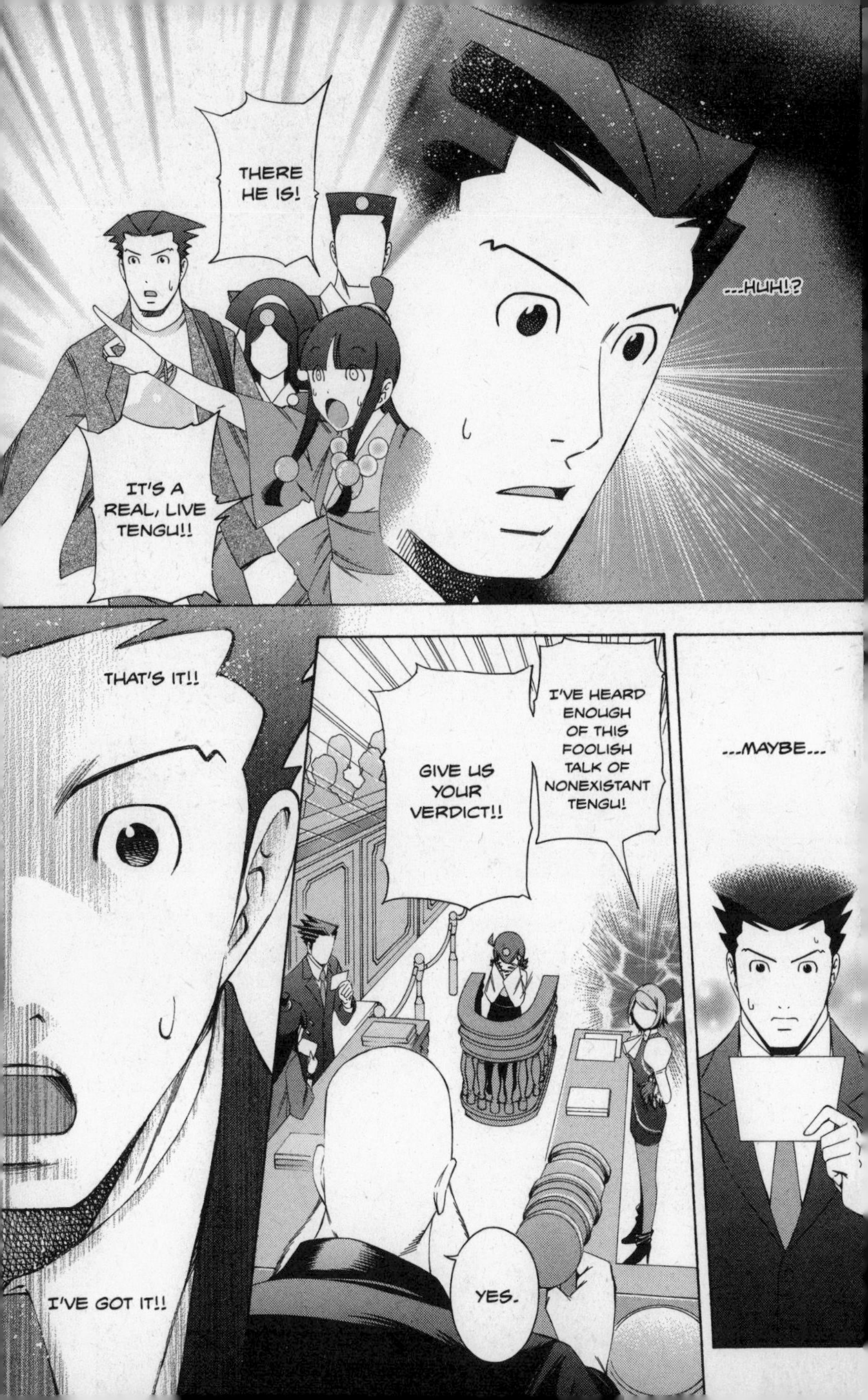
...HUH!?
THERE HE IS!
IT'S A REAL, LIVE TENGU!!
...MAYBE...
I'VE HEARD ENOUGH OF THIS FOOLISH TALK OF NONEXISTANT TENGU!
GIVE US YOUR VERDICT!!
YES.
THAT'S IT!!
I'VE GOT IT!!

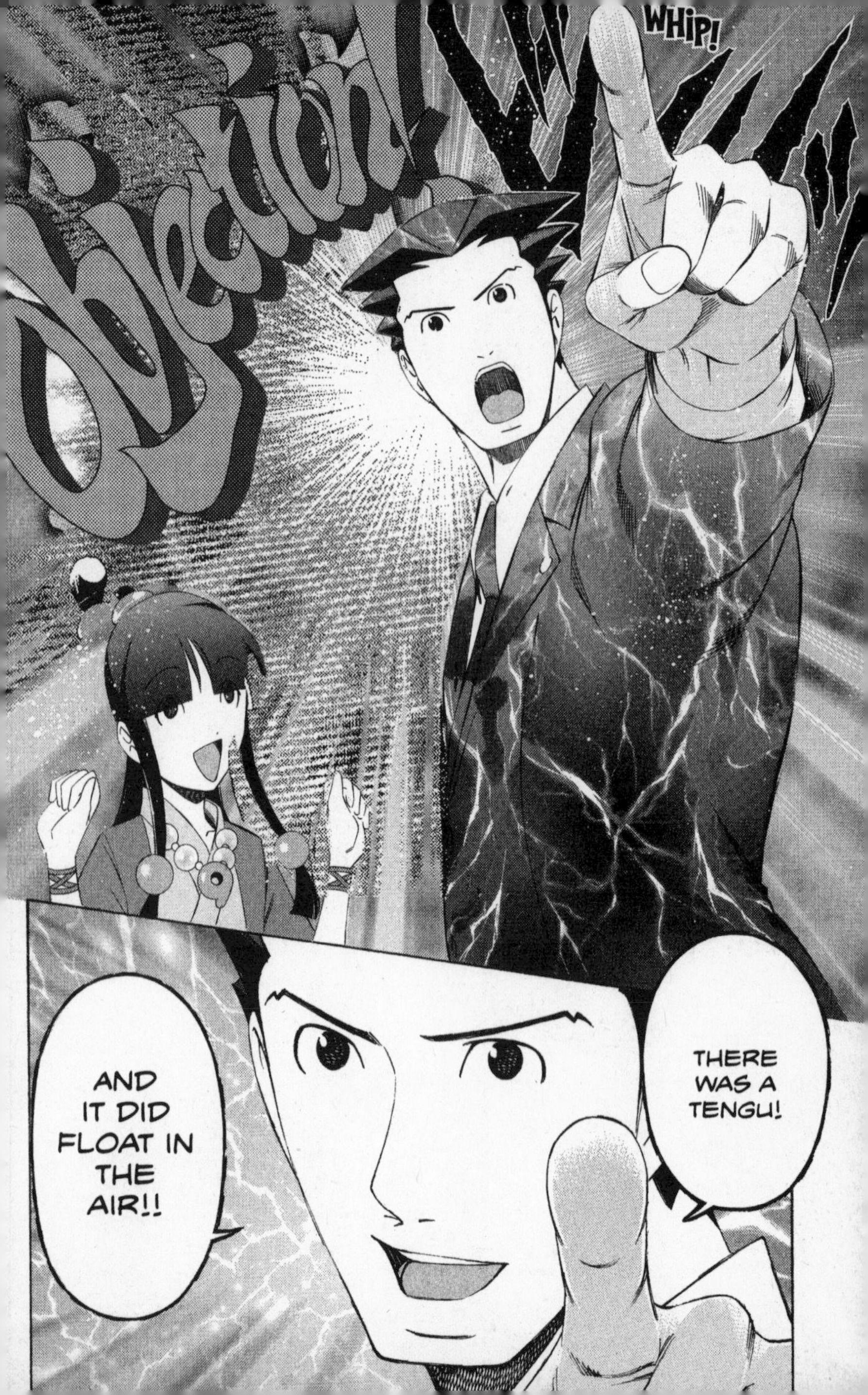
Objection!
WHIP!
THERE WAS A TENGU!
AND IT DID FLOAT IN THE AIR!!

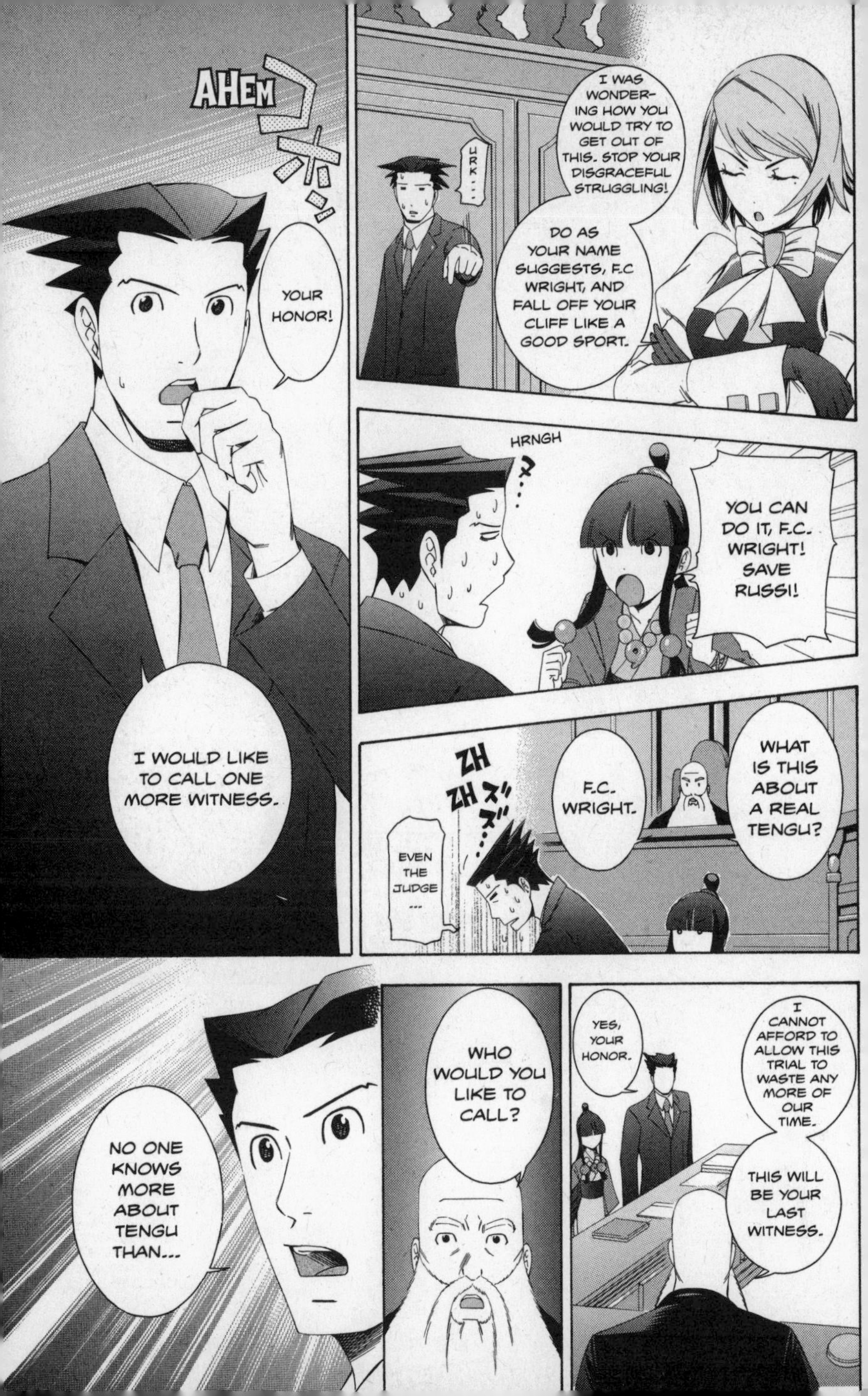
I WAS WONDERING HOW YOU WOULD TRY TO GET OUT OF THIS. STOP YOUR DISGRACEFUL STRUGGLING!
URK...
DO AS YOUR NAME SUGGESTS, F.C WRIGHT, AND FALL OFF YOUR CLIFF LIKE A GOOD SPORT.
YOU CAN DO IT, F.C. WRIGHT! SAVE RUSSI!
HRNGH
WHAT IS THIS ABOUT A REAL TENGU?
F.C. WRIGHT.
ZH ZH
EVEN THE JUDGE...
AHEM
YOUR HONOR!
I WOULD LIKE TO CALL ONE MORE WITNESS.
I CANNOT AFFORD TO ALLOW THIS TRIAL TO WASTE ANY MORE OF OUR TIME.
YES, YOUR HONOR.
THIS WILL BE YOUR LAST WITNESS.
WHO WOULD YOU LIKE TO CALL?
NO ONE KNOWS MORE ABOUT TENGU THAN...

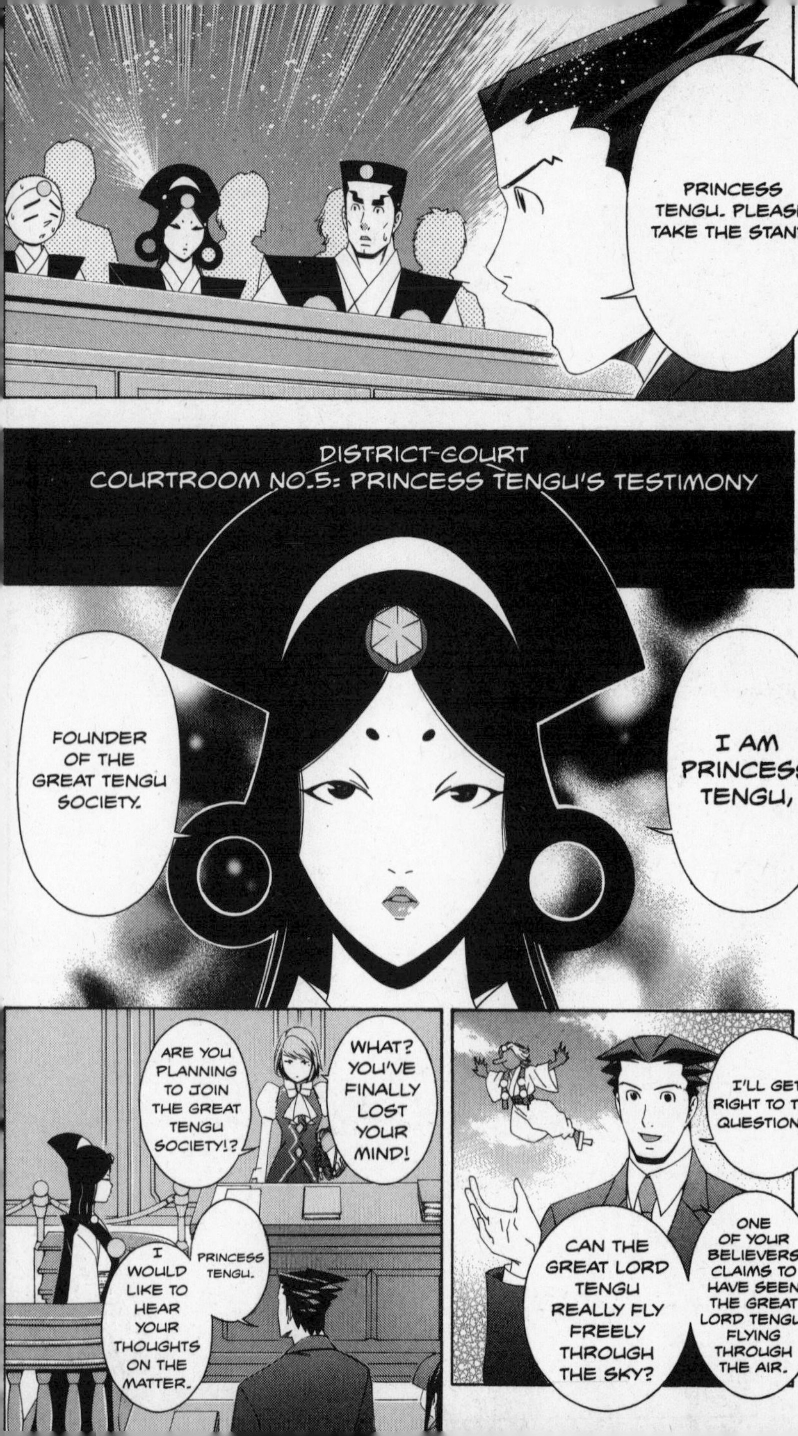
PRINCESS TENGU. PLEASE TAKE THE STAND.
DISTRICT COURT
COURTROOM NO. 5: PRINCESS TENGU'S TESTIMONY
I AM PRINCESS TENGU,
FOUNDER OF THE GREAT TENGU SOCIETY.
I'LL GET RIGHT TO THE QUESTIONS.
ONE OF YOUR BELIEVERS CLAIMS TO HAVE SEEN THE GREAT LORD TENGU, FLYING THROUGH THE AIR.
CAN THE GREAT LORD TENGU REALLY FLY FREELY THROUGH THE SKY?
WHAT? YOU'VE FINALLY LOST YOUR MIND!
ARE YOU PLANNING TO JOIN THE GREAT TENGU SOCIETY!?
PRINCESS TENGU.
I WOULD LIKE TO HEAR YOUR THOUGHTS ON THE MATTER.

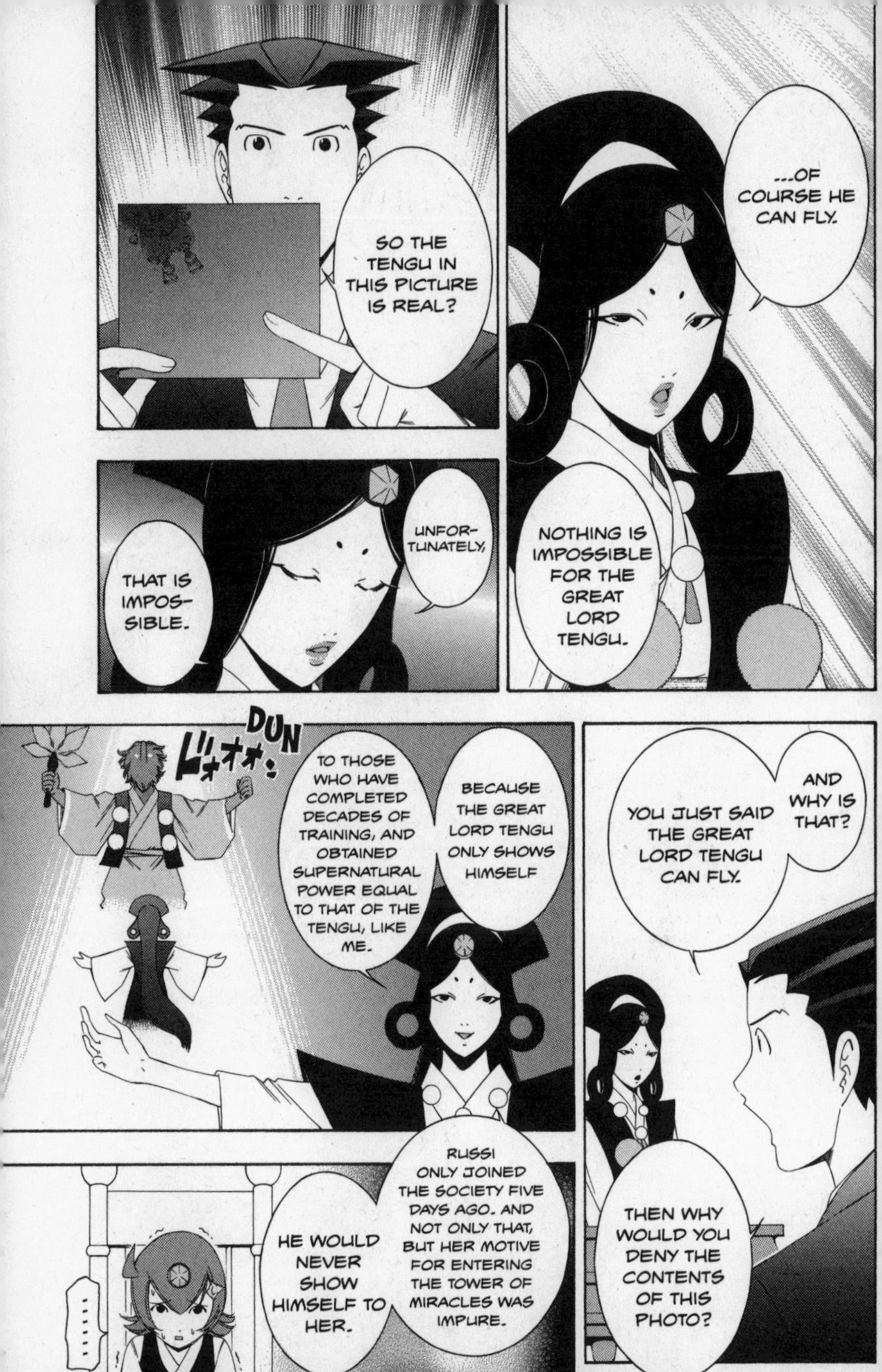
...OF COURSE HE CAN FLY.
NOTHING IS IMPOSSIBLE FOR THE GREAT LORD TENGU.
SO THE TENGU IN THIS PICTURE IS REAL?
UNFOR-TUNATELY,
THAT IS IMPOS-SIBLE.
AND WHY IS THAT?
YOU JUST SAID THE GREAT LORD TENGU CAN FLY.
THEN WHY WOULD YOU DENY THE CONTENTS OF THIS PHOTO?
DUN
BECAUSE THE GREAT LORD TENGU ONLY SHOWS HIMSELF
TO THOSE WHO HAVE COMPLETED DECADES OF TRAINING, AND OBTAINED SUPERNATURAL POWER EQUAL TO THAT OF THE TENGU, LIKE ME.
RUSSI ONLY JOINED THE SOCIETY FIVE DAYS AGO. AND NOT ONLY THAT, BUT HER MOTIVE FOR ENTERING THE TOWER OF MIRACLES WAS IMPURE.
HE WOULD NEVER SHOW HIMSELF TO HER.
......

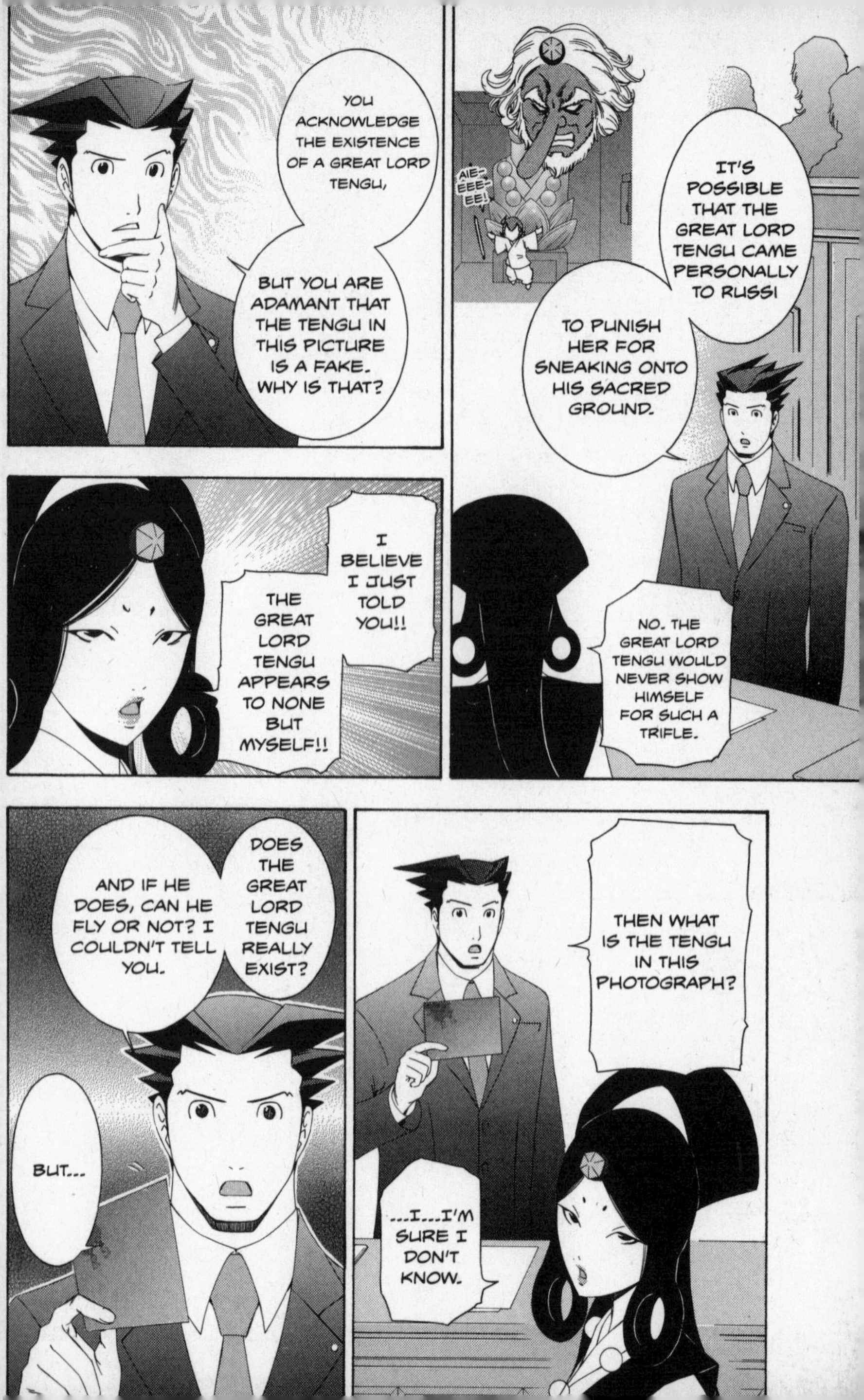
YOU ACKNOWLEDGE THE EXISTENCE OF A GREAT LORD TENGU,
BUT YOU ARE ADAMANT THAT THE TENGU IN THIS PICTURE IS A FAKE. WHY IS THAT?
I BELIEVE I JUST TOLD YOU!!
THE GREAT LORD TENGU APPEARS TO NONE BUT MYSELF!!
AIE-EEEE-EE!
IT'S POSSIBLE THAT THE GREAT LORD TENGU CAME PERSONALLY TO RUSSI
TO PUNISH HER FOR SNEAKING ONTO HIS SACRED GROUND.
NO. THE GREAT LORD TENGU WOULD NEVER SHOW HIMSELF FOR SUCH A TRIFLE.
THEN WHAT IS THE TENGU IN THIS PHOTOGRAPH?
...I...I'M SURE I DON'T KNOW.
DOES THE GREAT LORD TENGU REALLY EXIST?
AND IF HE DOES, CAN HE FLY OR NOT? I COULDN'T TELL YOU.
BUT...

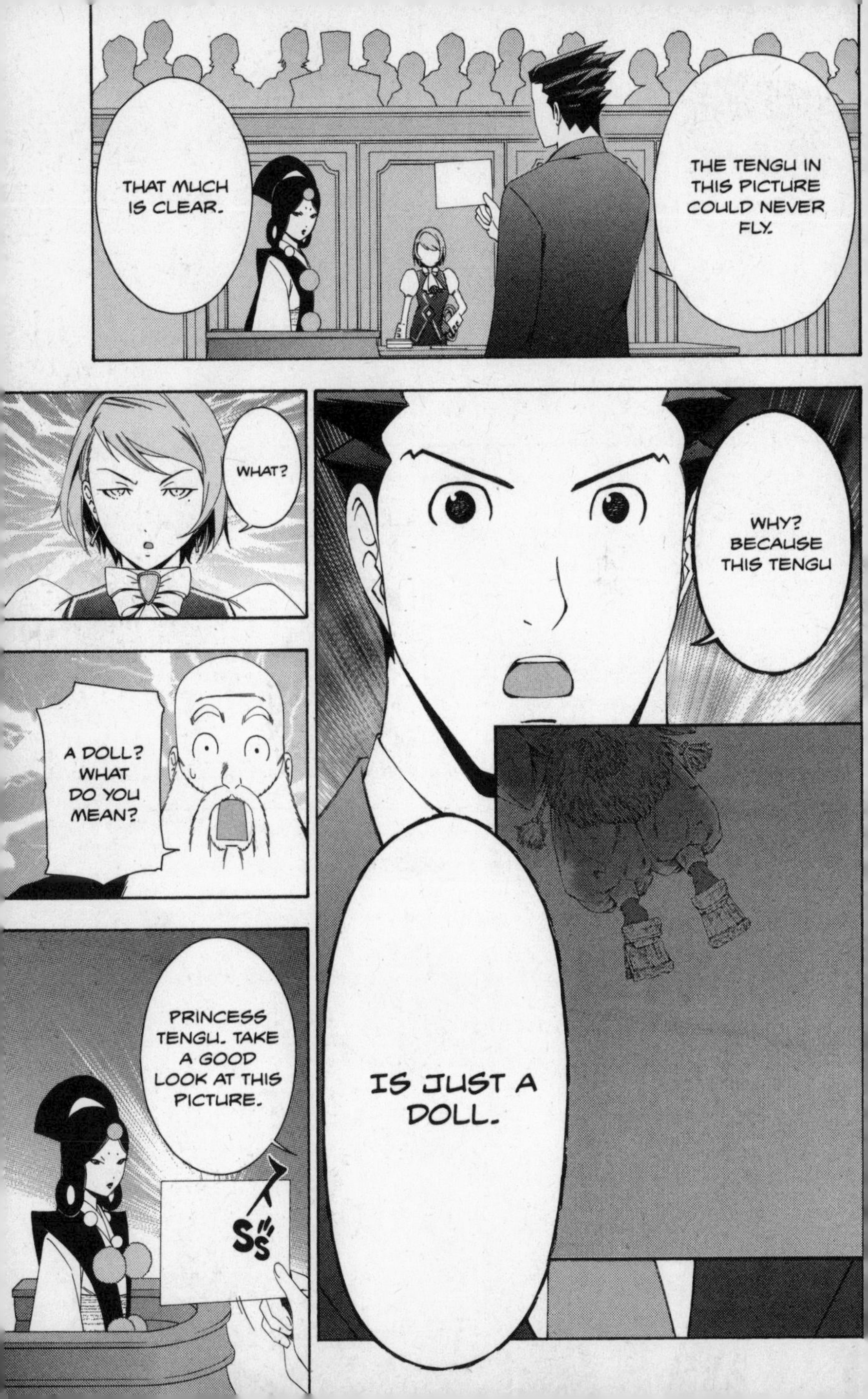
THE TENGU IN THIS PICTURE COULD NEVER FLY.
THAT MUCH IS CLEAR.
WHY? BECAUSE THIS TENGU
IS JUST A DOLL.
WHAT?
A DOLL? WHAT DO YOU MEAN?
PRINCESS TENGU. TAKE A GOOD LOOK AT THIS PICTURE.
SS

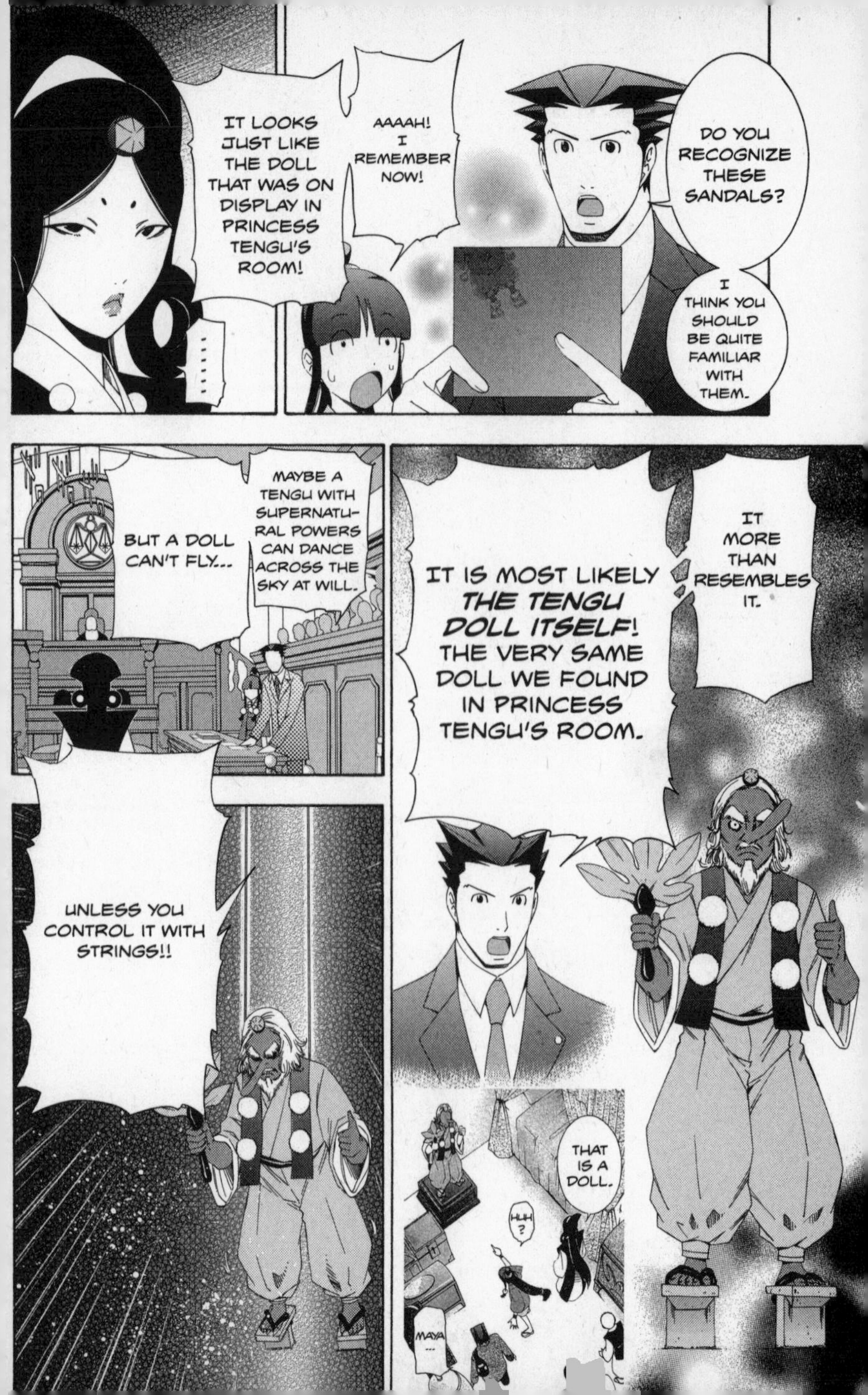
DO YOU RECOGNIZE THESE SANDALS?
I THINK YOU SHOULD BE QUITE FAMILIAR WITH THEM.
AAAAH! I REMEMBER NOW!
IT LOOKS JUST LIKE THE DOLL THAT WAS ON DISPLAY IN PRINCESS TENGU'S ROOM!
......
IT MORE THAN RESEMBLES IT.
IT IS MOST LIKELY *THE TENGU DOLL ITSELF*! THE VERY SAME DOLL WE FOUND IN PRINCESS TENGU'S ROOM.
THAT IS A DOLL.
HUH?
MAYA...
MAYBE A TENGU WITH SUPERNATURAL POWERS CAN DANCE ACROSS THE SKY AT WILL.
BUT A DOLL CAN'T FLY...
UNLESS YOU CONTROL IT WITH STRINGS!!

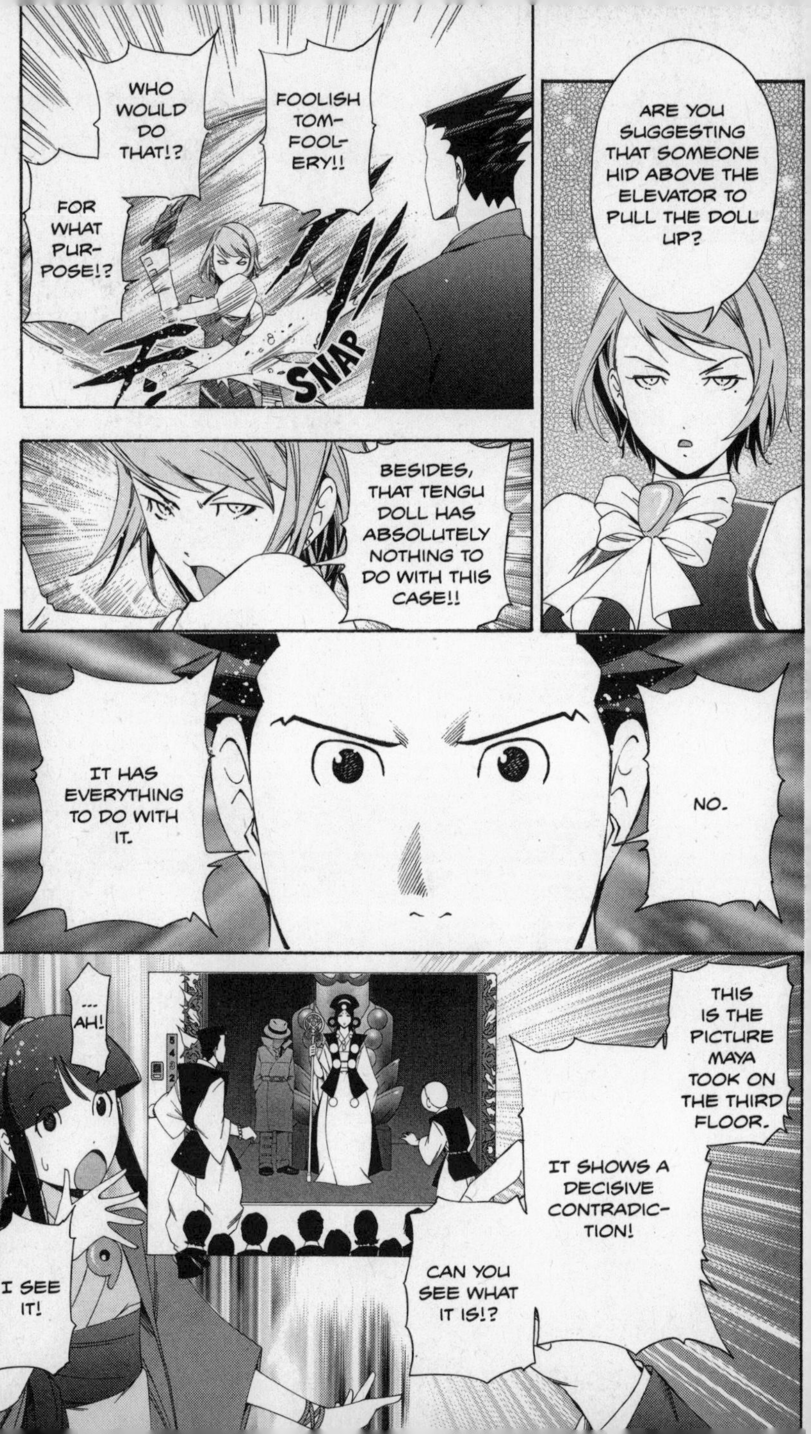
ARE YOU SUGGESTING THAT SOMEONE HID ABOVE THE ELEVATOR TO PULL THE DOLL UP?
FOOLISH TOM-FOOL-ERY!!
WHO WOULD DO THAT!?
FOR WHAT PUR-POSE!?
SNAP
BESIDES, THAT TENGU DOLL HAS ABSOLUTELY NOTHING TO DO WITH THIS CASE!!
NO.
IT HAS EVERYTHING TO DO WITH IT.
THIS IS THE PICTURE MAYA TOOK ON THE THIRD FLOOR.
IT SHOWS A DECISIVE CONTRADIC-TION!
CAN YOU SEE WHAT IT IS!?
...AH!
I SEE IT!

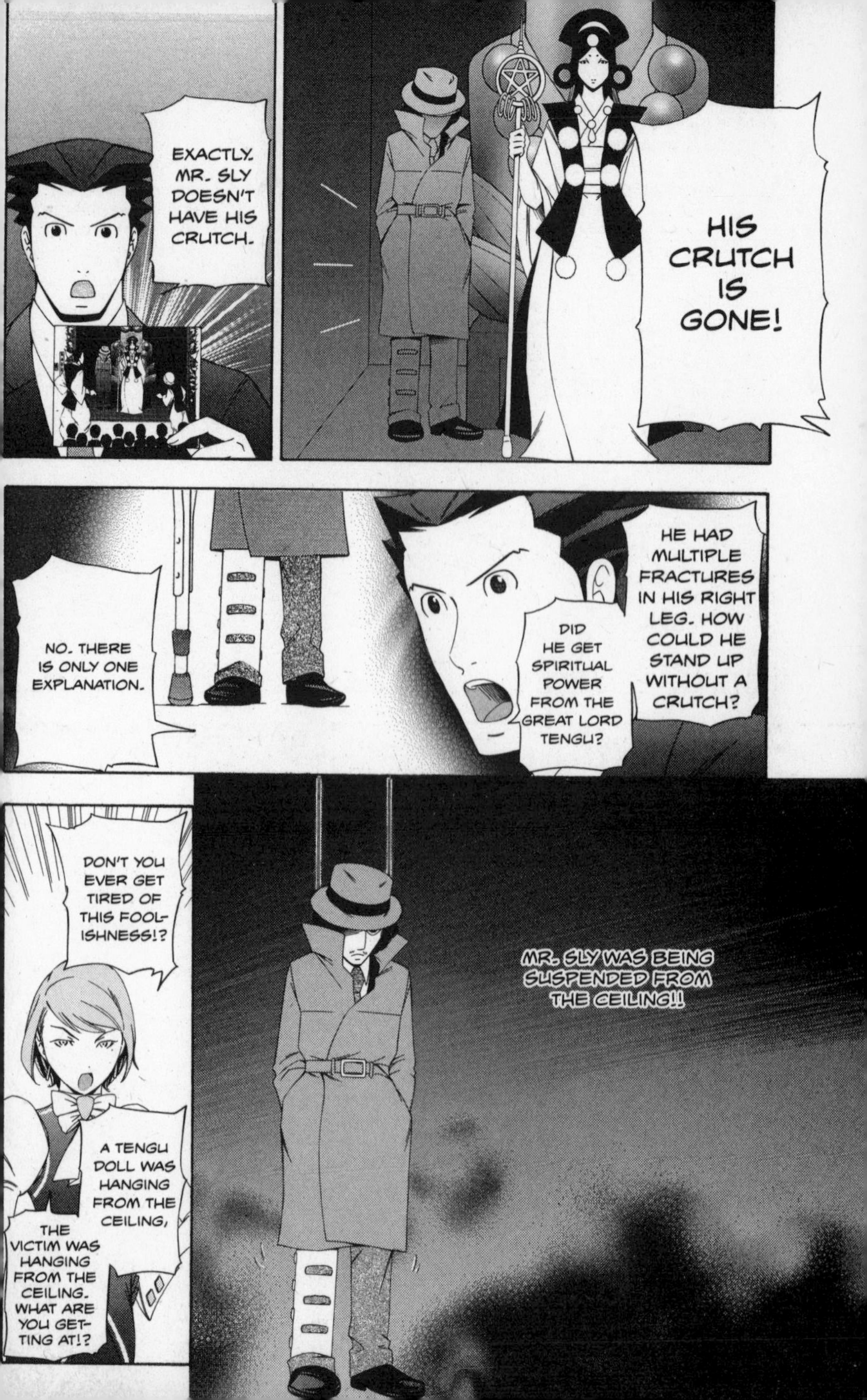
HIS CRUTCH IS GONE!
EXACTLY. MR. SLY DOESN'T HAVE HIS CRUTCH.
HE HAD MULTIPLE FRACTURES IN HIS RIGHT LEG. HOW COULD HE STAND UP WITHOUT A CRUTCH?
DID HE GET SPIRITUAL POWER FROM THE GREAT LORD TENGU?
NO. THERE IS ONLY ONE EXPLANATION.
MR. SLY WAS BEING SUSPENDED FROM THE CEILING!!
DON'T YOU EVER GET TIRED OF THIS FOOL-ISHNESS!?
A TENGU DOLL WAS HANGING FROM THE CEILING,
THE VICTIM WAS HANGING FROM THE CEILING. WHAT ARE YOU GET-TING AT!?

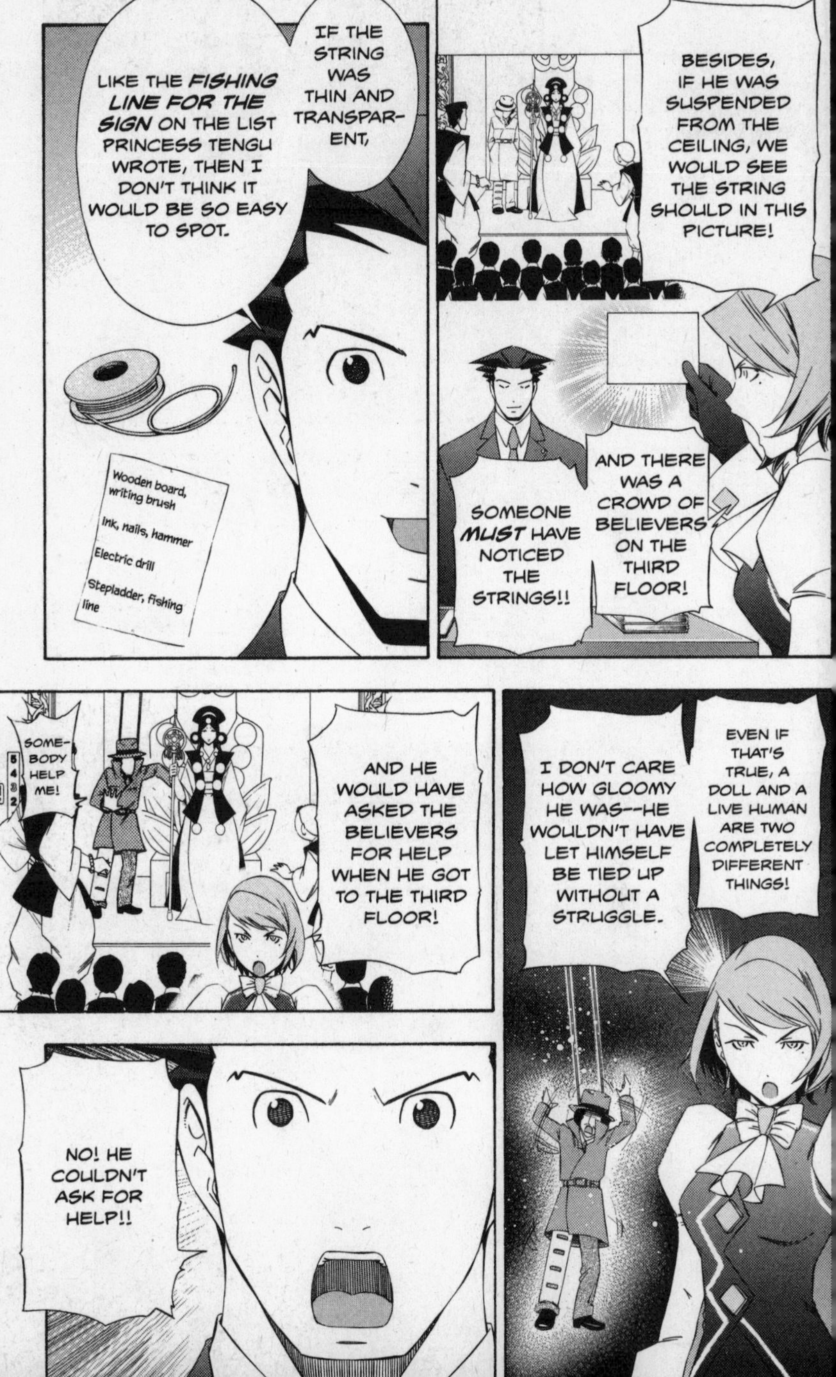
BESIDES, IF HE WAS SUSPENDED FROM THE CEILING, WE WOULD SEE THE STRING SHOULD IN THIS PICTURE!
AND THERE WAS A CROWD OF BELIEVERS ON THE THIRD FLOOR!
SOMEONE *MUST* HAVE NOTICED THE STRINGS!!
IF THE STRING WAS THIN AND TRANSPAR- ENT,
LIKE THE ***FISHING LINE FOR THE SIGN*** ON THE LIST PRINCESS TENGU WROTE, THEN I DON'T THINK IT WOULD BE SO EASY TO SPOT.
Wooden board, writing brush
Ink, nails, hammer
Electric drill
Stepladder, fishing line
EVEN IF THAT'S TRUE, A DOLL AND A LIVE HUMAN ARE TWO COMPLETELY DIFFERENT THINGS!
I DON'T CARE HOW GLOOMY HE WAS--HE WOULDN'T HAVE LET HIMSELF BE TIED UP WITHOUT A STRUGGLE.
AND HE WOULD HAVE ASKED THE BELIEVERS FOR HELP WHEN HE GOT TO THE THIRD FLOOR!
SOME- BODY HELP ME!
5
4
3
2
NO! HE COULDN'T ASK FOR HELP!!

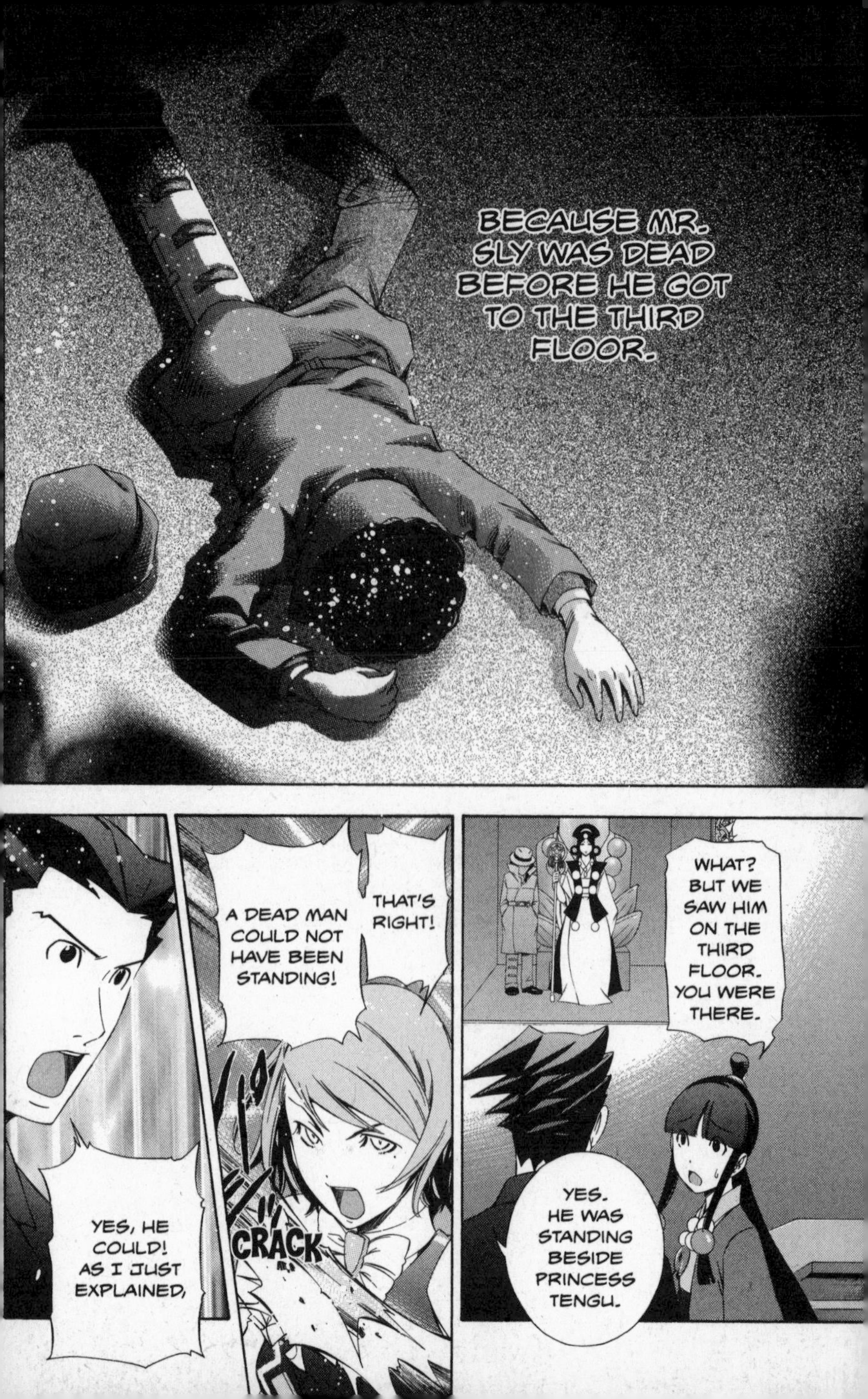
BECAUSE MR. SLY WAS DEAD BEFORE HE GOT TO THE THIRD FLOOR.
WHAT? BUT WE SAW HIM ON THE THIRD FLOOR. YOU WERE THERE.
YES. HE WAS STANDING BESIDE PRINCESS TENGU.
THAT'S RIGHT!
A DEAD MAN COULD NOT HAVE BEEN STANDING!
CRACK
YES, HE COULD! AS I JUST EXPLAINED,

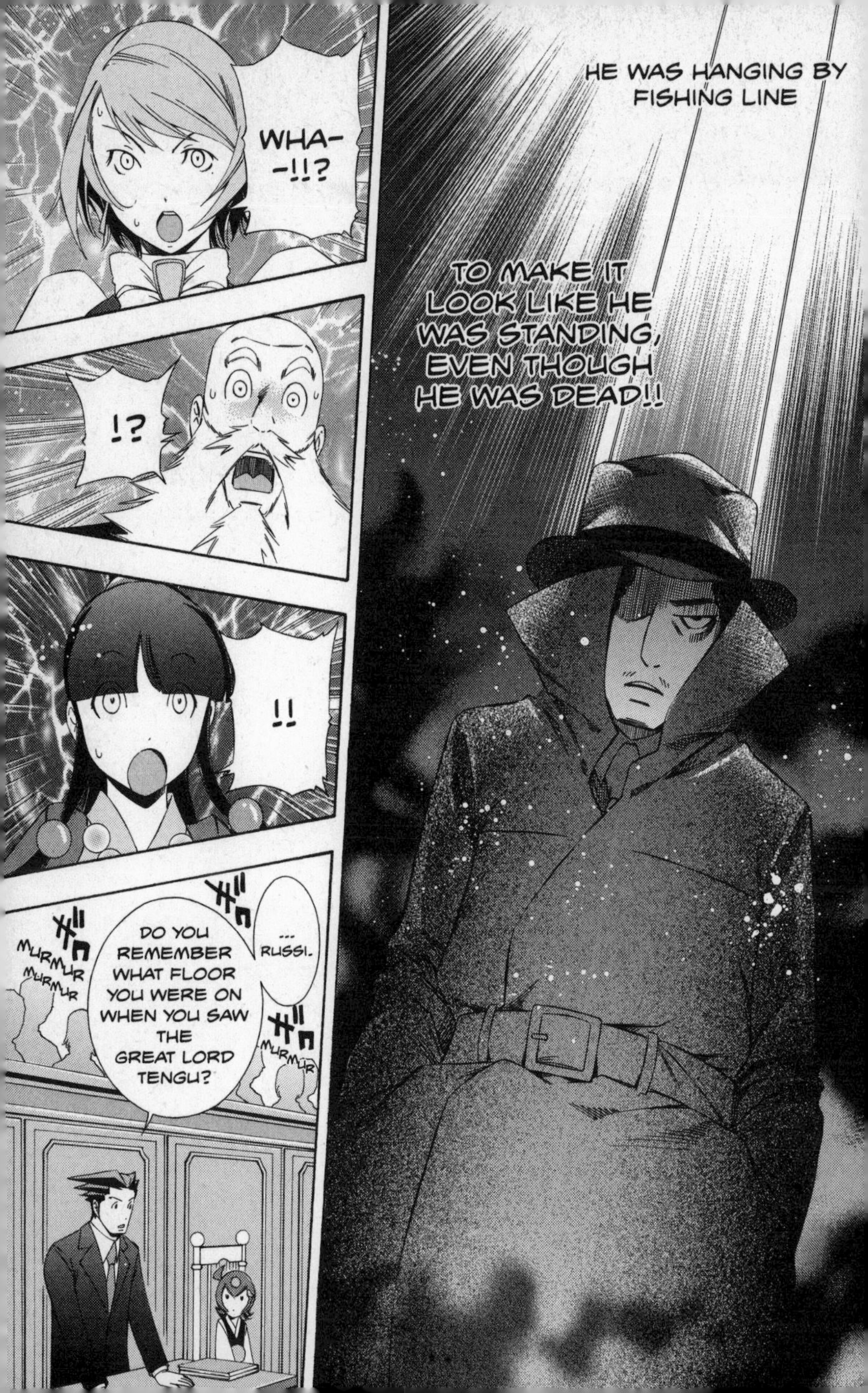
HE WAS HANGING BY FISHING LINE
TO MAKE IT LOOK LIKE HE WAS STANDING, EVEN THOUGH HE WAS DEAD!!
WHA- -!!?
!?
!!
... RUSSI.
DO YOU REMEMBER WHAT FLOOR YOU WERE ON WHEN YOU SAW THE GREAT LORD TENGU?
MURMUR
MURMUR MURMUR

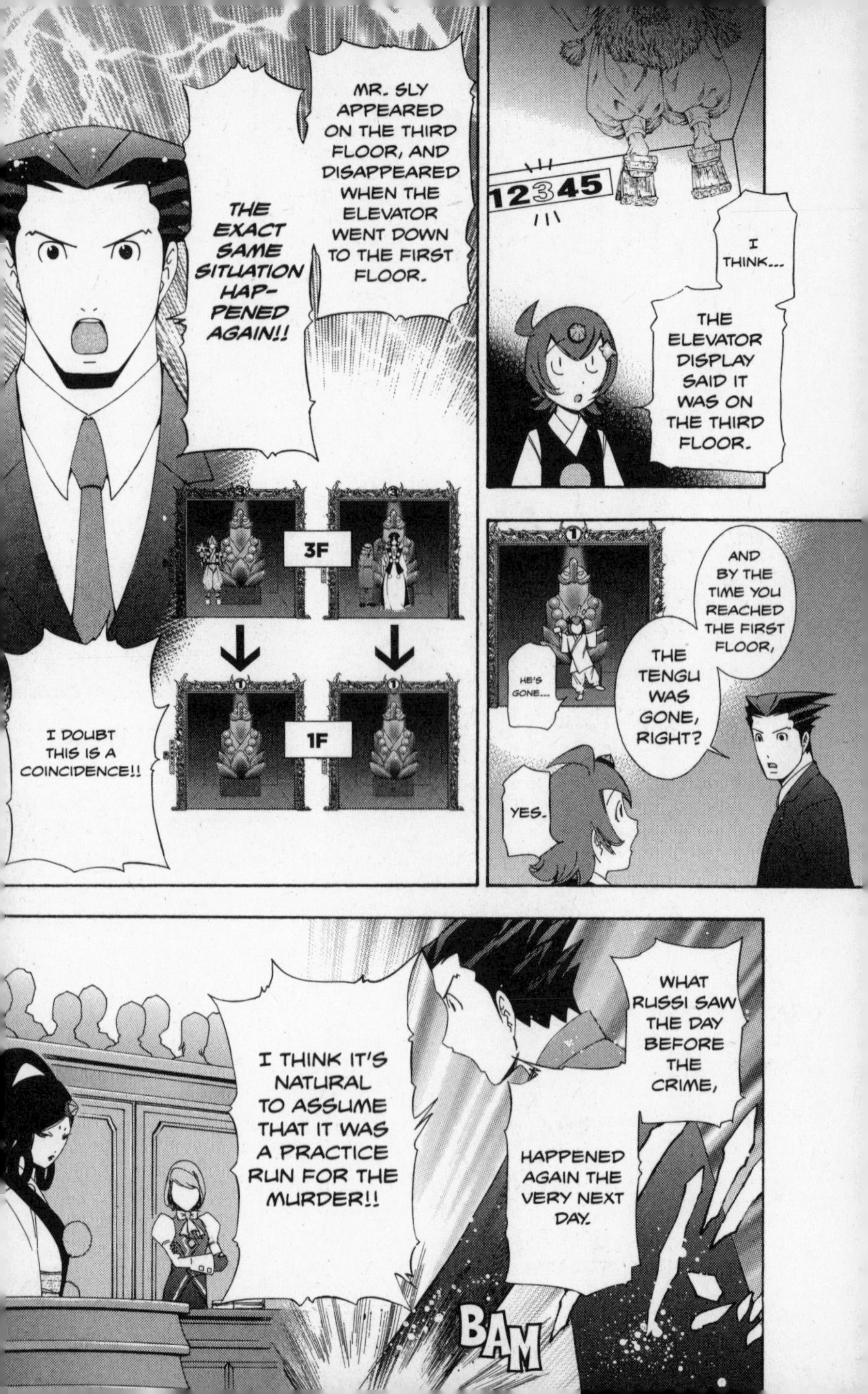

12345
I THINK...
THE ELEVATOR DISPLAY SAID IT WAS ON THE THIRD FLOOR.
AND BY THE TIME YOU REACHED THE FIRST FLOOR,
THE TENGU WAS GONE, RIGHT?
HE'S GONE...
YES.
MR. SLY APPEARED ON THE THIRD FLOOR, AND DISAPPEARED WHEN THE ELEVATOR WENT DOWN TO THE FIRST FLOOR.
THE EXACT SAME SITUATION HAP-PENED AGAIN!!
3F
1F
I DOUBT THIS IS A COINCIDENCE!!
WHAT RUSSI SAW THE DAY BEFORE THE CRIME,
HAPPENED AGAIN THE VERY NEXT DAY.
I THINK IT'S NATURAL TO ASSUME THAT IT WAS A PRACTICE RUN FOR THE MURDER!!
BAM

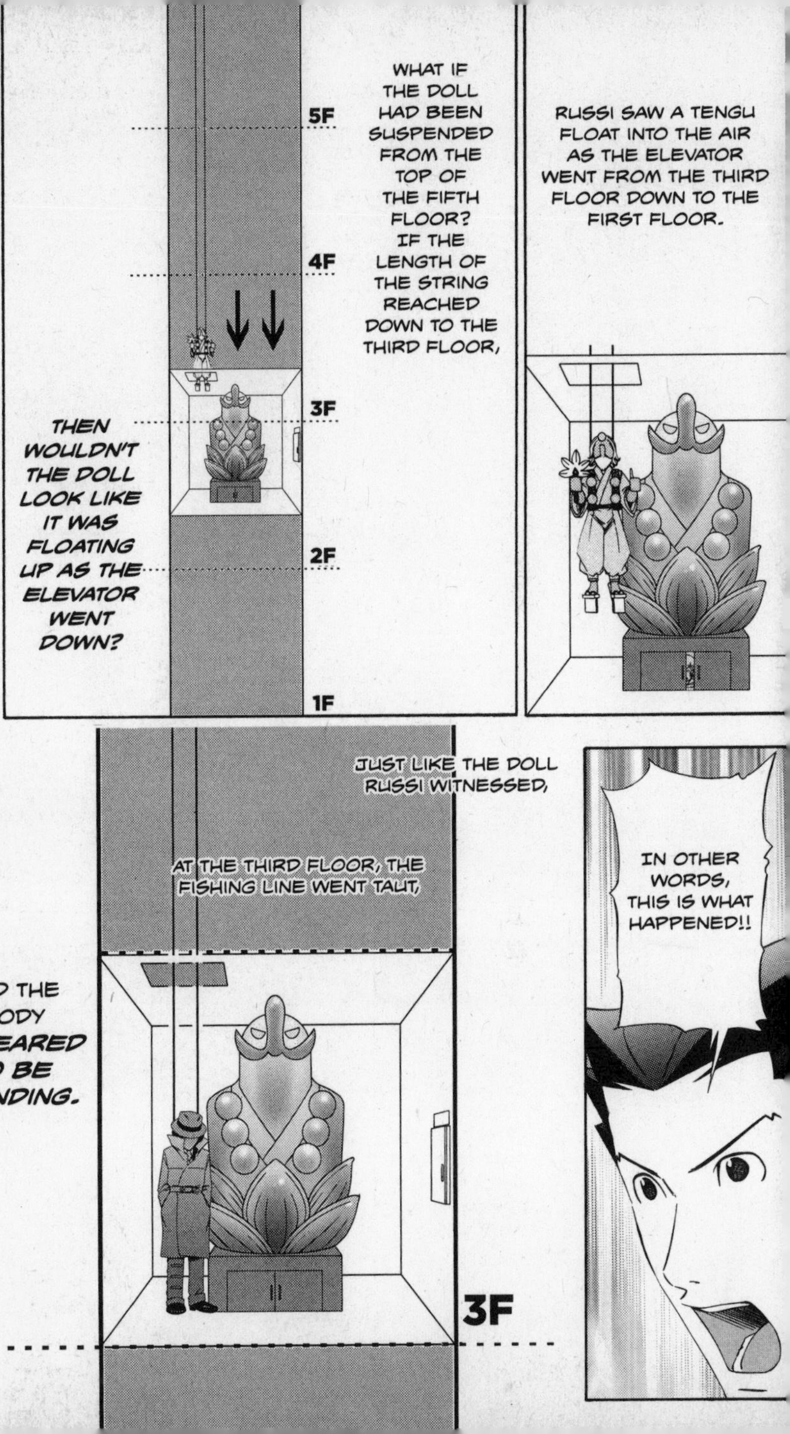
RUSSI SAW A TENGU FLOAT INTO THE AIR AS THE ELEVATOR WENT FROM THE THIRD FLOOR DOWN TO THE FIRST FLOOR.
WHAT IF THE DOLL HAD BEEN SUSPENDED FROM THE TOP OF THE FIFTH FLOOR? IF THE LENGTH OF THE STRING REACHED DOWN TO THE THIRD FLOOR,
5F
4F
3F
2F
1F
THEN WOULDN'T THE DOLL LOOK LIKE IT WAS FLOATING UP AS THE ELEVATOR WENT DOWN?
IN OTHER WORDS, THIS IS WHAT HAPPENED!!
JUST LIKE THE DOLL RUSSI WITNESSED,
AT THE THIRD FLOOR, THE FISHING LINE WENT TAUT,
AND THE BODY APPEARED TO BE STANDING.
3F

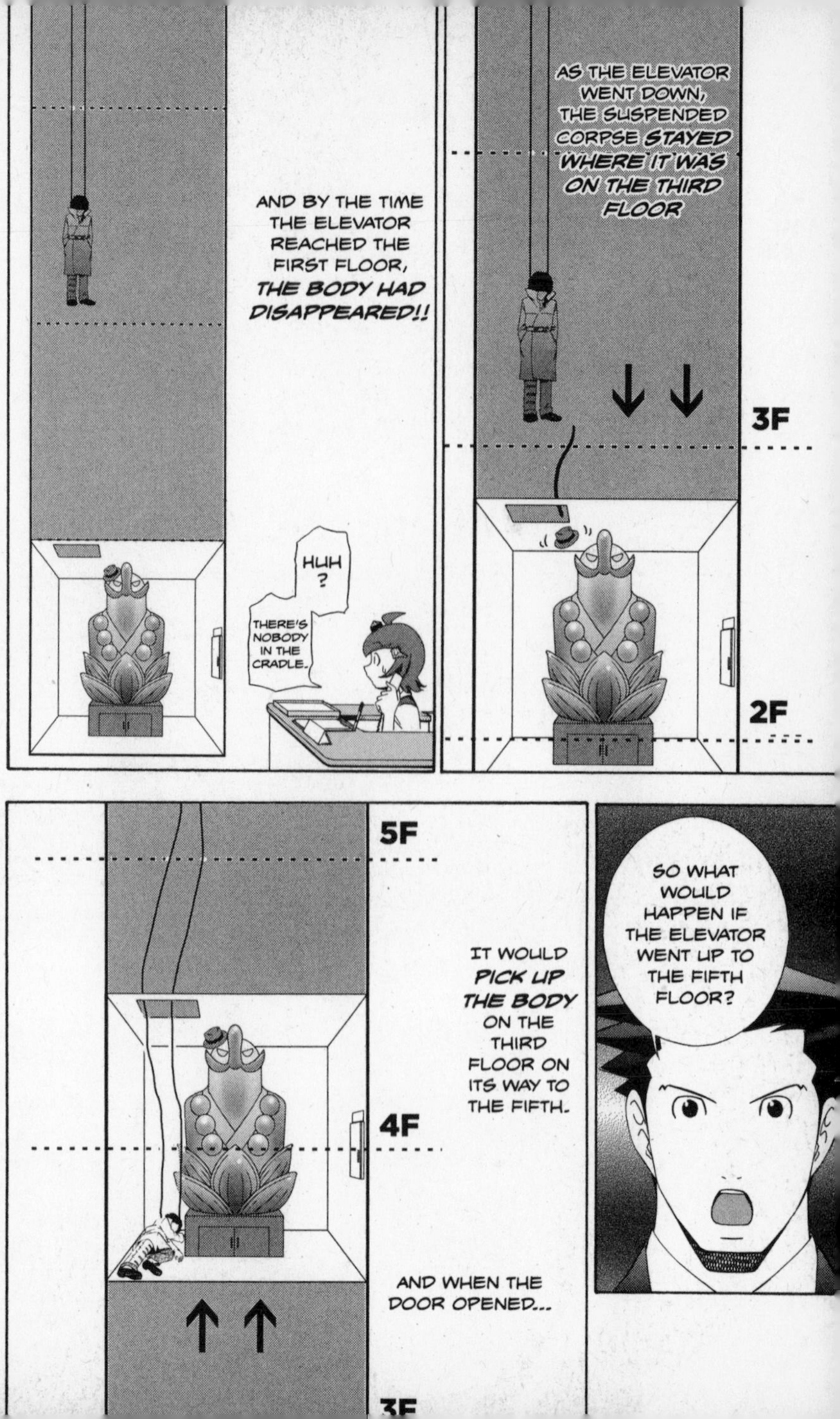
AS THE ELEVATOR WENT DOWN, THE SUSPENDED CORPSE *STAYED WHERE IT WAS ON THE THIRD FLOOR*
3F
2F
AND BY THE TIME THE ELEVATOR REACHED THE FIRST FLOOR, *THE BODY HAD DISAPPEARED!!*
HUH ?
THERE'S NOBODY IN THE CRADLE.
SO WHAT WOULD HAPPEN IF THE ELEVATOR WENT UP TO THE FIFTH FLOOR?
IT WOULD *PICK UP THE BODY* ON THE THIRD FLOOR ON ITS WAY TO THE FIFTH.
5F
4F
AND WHEN THE DOOR OPENED...
3F

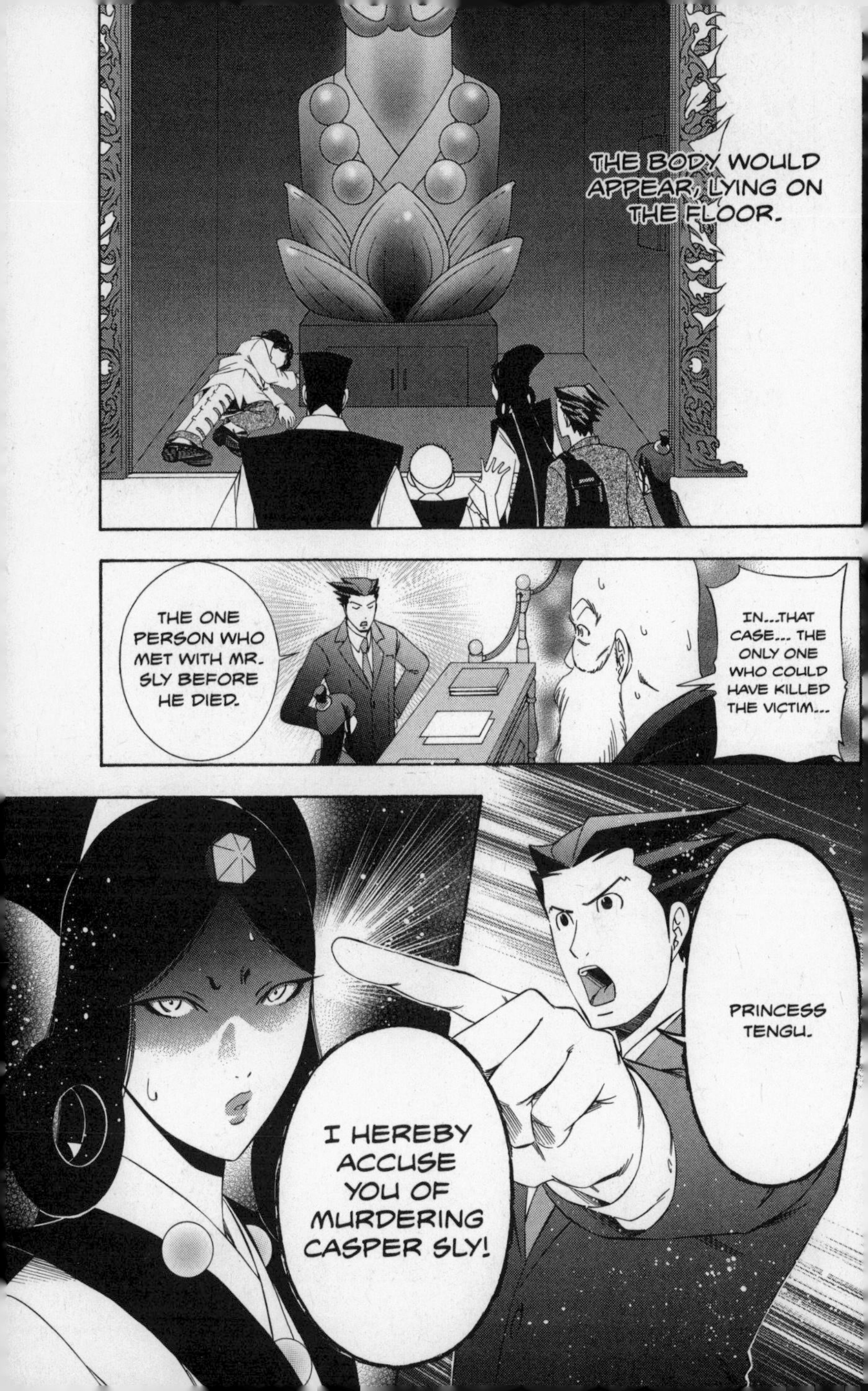
THE BODY WOULD APPEAR, LYING ON THE FLOOR.
IN...THAT CASE... THE ONLY ONE WHO COULD HAVE KILLED THE VICTIM...
THE ONE PERSON WHO MET WITH MR. SLY BEFORE HE DIED.
PRINCESS TENGU.
I HEREBY ACCUSE YOU OF MURDERING CASPER SLY!

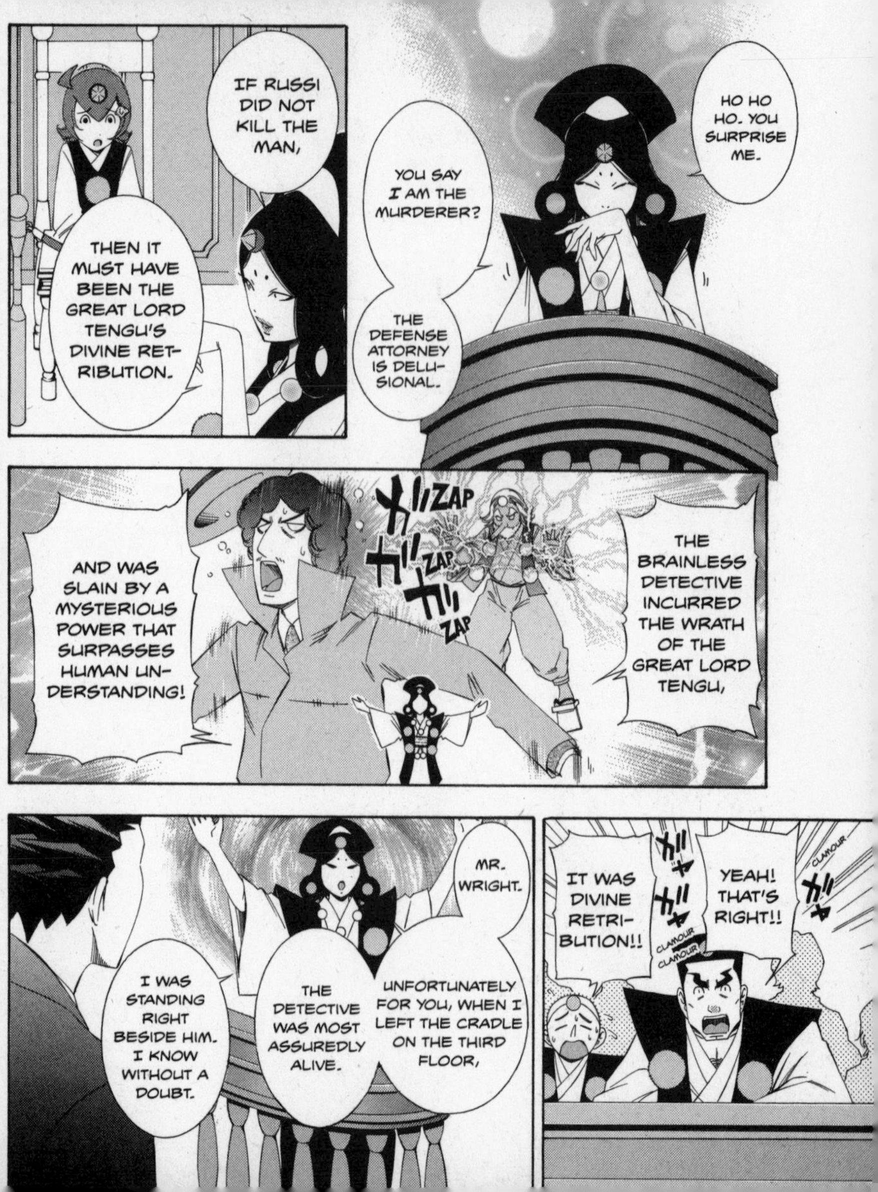
HO HO HO. YOU SURPRISE ME.
YOU SAY I AM THE MURDERER?
THE DEFENSE ATTORNEY IS DELUSIONAL.
IF RUSSI DID NOT KILL THE MAN,
THEN IT MUST HAVE BEEN THE GREAT LORD TENGU'S DIVINE RETRIBUTION.
THE BRAINLESS DETECTIVE INCURRED THE WRATH OF THE GREAT LORD TENGU,
ZAP
ZAP
ZAP
AND WAS SLAIN BY A MYSTERIOUS POWER THAT SURPASSES HUMAN UNDERSTANDING!
CLAMOUR
YEAH! THAT'S RIGHT!!
IT WAS DIVINE RETRIBUTION!!
CLAMOUR CLAMOUR
MR. WRIGHT.
UNFORTUNATELY FOR YOU, WHEN I LEFT THE CRADLE ON THE THIRD FLOOR,
THE DETECTIVE WAS MOST ASSUREDLY ALIVE.
I WAS STANDING RIGHT BESIDE HIM. I KNOW WITHOUT A DOUBT.

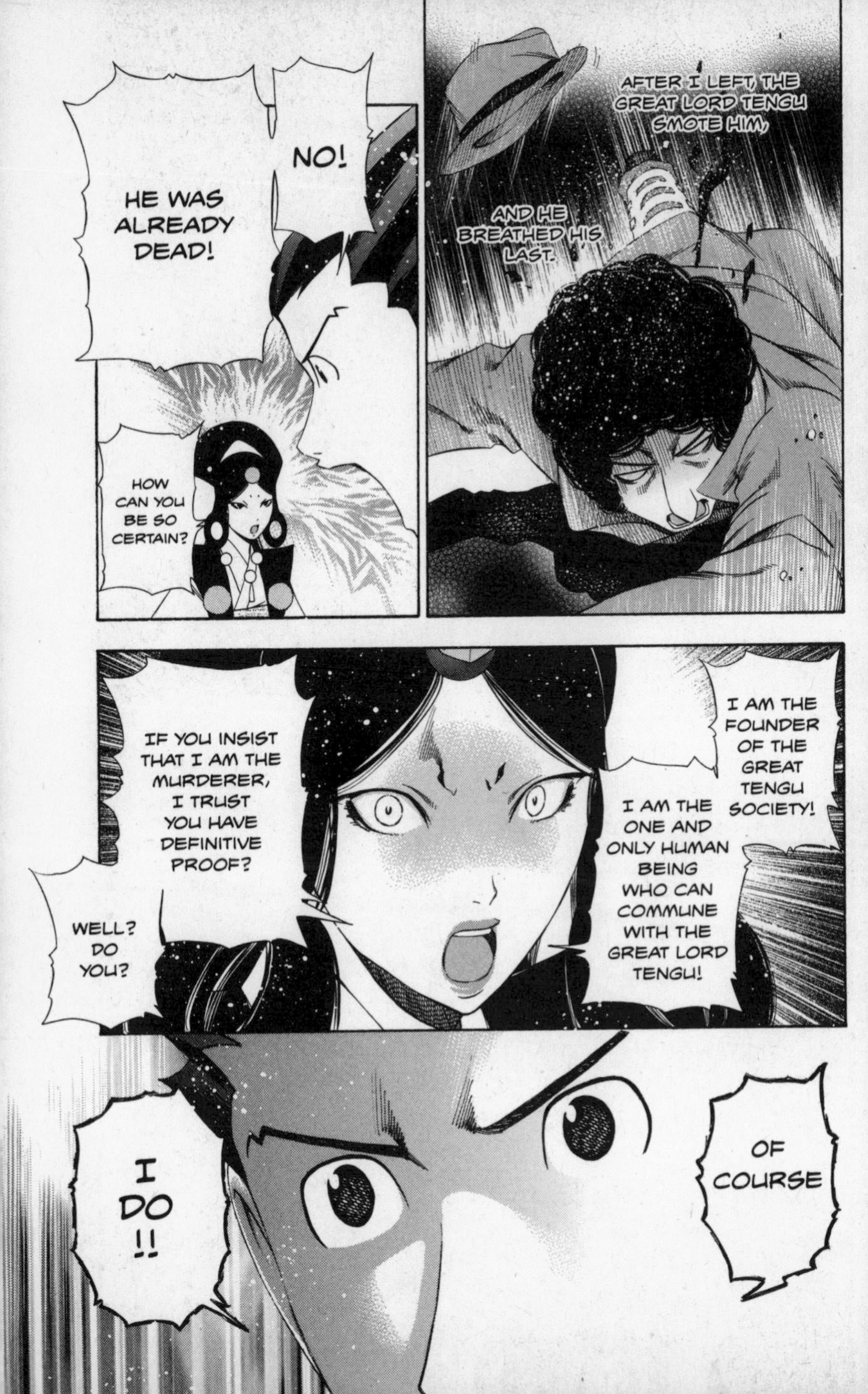
AFTER I LEFT, THE GREAT LORD TENGU SMOTE HIM,
AND HE BREATHED HIS LAST.
NO!
HE WAS ALREADY DEAD!
HOW CAN YOU BE SO CERTAIN?
I AM THE FOUNDER OF THE GREAT TENGU SOCIETY!
I AM THE ONE AND ONLY HUMAN BEING WHO CAN COMMUNE WITH THE GREAT LORD TENGU!
IF YOU INSIST THAT I AM THE MURDERER, I TRUST YOU HAVE DEFINITIVE PROOF?
WELL? DO YOU?
OF COURSE
I DO !!

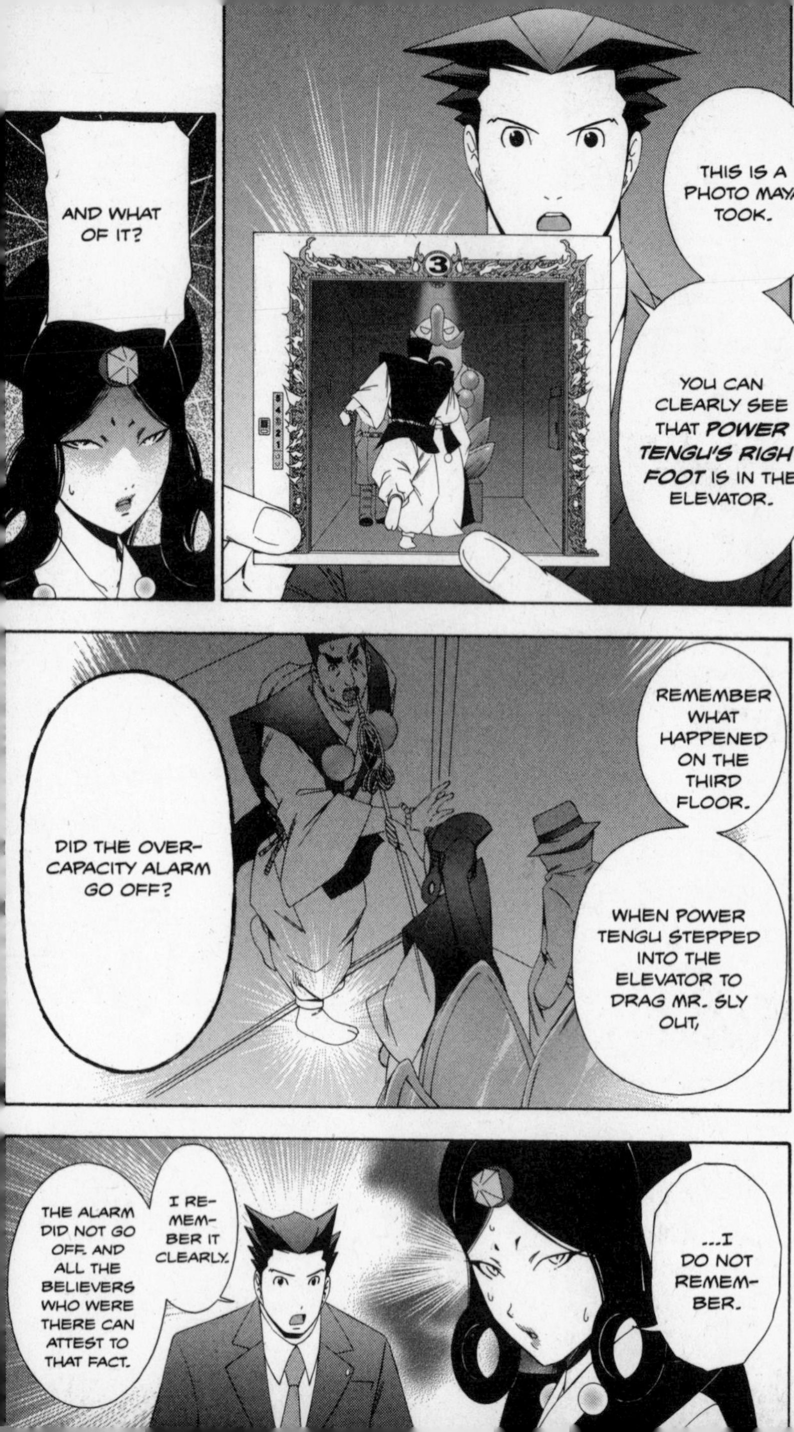
THIS IS A PHOTO MAYA TOOK.
YOU CAN CLEARLY SEE THAT *POWER TENGU'S RIGHT FOOT* IS IN THE ELEVATOR.
AND WHAT OF IT?
REMEMBER WHAT HAPPENED ON THE THIRD FLOOR.
WHEN POWER TENGU STEPPED INTO THE ELEVATOR TO DRAG MR. SLY OUT,
DID THE OVER-CAPACITY ALARM GO OFF?
...I DO NOT REMEMBER.
I REMEMBER IT CLEARLY.
THE ALARM DID NOT GO OFF. AND ALL THE BELIEVERS WHO WERE THERE CAN ATTEST TO THAT FACT.

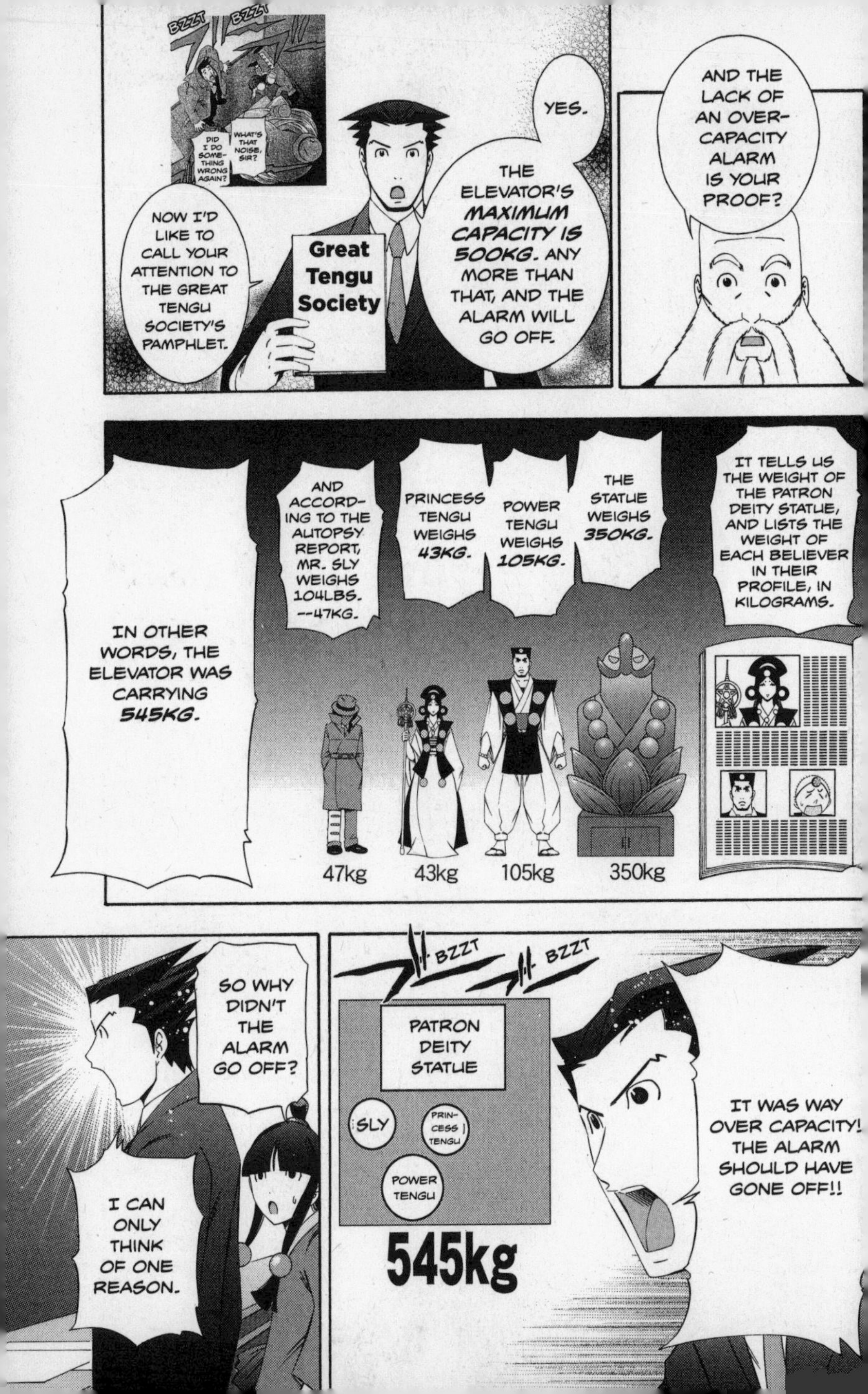
AND THE LACK OF AN OVER-CAPACITY ALARM IS YOUR PROOF?
YES.
THE ELEVATOR'S MAXIMUM CAPACITY IS 500KG. ANY MORE THAN THAT, AND THE ALARM WILL GO OFF.
BZZT
BZZT
WHAT'S THAT NOISE, SIR?
DID I DO SOMETHING WRONG AGAIN?
Great Tengu Society
NOW I'D LIKE TO CALL YOUR ATTENTION TO THE GREAT TENGU SOCIETY'S PAMPHLET.
IT TELLS US THE WEIGHT OF THE PATRON DEITY STATUE, AND LISTS THE WEIGHT OF EACH BELIEVER IN THEIR PROFILE, IN KILOGRAMS.
THE STATUE WEIGHS 350KG.
POWER TENGU WEIGHS 105KG.
PRINCESS TENGU WEIGHS 43KG.
AND ACCORDING TO THE AUTOPSY REPORT, MR. SLY WEIGHS 104LBS. --47KG.
IN OTHER WORDS, THE ELEVATOR WAS CARRYING 545KG.
47kg
43kg
105kg
350kg
BZZT
BZZT
IT WAS WAY OVER CAPACITY! THE ALARM SHOULD HAVE GONE OFF!!
PATRON DEITY STATUE
SLY
PRINCESS TENGU
POWER TENGU
545kg
SO WHY DIDN'T THE ALARM GO OFF?
I CAN ONLY THINK OF ONE REASON.

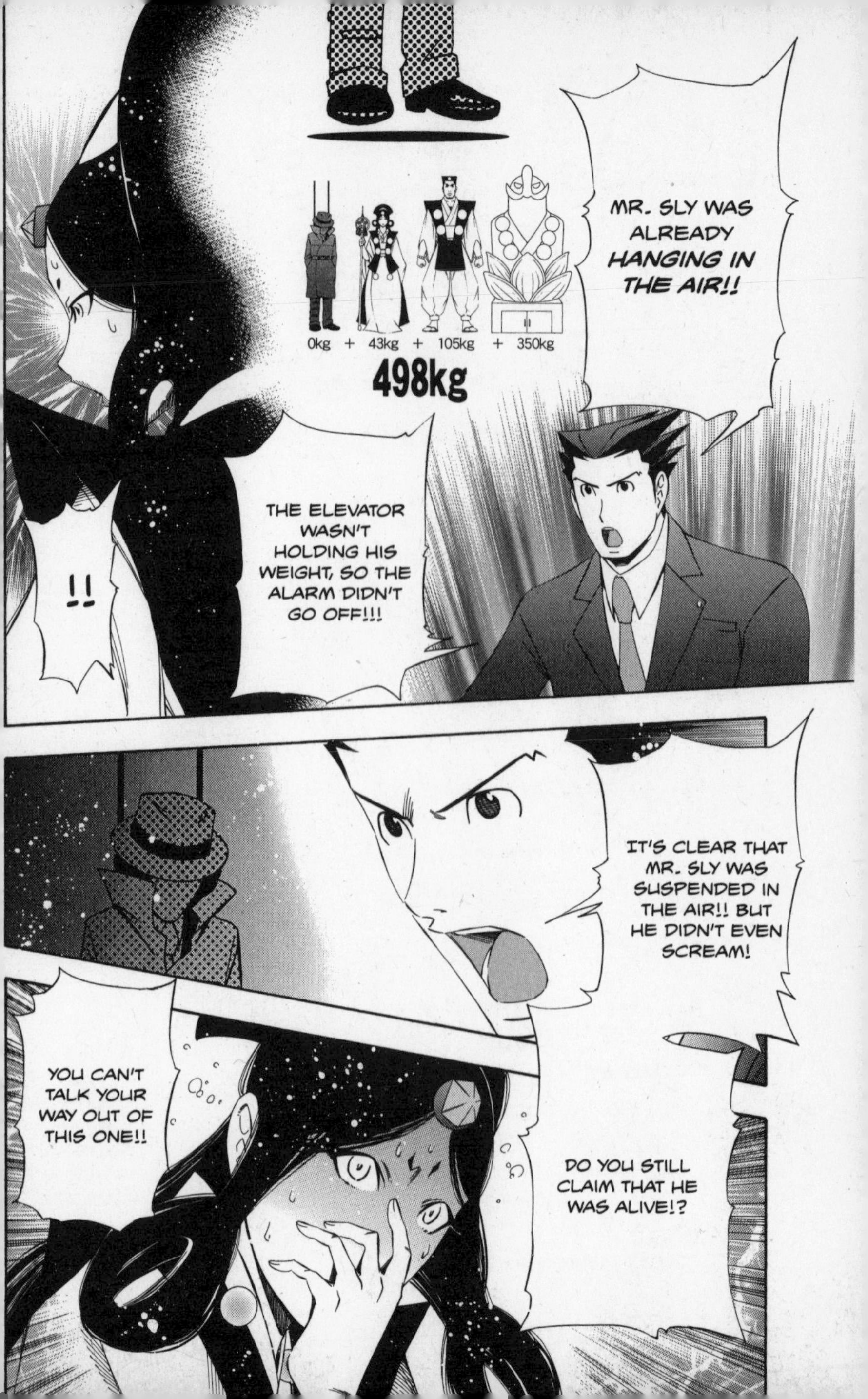
MR. SLY WAS ALREADY HANGING IN THE AIR!!
0kg + 43kg + 105kg + 350kg
498kg
THE ELEVATOR WASN'T HOLDING HIS WEIGHT, SO THE ALARM DIDN'T GO OFF!!!
!!
IT'S CLEAR THAT MR. SLY WAS SUSPENDED IN THE AIR!! BUT HE DIDN'T EVEN SCREAM!
DO YOU STILL CLAIM THAT HE WAS ALIVE!?
YOU CAN'T TALK YOUR WAY OUT OF THIS ONE!!

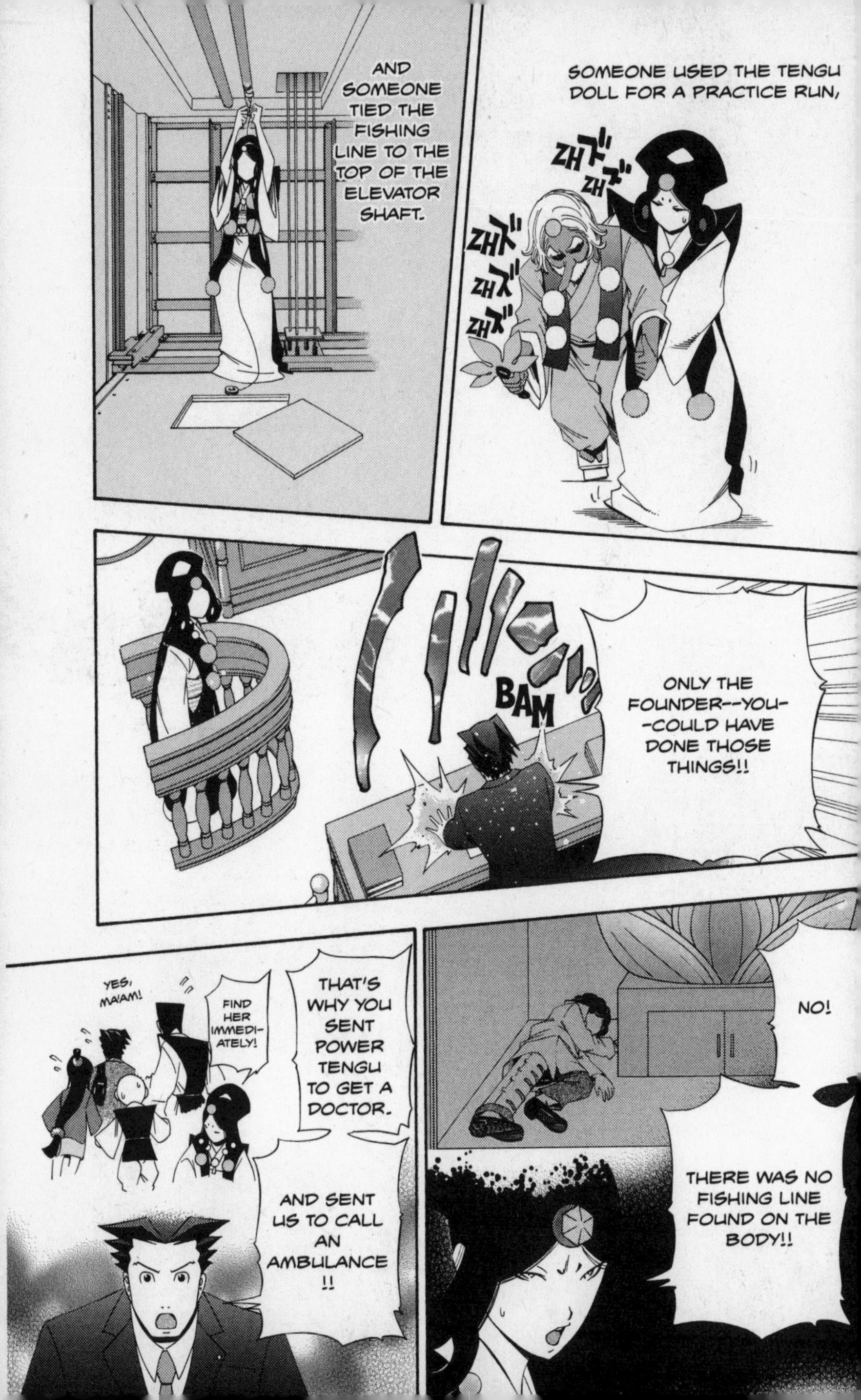
SOMEONE USED THE TENGU DOLL FOR A PRACTICE RUN,
ZH ZH
ZH ZH ZH
AND SOMEONE TIED THE FISHING LINE TO THE TOP OF THE ELEVATOR SHAFT.
ONLY THE FOUNDER--YOU--COULD HAVE DONE THOSE THINGS!!
BAM
THAT'S WHY YOU SENT POWER TENGU TO GET A DOCTOR.
FIND HER IMMEDIATELY!
YES, MA'AM!
AND SENT US TO CALL AN AMBULANCE!!
NO!
THERE WAS NO FISHING LINE FOUND ON THE BODY!!

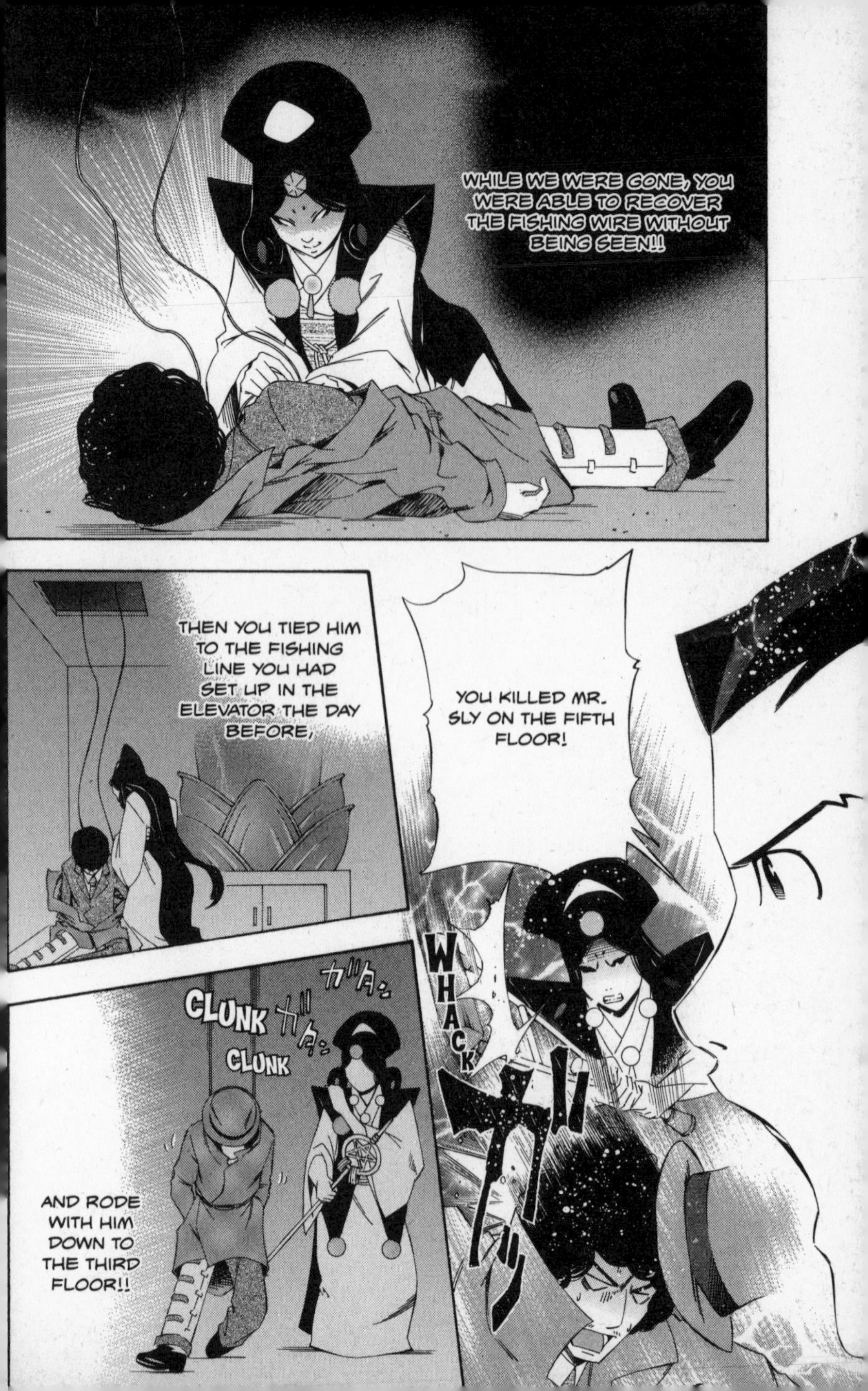
WHILE WE WERE GONE, YOU WERE ABLE TO RECOVER THE FISHING WIRE WITHOUT BEING SEEN!!
YOU KILLED MR. SLY ON THE FIFTH FLOOR!
WHACK
THEN YOU TIED HIM TO THE FISHING LINE YOU HAD SET UP IN THE ELEVATOR THE DAY BEFORE,
CLUNK
CLUNK
AND RODE WITH HIM DOWN TO THE THIRD FLOOR!!

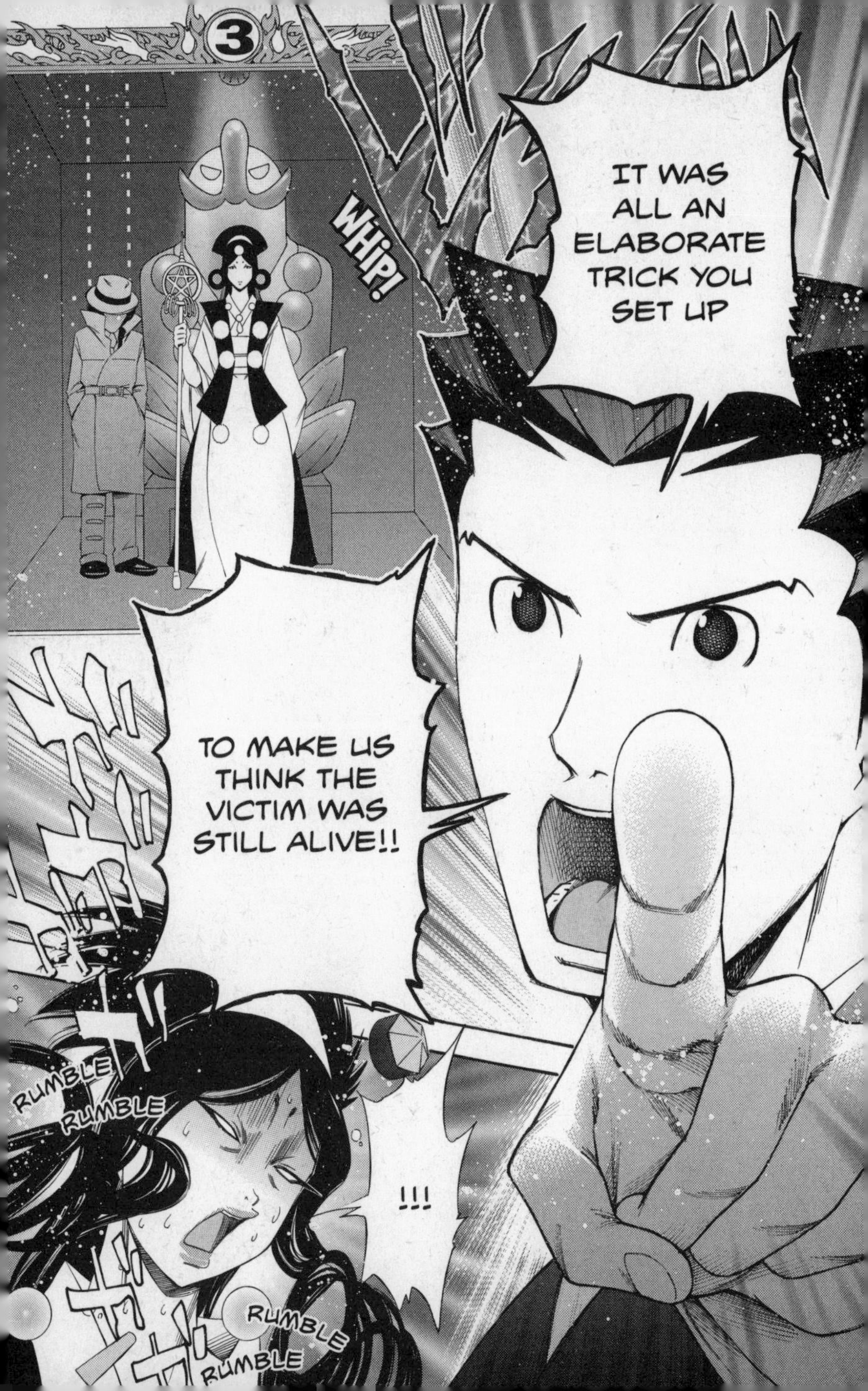
IT WAS ALL AN ELABORATE TRICK YOU SET UP
TO MAKE US THINK THE VICTIM WAS STILL ALIVE!!
3
WHIP!
RUMBLE RUMBLE
!!!
RUMBLE RUMBLE

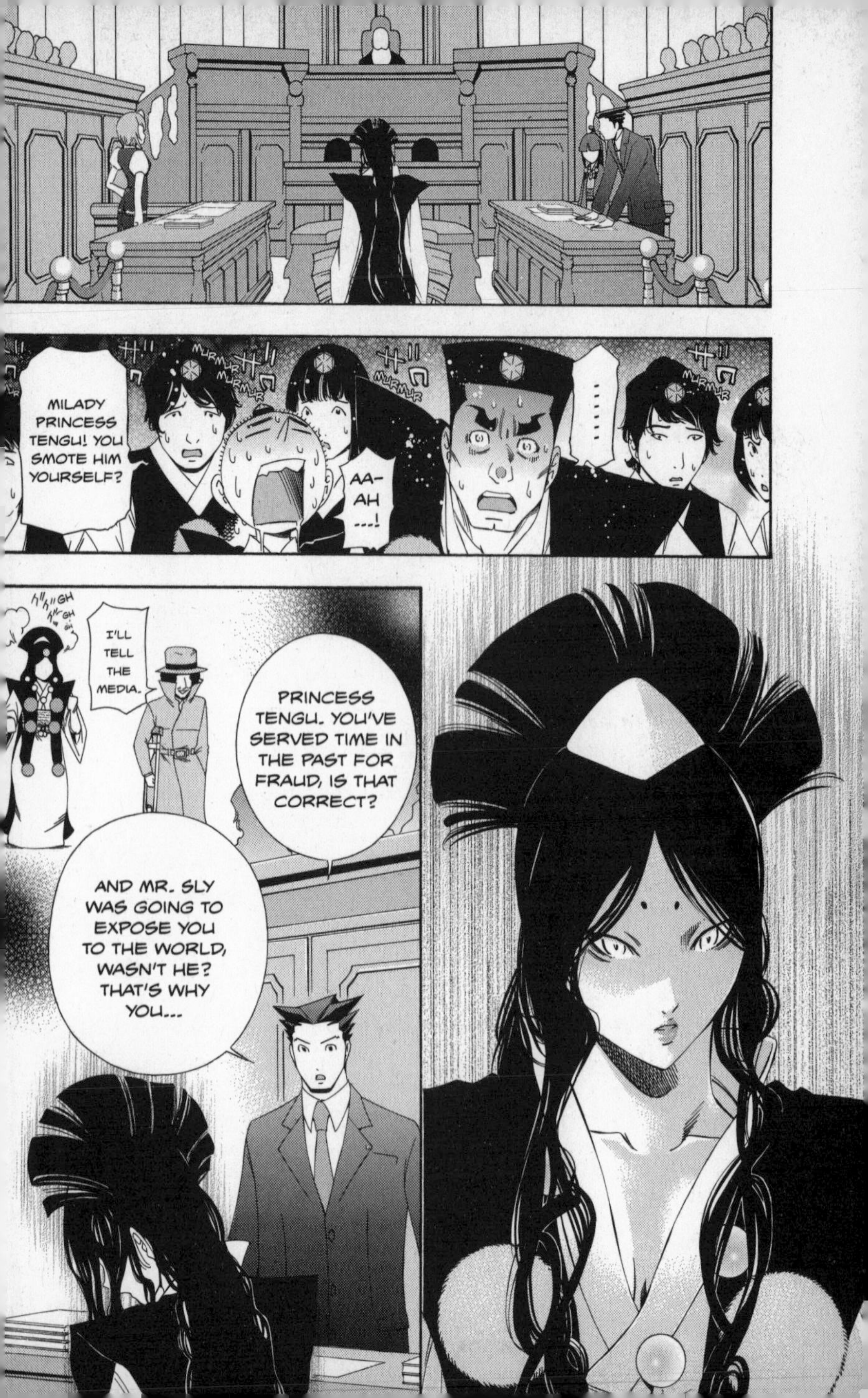
......
MURMUR
AA-AH ---!
MURMUR
MURMUR
MURMUR
MILADY PRINCESS TENGU! YOU SMOTE HIM YOURSELF?
GH GH GH
I'LL TELL THE MEDIA.
PRINCESS TENGU. YOU'VE SERVED TIME IN THE PAST FOR FRAUD, IS THAT CORRECT?
AND MR. SLY WAS GOING TO EXPOSE YOU TO THE WORLD, WASN'T HE? THAT'S WHY YOU...

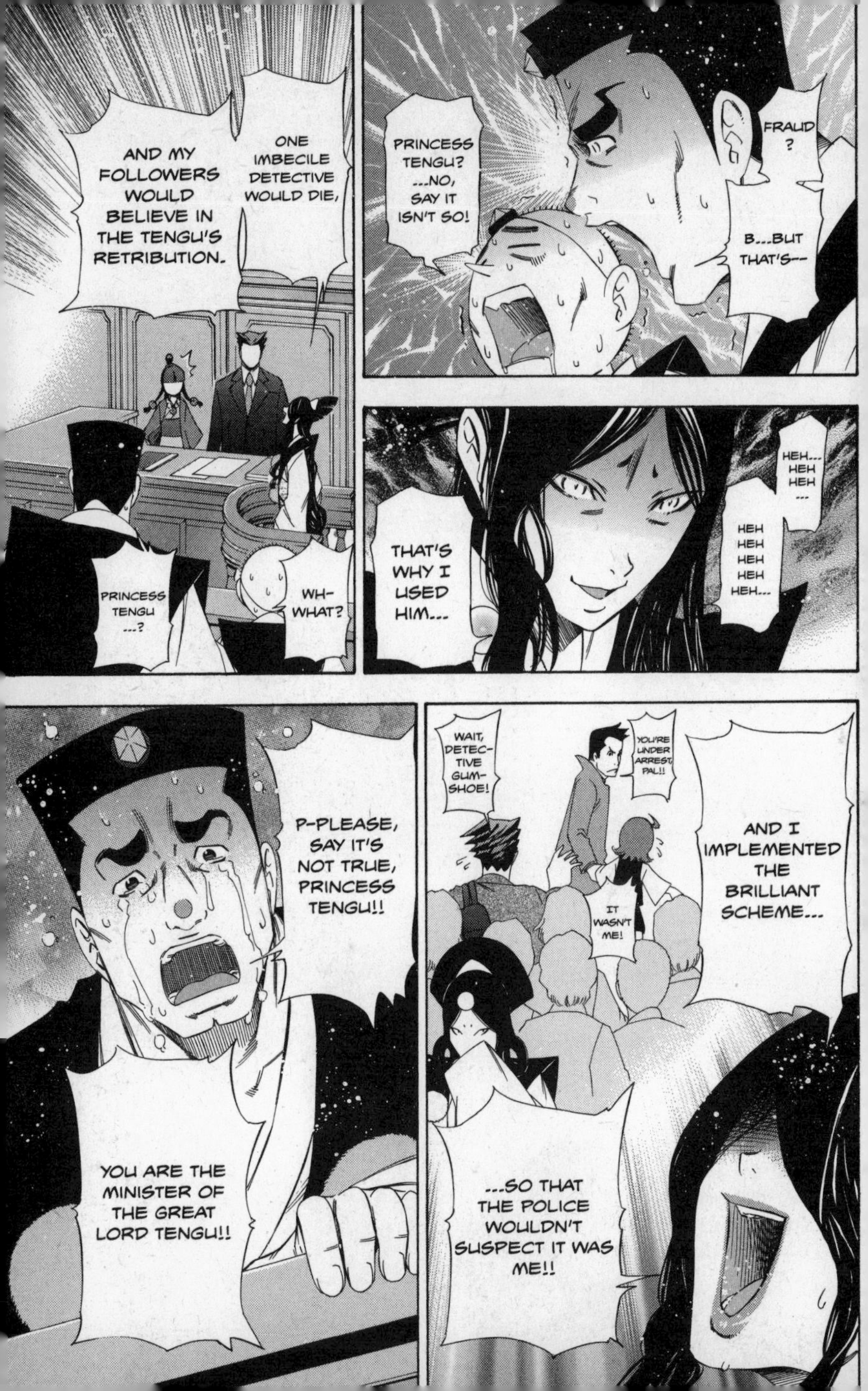
FRAUD?
PRINCESS TENGU? ...NO, SAY IT ISN'T SO!
B...BUT THAT'S--
HEH... HEH HEH ...
HEH HEH HEH HEH HEH...
THAT'S WHY I USED HIM...
ONE IMBECILE DETECTIVE WOULD DIE,
AND MY FOLLOWERS WOULD BELIEVE IN THE TENGU'S RETRIBUTION.
WH-WHAT?
PRINCESS TENGU ...?
AND I IMPLEMENTED THE BRILLIANT SCHEME...
YOU'RE UNDER ARREST, PAL!!
WAIT, DETEC-TIVE GUM-SHOE!
IT WASN'T ME!
...SO THAT THE POLICE WOULDN'T SUSPECT IT WAS ME!!
P-PLEASE, SAY IT'S NOT TRUE, PRINCESS TENGU!!
YOU ARE THE MINISTER OF THE GREAT LORD TENGU!!

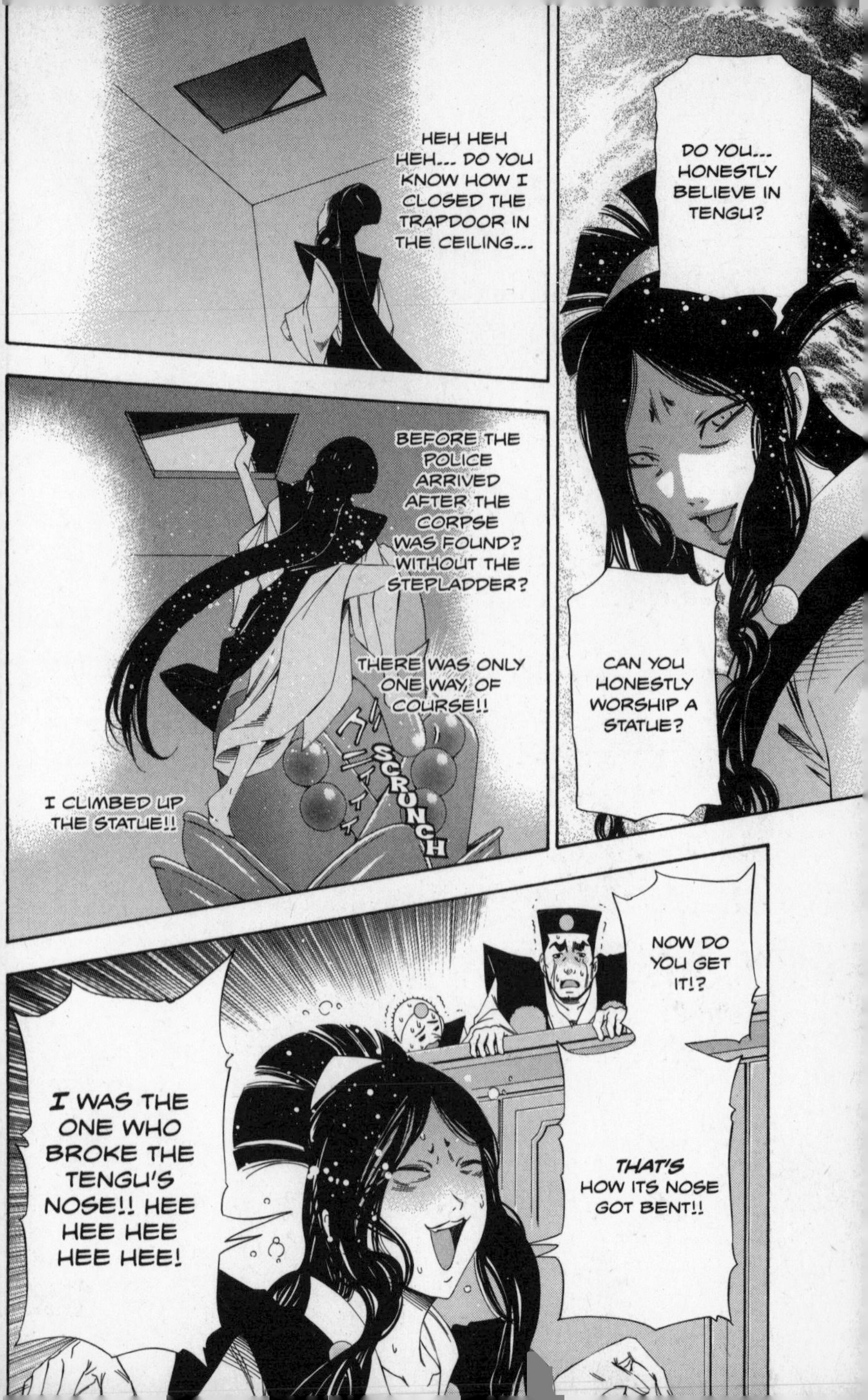

DO YOU... HONESTLY BELIEVE IN TENGU?
CAN YOU HONESTLY WORSHIP A STATUE?
HEH HEH HEH... DO YOU KNOW HOW I CLOSED THE TRAPDOOR IN THE CEILING...
BEFORE THE POLICE ARRIVED AFTER THE CORPSE WAS FOUND? WITHOUT THE STEPLADDER?
THERE WAS ONLY ONE WAY, OF COURSE!!
SCRUNCH
I CLIMBED UP THE STATUE!!
NOW DO YOU GET IT!?
THAT'S HOW ITS NOSE GOT BENT!!
I WAS THE ONE WHO BROKE THE TENGU'S NOSE!! HEE HEE HEE HEE HEE!

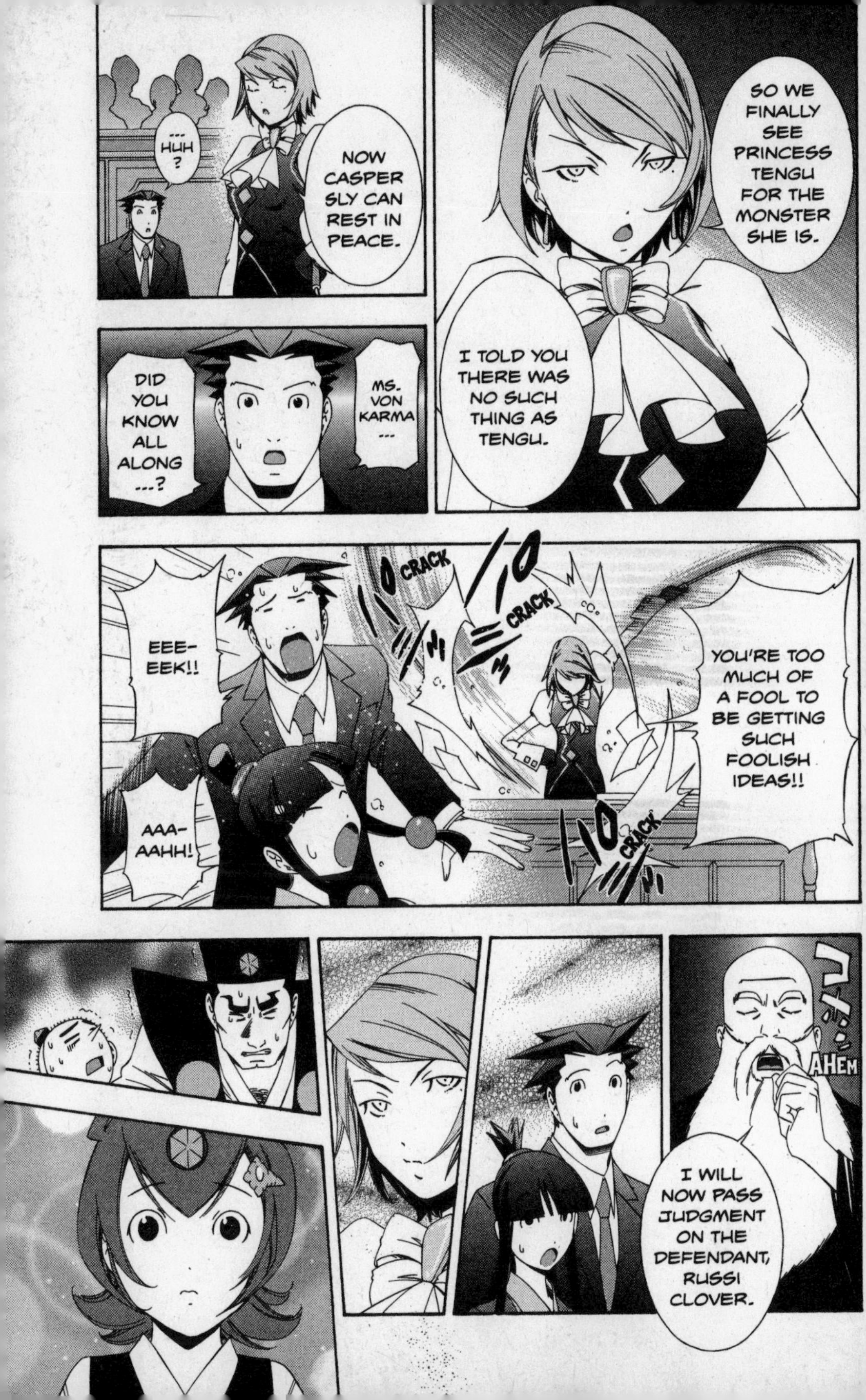
SO WE FINALLY SEE PRINCESS TENGU FOR THE MONSTER SHE IS.
I TOLD YOU THERE WAS NO SUCH THING AS TENGU.
NOW CASPER SLY CAN REST IN PEACE.
...HUH?
MS. VON KARMA...
DID YOU KNOW ALL ALONG...?
YOU'RE TOO MUCH OF A FOOL TO BE GETTING SUCH FOOLISH IDEAS!!
CRACK
CRACK
EEE-EEK!!
CRACK
AAA-AAHH!
AHEM
I WILL NOW PASS JUDGMENT ON THE DEFENDANT, RUSSI CLOVER.

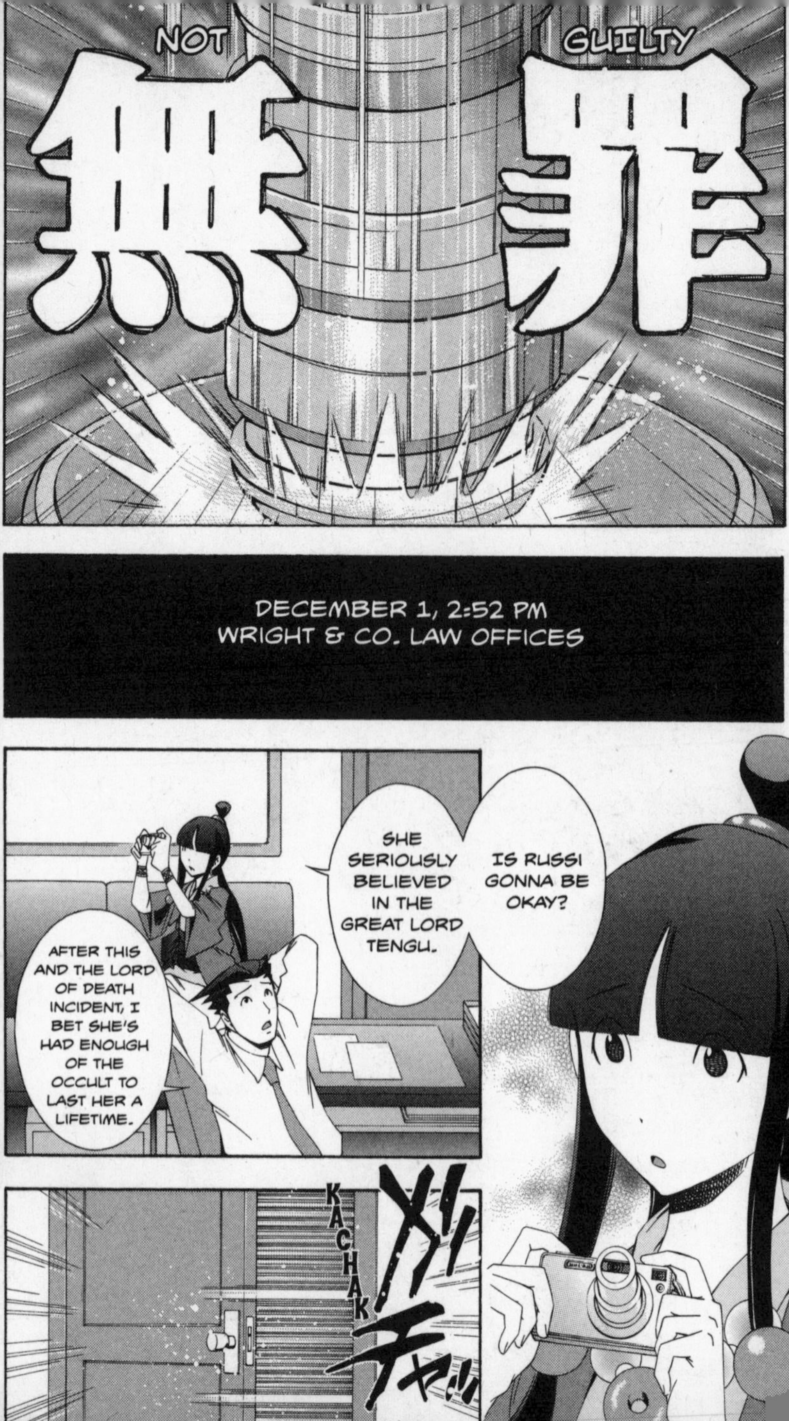
NOT
GUILTY
無罪
DECEMBER 1, 2:52 PM
WRIGHT & CO. LAW OFFICES
IS RUSSI GONNA BE OKAY?
SHE SERIOUSLY BELIEVED IN THE GREAT LORD TENGU.
AFTER THIS AND THE LORD OF DEATH INCIDENT, I BET SHE'S HAD ENOUGH OF THE OCCULT TO LAST HER A LIFETIME.
KACHAK

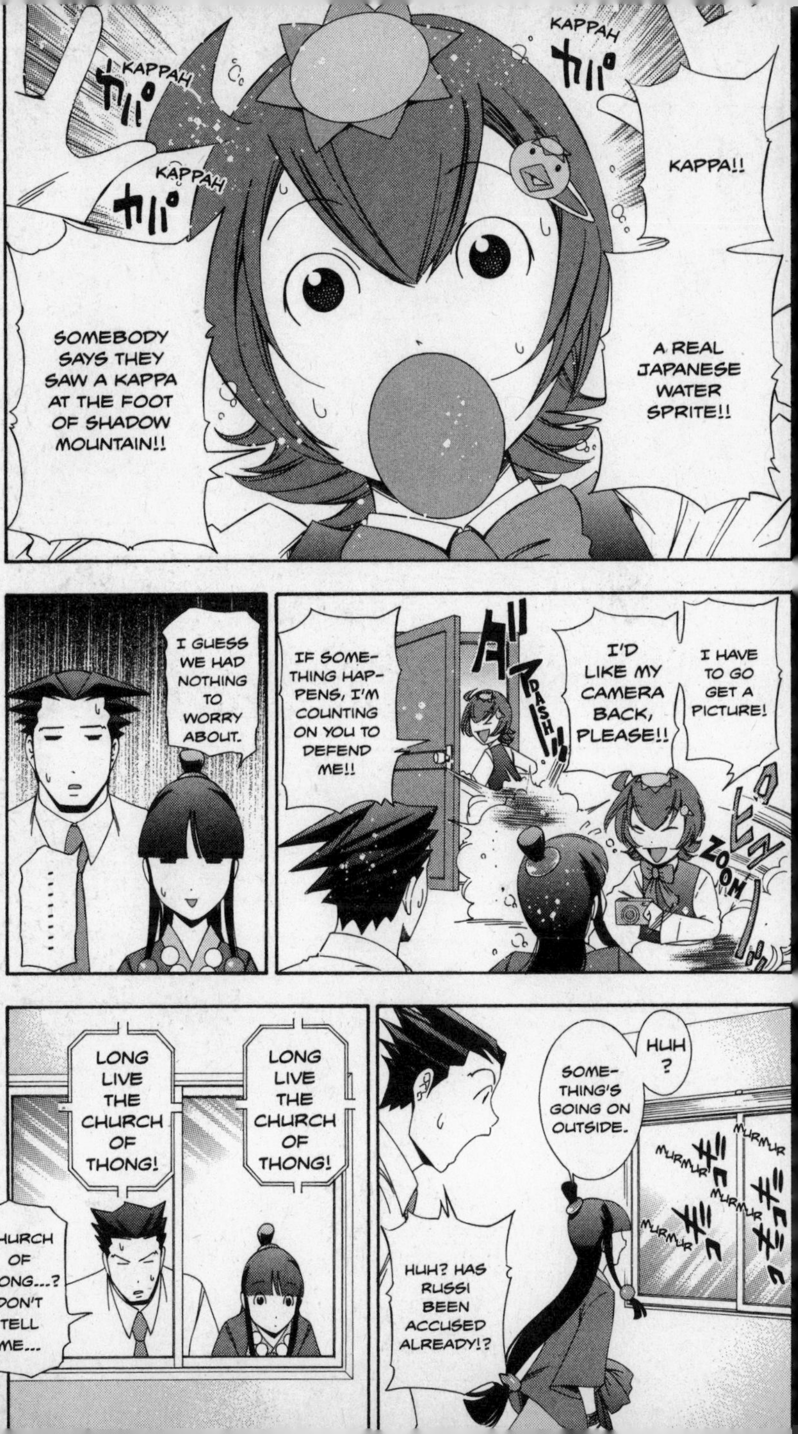
KAPPAH
KAPPA!!
A REAL JAPANESE WATER SPRITE!!
KAPPAH
KAPPAH
SOMEBODY SAYS THEY SAW A KAPPA AT THE FOOT OF SHADOW MOUNTAIN!!
I HAVE TO GO GET A PICTURE!
I'D LIKE MY CAMERA BACK, PLEASE!!
ZOOM
DASH
IF SOMETHING HAPPENS, I'M COUNTING ON YOU TO DEFEND ME!!
I GUESS WE HAD NOTHING TO WORRY ABOUT.
......
HUH?
SOMETHING'S GOING ON OUTSIDE.
MURMUR
MURMUR
MURMUR
MURMUR
HUH? HAS RUSSI BEEN ACCUSED ALREADY!?
LONG LIVE THE CHURCH OF THONG!
LONG LIVE THE CHURCH OF THONG!
CHURCH OF THONG...? DON'T TELL ME...

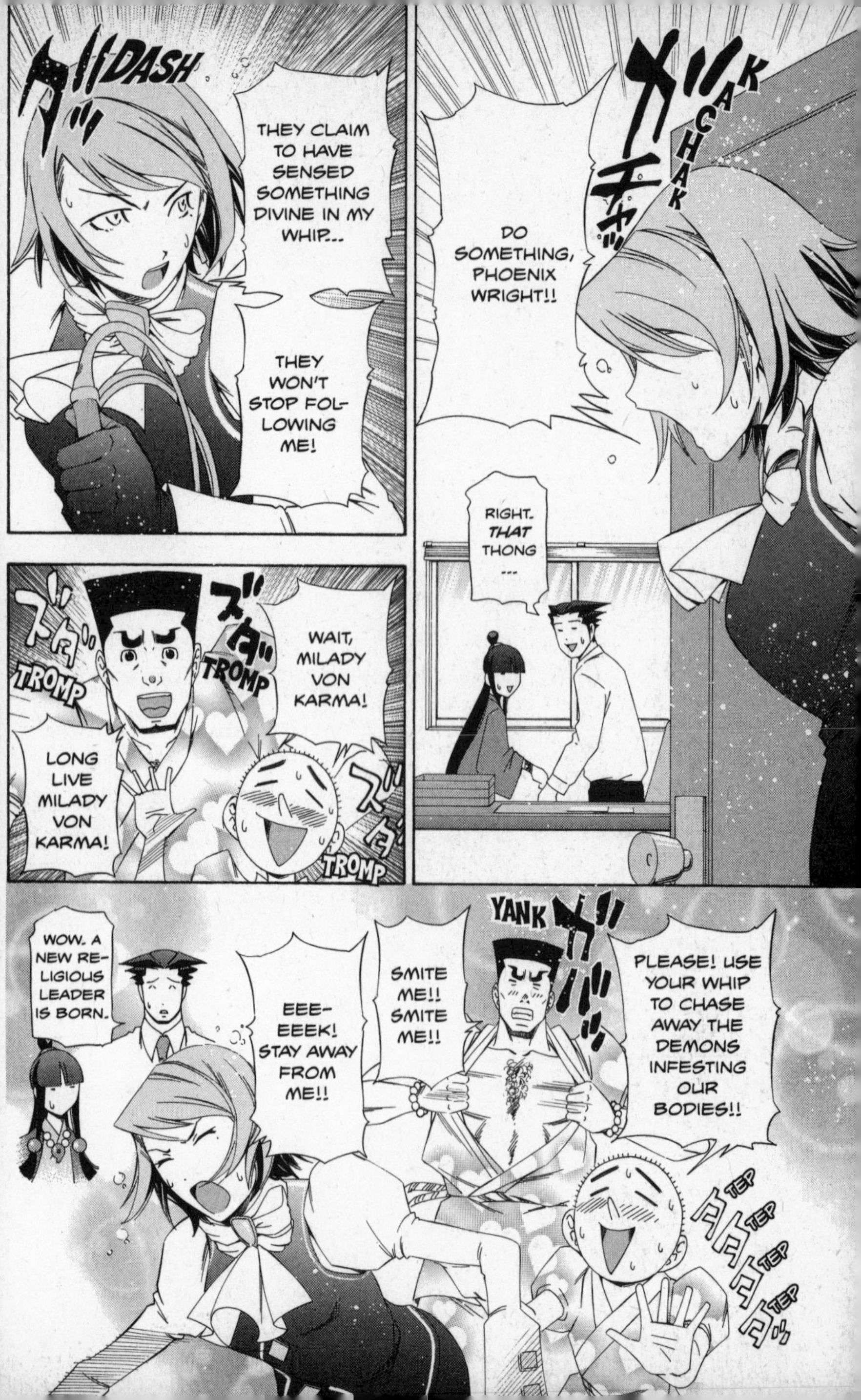
KACHAK
DO SOMETHING, PHOENIX WRIGHT!!
RIGHT. *THAT* THONG...
DASH
THEY CLAIM TO HAVE SENSED SOMETHING DIVINE IN MY WHIP...
THEY WON'T STOP FOL-LOWING ME!
TROMP
WAIT, MILADY VON KARMA!
TROMP
LONG LIVE MILADY VON KARMA!
TROMP
YANK
PLEASE! USE YOUR WHIP TO CHASE AWAY THE DEMONS INFESTING OUR BODIES!!
SMITE ME!! SMITE ME!!
EEE-EEEK! STAY AWAY FROM ME!!
WOW. A NEW RE-LIGIOUS LEADER IS BORN.
TEP TEP TEP TEP

Phoenix Wright
Ace Attorney™

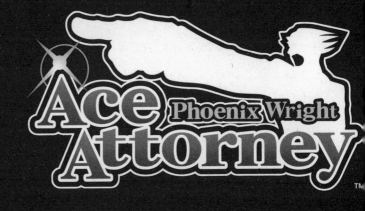

NEGIMA!
MAGISTER NEGI MAGI

BY KEN AKAMATSU

Negi Springfield is a ten-year-old wizard teaching English at an all-girls Japanese school. He dreams of becoming a master wizard like his legendary father, the Thousand Master. At first his biggest concern was concealing his magic powers, because if he's ever caught using them publicly, he thinks he'll be turned into an ermine! But in a world that gets stranger every day, it turns out that the strangest people of all are Negi's students! From a librarian with a magic book to a centuries-old vampire, from a robot to a ninja, Negi will risk his own life to protect the girls in his care!

Ages: 16+

Special extras in each volume! Read them all!

VISIT WWW.KODANSHACOMICS.COM TO:

• View release date calendars for upcoming volumes
• Find out the latest about new Kodansha Comics series

ANIMAL LAND

BY MAKOTO RAIKU

In a world of animals, where the strong eat the weak, Monoko the tanuki stumbles across a strange creature the likes of which has never been seen before–a human baby! While the newborn has no claws or teeth to protect itself, it does have the special ability to speak to and understand all different animals. Can the gift of speech between species change the balance of power in a land where the weak must always fear the strong?

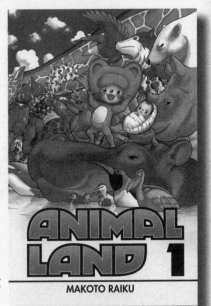

ANIMAL LAND 1

MAKOTO RAIKU

Ages 13+

You are going the wrong way!

Manga is a completely different type of reading experience.

To start at the beginning, go to the end!

That's right! Authentic manga is read the traditional Japanese way—from right to left, exactly the opposite of how American books are read. It's easy to follow: Just go to the other end of the book, and read each page—and each panel—from right side to left side, starting at the top right. Now you're experiencing manga as it was meant to be.